| Equals: | Less: | | | Plus: | Equals: |
|---|---|---|---|---|---|
| Net national product | Indirect business tax and nontax liability | Business transfer payments | Statistical discrepancy | Subsidies less current surplus of government enterprises | National income |
| 93.7 | 7.1 | 0.6 | 1.1 | −0.2 | 84.8 |
| 48.4 | 7.1 | .7 | .7 | −.0 | 39.9 |
| 82.2 | 9.4 | .5 | 1.4 | .4 | 71.4 |
| 91.0 | 10.1 | .4 | 1.1 | .4 | 79.7 |
| 115.0 | 11.3 | .5 | .6 | .1 | 102.7 |
| 147.3 | 11.8 | .5 | −.8 | .1 | 135.9 |
| 180.7 | 12.8 | .5 | −1.8 | .1 | 169.3 |
| 198.9 | 14.2 | .5 | 2.7 | .6 | 182.1 |
| 200.2 | 15.5 | .5 | 4.1 | .7 | 180.7 |
| 195.8 | 17.1 | .5 | .5 | .9 | 178.6 |
| 215.7 | 18.4 | .6 | 1.5 | −.2 | 194.9 |
| 239.3 | 20.1 | .7 | −1.6 | −.1 | 219.9 |
| 236.5 | 21.3 | .8 | .6 | −.3 | 213.6 |
| 263.0 | 23.4 | .8 | 1.3 | .1 | 237.6 |
| 303.6 | 25.3 | .9 | 3.2 | −.1 | 274.1 |
| 318.7 | 27.7 | 1.0 | 1.7 | −.3 | 287.9 |
| 335.8 | 29.7 | 1.2 | 2.3 | −.5 | 302.1 |
| 334.1 | 29.6 | 1.1 | 2.0 | −.3 | 301.1 |
| 365.3 | 32.2 | 1.2 | 1.3 | −.0 | 330.5 |
| 383.0 | 35.1 | 1.4 | −2.1 | .7 | 349.4 |
| 402.3 | 37.5 | 1.5 | −1.2 | .7 | 365.2 |
| 406.2 | 38.7 | 1.6 | .2 | 1.1 | 366.9 |
| 443.0 | 41.8 | 1.8 | −1.3 | .1 | 400.8 |
| 460.2 | 45.4 | 2.0 | −2.4 | .4 | 415.7 |
| 477.0 | 48.0 | 2.0 | −.1 | 1.7 | 428.8 |
| 516.1 | 51.6 | 2.1 | 2.1 | 1.8 | 462.0 |
| 546.1 | 54.6 | 2.4 | 1.7 | 1.1 | 488.5 |
| 584.8 | 58.8 | 2.7 | .1 | 1.7 | 524.9 |
| 635.0 | 62.6 | 2.8 | −1.2 | 1.6 | 572.4 |
| 695.3 | 65.3 | 3.0 | 1.4 | 2.5 | 628.1 |
| 733.7 | 70.2 | 3.1 | −.3 | 1.6 | 662.2 |
| 801.3 | 78.9 | 3.4 | −2.1 | 1.4 | 722.5 |
| 864.0 | 86.6 | 3.9 | −3.9 | 1.9 | 779.3 |
| 904.7 | 94.3 | 4.1 | −1.5 | 2.9 | 810.7 |
| 981.1 | 103.7 | 4.4 | 4.1 | 2.6 | 871.5 |
| 1,079.5 | 111.5 | 4.9 | 3.3 | 3.8 | 963.6 |
| 1,209.9 | 120.9 | 5.5 | .8 | 3.4 | 1,086.2 |
| 1,298.2 | 129.1 | 5.8 | 3.7 | 1.1 | 1,160.7 |
| 1,389.9 | 140.1 | 7.4 | 5.5 | 2.4 | 1,239.4 |
| 1,543.0 | 151.7 | 7.9 | 5.1 | 1.0 | 1,379.2 |
| 1,723.2 | 165.7 | 8.6 | 1.4 | 3.1 | 1,550.5 |
| 1,941.4 | 178.2 | 9.3 | −2.6 | 3.7 | 1,760.3 |
| 2,161.7 | 189.6 | 10.3 | −1.5 | 3.4 | 1,966.7 |
| 2,338.5 | 213.4 | 11.7 | 2.3 | 5.5 | 2,116.6 |
| 2,627.5 | 251.3 | 12.9 | 5.6 | 6.1 | 2,363.8 |
| 2,710.4 | 258.8 | 14.1 | −.5 | 8.8 | 2,446.8 |
| 2,927.7 | 280.4 | 15.6 | .5 | 15.6 | 2,646.7 |
| 3,258.4 | 304.3 | 17.3 | −8.2 | 14.4 | 2,959.4 |

# INTERMEDIATE MACROECONOMICS

MICHAEL R. DARBY
University of California, Los Angeles

MICHAEL T. MELVIN
Arizona State University

Scott, Foresman and Company
Glenview, Illinois    London, England

339
D21i

**Library of Congress Cataloging-in-Publication Data**

Darby, Michael R.
  Intermediate macroeconomics.

  Bibliography.
  Includes index.
  1. Macroeconomics.   I. Melvin, Michael,
II. Title
HB172.5.D37   1986   339   85-31716
ISBN 0-673-15999-X

# CONTENTS

# PREFACE

A good undergraduate macroeconomics text must meet several criteria. It must present the standard body of macroeconomic thought handed down through the years, but it should also include up-to-date material consistent with recent trends in macroeconomic research. Most importantly, all of this must be accomplished in a manner that students will find accessible and interesting. It helps no one—students nor faculty—to present a rigorously complete overview of macroeconomics that is written at a level too high for the average undergraduate student. In our text we strive for complete coverage of intermediate macroeconomic topics that is challenging yet easy to read.

It is not contradictory to say that the material is challenging and that the text reads easily. By presenting topics in an interesting manner and by blending traditional and modern approaches to macroeconomic theory with applications and real-world examples, the subject matter is made lively and interesting. However, we have taken great pains to ensure that the language is not too formal and is written for the student rather than the professor.

It is important that macro texts cover the basic tools of analysis used by macroeconomists for the past 40 years. Following the introductory material, the text proceeds to a presentation of the standard Keynesian short-run *IS-LM* model. Then we present the aggregate demand and supply analysis of the short-run determination of output and prices. Next a long-run equilibrium analysis of the level and growth of output and prices enables an understanding of the long-run trends in the economy. Finally, the dynamic adjustment of the economy to disturbances is analyzed. The dynamic analysis allows a view of the transition from the short-run equilibrium to the new long-run equilibrium that is missing in the static framework of *IS-LM* and aggregate demand and supply. Once the analytical structure is complete, we can turn to a consideration of economic policy, history, and international finance.

This text differs in many respects from others in the field. A most obvious way is the coverage of the dynamic adjustment of the economy. We believe that it is not enough to know where we started and where we wind up, because the nature of the economy's adjustment to some disturbance is critical to understanding the real-world cyclical behavior of the economy. In addition, this text is different from most in that many of the topics that monetarists and new classical macroeconomists believe are important are given full consideration here, yet are mentioned only briefly at best in the major competing texts. For example, we give special attention to the role of expectations, the roles of labor markets and inventories in producing a short-run aggregate supply curve, and the debate over the feasibility of stabilization policy.

While the differences between our text and the others are important in understanding the existing state of the macroeconomist's art, we would emphasize that the standard Keynesian approach to macroeconomics is given a careful treatment. Different users will, no doubt, choose to de-emphasize or omit portions of the text. While the text is written in a manner to allow a complete reading in one term, those who choose to skip some sections will find that easy to do.

## Acknowledgements

No major textbook ever reaches the market without the benefit of careful reviewing by colleagues. We are grateful to:

Jack E. Adams    University of Arkansas, Little Rock
David Aschauer    University of Michigan
Charles Britton    University of Arkansas, Fayetteville
Gregory Christainsen    California State University, Hayward
Russell Cooper    Iowa State University
Thomas J. Cunningham    Barnard College
Chris Ellis    University of Oregon
Pamela Labadie    Columbia University
John Martin    CUNY—Bernard Baruch College
Marjorie Rose    University of California, Los Angeles
Don Schlagenhauf    Arizona State University
Cliff Sowell    Berea College
Lee Spector    University of Iowa
Susan Woodward    Council of Economic Advisors

In addition, students at UCLA, the University of Rochester, and Berea College provided valuable field testing of the manuscript, resulting in several improvements in style and content. The enthusiastic participation of our acquisitions editor, George Lobell, accelerated the development of the final product—a text that students have found interesting and accessible, and instructors will find comprehensive and and up-to-date.

**CHAPTER EIGHT**

# AGGREGATE SUPPLY ISSUES **186**

# UNDERSTANDING U.S. MACROECONOMIC HISTORY  **368**

**CHAPTER SIXTEEN**

# MACROECONOMICS AND THE OPEN ECONOMY  412

# INTERMEDIATE
# MACROECONOMICS

# MACROECONOMIC ISSUES

## 1.1 WHAT IS MACROECONOMICS?

The study of macroeconomics addresses what most of us would consider to be the most important economic issues: inflation, unemployment, and the nation's output and income. At various times, most adults have wondered about the sorts of questions that will be answered here. Why are interest rates so high? How can the unemployment rate be high for a while and then fall? What causes recessions? Is there a way to avoid another Great Depression? Must we have inflation? It should already be apparent that macroeconomics is about the world in which we live. We will not be studying abstract theories or ivory-tower idealism. The macroeconomic theories introduced in these pages are applied to real world events. We will consider evidence from the historical record to evaluate the usefulness of these theories.

### THE HISTORICAL CHALLENGE

In the last 100 years, the United States has experienced many contractions of business activity, including a severe depression from 1929 to 1933. What is bad about business activity slowing? As output of goods and services falls, unemployment rises and household incomes tend to fall. Considering the tragic waste of human potential that occurs during economic contractions, it would seem that there must be a better way to "manage" an economy. But is the better method one of more active government intervention in economic matters or less intervention? We should note right now that macroeconomic policy is of great political importance in a democracy where politicians must run for election on a regular basis.

*The historical record of inflation and unemployment indicates that there is much room for improvement.*

A review of the historical record of unemployment is provided in Chapter 3, and the Great Depression is reviewed in Chapter 15. Considering the past record, it appears that there is much room for improvement. But unemployment is not the only problem faced by the economic policymaker. Inflation also has been a recurrent problem of the modern economy. Yet it is interesting to consider that from the ratification of the U.S. Constitution in 1789 until 1940, there was no particular trend in the general level of prices. Sometimes prices would rise for a few years, but this rise would be offset by a period of falling prices. We have undergone a fundamental change in the past 50 years. By 1983, prices were more than seven times higher, on average, than in 1940. We will be studying the forces that brought about this change in the inflationary environment.

## THE MACROECONOMIC APPROACH

The basic challenge of macroeconomics is to explain this historical record and find ways to improve on it. Macroeconomists respond to this challenge by developing models of the economy which explain the behavior of employment, output, and the price level in terms of their main determinants. If the behavior of these determinants or causes can be controlled or offset, then the historical record can be improved upon.

**aggregates**
Economywide measures of concepts like unemployment and inflation

The essential element of the macroeconomic approach of explaining the economy is the use of a relatively small number of **aggregates**. Aggregates are economywide measures of concepts like unemployment, prices, and output. Macroeconomics does not deal much with disaggregated data on particular industries or firms. Chapters 2 and 3 describe the major aggregates on which macroeconomists focus.

The study of economics is divided into two major fields—macroeconomics and microeconomics. Microeconomists study the smaller parts of the economy, like a particular industry or firm, assuming that the general level of prices and income is given. Macroeconomists analyze the general level of prices and income assuming that the structure of industry and the distribution of incomes over firms and individuals is given. The work of each branch of economics is complementary. By taking the issues considered by microeconomists as given, the macroeconomist has a more manageable problem to deal with.

## CONTROVERSIES

The history of macroeconomic thought has been marked by often bitter controversy among people who deeply cared about improving economic conditions but disagreed about how to do it. A historical perspective on the controversy may help. Through at least the mid-1930s, economists generally agreed that the dominant variable determining the price level and the business cycle was the quantity of money existing in a country. The United States established a central bank—the **Federal Reserve System**, or **Fed** for short—by the Federal Reserve Act of 1913. During the 1920s, many economists argued that the Fed's ability to control the money supply eliminated the threats of depression and inflation forever. The Great Depression of the 1930s came as quite a shock to these economists. It was thought that the Fed was doing all it could, yet this seemed to be no help at all.

**Federal Reserve System (Fed)**
The central bank of the United States

At the same time that the United States was in depression, so was Britain. In 1936 an English economist, John Maynard Keynes, published *The General Theory of Employment, Interest, and Money*. This book presented a view of a depression economy in which money was not very important. In the **Keynesian** analysis, investment, government spending and taxation, and exports are the key variables influencing the level of economic activity. Keynes' book had an immediate impact and was embraced by many economists who are now identified as Keynesians. The Keynesian view was the dominant force in macroeconomics well into the late 1960s.

**Keynesian**
A macroeconomic approach to the economy that stresses government guidance of aggregate investment, consumer expenditures, government taxing and spending, and export demand

All along, however, some economists remained unconvinced of the ability of the Keynesian view to explain real-world phenomena. The major band of dissenters came to be known as **monetarists**, and the leading monetarist was Milton Friedman of the University of Chicago. The term "monetarist" refers to the belief by this group in the **quantity theory of money** as a useful framework for analyzing economic fluctuations—much like the pre-Keynesian economists. The quantity theory of money may be summarized by the equation of exchange:

**monetarists**
A group of economists who stress the importance of the money supply as a determinant of macroeconomic fluctuations

**quantity theory of money**
$MV = Py$

$$MV = Py \qquad (1.1)$$

Equation (1.1) states that the quantity of money "$M$" times the velocity of money "$V$" is equal to the price level "$P$" times real income "$y$." While more precise definitions follow in later chapters, $M$ is the

**monetary policy**
The control of the money supply to stabilize the economy

**fiscal policy**
The control of government spending and taxation to stabilize the economy

In the 1960s and 1970s, macroeconomists were often labeled as Keynesians or monetarists.

amount of money available for spending and $V$ is the number of times the money stock "turns over," or the average number of times each dollar is spent. $P$ is the average level of prices in the economy and $y$ is the real output, or measure of real goods and services produced. If $V$ and $y$ are constant, then changes in the money supply will bring about corresponding changes in the price level. This emphasis on the quantity theory of money was reflected in the monetarist theory, emphasizing the role of **monetary policy** in stabilizing the economy. Monetarists emphasized the importance of Federal Reserve control of the money supply in determining the level of economic activity. This was opposite the Keynesian belief that monetary policy is relatively less important. Keynesians emphasized **fiscal policy**, which is government spending and taxation policy aimed at stabilizing the economy. The monetarist versus fiscalist debate often involved heated exchanges between the leading proponents in each camp.

Monetarists refined our understanding of the way in which monetary changes affect the economy. The development of the modern quantity theory of money was spurred greatly by a book published in 1963: *A Monetary History of the United States, 1867–1960*, by Milton Friedman and Anna Schwartz. With the publication of the Friedman and Schwartz volume, economists started to revise their view of what really occurred during the Great Depression. A challenge to traditional Keynesian economics was presented.

While a detailed view of history—including the Great Depression—is left until Chapter 15, here we must realize that Friedman and Schwartz's book initiated a "monetarist revolution" similar to the Keynesian revolution that followed Keynes' book. Throughout the 1960s and early 1970s, the debate between Keynesians and monetarists raged. By the late 1970s, economists were successfully introducing views which could be seen as syntheses of the Keynesian and monetarist positions. Today, the Keynesian or monetarist labels are not used as they once were and the macroeconomics profession is not conveniently divided into these two camps. Diversity still exists and there are many new issues to debate, but the old dichotomy between Keynesian and monetarist views has finally become passé.

## 1.2 MACROECONOMIC RELATIONSHIPS

### VARIABLES AND FUNCTIONS

**variables**
Values that can fluctuate over time

As in the study of any subject, the macroeconomics student encounters many new terms and methods of analysis. The economic aggregates that we study are called **variables** because their values may change over time. The key variables we examine are often related via **functional relationships**. For instance, in Chapter 4 we learn that consumption is a function of income. This means that changes in income will be associated with changes in consumption. We express such functional relationships using an equation like this:

$$c = a + by \qquad (1.2)$$

Equation (1.2) is a formal expression of the relationship between consumption $c$ and income $y$. The letter $a$ stands for some constant money value of consumption that is established independent of income, and the letter $b$ is a fraction between 0 and 1 that indicates the amount by which consumption changes when income changes. Suppose some hypothetical economy has a consumption function like this:

$$c = 100 + .8y \qquad (1.3)$$

At any level of income, consumer spending is equal to $100 plus 8/10 of the level of income. Therefore, if income is $900, $c = 100 + .8(900) = 820$.

The relationships considered in macroeconomics often are causal relationships. In fact, we can identify a causal relationship in the consumption function. If we believe that changes in income lead to changes in consumption, then income is said to be an **independent variable** and consumption a **dependent variable**—the value of consumption depends upon the value of income, which is free to vary.

Economists build **macroeconomic models**, or simplified views of the real world, to aid our understanding. Since the real world is much too complex to comprehend in its entirety, there are advantages to abstracting from reality to be able to focus on the issues of crucial importance. In the typical macro model, the consumption function is but one of many equations describing the fundamental relationships at work. In describing a macroeconomic model, we can identify variables as being either endogenous or exogenous. An **endogenous variable** is one that has its value determined by the interactions within the model. An **exogenous variable** is one whose value comes from outside the model. The values of exogenous variables are said to be "given" to the model. Typically, government spending is an exogenous variable as it may be set by government independently. Similarly, the money supply is usually considered exogenous since it may be set at any value desired by the Fed. The price level, on the other hand, is an endogenous variable, whose value is determined by the interaction of forces within the model.

**functional relationships**
Relations where one variable affects another

**independent variable**
A value whose fluctuation affects another variable

**dependent variable**
A value that depends on the fluctuation of another variable

**macroeconomic models**
Functional relationships between aggregate values

**endogenous variable**
A value determined by the interactions of other variables in a model

**exogenous variable**
A value determined by forces outside the variables of a model

## USING GRAPHS

We frequently use graphs to summarize important economic relationships. By using graphs, the functional relationships considered are seen more clearly. To be sure we understand the use of graphs, let's consider the graphical representation of the consumption function of equation (1.3). Figure 1.1 presents the hypothetical function. The positive slope of the function indicates that consumption is an increasing function of income. We measure consumption on the vertical axis and income on the horizontal axis. The point where the consumption function intersects the vertical axis is called the **intercept**. The intercept gives the value of $c$ when $y$ equals zero, which in this case is 100. The **slope** of the line refers to the change in the value of the variable measured on the vertical axis given a change in the value of the variable measured along the horizontal axis. If income changes from 500 to 600, this is a change of 100. When income equals 500, consumption is also equal to 500. At an income of 600, consumption equals 580. Since consumption increases by 80 when income increases by 100, the slope is 80/100 or .8. Notice that the slope of the consumption function is the same as the value of $b$ in equation (1.2). This will be true of all linear functions. The consumption function will be analyzed in more detail in Chapter 4. At this point we simply use it to illustrate the use of graphs.

**intercept**
A point on the axis formed by the intersection of a curve and the axis

**slope**
The steepness or flatness of a line or curve; positive slope is upward and negative slope is downward

Figure 1.1

A Hypothetical Consumption Function

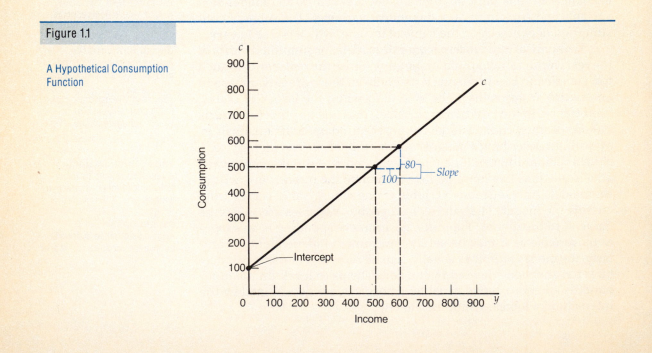

## STATICS AND DYNAMICS

Macroeconomists have different methodologies or ways of analyzing the economy. One method is that of **comparative statics**. A comparative-static analysis examines the economy at particular points in time—stopping time, you might say, to peek at the then existing situation. It is comparative because the analysis is repeated for alternative values of exogenous variables to see how the economy is affected. By doing this sort of analysis using the different exogenous variables for different points in time, the economist can see how variables change over time. This approach is similar to that of a motion picture—in which continuous motion is approximated by a series of still pictures.

> **comparative statics**
> Examining an economy at different, discrete points in time

These sequential static analyses can become quite cumbersome, especially when there are many changing exogenous variables or when many repetitions are required to trace out a prolonged process of adjustment. For those cases, macroeconomics has increasingly made use of dynamic analysis. A **dynamic analysis** traces the paths of variables through time on a continuous basis. Whereas a static analysis will indicate the location of key variables at points separated by time, a dynamic analysis will allow an analysis of how the variables reach these points. For instance, suppose we are analyzing how changes in interest rates affect the demand for money. We expect that higher interest rates will reduce money demand, as the rate of interest is the opportunity cost of holding money. The **opportunity cost** of undertaking some activity is the forgone next best alternative. In the case of holding money, the opportunity cost is the interest that could have been earned by holding some interest bearing money substitute instead of non–interest-bearing money. This is why we expect the quantity of money demanded to be inversely related to the interest rate.

> **dynamic analysis**
> Examining the continuous movement of an economy between points in time

> **opportunity cost**
> For any action taken, the next best alternative action that could have been taken and is now lost

If we observe a fall in interest rates, we expect money demand to rise. In a comparative static framework, we would first consider the demand for money prior to the interest-rate drop, and then consider the demand for money at some later time after the fall in interest rates, when money demand is higher than in the previous period. A dynamic analysis will consider the nature of the process of the rise in money demand in response to falling interest rates. We may be very interested in the pattern of the change—was there an abrupt rise to the new amount of money demanded; was there a steady, even rise drawn out through time; or was there still some other pattern?

There are some questions for which comparative-static analysis provides adequate answers, while others are most easily analyzed in a dynamic framework. As in other sciences, macroeconomics methodology must be tailored to fit the questions we ask.

## 1.3 WHAT LIES AHEAD

The first step required in a study of macroeconomics is to become familiar with the key variables used to measure and explain income, employment, and the price level. This will be the subject of Chapters 2 and 3.

The next step is to develop an understanding of simple macroeconomic models which can be used to explain changes in the key variables. The traditional Keynesian analysis is developed in Chapters 4 and 5. This Keynesian approach is a static approach where the aim is to explain the values of income and the interest rate at a particular point in time. Chapters 6, 7, and 8 develop an alternative comparative static framework that is based on the aggregate demand and supply in the economy. The approach used in these chapters will allow us to consider several pressing economic issues which cannot be investigated adequately in the traditional Keynesian framework. In particular, modern macroeconomists have placed great emphasis on the role of **expectations**. We will see that the ability of government policy to stabilize the economy depends upon what individuals expect the government to do as well as other factors. The role of expectations is first introduced in Chapter 7.

Through Chapter 8, we utilize the comparative static approach to economic analysis. Yet, as mentioned earlier, comparative statics is inappropriate to the important question of how we get from one equilibrium position to another. To fill this gap we must turn to a dynamic analysis. Chapters 9 and 10 provide a foundation for our dynamic analysis, as they introduce the determinants of the long-run growth trends in income and prices. In Chapters 11 through 13, a dynamic analysis of why and how the economy deviates from these long-run trends is presented.

With our understanding of the workings of the economy reasonably complete by Chapter 13, we address the role of government macroeconomic policy in Chapter 14 and United States macroeconomic history in Chapter 15. Finally, Chapter 16 considers international matters. In the modern world, it is no longer appropriate to treat countries as having **closed economies**, where the rest of the world may be ignored. Chapter 16 considers some issues of importance to the **open economy**: i.e., how international events affect our economy.

Throughout the text, end-of-chapter essays will focus on a particularly interesting topic related to each chapter. These essays will offer a view beyond the standard textbook coverage and should add depth to our understanding of macroeconomics.

---

**expectations**
The guesses consumers and business people make about future economic events that affect current actions

**closed economy**
An economy considered in isolation from the rest of the world

**open economy**
An economy considered in a larger context including transactions with the rest of the world

**SUMMARY**

1 Macroeconomics attempts to explain the causes of inflation, unemployment, and fluctuations in business activity.

2 The basic challenge of macroeconomics is to find ways to improve on the historical record.

3 The popular view that the quantity of money largely determined the business cycle was ended by John Maynard Keynes' *The General Theory of Employment, Interest, and Money* in 1936.

4 Keynesian economics emphasizes the importance of fiscal policy in determining business cycle fluctuations.

5 The publication of Friedman and Schwartz's *A Monetary History of the United States, 1867–1960* began to move macroeconomists away from Keynesian thought toward monetarism.

6 Monetarists emphasize the importance of Federal Reserve control of the money supply in determining the level of economic activity.

## EXERCISES

1. What is the difference between macroeconomics and microeconomics?

2. Using the equation of exchange of the quantity theory of money, explain how monetary policy can cause inflation.

3. How is a Keynesian different from a monetarist?

4. Suppose that consumption is a function of income, and the relation between consumption and income is detailed in the following table:

| C | Y |
|------|------|
| 1400 | 1000 |
| 3200 | 3000 |
| 5000 | 5000 |
| 6800 | 7000 |
| 8600 | 9000 |

   a. Graph the consumption function implied by this table.
   b. What is the slope of this consumption function?
   c. What is the intercept?

## REFERENCES FOR FURTHER READING

Friedman, Milton, and Walter W. Heller. *Monetary Versus Fiscal Policy*. New York: Norton, 1969.

Wolfson, Murray, and Vincent Buranelli. *In the Long Run We Are All Dead, A Macroeconomics Murder Mystery*. New York: St. Martin's, 1984.

# THE MACROECONOMIC POLICYMAKERS

Chapter 1 described macroeconomics and introduced the notion that economists and politicians try to devise policies that will provide high rates of noninflationary economic growth with low unemployment rates. Although much of the rest of the text will deal with the theory and practice of macroeconomic policy, here we want to introduce the major players in the policymaking game.

Macroeconomic policy is conveniently divided into fiscal policy and monetary policy. Fiscal policy refers to control of government spending and taxation, while monetary policy is the control of the money supply and credit. We will first discuss fiscal policy decisionmakers and then turn to monetary policy.

In the United States, fiscal policy is determined by laws that are passed by Congress and signed by the President. The relative roles of the legislative and executive branches in shaping fiscal policy vary with the political climate, but usually it is the President who initiates major policy changes. Different Presidents rely on different advisors for counsel on fiscal policy. These advisors usually include Cabinet officers such as the Secretary of the Treasury and the Director of the Office of Management and Budget. In addition, the President has a Council of Economic Advisors (CEA) that includes three economists and a support staff who monitor and interpret economic developments for the President. The influence of the Chairman of the CEA depends entirely upon his or her personal relationship with the President.

The President may believe that his advisors have made a convincing case for some fiscal policy action. What can the President do? The President must present the case to Congress, as Congress controls the purse strings and will ultimately set the level of government spending and taxes. So while the President may exercise a role of leadership in proposing a course of fiscal policy action, the actual authority to spend and tax resides in the Congress.

Monetary policy is determined by the Federal Reserve System. The Federal Reserve, or "**Fed**" as it is commonly called, is the central bank of the United States. This means that the Fed serves as a banker for the United States government and has the authority to regulate the nation's supply of money and credit. The Fed controls the growth of the money supply largely through its open-market operations or buying and selling of government bonds. The exact nature of this monetary control process is discussed later in the text; here we are more concerned with the actors than the process. The major actors in the determination of monetary policy are the seven members of the Board of Governors of the Federal Reserve System. The governors are appointed by the President and confirmed by the Senate and serve 14-year terms. The idea behind the long, nonrenewable terms is that the Governors should be free from political pressure to follow the course of action deemed appropriate on economic grounds. The central figure at the Fed is the Chairman of the Board of Governors (at the time of this writing, Paul Volcker). The Chairman's ability to exert leadership on the board and before Congress allows for considerable individual influence on United States macroeconomic policy.

Throughout the text, we will frequently make reference to fiscal and monetary policy and their effects. The analysis of macroeconomic theory and policy will unfold in the coming chapters. Our modest goal in this initial essay is to introduce the key players.

# CHAPTER TWO

# THE NATIONAL INCOME ACCOUNTS

In order to discuss the performance of an economy, there must be a common way to measure a nation's output of goods and services. This chapter discusses the conceptual problems associated with such measures and provides examples of the actual measures used. In microeconomics, discussions of the price and quantity of particular goods or services, like oranges or movies, are more meaningful in that they can be related to a student's past experiences. Such prior experience is missing when you first study macroeconomics: the price and quantity concepts appropriate for the economy as a whole may be somewhat nebulous. Therefore, Chapter 2 lays a foundation upon which future chapters will build. An intuitive feeling for the relationships of basic macro concepts will help you as we build macro theory models.

## 2.1 ECONOMIC ACTIVITY BY SECTORS

We all have firsthand knowledge of the complexities of modern economies. If our goal is to focus on a few important characteristics of an economy, we find that by abstracting from an actual economy the analysis is greatly simplified. We will therefore begin our investigation into the performance of an economy by describing how economic activity would occur in a simple economy consisting only of households and business firms. We will then build upon this very basic model economy in order to allow for a richer mix of economic "actors" and phenomena that more closely approximates reality.

## HOUSEHOLDS AND FIRMS

**factors of production**
The resources used to produce goods and services

**labor force**
All those people in the economy who are currently working or looking for work

**capital**
All manmade resources used in producing goods and services

In our initial simple economy, households own all the resources or **factors of production**. We may conveniently divide these resources into two groups: human resources, commonly referred to as the **labor force**, and non-human resources called **capital**. When you read the financial news and see that a firm is trying to "raise capital," this firm is trying to raise money or attract funds for its use. This is not the kind of capital commonly referred to in macroeconomics. For our purposes, capital refers to man-made resources that have been created by business firms for use in the production of other goods and services. In this sense, a stock certificate is unproductive, but a factory or a machine may be directly used to produce other goods and so is counted as part of the nation's capital stock.

**entrepreneurs**
Owners of business firms

**profits**
The financial return to a firm's owners minus the outlay to that firm's factors of production

**flows**
An amount per unit of time

Business firms employ the services of factors of production to produce final goods and services which are sold to the households. The owners of the business firms, or **entrepreneurs**, earn **profits** from the sale of their output. Their profits are the difference between their sales revenue and their payments for the factors of production hired from the households.

The buying and selling of goods, services, and factors of production, along with the incomes and profits earned are **flows**. That is, services of the factors of production flow from the households in exchange for payments from the firms which become household income. Goods and services flow from the firms to the households in exchange for household payments representing the firms' revenue. Figure 2.1 illustrates the circular nature of these flows; one sector's payments are the other sector's receipts.

As Figure 2.1 shows, there are two ways to measure the total value of the economic activity in this economy: (1) the value of the output of the business firms, as measured by total payments for goods and services, or (2) the value of the inputs to the productive process sold by the households, as measured by total payments for factors of production or household income. Where do the profits paid to the entrepreneurs fit in? We consider entrepreneurship to be a particular kind of labor resource involving risk taking and managerial ability; so profits are just another payment for another input, and are already included in Figure 2.1. We must realize that profits are not simply some kind of residual which is left over after all expenses are met, but a necessary cost which must be covered to attract entrepreneurial talent. To the entrepreneur, the opportunity cost of operating a business might be the wage that could be earned by working for

Figure 2.1

The Circular Flow of Economic Activity in a Simple Economy

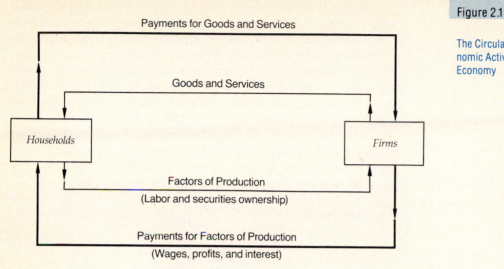

someone else. As long as the entrepreneur expects to just cover this alternative return and a compensation for risk, he or she will continue operating the business. In this event, the entrepreneur is said to be earning a **normal profit**—a profit that is sufficiently large to induce continued entrepreneurial effort and therefore should be considered a necessary cost of operating the business. Measured profits will exceed or fall short of normal profits in any given year depending on business conditions.

**normal profit**
That part of the financial return to a firm that pays the opportunity cost of running a firm

The bottom line of our aggregate circular flow is that *income equals output*. Business firms pay out their total revenue from sales of output as payments for the services of land, labor, capital, or entrepreneurship. To provide a concrete illustration of these rather abstract concepts, let's consider a numerical example of a simple economy like the one discussed.

▶ Let's suppose that our simple economy consists of a labor force of 1000 working people. One hundred members of this labor force are entrepreneurs who operate 100 identical firms. The other 900 workers each receive an annual wage of $10,000 and are employed by the 100 firms. In addition, each member of the labor force owns some capital goods in the form of 2 machines, which are rented to the firms for $1,000 each. Total wages paid and received in the economy would equal $900 \times \$10,000 = \$9,000,000$. Total rents paid to the 900 workers would equal $900 \times \$2,000 = \$1,800,000$.

**EXAMPLE 2.1**

Each of the identical firms pays wages of $9 \times \$10,000 = \$90,000$ for the 9 workers employed, and rents of $9 \times \$2,000 =$

$18,000 for the 18 machines rented from the workers. If the value of the entrepreneur's own machines and labor are the same as the other workers, then the entrepreneur must receive $12,000 from the firm (or else it would pay the entrepreneur to close the business and sell his or her services to another firm) in the form of profits. Thus each firm must produce an output worth $120,000 to cover the resource costs of labor, capital, and entrepreneurial ability ($90,000 + $18,000 + $12,000 = $120,000), and total firm profits in the economy equal 100 × $12,000 = $1,200,000. In terms of the income side of the circular flow, the aggregate income of this economy is found by summing the income received in the form of wages, rents and profits, or:

| **Aggregate Income** = | Wages | $9,000,000 |
|---|---|---|
| | Rents | 1,800,000 |
| | Profits | 1,200,000 |
| | | $12,000,000 |

The circular flow diagram, Figure 2.1, indicates that household payments or expenditures for the output of the business firms must also equal $12,000,000, and since we have 100 firms each selling $120,000 worth of goods and services, we see that this is true (100 × $120,000 = $12,000,000).

Let's assume that the households spend 90 percent of their income for consumption purposes and use 10 percent to buy new machines to add to the capital stock of the economy. Then aggregate expenditures, or the total payments for goods and services would be:

| **Aggregate Expenditures** = | Consumption | $10,800,000 |
|---|---|---|
| | Capital Goods | 1,200,000 |
| | | $12,000,000 |

So we have an example where total spending equals total income as in the circular flow diagram. ◼

Figure 2.1 and Example 2.1 point out an important truth of national income accounting: *total spending will always equal total income*. Having this basic fact behind us, let's move to a more realistic model of an economy.

## FINANCIAL MARKETS

First we alter our model economy to reflect a more accurate description of the ownership of capital. Rather than having capital owned by households and rented to firms, we will now assume that the capital goods (machines, factories, and the like) are owned by the firms. However, since a firm is ultimately owned by one or more individuals, we can say that the capital stock is indirectly owned by individuals. What is the evidence of this indirect ownership? If we assume that our business firms are corporations, then the **securities** issued by the firms give individuals indirect ownership.

The securities we speak of are bonds or stock certificates representing a firm's liability. Bonds are corporate debt. When a corporation sells bonds, it is borrowing money; the buyers of the bonds are thus corporate creditors. Stock certificates represent evidence of ownership; the stockholders of a corporation are its owners. Thus stocks and bonds represent claims on a firm's assets, including capital goods.

Our circular flow diagram must now be changed to incorporate the households' holdings of financial securities. Figure 2.2 indicates that now we have a new form of payment for factors of production:

**securities**
Stocks or bonds that are issued to finance a corporation

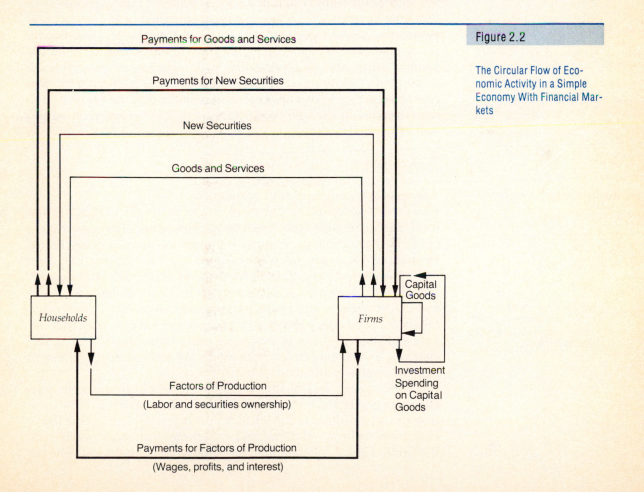

**Figure 2.2**

The Circular Flow of Economic Activity in a Simple Economy With Financial Markets

interest. Bondholders receive interest payments from the debtor firms. Households now receive payments from the following factor services they control: (1) labor, yields wage payments; (2) stock ownership, yields profit payments; (3) bond ownership, yields interest payments. Households no longer receive the rents directly from ownership of capital, yet they *are* receiving such rents indirectly through interest and profit payments. That is, the firms are using capital goods which generate income for the firms. In turn, the firm either pays out its income in the form of wages to its labor force, profits to its stockholders, or interest to its bondholders.

In the top half of Figure 2.2 we see that, as before, households spend their income with the business firms for goods and services. Only now, there is also a channel for new securities sold by the firms to the households. Furthermore, we should realize that now it is the business firms that will undertake **investment spending** to purchase capital, and not households as we had in Example 2.1. In Figure 2.2 we see that the firms both purchase and produce capital goods. Note that total firm receipts include payments for goods and services plus payments for new securities issues. Thus we see that it is possible for the firms to spend more, including investment spending, than the value of the goods and services they produce by issuing securities to households. Total output of the economy is now measured by total consumer expenditures on goods and services plus the value of business investment spending on capital goods. As before, total output will equal total income.

## GOVERNMENT

There remains one very important entity missing from our circular flow model: government. The government sector (federal, state, and local) interacts with both households and firms. The government employs workers and so provides wage income to households. Households also pay taxes to support the government and lend money when the government is borrowing. Such taxes and borrowing allow for government services such as national defense, police and fire protection, education, and **transfer payments**. Transfer payments are payments which are taken (taxed) from one set of individuals and then paid out to others for other than current productive services. Examples of transfer payments are social security, veteran's benefits, welfare, and unemployment benefits.

Government and business interact through government purchases of goods and services produced by firms, taxes paid by business firms (the ultimate burden of these taxes would fall on the firms' customers or input owners), and government services provided to the firms. Figure 2.3 illustrates the circular flow model with the ad-

**investment spending**
The purchase by business firms of capital

**transfer payments**
Outlays by government to individuals without any direct labor services rendered

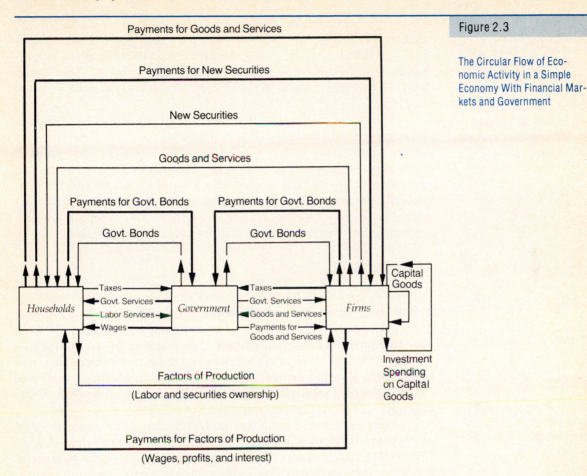

Figure 2.3

The Circular Flow of Economic Activity in a Simple Economy With Financial Markets and Government

dition of a government sector. The new features added in Figure 2.3 are placed in the middle of the diagram. Households now have an additional place to sell their labor for wages, and business firms have an additional market for their goods and services. Of course, the factors of production and goods and services purchased by the government must be paid for via government borrowing and taxes. Figure 2.3 shows that taxes are paid by both firms and households. Ultimately individuals bear the tax burden, as firms will charge higher prices, pay lower wages and interest, and/or earn lower profits for stockholders as a result of the taxes.

Figure 2.3 presumes that the government engages in **deficit spending**. A deficit occurs when government expenditures exceed tax revenues. In our model economy, the deficit is financed by the

**deficit spending**
Government spending in excess of taxes

budget surplus
Tax revenues in excess of government spending for some specified period


When government spending exceeds (is less than) tax revenues, a budget deficit (surplus) occurs.

sale of government bonds or borrowing. In the event of a government **budget surplus**—where tax revenues exceed government spending—outstanding bonds could be purchased back from the households, and the government debt reduced. In Figure 2.3, this would lead to a reversal of the direction of *Govt. Bonds* and *Payments for Govt. Bonds*.

Finally, we should note that there is one other avenue of financing a government budget deficit: money creation. Since the power to create money rests with the government, the excess of government spending over tax revenue could be made up by simply having the government create new money which would then be used by the government for purchases. While Figure 2.3 does not explicitly consider this money creation avenue, we will discuss at length governmental policy with regard to money in several later chapters.

## FOREIGN TRADE

There remains one sector left to consider. So far we have treated our model economy as a *closed economy*, one that does not trade with the rest of the world. One final bit of realism may be added by allowing for foreign trade. We will simplify the analysis by assuming that households and government are not engaged directly in international trade so that only business firms are buying and selling goods and services across international borders (this is not an unrealistic assumption in a capitalist country like the U.S.).

exports
Sales of goods and services to foreign buyers

imports
Purchases of foreign goods and services

balance of trade
Exports minus imports

Sales from our firms to foreign buyers are called **exports**, while purchases by domestic buyers of foreign goods are referred to as **imports**. Exports minus imports equals *net exports* or the **balance of trade**. A positive balance of trade, or trade surplus, means that we are selling more to the rest of the world than they are selling to us. The difference is paid for by foreigners shipping us securities. Conversely, if there is a negative balance of trade, or trade deficit, then our exports are less than imports and we will end up trading some of our securities to pay for the foreign goods and services in excess of our exports. If exports equal imports so that there is balanced trade, then the amount we pay for foreign imports will be just enough to allow foreigners to buy our exports.

In the likely event of unbalanced trade, where international flows of securities are needed to settle international debts, household securities holdings will change (either directly, as households purchase the foreign securities from foreign sources, or indirectly, as domestic business firms do so). A domestic trade surplus will increase stocks of foreign securities held by domestic households, while domestic trade deficits will reduce them.

Figure 2.4

The Circular Flow of Economic Activity in a Simple Economy With Financial Markets, Government, and International Trade

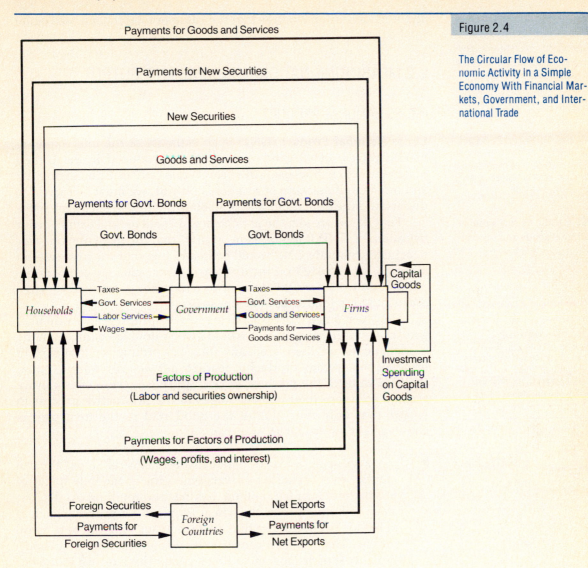

Figure 2.4 presents the complete circular flow model with international trade. Total spending, or **aggregate demand**, is equal to the sum of consumer spending for goods and services, business spending for investment in capital goods, government spending, plus net exports. Total income is found by summing wages (paid by both firms and government), interest, profits, and business taxes. Such an ac-

**aggregate demand**
Total spending of an economy, which is the sum of consumer expenditures, business investment, government spending, and net exports

Aggregate demand is given by the sum of consumer spending, investment, government spending, and net exports.

counting definition ensures that the value of total income will equal total output.

## 2.2 MEASURING NATIONAL INCOME AND OUTPUT

### GROSS NATIONAL PRODUCT

Gross National Product (GNP)
Total market value of all goods and services produced by an economy in a year

**Gross National Product (GNP)** is an estimate of the total value, at market prices, of all goods and services produced in the United States and sold to final users in a year. While GNP is the most popular and often cited measure of a nation's output, we must be careful to understand the limitations and problems inherent in such a measure.

GNP is the market value of all final goods and services produced in a year.

First, let's consider the importance of "sold to final users" in our definition of GNP. It might seem, at first, that the most obvious way to actually compute GNP would be to add together the total sales of all firms, as reported on income tax returns, plus government expenditures for labor (government purchases of goods and services are included in total sales of business firms).

double-counting
In GNP accounting, the mistake of adding the input costs of a product (such as raw material costs) to the final sale value of a finished product

However, since individual firms seldom produce an entire final good or service, this approach would involve **double-counting**. In the modern economy, there are many stages of production that exist in bringing the average product to market. Yet we only want to count the final value of the product for GNP purposes. How then can we account for these intermediate stages in the productive process to ensure that only the value of the good sold to the final user is counted? Let's consider an example.

EXAMPLE 2.2  ▶

Producing a loaf of bread involves several steps. We can identify four separate products emerging at the four stages of production: farming, milling, baking, and retailing. At the first stage, a farmer grows the wheat required for producing a loaf of bread. Let's suppose that the farmer sells the wheat to a mill for 25¢. The mill then converts the wheat into flour at an additional cost of 8¢ (cost including a competitive return to the entrepreneur) and so sells the flour to a baker for 25¢ + 8¢ = 33¢. The bakery produces baked bread at a cost of 12¢ plus the flour input cost of 33¢, and so sells the bread to a retailer for 45¢. The retailer sells bread to the ultimate consumer for 50¢. Thus the bread should add 50¢ to GNP, as it is the value to the final consumer that matters. If we consider the various stages of production, we can also arrive at the same 50¢ value by use of the **value added** approach. To see the value added at each stage of production we must construct the following table:

value added
The sales of a firm minus its costs of inputs purchased from other firms

| Product | Sales Price | Value Added |
|---|---|---|
| Wheat | $.25 | $.25 |
| Flour | .33 | .08 |
| Bread (wholesale) | .45 | .12 |
| Bread (retail) | .50 | .05 |
| | $1.53 | $.50 |

If we simply sum the value of sales at each stage of production we would attribute $1.53 to the value of the bread. This would seriously overstate the market value of the bread which is, of course, the final sales price of $.50. We could, however, take into account the activity at each stage of production by measuring the value added. We would have our national income accountants add up all sales minus the materials expenses of each firm—which equals the value added. ■

Besides the importance of the "final goods" distinction, we must also consider the meaning of measuring GNP "at market prices." First, we could modify our GNP definition to read "at legal market prices," as illegal transactions are not counted. Thus activity in illicit drugs, gambling, and prostitution is ignored in the GNP statistics except in places like Nevada, where gambling and some prostitution are legal. No doubt the level of illegal activity overlooked in the national income statistics is substantial. Some estimates are presented in the Underground Economy essay at the end of the chapter.

Illegal activity is not the only slip between reality and the national income accounts. A major area of importance is production within households. Remember, if it is not sold on a legal market, it generally isn't counted. This means that housework and other do-it-yourself activities, which are most certainly productive, are not counted in GNP. Barter transactions also escape the GNP accounts. For instance, if a plumber has a sick dog and a veterinarian needs his sink repaired, by trading services each can avoid taxation on the income that would have to be reported as a result of a monetary transaction. If the transaction's value is not recorded as taxable income, it will generally not appear in GNP.

GNP is measured in annual terms. Our definition states that we are counting the value of goods and services produced "in a year." In general, we usually consume something in the same year in which it is produced, but some goods, called consumers' **durable goods** last longer than a year. Since GNP is intended to measure the nation's output of goods and services, it is unrealistic to assume that the

**durable goods**
Products that last through repeated consumer use for more than one year

services of a refrigerator or a dishwasher are completely consumed in the year of purchase, yet in fact this is how they are treated. One major exception to this rule exists with owner-occupied housing. National income accountants *impute* a rental value of owner-occupied housing by estimating the value added as if the owners had rented the house to themselves and paid themselves the value added as profits.

There are three other areas where GNP values are imputed for goods and services produced but not explicitly purchased in the market:

1. Salary and wages paid in kind instead of by money—largely room and board provided by an employer.
2. Output consumed by the producer—largely home consumption of crops by farmers.
3. Services rendered by financial institutions in lieu of paying higher interest rates—generally measures the extent to which the services provided depositors are valued more highly than the actual interest paid (one way financial institutions compensate depositors is by charging them less than the full cost of services provided).

Keeping all these qualifications in mind, let's now look at some actual measures of the components of GNP for 1984. Table 2.1 shows the components of GNP in three different views: where it is produced, how it is purchased, and how it is claimed as income. As column 1 indicates, and as you would expect, the bulk of production (85 percent) occurs in business firms. Government adds but 10 percent of GNP value added, and households even less. While this is not true of all countries, the rest of the world is relatively unimportant as far as U.S. GNP accounting goes. Purchases of GNP are not as concentrated in one sector as is production. While household spending for consumption accounts for 64 percent of GNP, government spending is an important 20 percent, followed by business investment spending at 17 percent. In column 2 we also see that net exports are small but negative. We should remember that net exports can be (and often have been) positive when exports exceed imports. Column 3 indicates that the major claim on the nation's output is private income, followed by net taxes. Net taxes are all tax and non-tax payments to governments less transfer payments and interest paid on government debt. The other sizeable claim on output, **capital consumption allowance**, refers to the estimated amount of capital goods used up in production by depreciation, obsolescence, and accidental destruction.

**capital consumption allowance**
The depletion in value of the stock of capital goods each year

Table 2.1

**The Gross National Product
of the United States, 1984**

### (1) Output

| Where Produced | Amount | % of GNP |
|---|---|---|
| Households | 123.5 | 3 |
| Firms | 3117.6 | 85 |
| Government | 375.3 | 10 |
| Rest of the world | 44.9 | 1 |
| | 3661.3 | 100% |

### (2) Expenditures[a]

| Final Purchases | Amount | % of GNP |
|---|---|---|
| Consumer expenditures | 2342.3 | 64 |
| Gross investment | 637.3 | 17 |
| Government expenditures | 748.0 | 20 |
| Net exports | −66.3 | −2 |
| | 3661.3 | 100% |

### (3) Income

| Received as | Amount | % of GNP |
|---|---|---|
| Private income[b] | 2783.8 | 76 |
| Capital consumption | 402.9 | 11 |
| Net taxes[c] | 474.6 | 13 |
| | 3661.3 | 100% |

Amounts in billions of dollars. Totals may not add due to rounding.

Source: *Economic Report of the President, 1985*

Notes: [a] Purchases of final goods and services made by each sector.

[b] Computed as disposable personal income + undistributed corporate profits (with inventory and capital consumption adjustment) + wage accruals less disbursements − interest paid by consumers to business − personal transfer payments to foreigners (net) ≡ consumer expenditures + gross private saving − capital consumption.

[c] Computed as government purchases of goods and services + government surplus (national income and product accounts basis) + personal and government transfers to foreigners + government interest payments to foreigners + statistical discrepancy.

## NET NATIONAL PRODUCT

The capital consumption allowance of column 3 in Table 2.1 may be subtracted from the column 2 measure for gross investment to arrive at net investment. That is:

**Net Investment = Gross Investment − Capital Consumption Allowance**

We have already learned that investment is business spending on capital goods. Yet the presence of a capital consumption allowance reminds us that some of this investment spending is required to replace old capital goods that are no longer useful. By focusing on net investment, we see the extent to which the nation's capital stock is actually increased by current investment spending.

If gross investment was equal to the capital consumption allowance, then net investment would be zero and there would be no net additions to the capital stock.

Since used-up capital goods do not increase our ability to produce and consume, an alternative measure of how much we produce in a year that subtracts out the capital consumption allowance is net national product (NNP):

**Net National Product = Gross National Product − Capital Consumption Allowance**

To produce a table for NNP similar to the GNP Table 2.1, in our output column, we would subtract the capital consumption allowance from firm output. In the second column for expenditures, we would subtract the capital consumption allowance from gross investment to record net investment. Finally in the third column, the line for capital consumption allowance would be omitted. As with GNP, whichever way we compute it, NNP will be the same, and will equal $402.9 billion less than GNP, or $3,258.4 billion.

As was said above, capital consumption allowances represent no income to anyone. So NNP is perhaps a better way to measure national output and income than GNP, and we will use NNP as our preferred measure in the remainder of the book. It should be realized, however, that through the years, GNP and NNP have moved together so closely that they generally tell the same story, as illustrated in Figure 2.5.

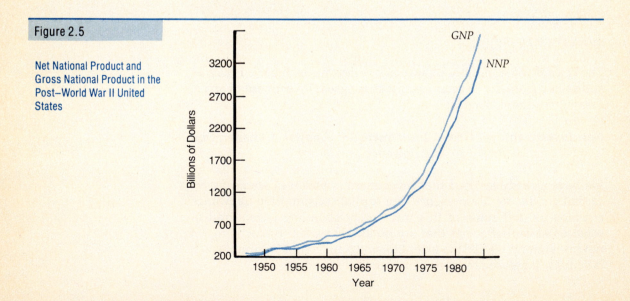

**Figure 2.5**

Net National Product and Gross National Product in the Post–World War II United States

## 2.3 NATIONAL INCOME ACCOUNTING IDENTITIES AND SAVING

**Saving** is the difference between private income and consumer expenditures. Private income is the income available for consumer spending, so that part of household income which is not spent is saved. Rather than repetitiously write these terms, we introduce convenient symbols which will stand for the various concepts. For instance, instead of writing the first two sentences of this paragraph, it is much easier to write and remember a simple **identity**. If private income is given the symbol $Y_N$, consumer expenditures $C$, and saving $S$, we define saving as:[1]

$$S \equiv Y_N - C$$

Note that the identity sign ($\equiv$) is used rather than the equal sign ($=$) in equation (2.1), because this relationship is always true by definition. In general, macroeconomists use identities to indicate definitions and use equal signs for relations based on human behavior (don't worry about this now; there will be plenty of examples later).

Recalling the circular flow analysis of Section 2.1, we know that saving is used to purchase new securities issues of firms and foreigners as well as government debt (and government issued money, although this was not explicitly introduced). Sales of existing securities and government bonds are not part of saving but rather a transfer of some assets in exchange for other assets. Saving, then, is used to finance business investment spending, net exports, and the government deficit. As Table 2.1 indicated, in terms of the income approach to GNP, total claims on output or income were equal to private income plus the capital consumption allowance plus net taxes. Since we will use NNP as our measure of national output or total income, we omit the capital consumption allowance and state that total income $Y$ is identically equal to private income plus net taxes, or:

$$Y \equiv Y_N + T \qquad (2.2)$$

From the expenditures approach, we know that total expenditures are identically equal to the sum of consumer expenditures $C$,

**saving**
Total consumer income minus consumer expenditures

**identity**
a relationship which is true by definition

---

[1]The more natural symbol for private income $Y_p$ is customarily used for another concept introduced below; the subscript $N$ is meant to remind us that private income is *net* of taxes.

investment $I$, government expenditures $G$, and net exports $X$, or:

$$Y \equiv C + I + G + X \qquad (2.3)$$

Since we are talking about $Y$ as NNP, we should think of investment, $I$, as net investment. Furthermore, since we know that total income always equals total expenditures, we can let $Y$ represent both total expenditures and total income—they are simply different ways of viewing the same concept.

Suppose we substitute the definition of $Y$ given in equation (2.2) into the $Y$ term on the left-hand side of equation (2.3). After the substitution we have:

$$Y_N + T \equiv C + I + G + X \qquad (2.4)$$

But since we know that private income, $Y_N$, must be used for either consumption or saving, we can define $Y_N$ as:

$$Y_N = C + S \qquad (2.5)$$

Now we can substitute $C + S$ into the $Y_N$ term in equation (2.4) to get:

$$C + S + T \equiv C + I + G + X \qquad (2.6)$$

The left-hand side of equation (2.6) tells us that total income is either spent for consumption, saved, or used to pay taxes. The right-hand side shows that final purchases of goods and services are composed of consumer spending, investment, government spending, and net exports. Since consumption appears on both sides of equation (2.6), we can subtract it from both sides leaving $S + T \equiv I + G + X$. A very useful way to express this identity is found by subtracting $T$ from each side of the equation, leaving us with:

Saving = Investment + Government Deficit + Net Exports

$$S \equiv I + G - T + X \qquad (2.7)$$

Realizing that $G - T$ "the difference between government spending and taxes" is the government deficit, equation (2.7) indicates that saving is equal to investment plus the government deficit plus net exports. This is always true by definition. We will find (2.7) to be useful as a check for the logical consistency of macroeconomic theories. If a particular theory predicts certain values for the individual elements of (2.7), in order for the theory to be reasonable, the predicted values must be consistent with (2.7).

The material of this chapter provides a foundation which, by itself, is rather unexciting. However, after adding the analysis of modern macroeconomics, you will realize a synthesis of this foundation with the following material until the major lessons of this chapter seem quite elementary. The goal, of course, is to understand the dynamics of key macroeconomic variables like unemployment and inflation.

**SUMMARY**

1  There are four major sectors of the U.S. economy:

a  Households: Sell labor for wages, hold securities and government debt for which they receive interest and profits, pay taxes, and receive government services.

b  Business firms: Own the capital stock and hire services of labor to produce goods and services which are sold to households, government, and the rest of the world. Firms also use household savings by selling securities to finance investment spending which builds the capital stock.

c  Government: Collects taxes and provides services to the other sectors.

d  Rest of world: Trades foreign goods and securities for U.S. goods and securities.

2  Total spending or aggregate demand in the economy is equal to total income.

3  Gross National Product (GNP) is the estimate of the total value at market prices of all goods and services produced in the U.S. in a year and sold to final users.

4  Net National Product (NNP) is equal to GNP minus capital consumption allowance. Capital consumption allowance measures the reduction in the capital stock due to depreciation and obsolescence.

5  Aggregate expenditures equal the sum of consumption plus investment plus government spending plus net exports.

6  Saving finances investment plus the government deficit plus net exports.

## EXERCISES

1. Why do we say that households "sell the services of their labor" rather than "sell their labor" to firms?

2. People often think of profits as some residual left over after a firm meets all of its expenses. Yet in this chapter profits were presented as a necessary return. What would happen if there were zero profits for a prolonged period of time? Which factor of production would be directly affected and how?

3. Why do you suppose we call stocks and bonds *securities*?

4. Using the *Survey of Current Business* or some other source, find the size of government transfer payments as a fraction of GNP for the years 1950, 1960, 1970, and 1980. How do you explain your finding?

5. Revise Figure 2.3 to explicitly show how government issued money could be incorporated. Be sure to explain your new circular flow model carefully.

6. If total spending always equals total income or output how can we ever have a recession where spending is too low to buy all the goods and services being produced? (If you can answer this question then either a) you have been reading ahead of the rest of the class, b) this is your second time through macroeconomics, or c) you should be teaching this class.)

7. How would the following items affect the current year's GNP:
   a. You sell your 1980 automobile to a friend.
   b. Instead of charging his usual $100 an hour consulting fee, an attorney agrees to counsel you for free.
   c. A U.S. computer manufacturer sells a computer system to a French firm for $2,000,000 and at the same time a U.S. newstand buys $1,000 of postcards from a French printer.
   d. A woman hires a gardener to maintain her property one day a week for $50.00 a week. She then marries him. After the wedding, he maintains the property without any payment.
   e. Prostitution is legalized.

8. If GNP is supposed to measure the total value of final output produced in a year, why use market prices as the measure of value for each individual good?

9. Use the following information to answer the questions below: (figures are in billions of dollars)

| | | |
|---|---|---|
| Consumer expenditures | = | 2412 |
| Capital consumption allowance | = | 334 |
| Net exports | = | 10 |
| Net investment | = | 423 |
| Government expenditures | = | 821 |
| Net taxes | = | 666 |

    **a.** Gross investment equals _____.

    **b.** GNP is equal to _____.

    **c.** Private income equals _____.

    **d.** NNP is equal to _____.

**10.** Produce a table like Table 2.1 for 1984 NNP.

**11.** If investment = $220 billion, there is a government budget surplus of $10 billion, exports = $175 billion, and imports = $185 billion, how much is saving?

**12.** What is the difference between saving and savings?

## REFERENCES FOR FURTHER READING

Jaszi, George. "An Economic Accountant's Ledger." *The Economic Accounts of the United States: Retrospect and Prospect.* Supplement to *Survey of Current Business*, July 1971, p. 218.

Kendrick, John W. "National Income and Product Accounts." In *International Encyclopedia of the Social Sciences*. London: Macmillan, 1968, vol. 11, pp. 19–34.

Rosen, Sam. *National Income and Other Social Accounts*. New York: Holt, 1972.

# THE UNDERGROUND ECONOMY

We all know that there is more going on in the U.S. economy than meets the eye via the national income accounts. As mentioned, in Chapter Two, generally only transactions occurring in a legal market are counted for GNP. What is missed is often referred to as the underground economy (also known as subterranean economy or irregular economy). The underground economy encompasses much more than simply illegal drugs, prostitution, and gambling. The musician who doesn't report his income when he is paid in cash, the retailer who "skims off the top" before reporting his sales, the waitress who reports only half of her tips, the illegal alien who takes his wage income back to Mexico are all part of the underground economy. Why don't people report their earnings— to avoid taxes, of course. As tax rates increase, we would expect a greater incentive for economic activity to "go underground." Just how large this sector is and the implications for economic policymaking are questions we want to address.

The two most widely publicized studies of the underground economy are by Edgar Feige of the University of Wisconsin and Peter Gutmann of the City University of New York. Gutmann estimated the size of the subterranean economy to be almost $200 billion in 1976, which is approximately 10 percent of 1976 GNP. Feige, using different assumptions, estimated the size of this activity at $369 billion in 1976, which is approximately 22 percent of GNP. Even more startling is Feige's estimate of the underground economy for 1980 of $704 billion, or 33 percent of GNP!

Before discussing the implications of such figures, we should understand how such guesses are achieved. After all, no one makes public announcements regarding how much income he failed to report, or what last month's cocaine revenues were. Economists have long believed that most illicit deals are transacted in cash, as cash leaves no traceable record like checks or credit cards do. Since World War II, there has been a pronounced growth in currency relative to demand deposits (the technical name for checking accounts), and the assumption of researchers like Gutmann and Feige, is that such growth in the popularity of currency reflects an expansion of illicit transactions that people want to hide. By using certain assumptions regarding the amount of transactions each illicit dollar will support along with a few additional qualifications, one can derive estimates for the value of the transactions being financed "underground."

It may be comforting to the skeptical that some corroborating evidence regarding the 1976 figures has been reported by the Internal Revenue Service. The IRS has estimated that in 1976 unreported legally earned income was approximately $100 billion, and that, in addition, no taxes were paid on $25 to $35 billion of individual income arising from illegal activities.

What does all this mean for understanding macroeconomics? It means, quite simply, that the reported GNP figures may considerably understate the true level of economic activity. If the underground economy has grown more rapidly than the growth reported in the national income accounts, then the U.S. economy is healthier than would appear at first glance. Feige suggests that because of the underground economy:

1. Official statistics on income will grossly understate the true growth of the overall economy.
2. Official unemployment statistics are almost certain to overestimate the true situation.
3. Official inflation statistics are likely to be substantial overestimates.

Before celebrating this revelation regarding the condition of the economy, be aware that other researchers, like Edward Denison of the Brookings Institution and Richard O. Porter and Amanda S. Bayer of the staff of the Federal Reserve Board claim that Gutmann's and Feige's estimates are excessive. Still we know that there is much unreported income and furthermore, this is not a unique condition to the U.S. As Feige says: "The Swedes have a 'hidden economy,' the English their 'fiddle,' the Italians their 'lavorno nero,' the French their 'travail au noir'." The incentive to engage in illegal activities or avoid taxation is universal. When considering the national income accounts, we do well to remember what is not there, as well as what is.

## REFERENCES

Bowsher, Norman. "The Demand for Currency: Is the Underground Economy Undermining Monetary Policy?" Federal Reserve Bank of St. Louis *Review*, January 1980, 11–17.

Denison, Edward F. "Is U.S. Growth Understated Because of the Underground Economy? Employment Ratios Suggest Not." *Review of Income and Wealth*, 28, (March 1982), 1–16.

Feige, Edgar L. "How Big Is the Irregular Economy?" *Challenge*, Nov./Dec. 1979, 5–13.

Gutmann, Peter M. "The Subterranean Economy." *Financial Analysts Journal*, Nov./Dec. 1977, pp. 26, 27, 34.

Porter, Richard O., and Amanda S. Bayer. "A Monetary Perspective on Underground Economic Activity in the United States." *Federal Reserve Bulletin*, 70, (March 1984), 177–90.

# CHAPTER THREE

# OTHER MACROECONOMIC VARIABLES

This chapter continues to develop our foundation material, introducing and defining the terms and concepts frequently encountered in macroeconomics. Many of the concepts you encounter in this chapter you will have already heard of. Aside from being a prerequisite for understanding the remaining chapters, Chapter 3 contains information that is basic for being an enlightened observer of current news.

## 3.1 PRICE INDICES AND THE MEASUREMENT OF REAL INCOME

### THE AVERAGE LEVEL OF PRICES

Macroeconomists study prices in a different manner than microeconomists. Microeconomics is concerned with the prices of individual goods and how these prices change relative to each other. Changes in *relative prices* are caused by factors that affect basic supply and demand conditions underlying each good's price, such as shifts in consumer preferences or in technology. On the other hand, macroeconomists focus on the *average price level* across the entire economy. Even though the price of shoes may rise relative to the price of books, during inflation the average of shoe, book, and other goods' prices tends to rise. It is this movement of prices in general, and not the behavior of prices in a single market, that concerns the macro-economist.

The macroeconomic concern with the average level of prices is, in part, a result of difficulties in interpreting the national income accounts. As we learned in Chapter 2, net national product (NNP) is measured as the dollar value of output or income. This means that NNP is composed of the actual quantity of goods and services produced times the prices of these goods and services. The dollar value of output could then rise either because more goods and services are being produced or simply because the prices of this output have risen.

The primary goal of national income accounting is to determine changes in the real amounts of goods and services produced. But any time prices change, NNP will be distorted in terms of reporting how the actual output changed. Table 3.1 provides an illustration of this effect. For simplicity, suppose that our economy only produces three goods. The total value of output is found by summing the quantity produced times the price of each good. For instance, in Year 0, we produced 100 units of Good 1 at $10 each, 300 units of Good 2 at $5 each, and 2,000 units of Good 3 at $1 each. The total value of output, then, is $1,000 + $1,500 + $2,000 = $4,500. As we move from Year 0 to Year 1, prices remain constant but a larger quantity of each good is produced. The increase in total income from $4,500 to $4,950 is all due to the increase in production of the three goods. As we move from Year 1 to Year 2, we can see the confusion introduced by price level changes. Even though output has fallen in Year 2, total income is unchanged. How can this be? The answer, of course, is that prices have risen just enough to offset the fall in production. Output in Year 2 is back to the same level as Year 0. When we measure national income or output in terms of current dollar values, we cannot distinguish between changes due to production and changes due to prices.

## DEFLATING NOMINAL NATIONAL INCOME

Since we are concerned about economic growth, where growth refers to increases in the production of goods and services, we must be able to distinguish price-level changes from changes in real output. We want to decompose *national income Y* into an index of the *price level P* and an index of the total *real quantity of goods and services y*. Since total national income is equal to the average level of prices times the quantity of goods and services produced, we can express this relationship as:

Price level changes must be distinguished from real output changes.

$$Y = Py \qquad\qquad (3.1)$$

The current dollar value of income $Y$ is commonly referred to as **nominal national income**. The index of real output of goods and services $y$ is called **real national income**. Another way of expressing the relationship between $Y$ and $y$ is found by dividing both sides of equation (3.1) by the price level $P$:

$$Y/P = y \tag{3.2}$$

Real national income is equal to nominal national income divided by the price level. We *deflate* nominal income by dividing by price. Our deflated real income is a measure of real output or income that holds prices constant. In fact, we sometimes refer to nominal NNP as **current dollar** NNP, while real NNP is called **constant dollar** NNP. The "constant dollar" term reflects the technique of holding prices constant. We pick a particular year to serve as a *base year*, then measure how real output changes through time, in terms of the base-year price level. This is what equation (3.2) actually computes.

To clarify the discussion, consider an example based on Table 3.1.

**EXAMPLE 3.1** ▶      The choice of base year is arbitrary, but let's use Year 0 as our base. To keep track of our different variables through time, we can use subscripts to denote year. That is, $Y_0$ refers to nominal income in Year 0, $P_2$ is the price level in Year 2, and so on. Since we are going to measure how real income changes measured in base-year dollars, it is always true that nominal income equals real income in the base year. But to illustrate this we must construct our price index. In the base year, Year 0, our price index equals 1. This is simply saying that prices in Year 0 are 100 percent of base-year (which is Year 0) prices, or Year 0 prices equal 1 times base-year prices. What about Year 1? Since prices are unchanged from the base year to Year 1, the price index is, once again, equal to 1 as prices in Year 1 are also equal to 1 times base-year prices. In Year 2, we see that prices have risen. In fact, they have risen by 10 percent. Since prices in Year 2 are 110 percent of base-year prices, the price index equals 1.10. To find real income in each year, we simply divide nominal income by price, or:

*Real income is equal to nominal income divided by the price level.*

$$Y_0 = Y_0/P_0 = \$4{,}500/1 \quad\;\; = \$4{,}500$$
$$Y_1 = Y_1/P_1 = \$4{,}950/1 \quad\;\; = \$4{,}950$$
$$Y_2 = Y_2/P_2 = \$4{,}950/1.10 = \$4{,}500$$

As we mentioned above, in the base year, real income and nominal income are identical. In Year 1, real income and nominal income are also identical, because prices are unchanged

Table 3.1

|  | Good 1 | | Good 2 | | Good 3 | | Income |
|---|---|---|---|---|---|---|---|
| Year | Quantity | Price | Quantity | Price | Quantity | Price | |
| 0 | 100 | $10 | 300 | $5 | 2000 | $1 | $4,500 |
| 1 | 110 | 10 | 330 | 5 | 2200 | 1 | 4,950 |
| 2 | 100 | 11 | 300 | 5.50 | 2000 | 1.10 | 4,950 |

**Prices and Quantities Produced in a Three-Good Economy**

from the base year. In Year 2, however, nominal income was the same as in Year 1, but real income fell back to the Year 0 level of $4,500. If we look at the quantities produced of each good, we see that in fact Year 2 output was identical to Year 0, so real income must be unchanged between the two years. Had we just looked at nominal income, we would have been misled in Year 2. The only reason that nominal income in Year 2 stayed at the Year 1 level was price increases. If we deflate nominal income to take out the influence of price changes, we find that real income indeed went down from Year 1 to Year 2. ∎

## VARIETIES OF PRICE INDICES

**LASPEYRES AND PAASCHE INDICES**   The example just covered had the convenient property of all prices rising proportionally. Since the prices of Goods 1, 2, and 3 all rose 10 percent, it was very straightforward to say that the price index equals 1.10, as Year 2 prices are 110 percent of base-year prices. Realistically, all prices do not increase proportionally. In fact, in any dynamic economy, we should expect some prices to rise as others fall. There are several ways to compute a price index to incorporate such changing relative prices. The two most popular are the **Laspeyres index** and the **Paasche index.** The Laspeyres index requires the identification of a standard basket of goods to represent average production or consumption in the economy. By determining the dollar cost of the total basket in the current year and comparing that with the dollar cost in the base year, we can determine how the average price level has changed. If the basket costs twice as much in the current year as the base year, then the index value would be two. So the Laspeyres index compares the cost over time of a basket of goods considered representative of base-year production or consumption.

The Paasche index computes the value of a basket of goods representative of current period consumption, and then compares this cost with what a similar basket would have cost in the base year. The difference, then, between the Paasche and Laspeyres index is that

**Laspeyres index**
A price index based on the quantities bought in a base year

**Paasche index**
A price index based on the quantities bought in the current year

the Laspeyres index weights prices by quantities representative of base year production or consumption while the Paasche index weights prices by current year production or consumption. These indices will generally yield different measures of prices and real income, since each is an imperfect attempt at measuring changes in the purchasing power of income.

Table 3.2 provides an example of the differences between the Laspeyres and Paasche index. Price and quantity data are given for Year 0, assumed to be the base year, and Year 4, assumed to be the current year. The Laspeyres index compares the dollar value of base-year quantities using current prices in each year. Dividing the Year-4 value of $4700 by the base-year value of $4500 gives an index value of 104.4 percent. The Paasche index compares the dollar value of Year-4 quantities using prevailing prices in each year. Dividing the Year-4 value of $4950 by the base-year value of $4750 yields an index value of 104.2 percent. While the two indexes generally provide different results, the measures are usually close.

**implicit GNP deflator**
A Paasche index implied by Commerce Department estimates of average prices

**IMPLICIT GNP DEFLATORS**   There are several measures of the "average price level." The **implicit GNP deflator** is a very broad-based measure of average prices and is the index actually used by the U.S. Department of Commerce for creating real GNP. The GNP deflator is a Paasche index that measures how prices change across the broad spectrum of the economy. Since it would be virtually impossible to

---

**Table 3.2**

**Alternative Measures of Price Indices**

| | Good 1 | | Good 2 | | Good 3 | |
|---|---|---|---|---|---|---|
| Year | Quantity | Price | Quantity | Price | Quantity | Price |
| 0 | 100 | $10 | 300 | $5 | 2000 | $1 |
| 4 | 95 | 11 | 340 | 5 | 2100 | 1.05 |

Laspeyres index (compare changing cost of base year quantities):

Base year:  $(100 \times \$10) + (300 \times \$5) + (2000 \times \$1) = \$4500$
Year 4:  $(100 \times \$11) + (300 \times \$5) + (2000 \times \$1.05) = \$4700$

Index value in Year 4 = $4700/$4500 = 1.044 or 104.4 percent

Paasche index (compare changing cost of current year quantities):

Base year:  $(95 \times \$10) + (340 \times \$5) + (2100 \times \$1) = \$4750$
Year 4:  $(95 \times \$11) + (340 \times \$5) + (2100 \times \$1.05) = \$4950$

Index value in Year 4 = $4950/$4750 = 1.042 or 104.2 percent

consider the individual price of every good produced, real GNP is estimated by sector, where a "sector" is a grouping of closely related products. Price indices and nominal output are estimated for each sector, like automobiles, and then by dividing the nominal output by the price index, deflated real output for that sector is estimated. By summing across sectors, we obtain real GNP for the entire economy.

CONSUMER PRICE INDEX    One of the best known average price measures is the **consumer price index**, or CPI. The CPI is a Laspeyres index, where the cost of a base-year basket of consumer goods and services is monitored. There are alternative indices for different consumer groups. For instance, the CPI for all urban consumers is a measure of the average prices of goods and services purchased by urban consumers (about 80 percent of the civilian population). The CPI is a narrower measure than the GNP deflator in that it considers fewer items. But the "correct" price index depends upon what use you have in mind. Since many labor contracts include provisions to raise wages to mirror changes in prices, such "cost of living" raises are usually based on changes in the CPI, as the CPI considers those goods and services consumed by households.

To determine which goods and how much of each to include in the base year, the Department of Commerce utilizes extensive surveys of consumer spending. In recent years, the many flaws associated with price indices in general, and the CPI in particular, have been widely publicized. The essay at the end of the chapter will consider these shortcomings.

**consumer price index**
A Laspeyres index based on a standardized sampling of consumer goods and services

PRODUCER PRICE INDEX    There is one additional price index that receives widespread attention: the **producer price index** (PPI). The PPI measures average prices received by producers of commodities (the PPI was formerly known as the Wholesale Price Index, or WPI). We generally focus on a PPI for a particular stage of production, such as finished goods. This avoids exaggerating price-level changes that occur at a primary stage of the production process and then become reflected in later stages, using the primary good as an input. For instance, an increase in the price of steel scrap would be reflected in higher sheet steel prices and ultimately would lead to higher automobile prices. Since produced goods include many goods that are used as inputs for producing other goods, focusing on one stage of production—finished goods—avoids the double-counting of price increases passed up from one stage of production to the other. Since the PPI reflects price changes at an earlier stage of production than the CPI, the upward or downward movement is sometimes cited as an early warning as to where the CPI might move in the months ahead.

**producer price index**
A Laspeyres index based on a standardized sampling of prices for basic commodities

Table 3.3

**Annual Percentage Change in the GNP Deflator, Producer Price Index, and Consumer Price Index**

| Year | GNP Deflator | PPI | CPI |
|------|------|------|------|
| 1965 | 2.2% | 1.7% | 1.7% |
| 1966 | 3.2 | 3.2 | 2.9 |
| 1967 | 3.0 | −1.2 | 2.9 |
| 1968 | 4.4 | 2.8 | 4.2 |
| 1969 | 5.1 | 3.7 | 5.4 |
| 1970 | 5.4 | 3.5 | 5.9 |
| 1971 | 5.0 | 3.1 | 4.3 |
| 1972 | 4.2 | 3.1 | 3.3 |
| 1973 | 5.8 | 9.1 | 6.2 |
| 1974 | 8.8 | 15.3 | 11.0 |
| 1975 | 9.3 | 10.8 | 9.1 |
| 1976 | 5.2 | 4.4 | 5.8 |
| 1977 | 5.8 | 6.5 | 6.5 |
| 1978 | 7.4 | 7.8 | 7.7 |
| 1979 | 8.6 | 11.1 | 11.3 |
| 1980 | 9.2 | 13.5 | 13.5 |
| 1981 | 9.6 | 9.2 | 10.4 |
| 1982 | 6.0 | 4.0 | 6.1 |
| 1983 | 3.8 | 1.6 | 3.2 |
| 1984 | 3.7 | 2.1 | 4.3 |

CPI is for all urban consumers beginning 1978; earlier data are for urban wage earners and clerical workers.

PPI is for total finished goods.
Data are percentage changes in the yearly average values of the indexes.

Table 3.3 and Figure 3.1 illustrate how the three measures of average prices have changed in recent times. Note that the producer price index is much more volatile than the GNP deflator or the CPI. This is due to the inherent differences between consumption and production. While households consume at a fairly even pace through good times and bad, production occurs on a more erratic basis. When firms face rising demand and lack of inventory, output and prices increase. But during periods of unexpectedly low demand and consequently rising inventories of unsold goods, output and prices decline.

## NOMINAL VERSUS REAL VALUES

We mentioned above the use of price indices for deflating nominal GNP to find real GNP. Many other macroeconomic variables are discussed in real terms. We divide the nominal values of these variables by an appropriate price index to obtain a real value. For instance, we may want to see how government spending has changed through the

Figure 3.1

Annual Percentage Change in the GNP Deflator, Producer Price Index, and Consumer Price Index

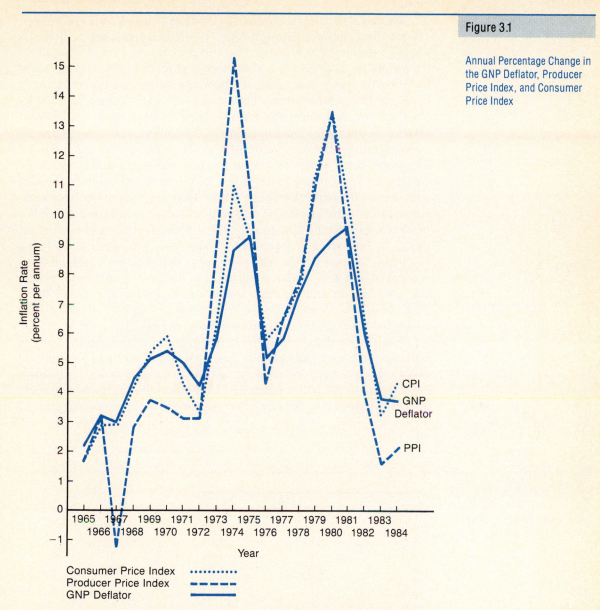

Consumer Price Index    ·········

Producer Price Index    ‑ ‑ ‑ ‑ ‑

GNP Deflator    —————

CPI is for all urban consumers beginning 1978; earlier data are for urban wage earners and clerical workers. PPI is for total finished goods. Data are percentage changes in the yearly average values of the indexes.

years in real terms, so we would divide nominal government spending by the price index to arrive at real government spending in real terms, we get a better idea of the change in the government's claim on real goods and services.

We can also use price indices to find how the real value of money, say a dollar, changes through time. While it is true that "a dollar is always a dollar," it is not true that the purchasing power of a dollar, its command over goods and services, is unchanging. By dividing $1.00 by the price index, we see how the value of a dollar changes through time. Our arbitrary choice of base year is once again irrelevant, but by definition the real value of $1.00 is $1.00 in the year chosen as our base. During inflationary times, when prices are on average rising, the real value of a dollar will be falling. Table 3.4 illustrates some computations of the real value of a dollar using the CPI as the appropriate price index. In the base year, where the CPI equals one, the real value is one dollar. In years prior to the base year, when prices were lower, the real value of a dollar exceeded $1.00. For instance, in 1963 the CPI equals .917 so that we may say on average, prices in 1963 were 91.7 percent of base year 1967 prices. Dividing $1.00 by .917, we find a real value of a dollar to be $1.09, in 1963 compared to a 1967 dollar. Another way of viewing this data, is that the same goods and services that could be purchased for $1.00 in 1967 could have been purchased for about $.92 in 1963. Based on the CPI value for 1983, these goods would have cost $3.11 in 1984.

While we will often discuss macroeconomic variables in terms of both nominal and real magnitudes, to help keep things straight we will follow a convention throughout the book of *representing nominal amounts by capital letters* (such as M for the nominal money supply) and *real amounts by lower case letters* (m for the real money supply).

---

**Table 3.4**

**The Real Value of a Dollar**

| Year | Price Index (CPI) | $1/CPI |
|------|-------------------|--------|
| 1961 | .896              | $1.12  |
| 1963 | .917              | 1.09   |
| 1965 | .945              | 1.06   |
| 1967 | 1.000             | 1.00   |
| 1969 | 1.098             | .91    |
| 1971 | 1.213             | .82    |
| 1973 | 1.331             | .75    |
| 1975 | 1.612             | .62    |
| 1977 | 1.815             | .55    |
| 1979 | 2.174             | .46    |
| 1981 | 2.724             | .37    |
| 1982 | 2.891             | .35    |
| 1983 | 2.984             | .34    |
| 1984 | 3.111             | .32    |

## 3.2 UNEMPLOYMENT

The popular way to describe the state of the labor market is to quote the **unemployment rate**. But just what is the unemployment rate? It is not, as some might think, the fraction of the total population out of work. The unemployment rate can be defined simply as the fraction of the labor force that is unemployed. But who is unemployed and who is classified as being in the labor force? To understand just what the unemployment rate measures, we must examine the definitions of the unemployed and the labor force. To be counted in the **labor force**, a person must either have a job, be looking for work, be waiting to report to work, or be in the military. Examples of individuals considered outside of the labor force would be students in school, those people doing housework in their own home, the retired, and others who have no job and are not looking for one.

To be considered as employed, yet not currently working, a person must be taking a temporary absence for such reasons as illness, vacation, strike, or bad weather. Unemployed persons must have looked for work within the past four weeks or else must be waiting for a job that will begin within 30 days. The definition of the unemployed is precise and narrow in order to accurately determine the state of the labor market based on reasonable wages. For example, nearly everyone not currently employed would say he or she wanted to work at some particular wage and position. A student or housewife with no current desire to enter the labor force would, we expect, be willing to work for a million dollars as, say, a cashier at a restaurant. By requiring that the unemployed at least claim to be actively seeking work, we separate those who dream of working at a wage no one would ever pay from those who believe they can find acceptable work at the going wage rate, and so are at least claiming to be actively seeking it.

To actually estimate the size of the labor force and the number unemployed, the Bureau of Labor Statistics surveys approximately 50,000 households each month. Once the estimates are known, the unemployment rate can be determined by dividing the number of unemployed by the number in labor force. Table 3.5 presents unemployment rate data for recent years. We can see from the table that teenagers tend to have much higher unemployment rates than older workers. Teenagers are generally the least skilled workers in the economy and so would be expected to have the highest rate of unemployment when employers must pay a minimum wage. We can also see that nonwhite unemployment rates are substantially higher than those for whites—once again likely due to skill differentials

**unemployment rate**
The fraction of the total labor force without a job and looking for work

**labor force**
Anyone who is employed or who is unemployed and looking for work

The unemployment rate is the fraction of the labor force unemployed.

Table 3.5

**U.S. Unemployment Rate**

|  | 1978 | 1979 | 1980 | 1981 | 1982 | 1983 | 1984 |
|---|---|---|---|---|---|---|---|
| Unemployment rate | 6.0% | 5.8% | 7.0% | 7.5% | 9.5% | 9.5% | 7.4% |
| Males 20 years and older | 4.3 | 4.2 | 5.9 | 6.3 | 8.8 | 8.9 | 6.6 |
| Females 20 years and older | 6.0 | 5.7 | 6.4 | 6.8 | 8.3 | 8.1 | 6.8 |
| Both sexes 16–19 | 16.4 | 16.1 | 17.8 | 19.6 | 23.2 | 22.4 | 18.9 |
| White | 5.2 | 5.1 | 6.3 | 6.7 | 8.6 | 8.4 | 6.5 |
| Non-white | 11.9 | 11.3 | 13.1 | 14.2 | 17.3 | 17.8 | 14.4 |

**labor participation rate**
The fraction of the adult civilian population who are members of the labor force

arising from several factors, including discrimination and the lack of momentum of a poor environment.

While the figures for the overall unemployment rate are generally considered to be reasonably accurate, the estimates for subgroups must allow for greater measurement error. The smaller the subgroup, the larger the potential error. This means that we must take greater care in making definitive statements about the circumstances of the various subgroups than about the overall rate.

The introduction to this section mentioned that the unemployment rate is not the percentage of the population out of work, but the percentage of the labor force out of work. As far as changes in the unemployment rate go, the distinction is not crucial because the fraction of the civilian population in the labor force has remained around 60 percent for quite some time. Table 3.6 presents data on the **labor participation rate** for all civilian workers as well as various subgroups. While the overall participation rate has hovered around 60 percent, there has been a slight upward trend since 1970. A most dramatic trend has occurred with respect to participation by sex. While adult male participation rates have been falling over time, adult female participation rates have risen. These figures mirror the changing social fabric of the nation with regard to the role of women in society. As you might expect, teenagers have lower participation rates than adults due to school attendance.

As with the national income accounts, there are pitfalls in the use of unemployment data. While the unemployment rate is frequently cited by politicians and economists as some kind of index of social welfare, we do well to consider its limitations. Just as the underground economy is unrecorded in GNP, so is it unrecorded in the unemployment rate. This suggests that the true unemployment rate is lower than the reported rate, as we know many individuals have

Table 3.6

**Labor Force Participation Rates** (Civilian labor force as percent of civilian population in each group)

|  | 1955 | 1960 | 1965 | 1970 | 1975 | 1980 | 1984 |
|---|---|---|---|---|---|---|---|
| All civilian workers | 59.3% | 59.4% | 58.9% | 60.4% | 61.2% | 63.8% | 64.4% |
| White males | 85.4 | 83.4 | 80.8 | 80.0 | 78.7 | 78.2 | 77.1 |
| White males 16–19 years | 58.6 | 55.9 | 54.1 | 57.5 | 61.9 | 63.7 | 59.0 |
| White females | 34.5 | 36.5 | 38.1 | 42.6 | 45.9 | 51.2 | 53.3 |
| White females 16–19 years | 40.7 | 40.3 | 39.2 | 45.6 | 51.5 | 56.2 | 55.4 |
| Black males | 85.0 | 83.0 | 79.6 | 76.5 | 71.9 | 71.5 | 70.8 |
| Black males 16–19 years | 60.8 | 57.6 | 51.3 | 47.4 | 42.9 | 43.5 | 41.7 |
| Black females | 46.1 | 48.2 | 48.6 | 49.5 | 49.4 | 53.6 | 55.2 |
| Black females 16–19 years | 32.7 | 32.9 | 29.5 | 34.1 | 35.6 | 35.9 | 35.0 |

jobs (both legal and illegal) which are not recorded by the Bureau of Labor Statistics. There is perhaps some offset to this overestimate of the unemployment rate insofar as some citizens have grown discouraged from prolonged unemployment and so have given up looking for work. These discouraged workers are not counted in the labor force even though they would take a job if one was offered. The point of this discussion is to remind us of the shortcomings of the unemployment rate. The fact that the unemployment rate had an upward trend through the 1970s does not necessarily mean that the United States was experiencing higher social costs relative to earlier periods. A world in which both spouses in a family are working can lead ultimately to higher unemployment than in the "old world" of one working spouse, because when one spouse is unemployed, there is less pressure to take a job not to the unemployed's liking. The presence and likely growth of the underground economy, along with a rising labor force participation rate, make the unemployment rate a questionable index of social welfare.

## 3.3 MONEY

### DEFINING THE MONEY SUPPLY

The term *money* is used in everyday language in three different ways: income (as, "He makes a lot of money."), wealth ("They have a lot of money."), and a particular type of asset ("She has lots of money in her pocket."). In economics, the term money is used *only* in the sense of a particular type of asset. An **asset** is a form in which wealth is

**asset**
Something of value that is owned by an individual or firm

held. A house, a government bond, and money are all assets, but money is only one kind of asset, albeit a very special kind. We may define money as those assets which can be used to make ultimate payment for goods, services, and debts. At different times and in different places, gold, seashells, stones, cigarettes, and other items have served as money. But what do we identify as money today?

We can all readily identify coins and currency as money, but beside this most obvious kind of money, what else should we count? Since the great majority of payments are made by check, we should consider checking accounts, or **checkable deposits** as they are formally called, an important part of our money supply. A check is a legal order for a bank to transfer a depositor's money to the payee of the check. The deposit is a legal liability of the bank which is controlled by the depositor. Current terminology (and Federal Reserve definitions) includes **demand deposits** and **other checkable deposits** as comprising checkable deposits. The distinction is that demand deposits pay no interest to the depositor while other checkable deposits do.

What about other kinds of bank deposits? The answer to this question was once much clearer than at present, as the dividing line between deposits used principally for making payments and deposits used primarily for financial investments was easier to draw. However,

**checkable deposits**
Bank deposits against which checks may be written

**demand deposits**
Those checking accounts that pay no interest to the depositor

---

**Table 3.7**

**Money Stock Measures and Components as of December 1984, Billions of Dollars, Not Seasonally Adjusted**

| | | |
|---|---|---:|
| M1 = | currency | 160.9 |
| | traveler's checks | 4.9 |
| | demand deposits | 257.4 |
| | other checkable deposits | 147.5 |
| | | 570.7 |
| | | |
| M2 = | M1 | 570.7 |
| | overnight repurchase agreements and Eurodollars | 57.5 |
| | money market deposit accounts (saving) | 415.1 |
| | small denomination time deposits | 886.4 |
| | savings deposits | 285.9 |
| | money market mutual funds (general purpose) | 168.1 |
| | | 2383.7 |
| | | |
| M3 = | M2 | 2383.7 |
| | large denomination time deposits | 417.5 |
| | term repurchase agreements and Eurodollars | 153.5 |
| | money market mutual funds (institution only) | 62.7 |
| | | 3,017.4 |

Source: Board of Governors of the Federal Reserve System.

several financial innovations in recent years have resulted in some
new financial assets that have both payment and investment characteristics. This situation is reflected in several alternative definitions
of the money stock, where the definitions may be ranked according
to their ability to serve the payment function required by money. The
narrowest definition of the money stock, known as the M1 definition,
is made up of currency held by the non-banking public (including
coins) plus checkable deposits; traveler's checks are also included.
Illustrating how the alternative definitions of money are related, Table 3.7 lists the components for each and their size as of December
1984. For our present purposes, the details of the components are
unimportant. What is important is a recognition that as we move
from M1 to M3, the assets included are increasingly oriented toward
financial investment rather than current payments.

From a macroeconomic viewpoint, the best definition of money
is the one that seems to work best in analyzing macroeconomic phenomena such as inflation and output. At this time, the choice among
M1, M2, and M3 is not settled, although it is fair to say that the bulk
of research has utilized M1. As a result, when we speak of money in
this book, we will mean M1, unless otherwise specified.

## THE MONEY SUPPLY PROCESS

Money in the U.S. is **fiat money**. This means that our legal money
supply is by government decree made up of pieces of paper and the
rights to pieces of paper (checking deposits). There have been times
when the U.S. had a **commodity money**, where physical commodities
such as gold served as money. While today's coins are made of metal,
they are called **token money** since their value in exchange exceeds the
commodity value of the metal. Although there is certainly no government guarantee of convertibility into gold or silver or any other commodity backing the U.S. dollar, money has value because people
believe they can exchange it for real goods and services and use it to
pay taxes. Money is backed strictly by confidence in its future value.
However, just as the price of apples goes down as the apple supply
rises (other things equal), so the value of money tends to fall as its
quantity increases. It is reasonable to believe that the price level and
inflation rate are closely related to the money supply. Therefore, it is
important to understand the how and why behind the creation of
money.

Changes in the U.S. money supply stem largely from changes in
**base money**, money issued by the federal government. Base money
is sometimes called ''high-powered money.'' This government-con-
trolled quantity of money can have a powerful influence on the economy. The supply of base money is controlled by the central bank of
the United States, the Federal Reserve System. The Fed, as it is

**fiat money**
Any money declared to exist by
the government

**commodity money**
Any money that also has equal-
valued use as a commodity
(such as gold or silver)

**token money**
Coins whose metallic value is
less than face value

**base money**
All money issued by the federal
government

called, is a quasi-independent agency of the government, and is headed by a Board of Governors appointed by the President of the United States. The Fed determines the monetary policy of the United States, and serves as a kind of banker's bank. Commercial banks keep deposits at their regional Federal Reserve District bank. Base money includes the Fed bank deposits and is defined as:

**Base money = coins + currency + commercial bank deposits at Fed**

The Fed determines the amount of coins and currency issued to the banking system and so has complete control over this component of base money. As for the deposits at the Fed, these are a small fraction of the value of total commercial bank deposits from the public. Other things equal, commercial banks want to lend all the deposits they can to maximize their interest earnings, but the Fed requires that a certain fraction of deposits be held as reserves (the bulk of which are deposited at Federal Reserve banks).

 Bank deposits are counted as part of the money supply (see Table 3.7), so when banks make loans, thereby creating new deposits, they are creating money. By altering the reserves of the banking system, the Fed controls the money-creating potential of commercial banks. We see, then, that the Fed can alter the money supply directly, by altering the coin and currency component of base money; or indirectly, by altering the reserves of the banking system, which then will lead to changed bank lending and consequently changes in the money stock.

 The relationship between base money and the larger money supply is often described by the following equation:

$$M = \mu B, \tag{3.3}$$

where $M$ is the money supply, $B$ is base money, and $\mu$ is the **money multiplier**. The money multiplier concept recognizes that the money supply tends to be a relatively constant multiple of base money, as can be seen in Table 3.8. What could cause changes in the multiplier, or the relationship between the money stock and base money? There are two factors that affect the money multiplier:

1. Changes in the *cash/deposit ratio*. This is the ratio of cash (currency and coin) held by the public to bank deposits. If this ratio rises, the money-lending/money-creating potential of the banking system falls because the increase in cash held by the public is outside of the banks. If the ratio falls, then the relative increase in deposits makes more money available to the banking system to lend.

*The Federal Reserve System controls the supply of base money.*

*When banks make loans, they create money.*

**money multiplier**
The numerical factor that relates base money to the money supply

Table 3.8

| Year | M1 Money Supply (*M*) | Base Money (*B*) | Money Multiplier ($\equiv M/B$) |
|------|------|------|------|
| 1960 | 141.9 | 44.5 | 3.2 |
| 1962 | 149.2 | 47.1 | 3.2 |
| 1964 | 161.9 | 51.9 | 3.1 |
| 1966 | 173.7 | 56.8 | 3.1 |
| 1968 | 199.4 | 64.8 | 3.1 |
| 1970 | 216.5 | 72.0 | 3.0 |
| 1972 | 251.9 | 84.2 | 3.0 |
| 1974 | 277.4 | 98.3 | 2.8 |
| 1976 | 310.4 | 112.0 | 2.8 |
| 1978 | 363.2 | 132.2 | 2.7 |
| 1980 | 414.5 | 155.0 | 2.7 |
| 1982 | 480.5 | 169.8 | 2.8 |
| 1983 | 525.3 | 185.0 | 2.8 |
| 1984 | 558.5 | 198.7 | 2.8 |

**Money Supply, Base Money, and the Money Multiplier** (December figures, billions of dollars)

2. Changes in the *reserve/deposit ratio*. If the fraction of deposits held as reserves increases, then the banking system can lend a smaller fraction of total deposits. If the reserve/deposit ratio falls, then some deposits which would previously have gone into bank reserves are now free to be loaned. The reserve/deposit ratio may rise due to a desire on the part of commercial banks to hold more reserves (even with an unchanged legal reserve requirement), or because of an increase in the legal reserve/deposit ratio. The Fed sets the legally required reserve/deposit ratio, and we now understand how changes in this *reserve requirement* will change the money supply.

Equation (3.3) indicates that changes in the money supply may occur because of changes in base money *B* and/or changes in the money multiplier $\mu$. We know the factors that can cause a change in $\mu$ but $\mu$ generally changes very slowly over time. Table 3.8 indicates that there has been a gradual decline in the money multiplier for M1. Such slow change in the multiplier suggests that in recent years, changes in the money stock have largely been a result of Federal Reserve induced changes in base money.

The Fed brings about changes in base money by Federal Reserve **open market operations**, the buying and selling of government bonds (U.S. Treasury bonds). When the Fed buys bonds on the bond market, the seller receives a Federal Reserve check which is deposited in a commercial bank. This new deposit will mean that bank reserves rise by the amount of the deposit, and this increase in base money will stimulate bank lending and the consequent growth of the money

**open market operations** The buying and selling of U.S. government securities by the Fed

supply. When the Fed is selling bonds on the open market, the buyer pays with a check, and the process just described is reversed: bank reserves and therefore base money fall, bank lending contracts, and consequently the money supply drops. The control of base money through the open market operations management of bank reserves is the way in which the U.S. money supply is managed by the Federal Reserve.

As we suggested earlier, there will be many occasions when we will deflate nominal values to look at real values. The money supply is a perfect example. We have been discussing and have seen tables depicting the nominal money supply. In later chapters we will often find it useful to talk about the real stock of money $m$, which is found by dividing the nominal money supply by the price level:

$$m = M/P \tag{3.4}$$

The real quantity of money measures the money supply in base-year dollars, and indicates the real goods and services for which the money stock could be exchanged.

## 3.4 BUSINESS CYCLES

**business cycles**
Fluctuations of growth and contraction in economic activity

**Business cycles** refer to fluctuations in economic activity. By economic activity, we mean national output and income. If we look at real NNP over time, we would see periods of expansion followed by periods of contraction which are then followed by another expansion, and so on. The economy cycles back and forth between boom and

**Figure 3.2**

The Business Cycle

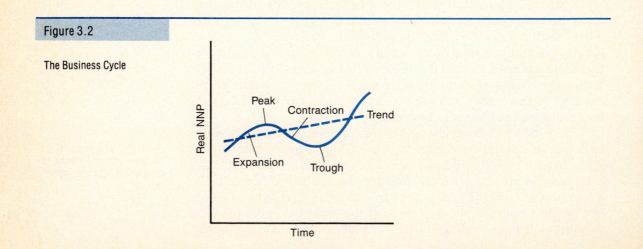

Table 3.9

| Trough | Peak | Trough | Peak |
|--------|------|--------|------|
| Dec. 1854 | June 1857 | Mar. 1919 | Jan. 1920 |
| Dec. 1858 | Oct. 1860 | July 1921 | May 1923 |
| June 1861 | Apr. 1865 | July 1924 | Oct. 1926 |
| Dec. 1867 | June 1869 | Nov. 1927 | Aug. 1929 |
| Dec. 1870 | Oct. 1873 | Mar. 1933 | May 1937 |
| Mar. 1879 | Mar. 1882 | June 1938 | Feb. 1945 |
| May 1885 | Mar. 1887 | Oct. 1945 | Nov. 1948 |
| Apr. 1888 | July 1890 | Oct. 1949 | July 1953 |
| May 1891 | Jan. 1893 | May 1954 | Aug. 1957 |
| June 1894 | Dec. 1895 | Apr. 1958 | Apr. 1960 |
| June 1897 | June 1899 | Feb. 1961 | Dec. 1969 |
| Dec. 1900 | Sept. 1902 | Nov. 1970 | Nov. 1973 |
| Aug. 1904 | May 1907 | Mar. 1975 | Jan. 1980 |
| June 1908 | Jan. 1910 | July 1980 | July 1981 |
| Jan. 1912 | Jan. 1913 | Nov. 1982 | |
| Dec. 1914 | Aug. 1918 | Source: National Bureau of Economic Research. | |

**Dates of Peaks and Troughs of Business Cycles in the U.S., 1854–1983**

bust, prosperity and hard times. Understanding why these fluctuations occur is the major challenge of macroeconomics.

Figure 3.2 presents the standard business cycle terminology.

When we plot NNP over time, we observe periods of *expansion* or economic growth when real NNP is rising. Eventually, a *peak* is reached, after which begins a period of falling NNP, or contraction. The contraction culminates in a *trough*, after which another expansion begins, and the story is replayed.

Note that while the economy is subject to these cyclical ups and downs, there is a long-run upward trend. On average, NNP has risen through time, but given the contractions, or *recessions* as they are often called, the time path of NNP is hardly smooth. Also, although the term "cycle" might suggest a regular, recurring pattern of ups and down, as we see in Table 3.9 there is nothing systematic about the period of expansion and contraction as the period between peaks and troughs is highly variable.

Much of our knowledge of business cycles is due to research sponsored by the National Bureau of Economic Research (NBER). The NBER is an independent organization that announces the beginning and end of a recession. The dates given in Table 3.9 are taken from the NBER reading of history. An expansion and the following contraction make up what is called a *reference cycle*. Table 3.9 provides the dates for the reference-cycle peaks, when a contraction begins, and for the reference-cycle troughs, when expansion starts. While the cycle lengths are very irregular, they average 3 to 4 years in length.

A reference cycle is made up of an expansion and contraction.

Since NNP and GNP are only published quarterly, you may wonder how the NBER can establish monthly dates for reference cycles. The dating is based on the month in which a majority of monthly "economic indicators" turn from positive to negative growth or vice versa. The assumption, one which experience shows is usually correct, is that the various monthly data series will tend to move in the same direction as real income.

The record of real economic growth in the U.S. is generally one of easily forgettable cyclical fluctuations around a long-run growth trend. However one fluctuation known to everyone is the Great Depression of the 1930s. Chapter 15 will be devoted to a detailed discussion of the Great Depression along with the experience of recent years in light of the macroeconomic knowledge gained in the following chapters. For now, we must realize the importance of understanding business cycles, since as Figure 3.3 indicates, the recent record of business fluctuations is quite volatile.

## 3.5 INTEREST AND INTEREST RATES

### THE CONCEPT OF INTEREST

**interest**
The income flow from saving or holding assets

**flow**
A rate of movement per unit of time

**stock**
A measure of amount at only a particular moment in time

**interest rate**
The ratio of income per year flowing from some asset to the total value of that asset

**Interest** may be thought of as income that flows from a stock of assets held. Before we delve any deeper into the concept of interest, we should be sure that we know the difference between stocks and flows. A **flow** is an amount measured per unit of time, while a **stock** is an amount measured at a particular point in time. For example, income is measured per year or per week, as in "I earn $100 per week," so income is a flow concept. The money supply, on the other hand, is measured as of a particular date. When we say that the money supply as of December, 1982 equals $478 billion, we are talking about the stock of money in existence at that point in time.

Getting back to interest, the interest income flowing from stocks of assets can be related to the assets by the concept of the **interest rate**. The interest rate $R$ may be defined as the ratio of income per year flowing from an asset to the value of the asset, or:

$$R = \frac{\text{income per annum}}{\text{value of asset}}$$

Suppose we have an asset valued at $1,000 that yields $100 per year in interest. The interest rate is then $100/$1,000 = .10. This is usually quoted as .10/year, or 10 percent per annum.

Figure 3.3

The Recent History of Business Fluctuations

Year

## SIMPLE VERSUS COMPOUND INTEREST

There are different formulas for computing interest rates. Let's first consider *simple interest*. Simple interest applies to single payment loans. In other words, money is loaned at time zero and is repaid later (say one year). The repayment includes both the interest and the principal (the amount originally lent). Let's look at one example to better illustrate the concept of simple interest.

▶        Suppose a $1,000 loan is made for one year at 10 percent interest, where interest and principal are due at the end of the year. Then the borrower must repay $100 interest plus the $1,000 principal at the end of the year. If $L_0$ is the original loan amount, $L_1$ the amount of principal and interest due in one year, and R the interest rate, then:

EXAMPLE 3.2

$$L_1 = (1 + R) L_0, \qquad (3.4)$$

or in this example,

$$\$1{,}100 = (1.10)\,\$1{,}000$$

This formula could be rearranged algebraically to compute $R$ if we know $L_0$ and $L_1$ as:

$$1 + R = L_1/L_0 \text{ or} \tag{3.5}$$
$$R = (L_1/L_0) - 1 \quad \blacksquare$$

Equation (3.5) is particularly useful in the case of *discount bonds*. Discount bonds are bonds that promise to pay the lender a certain amount at a specified future date. The bonds are sold at a discount from this future amount, the size of the discount determined by the current rate of interest. In this case $L_1$ and $R$ are given, so we rearrange our equation to solve for $L_0$, the amount paid by the lender to the borrower at time zero:

$$L_0 = L_1/(1 + R) \tag{3.6}$$

U.S. Treasury bills are the best known example of discount bonds. Suppose a $10,000 Treasury bill that matures in three months is sold for $9,756.10. How do we find the interest rate $R$? Since equation (3.5) applies to one year maturities, we must convert the three-month return into an annual equivalent. If we simply plug the Treasury bill data into equation (3.5), we find:

$$R = (\$10,000/\$9756.10) - 1 = .025.$$

But this is the return on a three-month bill. Since three months is one quarter of a year, we must multiply by four to find the annual yield equivalent, which is $4 \times .025 = .10$. Thus the annual rate of return is 10 percent per annum. In general, we can rewrite our interest rate formula to allow for any maturity period as:

$$R = \frac{[(L_z/L_0) - 1]}{z}, \tag{3.7}$$

where $z$ is the fraction of a year until maturity, and $L_z$ is the amount to be received upon maturity $z$ of a year from now.

So far we have been discussing simple interest. Suppose instead of a single payment loan, we have a loan which receives interest payments at regular intervals, and each interest payment received is allowed to accumulate or be reinvested with the original principal. An example here would be a bank deposit where the depositor (who is in effect lending money to the bank) will receive 5 percent interest paid each quarter on the amount deposited, and the interest is simply left in the account to be added to the initial deposit. This means that the depositor will be earning interest on both the initial deposit plus the accumulated interest payments. We call this compounding of the interest payments through time *compound interest*. To see the result of interest compounding, let's look at an example.

▶     Suppose a bank deposit pays 5 percent per annum interest, compounded quarterly. This means that at the end of each quarter year, the bank will pay $.05/4 = .0125$ or 1 1/4 percent of the account balance in interest. If we deposit $1,000 on January 1 and leave all interest receipts in the account for future compounding, through the year our account will grow as follows:

EXAMPLE 3.3

| Quarter | Beginning Balance | Interest Earned | Ending Balance |
|---------|-------------------|-----------------|----------------|
| 1 | $1,000.00 | $12.50 | $1,012.50 |
| 2 | 1,012.50 | 12.66 | 1,025.16 |
| 3 | 1.025.16 | 12.81 | 1,037.97 |
| 4 | 1.037.97 | 12.97 | 1,050.94 |

Had the account paid 5-percent simple interest, then the depositor would have earned only $.05 \times \$1,000 = \$50$ interest instead of $50.94. So compounding within the year results in a higher return for the depositor.■

Rather than actually compute the interest at each compound period to find the amount accumulated at a future data, we can use the formula:

$$L_{nz} = (1 + RZ)^n L_0, \qquad\qquad (3.8)$$

where $z$ is the compound interval (like every month, 1/12, or quarter, 1/4) and $n$ is the number of compoundings realized. In the example, $z$ equals 1/4 and $n$ equals 4. The quantity $nz$ tells us the number of years being considered.

Applying (3.8) to the data of Example 3.3, we have:

$$
\begin{aligned}
L_{(4)\,(1/4)} &= [1 + .05\,(1/4)]^4\,(\$1,000) \\
L_1 &= (1.0125)^4\,(\$1,000) \\
L_1 &= (1.05094)\,(\$1,000) = \$1,050.94.
\end{aligned}
$$

So the deposit balance in one year $L_1$ is $1,050.94, the same figure arrived at through the tedious process of Example 3.3.

**present value**
The worth now of some future payment amount

There is one additional concept we may pull from equation (3.8). What would you pay now to receive a certain sum $L_1$ in one year? In other words, what is the **present value** of the future payment $L_1$? It is of course $L_0$. Given the market rate of interest $R$, n compound periods of length $z$, and some future amount to be received $L_1$, by rearranging equation (3.8) we have our present value formula:

$$L_0 = L_{nz}/(1 + RZ)^n \tag{3.9}$$

In terms of the data of Example 3.3, we would pay no more than $L_0 =$ $1,000 to receive $1,050.94 in one year if the market rate of interest is 5 percent compounded quarterly. This process of determining the appropriate price to pay now for the right to receive a future payment is called *discounting*. We are discounting the future amount to be received in order to derive its present value.

While we have been referring to "the" market rate of interest, it should be realized that there is no single rate of interest representing "the market." There are different interest rates for the many different financial assets. Fortunately for macroeconomic analysis, interest rates tend to move together so that a focus on the changes in any particular interest rate, like the three-month Treasury bill rate, can usually be considered representative of interest rates in general.

## 3.6 WEALTH AND PERMANENT INCOME

**wealth**
The value of all assets owned, including one's labor

Consumers must make decisions subject to constraints. In particular, current and future spending is constrained by **wealth**. Wealth, a stock, may be thought of as the total resources available to support such spending. Total wealth includes the present and future value of labor as well as other assets like financial assets. Since the rights to all of one's future labor are not sold in a market, nor are many of the nonhuman assets readily traded, it is very difficult to measure wealth—both at the individual level and at the level of the economy.

**permanent income**
Income that would flow in the long run from all assets owned

**Permanent income** is an alternative measure of the total resources available for present and future consumption.[1] We learned

---

[1] Two important studies of the relationship between consumption and permanent income are Milton Friedman, *A Theory of the Consumption Function*, NBER General Series No. 63 (Princeton: Princeton University Press, 1957) and Michael R. Darby, "The Permanent Income Theory of Consumption—A Restatement," *Quarterly Journal of Economics*, 88 (May 1974), 228–50.

earlier that interest is the income flowing from an asset. Permanent income may be thought of as the value of income that would flow in perpetuity from the total stock of assets—both human and nonhuman. If $v$ is the real value of total wealth and $r_p$ is the appropriate interest rate for relating a real income flow to the real wealth stock, the real permanent income $y_p$ may be defined as the yield or interest earned from this wealth:

$$y_P \equiv r_p v \qquad (3.10)$$

We are saying that if $v$ is constant, then on average $y_P$ is the real income that would be earned. Realistically, of course, real income deviates from $y_P$ because of temporary changes and windfalls. As a result, we could categorize realized real income $y$ as consisting of two components: permanent income $y_P$ and *transitory income* $y_T$, so that

$$y = y_P + y_T \qquad (3.11)$$

During business-cycle expansions, we would expect $y_T$ to be positive so that real income for the entire economy exceeds $y_P$. During recessions we would expect negative transitory income so that $y$ is below $y_P$.

Over time, saving, investment, and technological progress should increase wealth, which implies an increase in permanent income also. We will learn more about permanent income and its uses in a later chapter. For now, we have introduced the basic terms and concepts which will allow us to begin a study of macroeconomics.

Permanent income measures the total resources available for present and future consumption.

## SUMMARY

**1**  Price indices measure average changes in economywide prices and are used to deflate nominal income to find real income—a measure of real goods and services produced.

**2**  The unemployment rate is defined as the number unemployed (those available for and seeking work) divided by the labor force (the number employed plus the number unemployed).

**3**  While there are several ways to define the money supply, the M1 definition consists of currency, checkable deposits, and traveler's checks.

**4**  The money supply is equal to base money (currency plus commercial bank deposits with the Federal Reserve) times the money multiplier.

5   The Federal Reserve (the U.S. central bank) controls the U.S. money supply by altering base money.

6   The Fed controls base money through open market operations (buying and selling government bonds).

7   The business cycle is characterized by an expansion to a peak followed by a contraction to a trough, with the process repeating at irregular intervals over time.

8   Interest is income that flows from a stock of assets and the interest rate is the annual amount of this income divided by the value of the assets.

9   Wealth is the total of all resources available for supporting current and future spending.

10   Because of the difficulty in measuring wealth, economists often use permanent income, the flow of income from wealth, to measure the consumer's wealth constraint.

## EXERCISES

1. In an economy with only two final goods, we observe the following output and prices:

| Year | Good 1 Quantity | Good 1 Price | Good 2 Quantity | Good 2 Price |
|------|-----------------|--------------|-----------------|--------------|
| 1 | 1,000 | $1.00 | 2,000 | $2.00 |
| 2 | 1,100 | .80 | 1,900 | 2.25 |

   a. Compute nominal income for each year.
   b. Computer a Laspeyres price index and then determine real income for both years (Year 1 is the base year).
   c. Compute a Paasche price index and then determine real income for both years (Year 1 is the base year).

2. It has been suggested that the unemployment data should include those "discouraged workers" who are not actively seeking work and are therefore excluded from the labor force by the current accounting method. What problems could you see arising from such a change? How would the Department of Labor identify the discouraged worker? What government policies could best insure against having more discouraged workers?

3. How can the number of employed individuals rise at the same time the unemployment rate is rising? When might you expect such an event to occur?

4. Rank your personal assets in order of their liquidity or "money-ness." Based on your personal spending habits, which of these assets would you count as part of your "money supply."

5. Using the *Federal Reserve Bulletin* or the latest *Economic Report of the President*, gather data on M1 and M2 for the past 15 years. What do you notice regarding the relationship between the two money definitions? Why has this occurred?

6. How will changes in the cash/deposit ratio and reserve/deposit ratio change the money multiplier? Armed with this knowledge, how would the growth of the "underground economy" affect the money multiplier?

7. Other things equal, how would each of the following situations tend to change the money supply (will the money supply increase, decrease, or be unchanged)?
   a. the Fed buys bonds on the open market
   b. the public wishes to hold less cash and so deposits cash in bank deposits
   c. the Fed lowers the reserve requirement for commercial banks
   d. commercial banks decide that it would be prudent to lend a smaller fraction of their deposits.

8. Since credit cards can be used to buy goods and services, are credit cards money? What do you suppose is the difference between money and credit.

9. If a particular bank has deposits (included in the money supply) of $100 million and holds $14 million in reserves (vault cash plus deposit at the Fed), how much money has this single bank "created?"

10. If the interest rate on a $10,000 three-month Treasury bill is 8 percent per annum, what would you expect the current selling price of the bill to be?

11. If you deposit $1,000 in a bank deposit paying 10 percent interest compounded semiannually, how much would your deposit balance be in two years if all the interest payments are allowed to accumulate in the deposit?

12. What would you pay now (the present value) to purchase the right to receive $5,000 in one year if the market rate of interest is 5 percent compounded annually?

## REFERENCES FOR FURTHER READING

*Economic Report of the President*. Washington, D.C.: U.S. Government Printing Office, 1984.

Gramley, Lyle E. "Financial Innovation and Monetary Policy." *Federal Reserve Bulletin*, July 1982, 393–400.

Meek, Paul. *U.S. Monetary Policy and Financial Markets*. New York: Federal Reserve Bank of New York, 1982.

Moore, Geoffrey H. *How Full is Full Employment? And Other Essays on Interpreting the Unemployment Statistics*. Washington, D.C.: American Enterprise Institute for Public Policy Research, 1973.

# THE CPI AND THE COST OF LIVING

If the CPI indicates an annual inflation rate of 6 percent, but you only receive a 4 percent raise, are you worse off? We often look to the consumer price index for an indication of how our cost of living is changing, but we must be careful not to read more into the CPI data than, in fact, is there.

First we must beware of month-to-month changes. Short-term changes in the CPI can be very misleading when used to indicate how average prices are changing. This is the reason that wage increases based on the CPI (so-called cost of living raises) are based on the change in the CPI over many months.

| | |
|---|---|
| All items | 100.000 |
| Food and beverages | 20.069 |
| Housing | 37.721 |
|   Shelter | 21.339 |
|     Renters' costs | 6.932 |
|       Rent, residential | 6.029 |
|       Other renters' costs | 0.904 |
|     Homeowners' costs | 13.881 |
|     Owners' equivalent rent | 13.490 |
|     Household insurance | 0.391 |
|     Maintenance and repairs | .526 |
|       Maintenance and repair services | .284 |
|       Maintenance and repair commodities | .242 |
|   Fuel and other utilities | 8.377 |
|   Household furnishings and operation | 8.005 |
|     Housefurnishings | 4.091 |
|     Appliances including TV and sound equipment | 1.208 |
|     Household appliances | 0.542 |
| Apparel and upkeep | 5.205 |
| Transportation | 21.791 |
| Medical care | 5.995 |
| Entertainment | 4.206 |
| Other goods and services | 5.014 |

Secondly, the CPI does not allow for consumer spending patterns to change in response to relative price changes. In other words, if the price of entertainment increases relative to other items in the consumer budget, we would expect households to shift their expenditures away from the more expensive entertainment towards other, now relatively cheaper, items. Since the current CPI is based on consumer spending surveys taken in 1972–73, there is no doubt that relative prices have changed. A new survey would produce different weights on the various categories of spending than the current weights given in Table E3.1.

A related problem is that the CPI figures do not take most quality changes into consideration. If the price of a good rises because a new, improved version of the good is now being sold, we should not refer to the price increase as inflationary. The price increase simply reflects the higher quality which consumers willingly pay for.

Now to answer the initial question: If the CPI indicates prices are rising faster than your income, are you worse off? The answer is maybe. Only if you spent your income precisely according to the CPI weights will the CPI represent your "cost of living." If the CPI rises one month because of a major change in gasoline prices, but you walk to work or school, then you are no worse off even though the CPI is rising. Since each household is different, it is difficult to say that someone is worse off due to CPI changes in the short run. However, if a divergence between CPI increases and income widened over time, it would eventually become quite clear that real consumer income had fallen.

# CHAPTER FOUR

# THE KEYNESIAN BUILDING BLOCKS

This chapter introduces the macroeconomic analysis that is labeled "Keynesian" economics. In 1936 John Maynard Keynes published a book, *The General Theory of Employment, Interest, and Money*, which caused a revolution in macroeconomics. While the fundamental aspects of this "Keynesian revolution" have been discussed in Chapter One, we should remember that the macro theory developed by Keynes and his followers is a theory that emphasizes total spending or aggregate demand as the determinant of a nation's income and output.

The Keynesian model is developed by investigating the individual elements of total spending separately, then adding these elements together to find aggregate demand. Chapter 4 will discuss the determinants of the individual spending components: consumption, investment, government spending, and net exports. Chapter 5 will then put these elements together in a framework that allows for an analysis of macroeconomic equilibrium.

First we will consider the three basic assumptions underlying the Keynesian model: (1) Adjustment to the equilibrium described by the model occurs in a short period of time. (2) The price level is a given constant. (3) Equilibrium is achieved through quantity adjustments.

> Keynesian economics emphasizes aggregate demand as the determinant of a nation's income and output.

## 4.1 THE UNDERLYING ASSUMPTIONS

### SHORT-RUN ANALYSIS

**equilibrium**
The point where quantity demanded equals quantity supplied

The Keynesian model is a model of *comparative statics*, focusing on the comparison of alternative macroeconomic equilibria at the same point in time. In microeconomics, **equilibrium** refers to the situation where quantity demanded equals quantity supplied, or markets are said to clear. The market fluctuates around this position. Similarly in macroeconomics we may think of equilibrium as the position towards which the economy naturally moves. We will develop the exact notion of macroeconomic equilibrium in this, and the next, chapter.

The short-run focus of the Keynesian model means that we can ignore the effects of flows on stocks. For example, while we realize that the capital stock grows as a result of investment spending, in the comparative static framework we assume that the capital stock is unchanged by current investment. Such an assumption allows us to ignore the values of the stock variables in the economy.

Realistically, this theoretical scenario would translate into a focus on the short-run economic time frame of a month or a quarter of a year—a period during which the effects of flows on stocks is negligible. To proceed through time, we must look at each successive period as a new comparative static exercise.

One of the major developments of modern macroeconomics has been the extension of the analysis to include *dynamic behavior, across time periods*, as we shall see. Still, the short-run Keynesian focus can be useful in understanding the behavior of the economy in the period immediately following an important event or change.

### CONSTANT PRICE LEVEL

The short-run Keynesian model treats prices as fixed. Practically, the given price level allows for an easy solution of the equilibrium. Realistically, since we are analyzing the economy at an instant in time, the constant price assumption is reasonable: Current events take time to influence prices of final goods because of the Keynesian assumption that wages are slow to change and product prices are determined by production costs. With unchanging prices, there is no useful distinction to make between nominal and real magnitudes.

### ADJUSTMENT THROUGH QUANTITIES

If total spending differs from the total output of the business firms, how does the economy adjust to this *disequilibrium*? We have already assumed that prices are fixed so we cannot rely on price adjustments to encourage more output and/or less spending or vice versa. Instead, the Keynesian model assumes that adjustment to equilibrium occurs through quantities rather than prices. If total spending or demand exceeds total output, business firms will expand production; if quantity demanded is less than what firms have produced, output will contract.

> The Keynesian model assumes adjustment to equilibrium occurs through quantities rather than prices.

Haven't we just raised a puzzle? In Chapter 2, we learned that actual total spending will always be equal to actual output, yet now we are talking about deviations in total spending from total output. The distinction is that national income accounting will always equate realized total spending and total output, but macro equilibrium turns on the relation between *planned expenditures* and actual output. Suppose that total planned spending across the economy equals $1,020 billion per year when total output is only $1,000 billion per year. Since actual output will always equal actual income and spending, actual expenditures are also $1,000 billion, which is $20 billion less than was planned or desired. The frustrated plans are reflected in *inventory investment* by business firms. Changes in inventories, like the rise in unsold cars on the auto dealer's lot, may be considered involuntary or unexpected investment. So investment spending includes more than just planned spending on capital goods; it also includes changes in inventories.

> Macroeconomic equilibrium requires that planned expenditures equal actual output.

The $20 billion excess of planned expenditures over actual output will be met by drawing down inventories. We can then say that inventory investment was $20 billion less than planned. As a result, business firms will employ more workers and utilize their capital stock more intensively to expand output and income equal to planned expenditures. In the case where planned expenditures are less than actual output, the process is reversed, as we would see inventory accumulation and a consequent reduction in output and income. The assumption is that the needed quantity adjustments will work to restore equilibrium within the short-run period of concern.

Now having introduced the underlying Keynesian assumptions, it is time to analyze the various categories which together comprise the aggregate expenditures variable (i.e., aggregate demand) central to Keynesian theory.

## 4.2 THE CONSUMPTION FUNCTION

### CONSUMPTION VERSUS CONSUMER EXPENDITURES

The term **consumption** includes more than just current purchases of nondurable goods and services. It also includes the consumption value of the services flowing from the existing stock of consumer durable goods. Even though you bought a refrigerator two years ago,

> **consumption**
> Current consumer nondurable purchases plus services from previously purchased durable goods

you did not consume all of the refrigerator services in that year, since such services are realized over the long life of the unit. Thus "consumption" includes the value of durable goods services that likely require no current outlay of cash by the household. However, this is not what Keynes meant by consumption.

consumer expenditures
Current consumer purchases

The Keynesian consumption function is in truth a **consumer expenditures** function, where consumer expenditures refer to all market purchases of goods and services. We see that consumer expenditures will not include the current consumption of the services provided by durable goods purchased earlier. We could, of course, impute a value for such durable goods service flows in the sense of an implicit rental value you would pay to rent such services, but insofar as current consumer spending does not include such values, a difference arises between consumption and consumer expenditures.

Realizing the difference between consumption and consumer expenditures, we nonetheless bow to tradition and use Keynes's term *consumption* for consumer expenditures. This is done because of the overwhelming use of the term "consumption function" in the macroeconomics literature.

## THE KEYNESIAN CONSUMPTION FUNCTION

Before proceeding, we should be sure that we know what is meant by consumption *function*. A function is a mathematical statement explaining how the value of one variable is determined by one or more other variables, as was discussed in Chapter 1. So a consumption function describes the variables considered to be important for explaining the value of consumption.

Keynes hypothesized a consumption function of elegant simplicity:

> The fundamental psychological law . . . is that men are disposed, as a rule and on average, to increase their consumption as their income increases, but not by as much as the increase in their income.[1]

In functional notation, we can express Keynes's idea as:

$$c = c_K(\overset{+}{y}),$$    (4.1)

---

[1] John Maynard Keynes, *The General Theory of Employment, Interest, and Money* (New York; Harcourt, Brace, 1936), p. 96.

where $c$ is real consumer expenditures, $y$ real income, and $c_K$ the Keynesian relationship between $y$ and $c$—as income rises, consumption rises, "but not by as much as the increase in income." Note that there is a positive sign over the $y$ in equation (4.1). This indicates that consumption is a positive function of income. We will indicate the direction of the effect of variables by including positive or negative signs when new functions are introduced.

The measure of the change in consumption given a change in income was called by Keynes the *marginal propensity to consume* (MPC). The word "marginal" refers to a small change in, while "propensity" is a natural inclination to do something. Thus the marginal propensity to consume describes the inclination of consumers to spend any given change in income. If we measure the change in consumption between period zero and period one as $(c_1 - c_0)$ and likewise measure the income change as $(y_1 - y_0)$, the MPC is defined as:

$$\text{MPC} \equiv \frac{c_1 - c_0}{y_1 - y_0}, \tag{4.2}$$

*The marginal propensity to consume measures the change in consumption given a change in income.*

or the change in consumption divided by the corresponding change in income. This is the ratio that Keynes suggested would be less than one.

Realistically, total income $y$ is not the relevant income concept for determining consumer expenditures. Instead, the income actually available to consumers for either spending or adding to wealth is private income $y_N$, which equals total income minus taxes $t$ or:

$$y_N \equiv y - t \tag{4.3}$$

We will henceforth use $y_N$ as the appropriate income measure, so that the Keynesian consumption function is:

$$c = c_K(y - t) \tag{4.4}$$

Figure 4.1 illustrates a hypothetical consumption function. Consumption functions are displayed graphically in consumption–income space. This is a recognition that income is a primary determinant of consumption. How does the MPC of equation (4.2) relate to Figure 4.1? The MPC is the slope of the consumption function. The slope of a line, remember, is the change along the vertical axis divided by the change along the horizontal axis as we move from one point to another point on the line. But moving from one point to another point on a consumption function gives us a change in consumption and a change in income, which is how we find the MPC.

Figure 4.1

The *MPC* as the Slope of the
Consumption Function

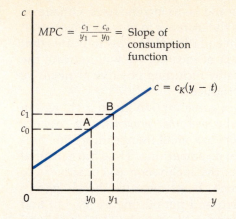

Figure 4.1 illustrates this fact. As with any straight line, we can find
the slope by looking at the change between two points on the line.
The movement from point $A$ to point $B$ along the consumption function in Figure 4.1 is caused by a rise in income from $y_0$ to $y_1$. At $y_0$,
consumption is $c_0$, while at $y_1$, consumption is $c_1$. So the change along
the horizontal axis is $(y_1 - y_0)$ and the change along the vertical axis is
$(c_1 - c_0)$. Thus the slope is $(c_1 - c_0)/(y_1 - y_0)$, which we learned in equation
(4.2) is also the MPC.

TAX EFFECTS    A typical assumption is that taxes are held constant
unless explicitly changed. Sometimes taxes are allowed to vary with
total income, but since this introduces little substantive difference in
the analysis, it is convenient to use the first assumption of constant
taxes unless we explicitly vary $t$ to focus on tax effects.

   If we do vary taxes, how is the consumption function affected?
A change in a determinant of consumption other than income, like
taxes, will alter the relationship between $c$ and $y$. Figure 4.2 demonstrates the impact of an increase in taxes from an initial level of $t_0$ to
the higher-level $t_1$. The effect of the higher tax is to shift the consumption function down and to the right. This means that at any
given level of $y$, the higher $t$, the lower $c$.

   Note that the new consumption function with $t_1$ is parallel to the
old. Since the slope of the consumption function is the MPC, we
would expect the two lines in Figure 4.2 to be parallel as both have
the same slope or MPC (remember the only change was a rise in
taxes). The vertical distance between the two consumption functions
indicates how much consumption falls at a given level of income due

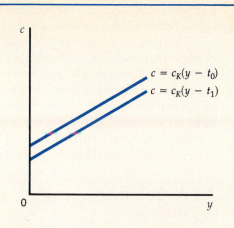

to the tax increase. We know that consumption changes by the MPC times the change in private income, or:

$$c_1 - c_0 = \text{MPC} \cdot [y_{N1} - y_{N0}] \qquad (4.5)$$

But private income is being changed by the amount of the change in taxes with total income $y$ remaining constant, so we now have:

$$c_1 - c_0 = \text{MPC} \cdot [(y - t_1) - (y - t_0)] \text{ or}$$

$$\qquad (4.6)$$

$$c_1 - c_0 = -\text{MPC} \cdot [t_1 - t_0]$$

So the vertical distance between the two consumption functions in Figure 4.2, representing the change in consumption at a constant $y$ with higher $t$, is found as the MPC times the change in taxes. It is, of course, not surprising that consumer expenditures are a decreasing function of taxes. But since, at any given level of income, the change in consumption given a change in taxes is determined by the MPC, the impact of government tax cuts aimed at stimulating consumer spending will be determined by the MPC. For instance, if the MPC equals .8, a $10 billion tax cut would initially stimulate consumer spending by 8 billion (.8 × $10 billion = $8 billion), but with an MPC of .4, the increase in spending would be only $4 billion (.4 × $10 billion = $4 billion).

   In the United States the short-run MPC has been about .4 or .5, even though consumption has averaged about 90 percent of private income for as far back as data are available. The explanation for this apparent paradox is that in addition to consuming about .9 of their permanent income $y_P$, "the income they expect to earn over the long run", households spend about .4 of their transitory income "temporary changes in income" primarily on long-lived goods such as refrigerators, automobiles, and clothes. If transitory income is negative, so that actually income is less than permanent income, these durable-goods expenditures are cut back by about .4 of this shortfall relative to normal income.[2] In the Keynesian short run, wealth and permanent income are fixed; so any changes in private income must be in transitory income. Thus short-run fluctuations in consumption are concentrated in durable goods and reflect a moderate MPC value.

## 4.3 INVESTMENT

*Net investment* is the rate of change in the stock of capital, so investment demand is derived from changes in the demand for capital. Remember that the demand for capital is a demand to hold a stock of capital goods, while investment demand is a demand to alter the stock of capital. The desired stock of capital is generally that stock at which the real return just covers the cost of financing the capital. If the real return on capital exceeded the financing cost, firms would have an incentive to purchase more capital. On the other hand, if the real return were less than the financing cost, firms would let the capital stock shrink by not replacing those machines that wear out. By changing the stock of capital, the return on capital is altered, other things remaining equal. If there is a fixed quantity of labor, by the law of diminishing returns, then the greater the stock of capital added to this labor, the lower the return from each additional unit of capital employed. Similarly, a reduction in the capital stock would increase the return from an additional unit of capital.

**real interest rate**
The nominal rate minus the inflation rate

The cost of financing capital for the overall economy is the **real interest rate.** The real interest rate is defined as the nominal rate $R$ less the rate of inflation $\hat{P}$. (Throughout the text, the symbol will be used to denote the growth rate of a variable. The growth rate or rate of change in prices is referred to as the inflation rate.) Subtracting $\hat{P}$ from $R$, we define the real rate of interest $r$ as

$$r \equiv R - \hat{P} \tag{4.7}$$

[2]References are to Milton Friedman, *A Theory of the Consumption Function*, NBER General Series No. 63 (Princeton: Princeton University Press, 1957); Michael R. Darby, "The Permanent Income Theory of Consumption—A Restatement," *Quarterly Journal of Economics*, 88 (May 1974), 228–50; and Michael R. Darby, "The Consumer Expenditure Function," *Explorations in Economic Research*, 4 (Winter–Spring 1977–78), 645–74.

While there will be further discussion of the real/nominal rate distinction at the end of the chapter, for now we should realize that it is the real rate $r$ that will be equal to the real return on capital.

With prices (and thus $\hat{P}$) given in the Keynesian analysis, we could look at the nominal rate of interest as a measure of the cost of financing capital. Equation (4.7) indicates that if $\hat{P}$ is given, $r$ changes with changes in $R$. Furthermore, since lower interest rates mean lower capital-financing costs, *there is an inverse relation between the stock demand for capital and the interest rate*, other things equal. One "other thing" that could affect the demand for capital is the quantity of labor used with the capital. In the short-run analysis of the Keynesian model, increases in the level of employment will increase real income. So we can use real income as another determinant of the desired capital stock, because the greater the level of employment or the higher real income, the greater the demand for capital to be used with the additional workers. Thus the demand for capital and real income are directly related. Now we can summarize the discussion by writing a function for the *desired capital stock $k^d$* as:

$$k^d = k^d \overset{- \ +}{(R,y)} \qquad\qquad (4.8)$$

Investment is the rate of change in capital, so the level of investment will reflect the difference between the actual capital stock and the desired capital stock.[3] Since in the short-run period being analyzed, the actual capital stock is constant, investment is determined by those factors which affect the desired capital stock: $R$ and $y$, or:

$$i = i \overset{- \ +}{(R,y)}, \qquad\qquad (4.9)$$

where investment is a decreasing function of the interest rate, since higher $R$ lowers the desired capital stock. Investment is also an increasing function of real income since higher $y$ increases the desired capital stock.

Figure 4.3 illustrates the investment function graphically. Note that this figure has investment on the vertical axis and income on the horizontal. The positive slope of the function reflects the fact that investment is an increasing function of income. For any given level of

> Investment demand depends on the interest rate and income.

---

[3]Because the costs of producing capital goods changes as their level of production is varied, variations in $k^d$ will be only partially reflected in $i$ over one short period: If it will cost less to invest next period, it may be worth it to give up one period's return in excess of the interest rate.

Figure 4.3

The Investment Function

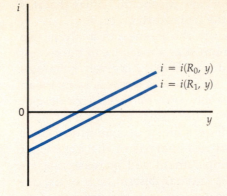

income, the higher the interest rate, the lower is investment. In Figure 4.3, $R_1$ is higher than $R_0$, so the investment function with $R_1$ lies below that with $R_0$. For simplicity, the investment function, like the consumption function, is drawn as a straight line. Realistically, there is nothing to require a rigid linear relation between $i$ and $y$.

## 4.4 GOVERNMENT SPENDING

Government spending differs from the other elements of total spending in that it is treated as exogenous. In other words, since government spending is determined by the discretionary powers of government officials, government spending is considered a given amount $g$. Figure 4.4 illustrates what this exogenous government spending looks like when graphed against $y$ for a particular value $\bar{g}$.

While we view $g$ as constant in Figure 4.4, it should be realized that we often examine the effect of exogenous changes in $g$. We shall consider later, in comparative static exercises, how changes in government spending lead to changes in income or other macroeconomic variables.

## 4.5 NET EXPORTS

Net exports are equal to exports minus imports.

Real *net exports* account for only a small fraction of total expenditures in the U.S. In smaller, more open economies, net exports can be a much more substantial element of spending. Net exports are unique among the spending components in that they may take on either a positive or negative value. Countries that export more than they import will have positive net exports, while those that import more than they export have negative net exports.

Figure 4.4

The Government Expenditure Function

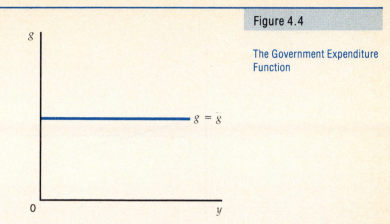

We subtract total imports from total exports to obtain this final part of total expenditures on domestic output. The reason that total imports are subtracted is that they represent that portion of consumer, investment, and government expenditures that is not spent on domestic output.

Since our Keynesian model holds prices constant, the only factors affecting real net exports will be domestic and foreign real income. Since foreign real income is considered exogenous, the ability of foreigners to buy domestic goods is considered fixed so that domestic exports are a given constant. Domestic imports however will increase with domestic income. As domestic income rises, both consumption and investment spending increase. Part of this increased spending is for foreign goods, so we have the positive effect of domestic income on imports.

Figure 4.5 shows a net exports graph. Since exports are treated as exogenous and imports vary with domestic income, as income increases, imports increase so that net exports fall. Thus net exports are a decreasing function of real income, or

$$x = x\,(\overset{-}{y}) \tag{4.10}$$

## 4.6 THE AGGREGATE EXPENDITURE FUNCTION

Total spending, (or aggregate expenditures), is equal to the sum of consumer expenditures, investment, government expenditures, and net exports: $c + i + g + x$. Using the functions discussed for each individual component of spending we can express aggregate expenditures a as:

*Consumer expenditures plus investment, government expenditures, and net exports equal aggregate expenditures.*

$$a = c + i + g + x = c_K\,(y - t) + i\,(R,y) + g + x(y) \tag{4.11}$$

Figure 4.5

The Net Export Function

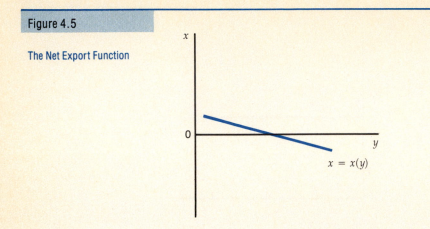

So we see that total spending is a function of the endogenous varia-bles $y$ and $R$, and the exogenous variables $t$ and $g$. We could then write our aggregate expenditure function as:

$$a = a(\overset{+}{y}, \overset{-}{R}; \overset{+}{g}, \overset{-}{t}) \tag{4.12}$$

To determine the effect that each of these variables will have on aggregate expenditures, we must consider their impact on the indi-vidual spending components. Increases in income cause consump-tion and investment to increase and net exports to decrease. But since the decrease in net exports is due to a small part of consumption and investment spending being devoted to imports, we may assume that aggregate expenditures as a whole are an increasing function of real income. The nominal interest rate $R$ only affects investment, and since increases in $R$ lower investment, aggregate expenditures are a decreasing function of $R$. While real government expenditures $g$ and taxes $t$ are given to the model by the government decision makers, changes in $g$ and $t$ are often used for comparative static investiga-tions. Increases in $g$ raise aggregate expenditures by an equal amount, other things equal. Increases in $t$ lower aggregate expendi-tures by the amount of the increase times the marginal propensity to consume.

If we graph all four components of aggregate spending and then vertically sum them, we arrive at our aggregate expenditure func-tion. Figure 4.6 and the accompanying table provide a concrete illus-tration of aggregate expenditures for a hypothetical economy. The data for each spending element are presented in the table and then

Figure 4.6

The Aggregate Expenditure Function

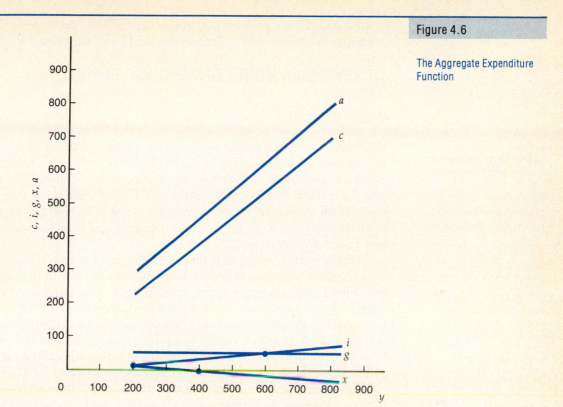

Table 4.A

| $y$ | $t$ | $R$ | $c$ | $i$ | $g$ | $x$ | $a = c + i + g + x$ |
|---|---|---|---|---|---|---|---|
| $ 200 | $50 | 10% | $220 | $10 | $50 | $ 10 | $ 290 |
| 400 | 50 | 10% | 380 | 30 | 50 | 0 | 460 |
| 600 | 50 | 10% | 540 | 50 | 50 | − 10 | 630 |
| 800 | 50 | 10% | 700 | 70 | 50 | − 20 | 800 |
| 100 | 50 | 10% | 860 | 90 | 50 | − 30 | 970 |
| 1200 | 50 | 10% | 1020 | 110 | 50 | − 40 | 1140 |

The exact functions underlying the figure and table are:

$$c = 100 + .8\,(y - t)$$
$$i = 10 - 200R + .ly$$
$$x = 20 - .05y$$

plotted against income in the graph. By adding each element of spending, we find *a*, our aggregate expenditures function.[4]

## 4.7 KEYNESIAN MONEY DEMAND AND SUPPLY

### MONEY DEMAND

barter
Trade of goods and services
for other goods and services

Barter requires a double co-incidence of wants that monetary exchange avoids.

Without money, we would have to use **barter**—trading goods and services for other goods and services. Barter is inefficient, relative to monetary exchange, in that it requires a double coincidence of wants: you must want whatever I produce and I must want what you produce. With money, we have a common unit of value that can be used in all transactions: I sell my output for money and then use money to buy goods and services.

While money is desirable for facilitating exchange and providing a way to store purchasing power, what determines how much money households and business firms wish to hold? It is not true that we want "all the money we can get." Such statements confuse money with wealth. While we may want "all the wealth we can get," money is but one form in which we can hold this wealth. The problem is one of allocating our wealth among the many alternatives like money, physical goods, or other financial assets like stocks and bonds.[5]

Traditionally, it is assumed that there is no interest paid on money. However, as we learned in Chapter 3, there are several alternative definitions of money which include interest–bearing deposits. Certainly, currency yields no interest, but many commercial bank checking accounts do, so that today it is not true that checking accounts yield no interest. However, if close substitutes for money, like bonds, pay a higher rate of interest, then the difference between the bond interest rate and the rate paid on money is the opportunity cost

---

[4]We assume particular values for $R, g,$ and $t$ for this example; different values would shift the graph.

[5]There is a very large literature on the demand for money. Some useful surveys of this literature are: John P. Judd and John L. Scadding, "The Search for a Stable Money Demand Function: A Survey of the Post-1973 Literature," *Journal of Economic Literature*, 20 (September 1982), 993–1023; David E. W. Laidler, *The Demand for Money: Theories and Empirical Evidence* (New York: Harper and Row, 1977); and David E. W. Laidler, "The Demand for Money in the United States—Yet Again," Carnegie-Rochester Conference Series on Public Policy, *On the State of Macroeconomics*, Karl Brunner and Allan H. Meltzer, eds. (Amsterdam: North Holland, 1980), 219–71.

of holding money. In other words, by holding money an individual foregoes the higher return available from bonds, and this is rightly considered a cost associated with holding money. So one determinant of the demand for money is the difference between the interest paid on bonds $R$ and the return from holding money $R_M$; so this determinant can be summarized as $(R - R_M)$.

We said that money was used to facilitate exchange by making transactions easier to carry out. It stands to reason then that the more transactions, or the higher the value of the transactions an individual faces, the more money is desired, other things equal. This is known as the **transactions demand** for money. Since real income is a measure of the level of transactions taking place, we expect money demand to be an increasing function of real income.

Besides this transactions demand for money, we can also identify an **asset demand**. While the transactions demand for money is related to the amount of work to be done by money in facilitating exchange, the asset demand considers the desire to hold money as a financial asset in a wealth portfolio. Just as wealth constrains the quantity of stocks and bonds held, it constrains the amount of money held. Other things equal, we would expect a wealthy household to have larger money balances than a poor household, just as the wealthier household would tend to have larger financial asset holdings in general. As a result, we expect money demand to be a positive function of income in terms of the asset demand.

In functional notation we can write our money demand function as:

$$m^d = m^d \overset{+ \quad -}{(y, R - R_M)} \tag{4.13}$$

> **transactions demand**
> The money desired to make current purchases of goods and services

> **asset demand**
> The money held for its potential value

> The demand for money depends on income and interest rates.

Money demand could be graphed in $mR$ space as in Figure 4.7a, or in $my$ space as Figure 4.7b. When graphed with the interest rate, the money demand curve has a negative slope—the higher the interest rate, the lower the quantity of money demanded (remember that we are holding all other things constant in such a graph, including $R_M$, the return on money.) Increases in income would shift the money demand curve in Figure 4.7a to the right so that at any level of interest the quantity of money demanded increases. Decreases in income would shift the curve to the left. In Figure 4.7b, the positive slope reflects the fact that money demand is an increasing function of income. In this case, increases in the interest rate shift the money demand curve to the left, decreasing money demand, while decreases in $R$ will cause increases in money demand. In future chapters we will consider how $R_M$ may vary with $R$ and how this affects money demand.

**Figure 4.7**

The Money Demand Function

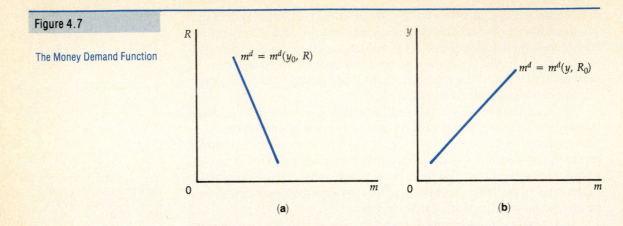

(a)                                              (b)

## MONEY SUPPLY

Like real government expenditures, we assume that the nominal supply of money is determined by decisions of government officials (the Federal Reserve) and is, therefore, exogenous. In other words, the nominal money supply is a given constant. Of course, this constant value can be altered by the government decision makers at will, but at any point in time we will have the **money supply** $M^s$ given as:

**money supply**
The total amount of money existing in an economy

$$M^s = M \tag{4.14}$$

Since prices are given in our Keynesian model, controlling the nominal money supply is the same as controlling the real money supply. With prices constant at $\bar{P}$, dividing nominal money by price gives real money, as in equation (4.15):

$$m^s = M^s/\bar{P} = M/\bar{P} = m \tag{4.15}$$

By altering $M$, the monetary authorities can alter $m$ since $\bar{P}$ is a constant. We will later study how changes in money demand can alter the price level and the real value of money balances, but for now we stick with the Keynesian assumption of fixed prices.

Figure 4.8 illustrates how the money supply function would look in $mR$ space. Since the Federal Reserve can make the money supply whatever it chooses, we will assume that the money supply is independent of the interest rate and is therefore a vertical line at the given level $m$. The assumption of a constant money supply allows for a simpler development of our macroeconomic models. Later, in the Chapter 14 discussion of macroeconomic policy we will consider how the money supply is altered in response to changes in other variables.

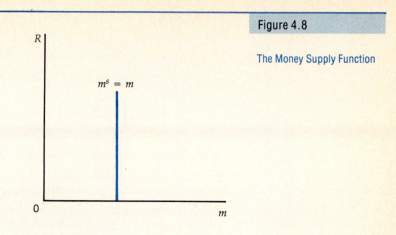

Figure 4.8

The Money Supply Function

**SUMMARY**

1   "Keynesian economics" refers to the body of thought and literature that began in 1936 with the publication of John Maynard Keynes's *The General Theory of Employment, Interest, and Money*.

2   The Keynesian approach focuses on the individual elements that together make up aggregate demand and is a short-run, fixed-price approach.

3   Consumption is a function of private income, which is income minus taxes. The change in consumption given a change in private income is measured by the marginal propensity to consume.

4   Investment, the rate of change in the capital stock, is a function of the interest rate and income.

5   Government spending is an exogenous variable given by government policymakers.

6   Net exports may be positive or negative, and taking foreign purchases of domestic goods as exogenous, will be a function of domestic income.

7   Aggregate expenditures are an increasing function of income, a decreasing function of the interest rate, an increasing function of government expenditures, and a decreasing function of taxes.

8   Money demand is a function of income and the difference between the interest paid on bonds and the interest paid on money.

9   Money supply is an exogenously given constant determined by the monetary authorities.

## EXERCISES

1. What is the value of the MPC in the following examples?

   a. Private income rises by $500 and consumption then rises by $250.

   b. Taxes fall by $100 and consumption rises by $80.

   c. The slope of the consumption function equals 3/4.

   d. Households want to save 1/10 of any extra income.

2. Using data from the *Federal Reserve Bulletin* or some other source, compute the realized real interest rate on 3-month Treasury bills for three or four recent years. You will subtract the realized rate of inflation from the T-bill yield over each 3-month period to construct the realized rate of return. Are there any curious results? Chapter 4 said that investment was a function of the real rate of interest. Would you expect any particular investment behavior to result from the real interest rates you constructed? Why or why not?

3. Illustrate graphically the effects on the net export function of:

   a. a tariff or tax placed on imports.

   b. an exogenous increase in foreign income.

   c. an increase in domestic income from $y_0$ to $y_1$.

4. Use the following table to answer the questions below:

| Y | t | R | C | i | g | x |
|---|---|---|---|---|---|---|
| $1000 | 200 | 10% | 400 | 0 | 200 | 40 |
| 2000 | 200 | 10% | 900 | 50 | 200 | 30 |
| 3000 | 200 | 10% | 1400 | 100 | 200 | 20 |
| 4000 | 200 | 10% | 1900 | 150 | 200 | 10 |
| 5000 | 200 | 10% | 2400 | 200 | 200 | 0 |

   a. What is the value of the MPC?

   b. Find aggregate expenditures at each level of income.

   c. If taxes fall to 50, what happens to aggregate expenditures and why?

   d. Graph the total expenditures function both before and after the tax decrease.

   e. *optional* What are the linear equations describing the consumption function, investment function, net exports functions, and government expenditures function?

5. **a.** Suppose that the consumption function is $c$ = $500 billion/
   year + $0.3y$. If $i + g + x$ were somehow fixed at $500 billion
   per annum, at what level of real income would $c + i + g + x$
   $= y$?

   **b.** If $i + g + x$ were instead fixed at $600 billion per annum, at
   what level of real income would $c + i + g + x = y$?

   **c.** What MPC is assumed in the consumption function?

6. Why is the effect on net exports of an increase in income less in
   absolute amount than the effect on $c + i$?

## REFERENCES FOR FURTHER READING

Will appear at the end of Chapter 5 since those references are also
applicable to Chapter 4.

## THE FISHER EQUATION: INFLATION AND INTEREST RATES

The concept of the real interest rate was introduced in Chapter 4 as a determinant of investment spending. The real rate of interest $r$ is generally thought of as the nominal interest rate $R$ less the rate of inflation $\hat{P}$. Another way of expressing this relationship is to write the nominal rate as being equal to the sum of the real rate plus the rate of inflation:

$$R \equiv r + \hat{P}$$

This equation is often called the **Fisher equation** after the famous Yale economist, Irving Fisher, who was a pioneer in the study of interest rates in the early twentieth century.

The Fisher equation states that the nominal interest rate on loans will equal the real interest rate (the rate which would be quoted if the inflation rate were zero) plus the actual inflation rate. As inflation rises, lenders demand the higher nominal interest rate to offset the declining real value of the nominal principal amount. Borrowers are willing to pay the higher interest rates because they know that they will be paying back less valuable dollars. Consider, for example, a loan of $100 to be repaid in one year at 10 percent simple interest. In one year the borrower may pay the lender $110. If the inflation rate for the year is zero, then the lender will earn a 10 percent real return. If the inflation rate is 10 percent, then the lender's real return is zero. At a 10 percent rate of inflation, you need $110 in one year to purchase what $100 would buy today. So if the loan yields a 10 percent nominal rate of interest when the inflation rate is 10 percent, the lender is being repaid 10 percent more dollars than originally loaned, but these dollars have the same purchasing power as the original principal amount. So in order to earn some positive real return, the lender must earn a nominal rate of interest in excess of the rate of inflation.

In recent years there has been some discussion over whether the real rate of interest is constant or variable. A look at past realized real rates indicates variability, as Table E4.1 below shows. Not only has the real rate of return on 6-month T-bills varied, but it was often negative between 1972 and 1980. Do these figures then indicate that the Fisher equation in nonsense? It is obvious that interest rates did not rise in line with the inflation rate in order to keep the real return constant, but this does not invalidate the Fisher hypothesis regarding the adjustment of the nominal interest rate.

First it must be realized that theoretically, the real rate of interest can vary over time. As we will learn later, the real rate of interest depends upon the expected productivity of capital, which certainly can vary. If the

| | 6-Month U.S. T-billNominal Interest Rate | Rate of CPI Inflation Over 6-Month Period | Realized Real Rate of Interest |
|---|---|---|---|
| June 1965 | 3.872% | 1.563% | 2.309% |
| Dec. 1965 | 4.523 | 3.416 | 1.106 |
| June 1966 | 4.696 | 3.195 | 1.501 |
| Dec. 1966 | 5.108 | 2.252 | 2.856 |
| June 1967 | 3.816 | 4.012 | −0.196 |
| Dec. 1967 | 5.562 | 4.130 | 1.432 |
| June 1968 | 5.652 | 5.202 | 0.450 |
| Dec. 1968 | 6.014 | 5.822 | 0.192 |
| June 1969 | 6.725 | 6.022 | 0.703 |
| Dec. 1969 | 7.788 | 5.669 | 2.119 |
| June 1970 | 6.907 | 5.168 | 1.739 |
| Dec. 1970 | 4.848 | 3.862 | 0.986 |
| June 1971 | 4.890 | 2.801 | 2.089 |
| Dec. 1971 | 4.199 | 3.087 | 1.112 |
| June 1972 | 4.270 | 3.680 | 0.590 |
| Dec. 1972 | 5.287 | 8.013 | −2.726 |
| June 1973 | 7.234 | 9.215 | −1.981 |
| Dec. 1973 | 7.444 | 12.130 | −4.686 |
| June 1974 | 8.232 | 11.845 | −3.613 |
| Dec. 1974 | 7.091 | 5.913 | 1.178 |
| June 1975 | 5.463 | 8.115 | −2.652 |
| Dec. 1975 | 5.933 | 3.479 | 2.454 |
| June 1976 | 5.784 | 6.368 | −0.584 |
| Dec. 1976 | 4.513 | 7.200 | −2.687 |
| June 1977 | 5.198 | 5.847 | −0.649 |
| Dec. 1977 | 6.377 | 8.789 | −2.412 |
| June 1978 | 7.200 | 9.035 | −1.835 |
| Dec. 1978 | 9.397 | 12.181 | −2.784 |
| June 1979 | 9.062 | 13.704 | −4.642 |
| Dec. 1979 | 11.847 | 14.038 | −2.191 |
| June 1980 | 7.218 | 10.040 | −2.822 |
| Dec. 1980 | 14.770 | 8.635 | 6.135 |
| June 1981 | 13.947 | 8.869 | 5.078 |
| Dec. 1981 | 11.471 | 5.662 | 5.809 |
| June 1982 | 12.310 | 1.239 | 11.071 |
| Dec. 1982 | 8.225 | 1.094 | 7.131 |
| June 1983 | 8.890 | 3.383 | 5.507 |
| Dec. 1983 | 9.140 | 2.787 | 6.353 |
| June 1984 | 10.550 | 3.572 | 6.978 |
| Dec. 1984 | 8.360 | 2.423 | 5.937 |

real rate of interest falls, then the nominal interest rate has risen less than the inflation rate. Second, we must understand that the real rates of interest shown in the table are realized "after the fact." A 6-month T-bill issued today will offer a particular rate of interest based on the current real rate of interest along with the current *expected* rate of inflation. No one knows with certainty what the actual inflation rate will be over the next 6 months, so the current nominal yield on the T-bill will reflect expected inflation. If 6 months later the actual inflation rate exceeded our expectations, then we would earn a lower real rate of interest than we expected to earn. For instance, in referring to our table on real interest rates, economists often call such rates *ex-post* real rates. *Ex-post* means "after the fact." So the real rates shown in the table are the returns that investors would have actually received from holding the T-bills over each 6-month period. Only with perfect foresight would these *ex-post* real rates equal the real rates investors expected to earn *ex ante*, or prior to the 6-month holding period. An investor holding a T-bill for 6 months following June 1975 would have earned a negative 2.652 percent. Did investors buying T-bills in December 1975 expect to earn negative real returns? While we cannot observe such subjective expectations, it is safe to say that throughout the 1970s, there were many episodes of surprisingly high inflation rates which could have led to surprisingly low real returns to investors.

The Fisher equation introduced above misses a very important effect—the effect of taxes. In a 1975 study, Michael Darby showed how the standard Fisher equation should be modified to incorporate taxes. Since nominal interest receipts are taxable income to the lender, the nominal interest rate must rise by more than the inflation rate to keep the *after-tax* real rate constant. To see this, let's rewrite our Fisher equation subtracting taxes from it to arrive at the after-tax real return $r_A$:

$$r_A = R(1 - t) - \hat{P}$$

where $t$ is now the tax rate applied to ordinary income. If $t$ is 1/3, then only $1 - 1/3 = 2/3$ of nominal interest receipts are kept after taxes. Rearranging this equation to put $R$ on the left hand side we have:

$$R = (r_A + \hat{P})/(1 - t)$$

This indicates that $R$ must rise by $1/(1 - t)$ times any increase in $\hat{P}$ to leave the after tax real return $r_A$ constant. So while the simple Fisher equation suggests that nominal interest rates will rise by as much as inflation, when we consider taxes, the rise will be by more than the increase in inflation. If $t = 1/3$, then $1 - t = 2/3$, so that $R$ will rise by $1/(2/3) = 3/2$ times the rise in inflation. Therefore, if expected inflation increases one percentage point, the nominal interest rate will have to increase 1.5 percentage points to keep the after-tax real rate constant.

Another way of writing the tax-adjusted Fisher equation, which is perhaps easier to remember, is

$$R = r + \hat{P} + \frac{t}{1 - t}\,\hat{P}$$

The first two terms represent the before-tax real interest rate $r_A/(1 - t)$ and the amount needed to offset the effect of inflation on the purchasing power of the amount lent. The third term is the amount of tax liability transferred from borrower to lender in making that offset, or the additional increase in $R$ required to compensate for the effect of taxes. This increase in the nominal interest rate in excess of the inflation rate has come to be called the *Darby effect*. Several studies that tested for its significance concluded that nominal interest rates do indeed adjust to incorporate tax effects rather than simply adjusting proportionally to inflation as suggested by the simple Fisher equation.[1] Thus the nominal interest rate can be thought of as the sum of three components: the (before-tax) real interest rate, the inflation rate or Fisher effect, and the Darby effect.

---

[1] While there have been numerous studies with conflicting results, two recent studies may settle the issue: Michael Melvin, "Expected Inflation, Taxation, and Interest Rates: The Delusion of Fiscal Illusion," *American Economic Review*, September 1982, 841–43, and Robert Ayanian, "Expectations, Taxes, and Interest: The Search for the Darby Effect," *American Economic Review*, September 1983, 762–65. The original statement of the Darby effect is in Michael R. Darby, "The Financial and Tax Effects of Monetary Policy on Interest Rates," *Economic Inquiry*, June 1975, 266–76. An interesting attempt to understand the unusual behavior of the after-tax real rate during 1972–1980 is reported by A. Steven Holland, "Real Interest Rates: What Accounts for Their Recent Rise?," *Federal Reserve Bank of St. Louis Review*, December 1984, 18–29.

# THE *IS–LM* MODEL: EQUILIBRIUM INCOME AND INTEREST RATE IN THE SHORT RUN

## 5.1 SOLVING THE *IS–LM* MODEL

### THE OVERALL APPROACH

In Chapter 5 we draw together the various pieces of the Keynesian model introduced in Chapter 4. The model developed in this chapter is known as the *IS–LM* model for reasons that will soon become obvious. The model, developed in 1937 by the English economist Sir John Hicks,[1] provides a useful set of graphs for determining macroeconomic equilibrium and the impact of various macroeconomic shocks in the short run. Specifically, the *IS–LM* model shows how real income and the nominal interest rate adjust so that the desired level of aggregate expenditures equals real income at the same time that the real quantity of money demanded equals the amount supplied. When these states are achieved, the economy is in equilibrium.

The *IS–LM* approach divides the determinants of equilibrium into two largely separate groups—the income-expenditures sector and the monetary sector. Each sector is summarized by a single equation algebraically, or by a single line graphed in $yR$ space. Since the

---

[1]John R. Hicks, "Mr. Keynes and the 'Classics': A Suggested Interpretation," *Econometrica*, 5 (April 1937), 147–59.

only variables that directly affect both the income-expenditures and monetary sectors simultaneously are real income and the nominal interest rate, it is possible to draw one line showing all combinations of real income and the nominal interest rate for which the income-expenditures sector is in equilibrium. The other line shows all combinations of income and interest rates in which the monetary sector is in equilibrium. By plotting the two lines in the same $yR$ graph, we find their point of intersection, which is the only combination of real income and the nominal interest rate where both sectors are in equilibrium.

## THE BASIC KEYNESIAN EQUATIONS

The basic model can be described by five equations given in Table 5.1. There are five unknown or endogenous variables that must be simultaneously determined by the system of five equations: real income $y$, the nominal interest rate $R$, aggregate expenditures $a$, the real quantity of money demanded $m^d$, and the real quantity of money supplied $m^s$. There are also three exogenous policy variables: real government spending $g$, real taxes $t$, and deflated nominal money $m = M/\bar{P}$, which are given to the model and are held fixed in determining the model's solution. Since there are five equations and five unknowns, a unique solution is possible.

Equations (5.1), (5.3), and (5.4) were introduced in Chapter 4.[2] Equations (5.2) and (5.5) are the equilibrium conditions in the in-

---

[2]In Chapter 4 we introduced the money demand function as being $m^d = m^d (y, R - R_M)$, where $R_M$ is the interest paid on money balances. For a given $R_M$, we will use the simpler money demand function of equation (5.3) from now on so we can concentrate on the equilibrium levels of $y$ and $R$. It should be realized, however, that changes in $R_M$ would cause shifts in the money demand function drawn in $mR$ or $my$ space.

**Table 5.1**

**The Basic Keynesian Equations**

| Equation | Description | Number |
|---|---|---|
| $\overset{+\ -\ +\ -}{a = a(y,R; g,t)}$ | Aggregate expenditures | (5.1) |
| $a = y$ | Income-expenditures equilibrium | (5.2) |
| $\overset{+\ -}{m^d = m^d(y,R)}$ | Demand for money | (5.3) |
| $m^s = m$ | Supply of money | (5.4) |
| $m^d = m^s$ | Monetary equilibrium | (5.5) |

come-expenditure sector (also known as the goods sector) and the monetary sector, respectively. Equation (5.2) recognizes that in equilibrium, the determinants of planned aggregate expenditures ($y,R$; $g,t$) will adjust so that planned expenditures equal actual expenditures. Equation (5.5) similarly ensures that the quantity of money demanded equals the quantity supplied.

As we learned from the circular flow analysis of Chapter 2, in addition to goods and money, there is a third market: the securities or "bond" market, which is omitted from consideration in Table 5.1. We are able to do this because equilibrium in the goods and money markets implies equilibrium in the bond market. This is true because the only way that people can plan to buy more bonds than are issued is to plan to spend less than they receive as income or decrease money balances below the amount supplied, or both. The funds available for purchasing bonds come either from current income or existing money balances. As a result, if all income received is spent and the amount of money demanded equals the amount supplied, then the demand and supply of bonds must be in equilibrium. Since the aggregate expenditure, money demand, and money supply functions all implicitly reflect bond demand and supply, we need not explicitly consider the bond market.

## THE *IS* CURVE

If we substitute equation (5.1) into (5.2), our income-expenditures equilibrium can be written as:

$$a\,(y,R;\,g,t) - y = 0\cdot \tag{5.6}$$

Since $a(y,R;\,g,t)$ represents the amount of goods demanded, and $y$ is the amount actually produced, equation (5.6) states that in equilibrium the excess demand for goods must be zero. Since $g$ and $t$ are given to the model, $y$ and $R$ must vary so that the excess demand for goods is zero. Assuming equilibrium in the goods market, this relationship between $y$ and $R$ in (5.6) defines the **IS curve**. The actual term "*IS*" was adopted by early Keynesian writers because their models typically excluded government spending and net exports and so concentrated on the equality of investment and saving; hence the *I* and *S* label.

*IS* curve
A curve derived from equilibrium between saving and investment

To illustrate the *IS* curve graphically, we must first consider how aggregate expenditures depend on $R$, the nominal interest rate. If we graph the aggregate expenditure function in $ya$ space for a given interest rate $R_0$, we find a particular equilibrium income level $y_0$ as seen in Figure 5.1. The line labeled 45° in Figure 5.1 cuts the $ya$ space in half. The significance of this line is that at any point along the line

Figure 5.1

The Effect of Alternative Interest Rates on Equilibrium Real
Income

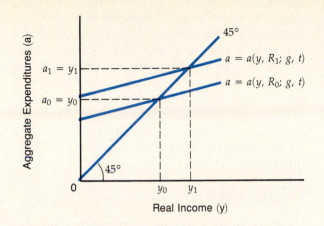

$a = y$. We can therefore use the 45° line to find equilibrium: the point of intersection between the 45° line and the aggregate expenditures line is the equilibrium point of aggregate expenditures.

If the interest rate falls from $R_0$ to a lower rate $R_1$, aggregate expenditures will rise since aggregate expenditures depend negatively upon the interest rate. The new aggregate expenditure line lies above the old line in Figure 5.1, and we see that when spending increases, the equilibrium level of income increases to $y_1$.

The *IS* curve is drawn in $yR$ space and indicates the set of $yR$ points (the values for $y$ and $R$) for which the goods market is in equilibrium. Figure 5.2 portrays an *IS* curve, showing all combinations of real income and the nominal interest rate for which planned

The IS curve shows all combinations of real income and the nominal interest rate for which planned expenditures equal actual expenditures.

Figure 5.2

The *IS* Curve: Income–
Expenditures Equilibrium

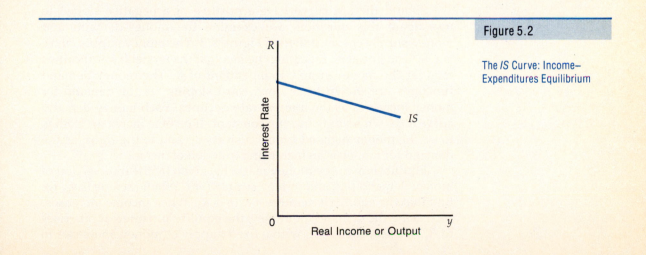

expenditures equal actual expenditures. The curve is negatively sloped because, as was illustrated in Figure 5.1, the higher the interest rate the lower the equilibrium level of income. If we take a particular level of income $y_0$ and find the interest rate at which equation (5.6) holds, we would have some particular rate $R_0$ so that $a(y_0, R_0; g,t) - y_0 = 0$. If we now consider a higher level of income $y_1$, holding everything but $R$ constant, $R$ must fall to some lower level $R_1$ in order to maintain equilibrium where $a(y_1,R_1; g,t) - y_1 = 0$. Because the *IS* curve is drawn holding government spending $g$ and taxes $t$ constant, we will always find *IS* curves negatively sloped, since $y$ is a negative function of $R$.

## THE *LM* CURVE

If we substitute equations (5.3) and (5.4) into (5.5), we can write our monetary equilibrium condition as:

$$m^d(y,R) - m = 0 \cdot \tag{5.7}$$

This says that in equilibrium, the excess demand for money must be zero. Since the money supply is given to the model by the discretionary powers of the monetary authority, real income $y$ and the nominal interest rate $R$ must adjust so that real money demand equals the real money supply. Equation (5.7) defines the **LM curve** as the set of $yR$ points giving equilibrium in the money market. The origin of "*LM*" is found in the notation used by Keynes. Keynes used $L$ to represent the money demand function (which he termed the *liquidity preference function*) and $M$ for the money supply. Hence *LM* was a descriptive label for the curve representing the $yR$ points consistent with equilibrium between money demand and money supply.

*LM* curve
A curve derived from equilibrium between money demand (*L*) and money supply (*M*)

Should the *LM* curve have a positive or a negative slope? To investigate this question, we examine the money-demand and money-supply curves drawn in Figure 5.3. The money supply curve is a vertical line at $m$, reflecting the fact that the monetary authorities may set the money supply independent of $R$. The money demand functions are shown to be downward sloping, as the demand for money increases as the interest rate declines. Each money demand curve is drawn holding income constant. If income increases from $y_0$ to $y_1$, the money demand function shifts up and to the right, as the demand for money is an increasing function of income.

Equilibrium in the money market is given by the intersection of money demand ($m^d$) and money supply ($m^s$). When income is $y_0$, we find that the equilibrium interest rate is $R_0$. When income increases, increasing the demand for money, the equilibrium interest rate rises to $R_1$. We see, then, that with a fixed supply of money, increases in

Figure 5.3

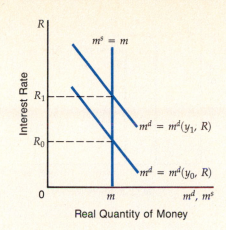

income will be associated with higher interest rates to maintain money market equilibrium.

The preceding analysis indicates that the *LM* curve, the set of all $yR$ points for which the money market is in equilibrium, will be upward sloping as in Figure 5.4. This positive slope illustrates that at higher interest rates, the quantity of money demanded is lower so income must rise to maintain the money market equilibrium. The *LM* curve will be steeper: (a) the greater the increase in money demand for a given increase in real income and (b) the smaller the decrease in money demand for a given increase in the nominal interest rate. The curve is steeper because with either of these conditions, small increases in $y$ will be associated with larger increases in the interest rate.

The LM curve shows all combinations of real income and the nominal interest rate for which money demand equals money supply.

Figure 5.4

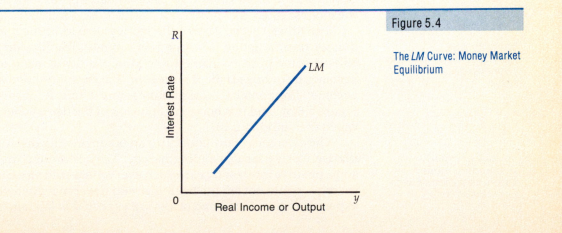

Figure 5.5

Perfectly Interest Inelastic
Money Demand (a) and the
Corresponding *LM* Curve (b)

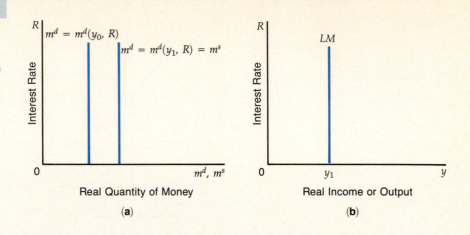

**(a)**                          **(b)**

## SPECIAL CASES OF THE *LM* CURVE

Keynes has suggested that the upward sloping *LM* curve of Figure 5.4 is modified to reflect a couple of possible special cases. The special cases of the *LM* curve result from two extreme cases of money demand: a perfectly **interest-inelastic money demand** and the *liquidity trap*.

**interest-inelastic money demand**
The vertical money demand curve that results when interest rates have no effect on money demand

    Perfect interest inelasticity means that changes in interest rates will have no effect on the demand for money. This will result in a vertical money demand curve as in Figure 5.5(a). At one level of income, money demand and supply will coincide regardless of the interest rate. If income increases from some level $y_0$ to a higher level $y_1$, then money demand increases correspondingly. If $y_1$ is the income level at which money demand equals money supply, then the *LM* curve will be a vertical line at $y_1$ as in Figure 5.5(b). As long as income equals $y_1$, the money market will be in equilibrium independent of the interest rate.

**liquidity trap**
The points at which demand for money becomes infinitely elastic

    The other special case of the money demand function is the liquidity trap, a notion developed by Keynes. The **liquidity trap** results at some positive interest rate at which the demand for money becomes infinitely elastic. This means that the money demand curve becomes horizontal at a minimum interest rate $R_{min}$, as shown in Figure 5.6(a), and this horizontal portion of the demand for money is called the liquidity trap.

**speculative motive for demanding money**
Current money demand for future spending needs

    The existence of the liquidity trap is supposedly due to the **speculative motive for demanding money**. Keynes argued that there is some positive interest rate at which everyone would agree that interest rates would not fall further but would rise. But if interest rates are expected to rise, then bond prices are expected to fall, and so no one

Figure 5.6

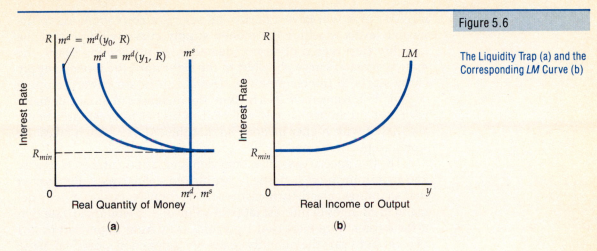

The Liquidity Trap (a) and the Corresponding *LM* Curve (b)

**(a)**   **(b)**

will want to hold bonds and the demand for money will become unlimited (the infinite elasticity).[3]

We should note that, as carefully documented by Axel Leijonhuvud,[4] Keynes himself never claimed that the liquidity trap had ever actually existed, but, in *The General Theory of Employment, Interest, and Money* (p. 207), Keynes suggested that the liquidity trap could occur in the future. While we have never observed such an occurrence, if in fact a liquidity trap existed, we would have a money demand curve as pictured in Figure 5.6(a). Although increases in income will shift the money demand curve to the right, at some low level of interest rates $R_{min}$, the money demand function is horizontal. This means that different levels of income may be associated with the same interest rate $R_{min}$ as long as the money supply intersects both money demand functions in their liquidity trap regions. The result-

The liquidity trap is an infinitely elastic money demand.

---

[3]An alternative explanation of the speculative motive was offered by James Tobin "Liquidity Preference as Behavior Towards Risk," *Review of Economic Studies*, 25 (Feb. 1958), 65–86). Tobin argued that individuals must be compensated for the risk of holding bonds—higher interest rates compensate for higher risk. At low interest rates we would expect the demand for money to increase as individuals shift away from risky bonds to riskless money (riskless in terms of the probability of changes in nominal value). While Tobin's argument provides an additional theoretical basis for a downward sloping money demand curve, only under special assumptions does this approach imply that a liquidity trap exists.

[4]Axel Leijonhuvud, *On Keynesian Economics and the Economics of Keynes* (New York: Oxford University Press, 1968).

ing *LM* curve will have a horizontal segment corresponding to the income levels at which the money supply curve will intersect the liquidity trap region of money demand. As income increases, the money demand curve will shift to the right until the money supply curve starts to intersect money demand in its downward sloping region. As income increases further, the increases in money demand with a given money supply will lead to higher interest rates being associated with higher income, so that the *LM* curve then takes the standard positive slope.

The two special cases of money demand, a zero interest elasticity and an infinite interest elasticity, are indeed special cases. Remember that an interest elasticity measures the responsiveness of money demand to changes in interest rates. A value of -0.5 would indicate that if the interest rate increased 1 percent, (say, from 10 percent to 10.1 percent per year) the quantity of money demanded would fall by ½ percent. Researchers have usually found estimates of the interest elasticity to lie in the range of -0.1 to -0.8. While it would be comforting to be more precise, the variety of studies done reflect the different methodologies used and personal views of the individual researchers to the extent that Cooley and LeRoy, in a critique of the literature on money demand, were led to the pessimistic conclusion that "it is next to impossible to say anything about the interest elasticity of money demand."[5]

The latter statement is likely to overestimate our lack of knowledge regarding the interest elasticity of money demand. While some studies have not been able to reject the hypothesis of zero interest elasticity, the evidence regarding a liquidity trap is more clear cut. After a careful review of the studies testing for a liquidity trap, a well-known authority on money demand, David Laidler, concludes, with but slight reservations, that "the liquidity trap is of no empirical significance."[6] Furthermore, the bounds for the interest elasticity identified by Cooley and LeRoy suggest nothing even close to an infinitely interest elastic demand for money. The current state of knowledge then points to a downward sloping money demand curve. While we cannot altogether rule out a zero interest elasticity, we may comfortably rule out a liquidity trap of infinite elasticity. It is there-

---

[5]Thomas F. Cooley and Stephen F. LeRoy, "Identification and Estimation of Money Demand," *American Economic Review*, 71 (Dec. 1981), 825–44.

[6]David E. W. Laidler, *The Demand for Money* (New York: Harper and Row, 1977), p. 133.

fore expected that the *LM* curve will have the standard positive slope of Figure 5.4, so that the vertical *LM* of Figure 5.5(b) and the horizontal region of Figure 5.6(b) are best considered curious special cases—theoretical possibilities with little or no empirical relevance.

## *IS–LM* EQUILIBRIUM

The *IS* curve gives all possible combinations of real income and the nominal interest rate for which the goods market is in equilibrium. The *LM* curve gives all real income and nominal interest rate combinations for which the money market is in equilibrium. When we put both the *IS* and the *LM* curve together on the same graph, as in Figure 5.7, the point where the two lines intersect is the only combination of real income and nominal interest rate at which both the goods market and the money market are in equilibrium simultaneously. The equilibrium real income is denoted $y_e$ and the equilibrium interest rate $R_e$.

> The equilibrium interest rate and income is determined by the intersection of the IS and LM curves.

To be sure we understand the concepts behind the ***IS–LM* equilibrium**, let's consider the situation for points away from equilibrium. Point *A* in Figure 5.8 is one such disequilibrium point. We see that point *A* lies on the equilibrium interest rate $R_e$, but at a lower level of income than $y_e$. Regarding the *IS* curve, when income is below $y_e$ at $y'$, the aggregate expenditures curve is above the 45° line in terms of the analysis of Figure 5.8 (A1), indicating an excess demand in the goods market (denoted *ED* in the diagram). Since point *A* also lies off the *LM* curve, we know that there will also be a disequilibrium in the money market. Figure 5.8(A2) indicates that this situation of an equilibrium interest rate $R_e$ with a lower-than-equilibrium income

> ***IS–LM* equilibrium**
> The point where the goods market and money market are in equilibrium simultaneously

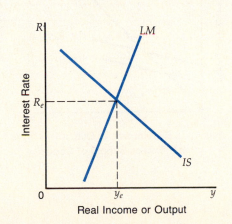

**Figure 5.7**

The Equilibrium Real Income and Nominal Interest Rate

Figure 5.8

Disequilibrium in the *IS–LM* Diagram

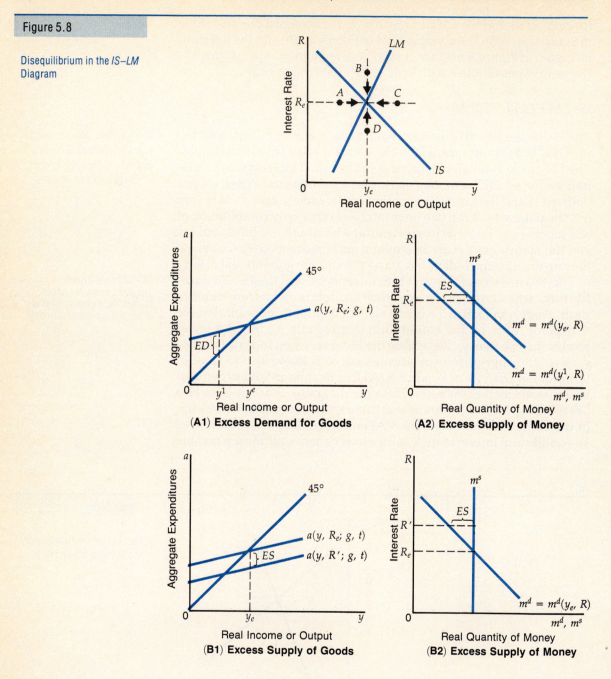

(A1) **Excess Demand for Goods**

(A2) **Excess Supply of Money**

(B1) **Excess Supply of Goods**

(B2) **Excess Supply of Money**

$y'$ gives an excess supply of money, denoted *ES* in the diagram. Thus the disequilibrium point *A* in the *IS–LM* diagram is associated with an excess demand in the goods market and an excess supply in the money market. The excess demand for goods and excess supply of money both tend to increase output and thereby raise income. If income would rise to $y_e$, both markets would again be in equilibrium. If the economy were actually to move from a point like *A*, the adjustment might not be direct: the interest rate might fall temporarily below $R_e$, for example, until $y$ reached $y_e$.

We can similarly consider the disequilibrium situations given by points *B*, *C*, and *D*. At point *B*, we have the equilibrium income $y_e$, but the interest rate is higher than equilibrium. In the goods market we have the situation depicted in Figure 5.8(B1). At the higher interest rate $R'$, the aggregate expenditures curve shifts downward (remember investment is a decreasing function of the interest rate), so

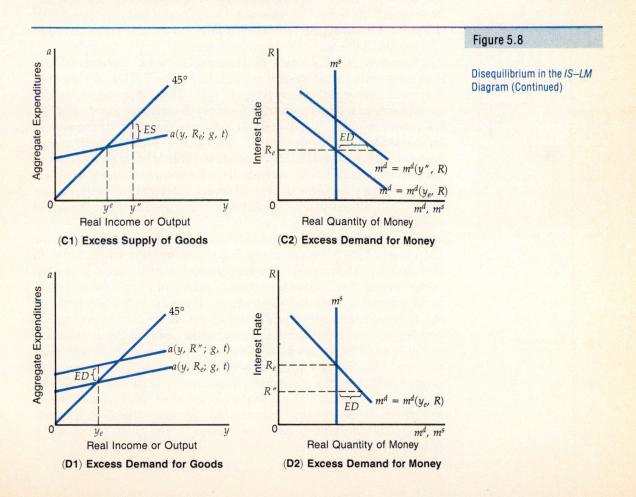

**Figure 5.8**

Disequilibrium in the *IS–LM* Diagram (Continued)

(C1) **Excess Supply of Goods**

(C2) **Excess Demand for Money**

(D1) **Excess Demand for Goods**

(D2) **Excess Demand for Money**

that there is an excess supply in the goods market at $y_e$. In the money market, the interest rate $R'$ is above the equilibrium rate $R_e$, giving an excess supply of money. So point $B$ is associated with an excess supply of both goods and money that would be eliminated by a drop in the interest rate to $R_e$. How does the lower interest rate come about? As people attempt to rid themselves of their excess money balances, they exchange some of this money for bonds. Increased demand for bonds raises bond prices and lowers the interest rate. When the interest rate falls to $R_e$, the quantity of money demanded just equals the quantity supplied and investment spending has been stimulated to where the excess supply of goods is eliminated.

Point $C$ occurs at the equilibrium interest rate $R_e$ and at an income higher than equilibrium, which we will call $y''$. With this higher-than-equilibrium income, there will be an excess supply in the goods market as in Figure 5.8(C1), and an excess demand in the money market as in Figure 5.8(C2). If income would fall back to $y_e$, the *IS–LM* equilibrium would be restored. This is really just the opposite of the point $A$ analysis, so here output falls as business firms cut back production in the face of rising inventories.

Finally, at point $D$ we see that income is at $y_e$ but the interest rate is at some lower level we will call $R''$. In Figure 5.8(D1) we see that the lower-than-equilibrium interest rate causes the aggregate demand curve to increase, giving an excess demand for goods at $y_e$. In the money market, Figure 5.8(D2) indicates that at $R''$ there will be an excess demand for money. So point $D$ is associated with excess demands in both markets that would be eliminated by an increase in the interest rate to $R_e$. As individuals sell nonmoney financial assets to build money balances to desired levels, interest rates will rise. As $R$ rises to $R_e$, money market equilibrium is restored as is goods market equilibrium.

Summarizing our findings for Figure 5.8: points to the left of the *LM* curve $(A,B)$ have an excess supply of money, while those to the right $(C,D)$ have an excess demand for money; points to the left of the *IS* curve $(A,D)$ have an excess demand for goods, while points to the right $(B,C)$ have an excess supply of goods. While any point on the *IS* curve represents equilibrium in the goods market and points on *LM* give equilibrium in the money market, only at the intersection of the *IS* and *LM* curves do we find simultaneous equilibrium in all markets. This *IS–LM* equilibrium is for a given state of the world or given solution to the set of five equations, (5.1) through (5.5). The usefulness of the *IS–LM* apparatus is the ease with which we can analyze changes in the macro economy. We can use the *IS–LM* theory for comparative static analyses of changes in the given values of the five-equation model.

# 5.2 SHIFTS IN THE GOODS MARKET

For the **aggregate expenditure function** to shift, one or more of the components of spending must change. A shift could occur in the consumer expenditure function, investment, government spending, or net exports. Given the relatively small size of net exports in the U.S., comparative static *IS–LM* analyses generally focus on a change in one of the first three components of spending. In the spirit of the Keynesian model, the *IS–LM* framework is used to analyze the short-run impacts of changes in spending. In the short run, expectations and plans are being held constant. We may think of the *IS–LM* model as considering the short-run effect of unexpected macroeconomic changes or shocks. In later chapters, we will discuss the important role of expectations and the different impacts of expected versus unexpected changes that more modern macro approaches allow.

aggregate expenditure function
Aggregate demand

## SHIFTS IN THE COMPONENTS OF AGGREGATE EXPENDITURE

Shifts in the income-expenditure sector operate through their effect on the aggregate expenditure function. Therefore, to analyze how a change in any component of spending affects the *IS–LM* equilibrium, we will first consider the impact on the aggregate expenditure function. It is useful to organize the possible exogenous changes according to whether they increase or decrease aggregate expenditures. Table 5.2 lists the sources of such changes in two columns: factors that increase desired aggregate expenditures and factors that decrease desired aggregate expenditures. Figure 5.9 illustrates these changes in the five graphs drawn, where curves labeled *1* portray the increases in the particular spending component and curves labeled *2* portray the decreases relative to the original position labeled *0*.

Case (a) is a change in real government expenditures financed by borrowing. Fiscal policy is set by government officials and may be changed at will. The phrase "financed by borrowing" is important, as changes in taxes affect consumption spending. By matching the government spending change with borrowing, rather than taxes, we assume that consumer expenditures are unaffected (in a later chapter we will reconsider this assumption). An exogenous increase in real government expenditures is represented graphically by a shift from $g_0$ to $g_1$ in Figure 5.9(a), while a decrease is shown by the shift from $g_0$ to $g_2$.

Case (b) is a change in real taxes financed by borrowing. By matching the change in taxes with borrowing, we can hold the level of government spending constant and concentrate on the shift in the

Table 5.2

| Factors That Increase Desired Aggregate Expenditures | Case | Factors That Decrease Desired Aggregate Expenditures |
|---|---|---|
| An increase in real government expenditures financed by borrowing. | (a) | A decrease in real government expenditures allowing reduced borrowing. |
| A decrease in real taxes financed by borrowing. | (b) | An increase in real taxes allowing reduced borrowing. |
| An autonomous upward shift in investment demand due to more favorable expectations. | (c) | An autonomous downward shift in investment demand due to less favorable expectations. |
| An autonomous upward shift in the consumption function. | (d) | An autonomous downward shift in the consumption function. |
| An autonomous upward shift in net exports due, for example, to increased foreign real income. | (e) | An autonomous downward shift in net exports due, for example, to decreased foreign real income. |

consumption function associated with the change in taxes. A decrease in taxes will cause the consumption function in $cy$ space to shift up from $c_0$ to $c_1$ in Figure 5.9(b). Now at every level of income, consumers want to spend more. An increase in taxes will shift the consumption function down like the move from $c_0$ to $c_2$.

Case (c) is an autonomous change in investment spending. Keynes argued that the position of the investment demand function depended upon expectations regarding the future profitability of investment. He believed that the psychology of business decision-makers was subject to sudden changes between optimism and pessimism over expected future returns and thus the investment function may be expected to shift considerably in the short run. If the returns to capital are expected to be higher in the future, the demand for investment should increase, as in the shift from $i_0$ to $i_1$ in Figure 5.9(c). Conversely, pessimism regarding the future returns would cause a decline in investment from $i_0$ to $i_2$ in the figure. While the susceptibility of entrepreneurial expectations to short-run shifts is an empirical question, there is no doubt that such changes in expectations would lead to changes in investment. This is the only consideration given to changing expectations in our Keynesian model.

Case (d), autonomous shifts in the consumption function, while theoretically possible, do not seem to be empirically relevant for the U.S. For the consumption function to shift autonomously, something must happen to change the spending habits of the nation as a whole. Events which might lead to an upward shift of the consumption function, say from $c_0$ to $c_1$ in Figure 5.9(d), would include an increase in

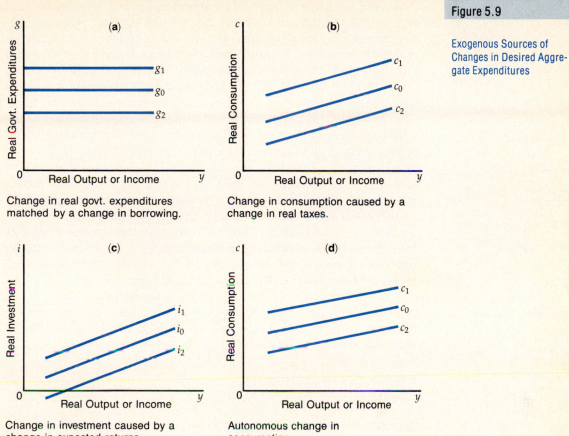

Figure 5.9

Exogenous Sources of Changes in Desired Aggregate Expenditures

**(a)**

Change in real govt. expenditures matched by a change in borrowing.

**(b)**

Change in consumption caused by a change in real taxes.

**(c)**

Change in investment caused by a change in expected returns.

**(d)**

Autonomous change in consumption.

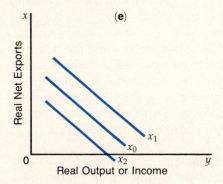

**(e)**

Change in net exports caused by a change in foreign real income.

perceived wealth or permanent income. The Keynesian consumption function is a short-run function that relates current consumer expenditures to current income. If consumers believe that their permanent income (see Chapter 3 for a discussion of permanent income) has increased, then we would expect them to spend more at any given level of current income. A decrease in permanent income would lead to a downward shift in the short-run consumption function, as from $c_0$ to $c_2$ in Figure 5.9(d). Since permanent income tends to change slowly over time, such short-run autonomous shifts in the consumption function are of little practical importance.

Finally, case (e), shifts in net exports, is also relatively unimportant for a large economy like the U.S. For smaller, more open economies, however, shifts in net exports may be very important. Figure 5.9(e) shows an increase in net exports by the change from $x_0$ to $x_1$. Such change could be caused by an increase in foreign real income as foreign residents spend some of this income increase on domestically produced goods. A decrease in foreign real income could cause a fall in net exports, like the shift from $x_0$ to $x_2$ in Figure 5.9(e).

While the origin of *IS*-curve shifts is found in the shifts of the individual components of aggregate expenditures, as just covered, we must consider the implications of alternative aggregate expenditure functions to understand the link between such shifts.

## THE EFFECTS OF ALTERNATIVE AGGREGATE EXPENDITURE FUNCTIONS

Consider two alternative aggregate expenditure functions:

$$a = a_0 (y, R; g_0, t_0) \tag{5.8}$$
$$a = a_1 (y, R; g_1, t_1) \tag{5.9}$$

and assume that for any given values of real income and the nominal interest rate, the aggregate expenditure function $a_0$ implies lower desired aggregate expenditures than $a_1$ as shown in Figure 5.10. Realistically, $a_0$ could be lower than $a_1$ for any of the reasons found in Table 5.2. Cases (a) or (b) change the $g$ or $t$ arguments of the function $a$ (. . .) while cases (c), (d), and (e) change the function of $a$ (. . .) itself.

For any given interest rate $\overline{R}$, the $a_1$ aggregate expenditure function will lie above the $a_0$ function when graphed in $ya$ space. As a result, at the given interest rate $\overline{R}$, there will be a higher equilibrium level of income associated with $a_1$. Recalling that the *IS* curve represents all points in $yR$ space for which the goods market is in equilibrium, and since for any $R$, a higher equilibrium $y$ occurs in the case of $a_1$, the *IS* curve associated with $a_1(IS_1)$ lies to the right of the *IS* curve associated with $a_0$ $(IS_0)$ as shown in Figure 5.11.

Figure 5.10

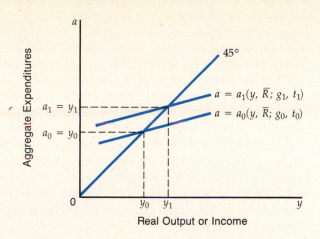

To find the impact of alternative aggregate expenditure functions on equilibrium real income and nominal interest rates, we must examine the changes in *IS–LM* equilibrium. Since the money market, and therefore the *LM* curve, is unaffected by the factors that changed the aggregate expenditure function, we may assume that the *LM* curve is held constant. Figure 5.12 shows that the equilibrium values of both real income and the nominal interest rate are higher with the $a_1$ aggregate expenditures function in the normal case of an upward sloping *LM* curve. For any given shift in the *IS* curve, the magnitude of the change in equilibrium $y$ and $R$ will depend upon the slope of

The effect of a shift in the aggregate expenditure function will depend on the shape of the LM curve.

Figure 5.11

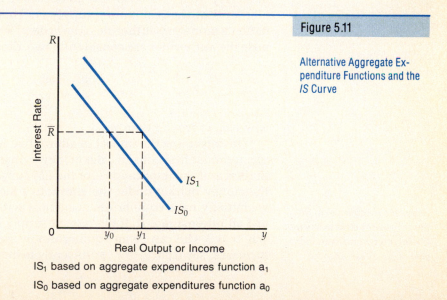

$IS_1$ based on aggregate expenditures function $a_1$

$IS_0$ based on aggregate expenditures function $a_0$

the *LM* curve. *The steeper LM, the greater the change in R and the smaller the change in y.* As *R* increases, investment spending falls so that equilibrium income increases less than would be the case if the interest rate were unchanged. In the special case of a vertical *LM* curve (*LM'* caused by a perfect interest inelasticity of money demand), the shift in the *IS* curve from $IS_0$ to $IS_1$ in Figure 5.12 has no effect on *y*. Since real money demand is unaffected by the interest rate in the case of the vertical *LM* curve, money demand can be equal to money supply at only one level of real income. An *LM* curve like *LM'*, as discussed earlier, does not seem as consistent with real world behavior as *LM* in Figure 5.12. We expect an upward shift in the aggregate expenditures curve to have some positive effect on real income. The exact slope of the *LM* curve, and thus the interest elasticity of money demand, is an empirical question which, as was pointed out earlier, has not been settled.

In summary, a shift upward in the aggregate expenditures function will shift the *IS* curve to the right and bring about higher equilibrium real income and a higher equilibrium nominal interest rate. A decrease in the aggregate expenditures function will shift the *IS* curve to the left, causing lower equilibrium real income and a lower equilibrium nominal interest rate.

## 5.3 SHIFTS IN THE MONEY MARKET

### MONETARY POLICY AND THE MONEY SUPPLY

Monetary policy in the *IS–LM* model refers to the choice of a particular level of the real money supply *m*. This choice is made by the nation's monetary authorities (the Federal Reserve in the U.S.). Suppose the authorities are considering two alternatives:

$$m^s = m_0 \qquad \qquad (5.10)$$
$$m^s = m_1 \qquad \qquad (5.11)$$

where $m_1$ is greater than $m_0$.

To determine the impact of alternative levels of the money supply, we must first consider the money demand–money supply equilibrium and the implications for the *LM* curve. Figure 5.13(a) depicts the money market under the alternative money supplies. Suppose we initially have equilibrium at point *A* with a money supply of $m_0$ and an interest rate $\overline{R}$. If the money supply increases to $m_1$ the only way that $\overline{R}$ still can be an equilibrium interest rate is if real income increases, say from $y_0$ to $y_1$, sufficiently to increase money demand so

Increases (decreases) in the money supply tend to lower (raise) interest rates and increase (decrease) income.

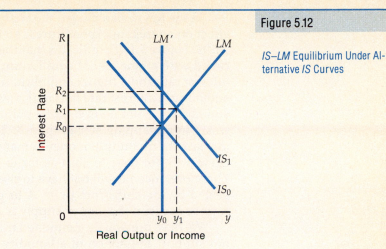

**Figure 5.12**

*IS–LM* Equilibrium Under Alternative *IS* Curves

that the money-supply and money-demand curves intersect at point *B*. The increase in money supply causes an excess supply of money at the original *y* and *R*, which is reflected in increased spending. The higher spending level raises income to the level at which all money is willingly held, or the quantity of money demanded equals the quantity of money supplied $m_1$. But since $m_1$ implies a higher level of income for any given interest rate, the *LM* curve associated with $m_1$ must lie to the right of the *LM* curve for $m_0$, as in the difference between $LM_0$ and $LM_1$ in Figure 5.13(b).

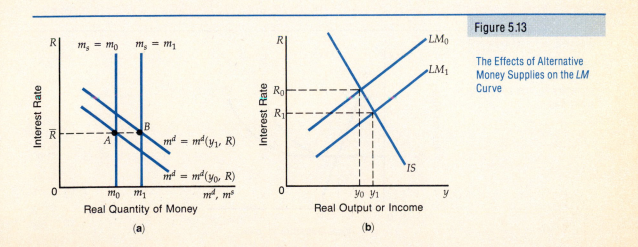

**Figure 5.13**

The Effects of Alternative Money Supplies on the *LM* Curve

In the Keynesian model, the change in the money supply has no effect on aggregate expenditures, so the *IS* curve is constant as *LM* shifts. Figure 5.13(b) indicates that the higher money supply is associated with a new *IS–LM* equilibrium, yielding a lower equilibrium interest rate and a higher equilibrium real income. The fact that the equilibrium interest rate falls indicates that the actual money market equilibrium is not point *B*, but a point to the left and lower ("southwest" in a mapping sense) than *B*. The drop in interest rates will increase the quantity of money demanded so that the money demand curve will not have to shift as far to the right as in Figure 5.13(a). Therefore, income will not have to rise by as much as originally suggested by the shift from point *A* to point *B* in the figure. Just the reverse occurs if the money supply is decreased: *y* falls and *R* rises.

We have previously mentioned that the real world evidence does not support the notion of a liquidity trap, or an infinitely interest elastic region of the money demand curve. Still, due to the popularity of this special case among Keynesian economists until the 1960s, we should consider the implications of a liquidity trap for monetary policy. As Figure 5.6 indicated, a liquidity trap would be reflected in a horizontal region of the *LM* curve. As Figure 5.14 shows, if the *IS* curve intersects the *LM* curve in this region, then increases in the money supply would have no effect on the equilibrium values of real income or the nominal interest rate. The liquidity trap argument was frequently invoked in the past to argue that monetary policy would be an ineffective means of changing real income. The probability that money demand would adjust to accommodate money supply with no income change is considered too low to warrant support or discussion by modern macroeconomists. As a result, the short-run situa-

---

**Figure 5.14**

The Effects of Alternative Monetary Policies With a Liquidity Trap

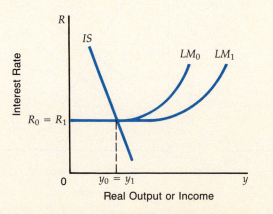

tion depicted in Figure 5.13 is the generally accepted view of the short-run *IS–LM* response to an increase in the money supply.

## MONEY-DEMAND SHIFTS

Shifts in money demand have generally not been important in Keynesian *IS–LM* analysis. However, if a decrease in money demand did occur, we can see in Figure 5.15 that the effect would be similar to an increase in the money supply. In Figure 5.15(a) we see that if money demanders' preferences changed (due, let's say, to an increased use of credit cards) so that the demand for money falls, then even with unchanged income, there will be a lower equilibrium interest rate. This indicates that the *LM* curve after the decrease in money demand ($LM_1$) will lie to the right of the original *LM* curve ($LM_0$). The end result will be a lower equilibrium interest rate and higher equilibrium income, just as if the money supply had risen. If money demand increased, we would observe just the opposite effects.

Increases (decreases) in money demand tend to raise (lower) interest rates and lower (raise) income.

There is really no problem in distinguishing between the ultimate effects of shifts in money demand versus shifts in money supply. In general, we must simply consider what happens to the excess supply of money at the original $y$ and $R$. If a change in the money market results in an increase in the excess supply of money at the initial $y$ and $R$, then the *LM* curve shifts to the right (as in Figures 5.15 and 5.13). If a change in the money market causes a decrease in the excess supply of money at the initial $y$ and $R$ (an excess demand is considered as a negative excess supply), then the *LM* curve shifts to the left.

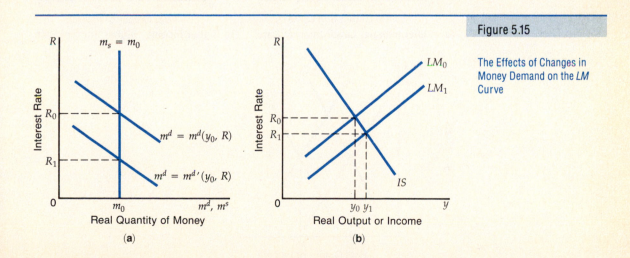

Figure 5.15

The Effects of Changes in Money Demand on the *LM* Curve

## FINANCING INCREASED GOVERNMENT EXPENDITURES BY MONEY CREATION

Suppose a $10 billion increase in government spending over the short period were financed by creating an additional $10 billion of base money instead of increasing taxes or borrowing. If the money multiplier equals 2.5, this would cause a $25 billion increase in the money supply. The increase in government spending will cause the *IS* curve to shift to the right, while the increase in the money supply will cause the *LM* curve to also shift right. What is the end result of such policy on equilibrium real income and nominal interest? As Figure 5.16 shows, when both *IS* and *LM* shift to the right, real income unambiguously increases while the new nominal interest rate is indeterminate. In other words, there is no way that both *IS* and *LM* can shift

**Figure 5.16**

The Effect of Financing Increased Government Expenditures by Money Creation

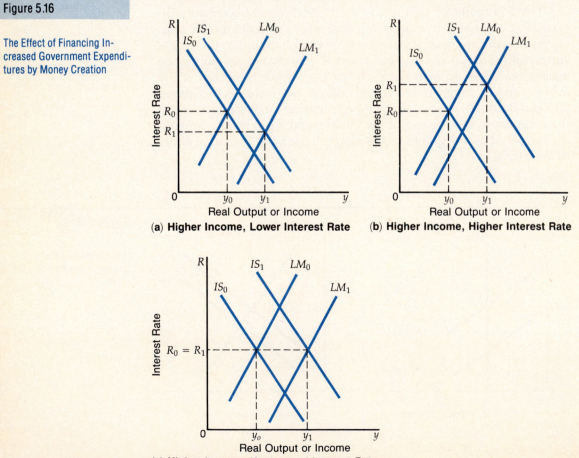

right without the equilibrium real income increasing. However, what happens to the equilibrium interest rate depends upon the magnitude of the shifts in the *IS* and *LM* curves. In Figure 5.16(a) the rightward shift in *LM* is large relative to *IS* so the nominal interest rate falls. In 5.16(b) *IS* shifts more than *LM*, so the interest rate rises. Finally, in Figure 5.16(c) the increases in *IS* and *LM* are similar in magnitude so that while income increases, there is no change in the nominal interest rate.[7] There are always problems of indeterminate solutions when both the *IS* and *LM* curves shift. Without information on the magnitudes of the shifts in the individual curves, we must be careful in drawing conclusions regarding changes in equilibrium real income and the nominal interest rate.

The *IS–LM* apparatus developed in this chapter can be very useful, but we must remember its limitations. It is appropriate for analyzing the short-run impact of changes in macroeconomic variables. By short run we mean a period during which changes in flow variables do not affect stock variables,[8] prices are fixed, and expectations are unchanged. How short is this period? If we used *IS–LM* graphs to analyze the impact effect of macroeconomic shocks, we can generally be comfortable with our findings. To pass beyond the immediate effects we must turn to a dynamic approach to macroeconomics. Such an approach will be developed beginning in Chapter 9.

A concrete example of the usefulness of *IS–LM* analysis will be provided by the essay at the end of the chapter. There we will apply our *IS–LM* techniques to investigate the potential for government spending to ''crowd out'' or replace private-sector spending in the economy. As we shall see, *IS–LM* graphs provide a neat, understandable structure in which a potentially confusing issue can be analyzed.

---

[7] We generally do not consider the many modifications to the standard Keynesian model which have been proposed over the years, since more complete models are presented in later chapters. However, one possible amendment should be noted: The ''real balance effect'' (also sometimes known as the Pigou or Patinkin or Haberler effect) is based on the proposition that a higher real money stock will increase desired consumer spending directly, other things equal. This implies that an increase in *m* shifts both the *LM* and *IS* curve to the right even if the increased money is used to finance decreased borrowing (the standard case) and not increased *g* as just analyzed in the text. As a result, the real balance effect implies that Figure 5.16 is appropriate to the analysis of increases in *m* even if *g* and *t* are unchanged. Historically, the real balance effect was used to show that increases in *m* would increase *y* even if the economy were to be caught in the liquidity trap.

[8] An exception is made for base money and money that can be changed very quickly by accounting entries.

## SUMMARY

**1**   The *IS–LM* model shows how real income and the nominal interest rate adjust to maintain both goods-market and money-market equilibrium.

**2**   The *IS* curve includes the set of real income and nominal interest rate combinations for which the goods market is in equilibrium.

**3**   The *LM* curve is the set of real income and nominal interest rate combinations associated with money-market equilibrium.

**4**   If the demand for money is perfectly interest inelastic, then the *LM* curve is a vertical line at a given level of income.

**5**   If the demand for money is infinitely elastic with respect to the interest rate (this is called the liquidity trap), the *LM* curve is a horizontal line at a particular nominal interest rate.

**6**   The *LM* curve is generally accepted as an upward sloping line in $yR$ space, while the *IS* curve has a negative slope.

**7**   Shifts in the *IS* curve are caused by shifts in one of the components of aggregate expenditures: consumer expenditures, investment, government spending, or net exports.

**8**   An excess demand in the goods market, which shifts the *IS* curve to the right, will lead to higher real income and nominal interest rates.

**9**   Shifts in the *LM* curve are caused by changes in the money supply or money demand.

**10**   An excess supply of money will cause the *LM* curve to shift to the right and bring about a higher equilibrium real income and a lower equilibrium interest rate.

**11**   When both the *IS* and *LM* curves shift, there is generally some indeterminacy regarding either the new equilibrium income or interest rate, unless we have some information on the magnitude of the shifts.

## EXERCISES

**1.** The model used in this chapter contains a money market and a goods market. Yet we also have a bond market which is not explicitly considered. Suppose we now want to add a *BB* curve to our *IS–LM* diagram, representing all income and interest rate combinations for which the bond market is in equilibrium. Draw such a *BB* line in an *IS–LM* graph. (Hint: Consider the discussion of adjustment to disequilibrium surrounding the *IS–LM* graph of Figure 5.8.)

2. What are the implications for fiscal policy (government spending and taxation) of:

   **a.** a perfectly interest inelastic money demand,

   **b.** a liquidity trap.

3. What will happen to the equilibrium level of real income and the nominal interest rate if (illustrate your conclusion using *IS–LM* graphs):

   **a.** There is an autonomous downward shift in the consumption function.

   **b.** The Federal Reserve decreases the money supply.

   **c.** Real government expenditures increase (and the increase is financed only by borrowing) at the same time that the Federal Reserve increases the money supply by buying government bonds.

   **d.** There is an autonomous downward shift in the investment function at the same time that the Federal Reserve increases the money supply.

   **e.** Foreign real income increases at the same time that the Federal Reserve decreases the U.S. money supply.

4. Suppose that the aggregate expenditure function is

   $$a = 1000 + g - 0.4t + 0.6y - 100R$$

   where $a$, $g$, t, and $y$ are in real terms, measured in $billions per annum, and $R$ is in percentage points per annum.

   **a.** If $g$ = $105 billion and $t$ = $100 billion, complete this table of points on this *IS* curve:

   | $R$ | 1% | 2% | 3% | 4% | 5% |
   |-----|----|----|----|----|----|
   | $y$ |    |    |    |    |    |

   **b.** Use the points in the table to draw an *IS* curve on graph paper.

5. Suppose the aggregate expenditure function in Exercise 4 is changed to:

   $$a = 1250 + g - 0.4t + 0.6y - 200R$$

   Graph the implied *IS* curve and compare it to the one drawn for the previous exercise. If the difference in aggregate expenditures is due to a greater sensitivity of investment spending to the nominal interest rate in the present case, explain why this change should lead to the change in the slope of the *IS* curve observed.

6. Suppose a $10 billion increase in real government spending would shift the *IS* curve to the right by $20 billion. Compare the effects on real income and the nominal interest rate according to whether the *LM* curve is flat or steep. What is the common sense reason for these differences?

7. Show that a decrease in money demand for any given level of real income and the nominal interest rate would shift the *LM* curve to the right.

8. In a strict comparative statics model, it makes no sense to talk about a $10 billion increase in real base money financing a $10 billion increase in the rate of government expenditure. Why?

## REFERENCES FOR FURTHER READING

Brunner, Karl, and Allan H. Meltzer. "Mr. Hicks and the 'Monetarists.' " *Economica*, February 1973, 44–59.

Coddington, Alan. "Keynesian Economics: The Search for First Principles." *Journal of Economic Literature*, 14 (December 1976), 1258–73.

Keynes, John Maynard. *The General Theory of Employment, Interest, and Money.* New York: Harcourt, Brace, 1936.

Leijonhuvud, Axel. *On Keynesian Economics and the Economics of Keynes.* New York: Oxford University Press, 1968.

Smith, Warren L. "A Graphical Exposition of the Complete Keynesian System." *Southern Economic Journal*, 23 (October 1956), 115–25.

## CROWDING THE PRIVATE SECTOR OUT WITH GOVERNMENT SPENDING[1]

The debate over the degree to which government spending displaces private spending reached new heights during the Reagan administration. The forecasts of continued, rising government spending and large federal budget deficits brought many a politician and economist into the fray. Economists, both in and out of government, were warning that unless government spending came under control, private spending would be forced to decline. What is the mechanism whereby government spending *crowds out* private spending? Should the often-voiced fears of crowding out concern responsible citizens? These are questions that we will address in this essay.

How can we tell when crowding out occurs? If an increase in government expenditures financed by taxes or borrowing does not increase equilibrium real income by an equal or greater amount, then we may infer that the private sector has been "crowded out" at least to some extent. This is because real income equals the sum of government and private sector expenditures; so if real income goes up by less than government expenditures, private expenditures must fall. If there is no change in real income so that private expenditures fall by the full amount of the increase in government expenditures, we say that there is *complete* crowding out. We assume that the money supply is held constant so that only fiscal policy is changed. As stated then, the conditions under which partial or complete crowding out occurs within the initial short period can be usefully discussed in terms of the *IS–LM* framework. While our discussion is not intended to exhaust the possibilities, we will offer several alternative *IS–LM* cases consistent with crowding out, and then briefly consider the empirical validity of each. Over time, other forces—such as changes in prices and expectations—may become more important; so long-run crowding out may be more nearly complete than in the short run considered here. These longer run adjustments are the subject of later chapters.

## VERTICAL *LM* CURVE

If the interest elasticity of money demand is zero, so that the *LM* curve is vertical, as in Figure E5.1, then shifts in the *IS* curve will have no effect on equilibrium real income. If real government spending increases, then the *IS* curve shifts to the right, like the move from $IS_0$ to

---

[1] This essay draws heavily on the *IS–LM* analysis used by Keith M. Carlson and Roger W. Spencer in "Crowding Out and Its Critics," *Federal Reserve Bank of St. Louis Review*, December 1975.

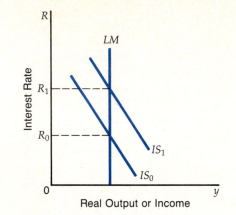

*IS*$_1$. The result of this shift is to raise the equilibrium nominal interest rate to $R_1$.

As we learned in Chapter 1, the equation of exchange ($MV = Py$) indicates that real income will increase (remember the price level $P$ is constant in Keynesian *IS–LM* analysis) only if the money supply $M$ or the velocity of money $V$ increases. But with perfectly interest inelastic money demand, higher interest rates have no impact on money demand, and therefore velocity is unchanged. This means that while government spending is increased, some other component of aggregate expenditures falls so that the aggregate expenditures function is unchanged on balance. In this case we have complete crowding out.

This has often been called "the Classical" or "monetarist" case in that it states that only a change in the money supply could change real income, as fiscal policy is ineffective. While it is not clear that many monetarists have ever embraced such a theory, it is clear that leading monetarists like Milton Friedman have not. Friedman clearly states, "I know no empirical student of the demand for money who denies that interest rates affect the real quantity of money demanded" and "in my opinion no 'fundamental issues' in either monetary theory or monetary policy hinge on whether the estimated elasticity can for most purposes be approximated by zero or is better approximated by $-.1$ or $-.5$ or $-2.0$, provided it is seldom capable of being approximated by $-\infty$."[2] In

[2] The first quotation is found in Milton Friedman, *The Optimum Quantity of Money and Other Essays* (Chicago: Aldine, 1966), p. 142. The second quotation is from Milton Friedman, "Comments on the Critics," in Robert J. Gordon (ed.), *Milton Friedman's Monetary Framework* (Chicago, University of Chicago Press, 1974), p. 138.

the first quotation, Friedman is arguing against the existence of a perfectly interest inelastic demand for money with its corresponding vertical *LM* curve. The second quotation argues that only an infinitely elastic money demand curve, or a liquidity trap, will cause problems for the effectiveness of monetary versus fiscal policy. We see then that labeling the vertical *LM* curve as being a monetarist representation would not be accurate. Aside from such matters, we must generally be quite dubious about the possibility of a vertical *LM* curve until such time as more convincing evidence has been presented to support a perfect interest inelasticity of money demand.

## HORIZONTAL *IS* CURVE

If the investment function is perfectly interest elastic, then it is possible to have a horizontal *IS* curve as depicted in Figure E5.2. How could the investment demand curve be drawn as a horizontal line at a fixed interest rate? Keith Carlson and Roger Spencer have argued that such an *IS* curve may be supported by the work of the late Frank Knight of the University of Chicago.[3] They interpret Knight as arguing that there may be no diminishing returns from investment because of two factors. First, the quantity of capital is so large relative to the additions to it that these additions should not be expected to have much of an effect on reducing the return to capital; second, investment spending is accompanied by increases in knowledge as a result of research and development expenditures. The associated technological advances will work

---

[3] Carlson and Spencer, "Crowding Out and Its Critics," p. 6.

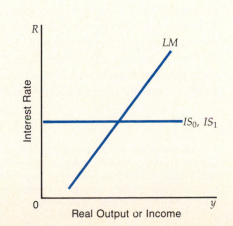

Crowding Out With a Horizontal *IS* Curve

to offset any reduction in the productivity of capital due to a growing capital stock. This would make further investment still profitable at the existing interest rate.

With a horizontal *IS* curve, there is no shift to the right in *IS* when government spending increases. The *IS* curve after the fiscal policy action $IS_1$ is the same as the original curve $IS_0$. In this framework, any increase in government spending is matched by a reduction in investment spending so that real income remains unchanged. Again complete crowding out occurs. While the vertical *LM* curve is sometimes (mistakenly) referred to as the monetarist case, we see that in this case also, only monetary policy can change real income.

How relevant or realistic is the notion of an infinitely elastic demand for investment? If it has any empirical relevance at all, it can only be in the long run, when the technological change discussed by Knight may be realized. In the short period of analysis associated with *IS–LM* graphs, the probability of observing a perfectly interest elastic investment function is very remote. Nonetheless, the flatter the *IS* curve (or the steeper the *LM* curve), the smaller will be the effect of an increase in *g* on *y* and the more nearly complete will be crowding out.[4]

As we attempt to incorporate other explanations of crowding out into the *IS–LM* framework, we find ourselves moving away from the strict *IS–LM* model developed in Chapter 5. Since we will be appealing to additional factors outside the purview of the standard *IS–LM* model, we are in effect demonstrating its limitations and weaknesses. Still it is common to stretch the applicability of the model to consider other cases of crowding out.

## ULTRARATIONALITY AND DIRECT SUBSTITUTION EFFECTS

In 1974 Paul David and John Scadding[5] published a paper arguing that crowding out could be caused by the private sector considering the public sector to be an extension of itself. This assertion of *ultrarationality* on the part of the private sector presumes that increases in government spending financed by borrowing are substituting directly for private sector consumption and investment. Households view the increased government spending as providing benefits similar to those that would flow from private expenditures. This is based on the assumption that households regard the corporate and government sectors as acting in their

---

[4] These slopes will depend, in part, on whether our short period is a year or a quarter: Investment demand is more interest elastic—and the *IS* curve flatter—over a year than over three months.

[5] "Private Savings, Ultra-rationality, Aggregation, and 'Denison's Law,'" *Journal of Political Economy*, March/April 1974, 225–50.

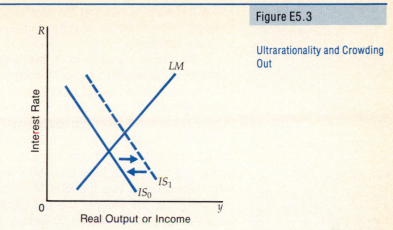

private interest. As a result, when government spending for capital goods (say, dams or office buildings) increases, shifting the aggregate expenditures curve upward, investment spending falls so that there is no net impact on aggregate expenditures. We may think of the *IS* curve as implicitly shifting out from $IS_0$ to the dashed line $IS_1$ in Figure E5.3, and then shifting back in so that there is no net change. Once again we have complete crowding out.

Similarly, we may think of increases in government expenditures for consumption goods (social workers or school lunches) financed by borrowing as substituting for private consumption. The idea here is that these government expenditures are valued in terms of their consumption benefits and so displace an equivalent amount of consumption expenditures. Once again we would have no net shift in the aggregate expenditures function or the *IS* curve.

While the assumption of ultrarationality may at first appear to be rather farfetched, David and Scadding point out that it may be used as an explanation of what has come to be called *Denison's Law*. In 1958 Edward Denison published a paper showing how the ratio of gross private saving to GNP had been remarkably constant in the U.S.[6] If ultrarationality is true, then there should be no change in macroeconomic values, such as the ratio of gross private saving to GNP, as a result of government activity. The activity of the public sector simply substitutes for the private sector. Even though Denison's Law, the constancy of the ratio of gross private saving to GNP, may be consistent with ultraration-

[6] Edward F. Denison, "A Note on Private Saving," *Review of Economics and Statistics*, August 1958, 261–67.

ality, it is safe to say that the economics profession has not been convinced that ultrarationality describes real world behavior to any significant degree.

The cases considered in this brief essay are best considered as extremes. Rather than perfectly horizontal or perfectly vertical *IS* or *LM* curves we should expect to see fairly flat or relatively steep curves. In other words, the three cases considered here all resulted in complete crowding out. If short-run crowding out is a significant phenomena (which, we must realize, has not been proven), we should not expect it to be complete. The steeper the *LM* or the flatter the *IS*, the greater the crowding out possibilities; so even if we have less than complete crowding out we could use the *IS–LM* model for illustration—in any period, for instance, the steeper the *LM* curve, the less expansionary will be any increase in *IS* caused by greater government spending. Crowding out most likely occurs in varying degrees: sometimes there is little crowding out of private spending by public spending and at other times the problem may be more severe. While it would be nice to identify various historical episodes as concrete evidence of significant short-run crowding out, practical limitations on economic researchers will not allow such conclusions.

<br>

# CHAPTER SIX

# LONG-RUN EQUILIBRIUM

The basic variables explained by macroeconomic theory are real income and prices. Chapter 6 discusses the main forces that determine their levels. Later, in Chapters 9 and 10, we will see how gradual changes in the determinants can cause growth in income and increases in price levels. The new feature of this chapter is an analysis of an economy in long-run equilibrium. **Long-run equilibrium** refers to the position of the economy when the temporary effects of unexpected changes in macroeconomic conditions have been eliminated. This is an ultimate ''resting point'' of the economy after we pass beyond the short-run period covered by the *IS–LM* analysis of Chapters 4 and 5. We may consider Chapter 6 a continuation of Chapters 4 and 5 that will answer the equation: Where does the economy wind up in the long run?

The underlying forces determining equilibrium can be usefully split into two separate groups: the real and the monetary. Real income or output—the total final goods and services produced—is determined by (1) existing resources of labor and capital, (2) technology and institutions which govern the possible ways in which these resources can be combined to produce final output, and (3) tastes, which influence both the composition of goods actually produced and the amount of labor services made available. Monetary factors are negligible in the long-run determination of real income, but are essential to the determination of the price level.

**long-run equilibrium**
The ''base line'' operation of the economy when short-term fluctuations are removed

119

## 6.1 THE LABOR MARKET

### DEMAND

**aggregate production function**
A function relating labor and capital to total output

To begin our analysis, we must introduce the concept of the **aggregate production function**. An aggregate production function relates quantities of inputs like labor $\ell$ and capital $k$ to the quantity of output $y$ produced. We can express our aggregate production function as:

$$y = f(k, \overset{+}{\ell})^{+}$$

$$(6.1)$$

The exact output produced by $k$ and $\ell$ will depend upon existing technology. Given any particular technology, output will vary with the $k$ and $\ell$ used. Therefore, to understand the determination of real income, we must examine the demands for and supplies of the factors of production. Let us begin with the demand for labor.

**demand for labor**
Total amount of labor desired in the economy

**Law of Diminishing Returns**
Holding fixed some inputs; as one adds further variable inputs, the extra output per unit declines

For any given production function and stock of capital, we can derive a **demand for labor**. First we consider how much output could be produced by using various amounts of labor combined with our fixed stock of capital. Figure 6.1 illustrates the typical result. If the capital stock is fixed at some value $k_0$, as we add labor in increasing quantities, output increases but at a decreasing rate. This is the **Law of Diminishing Returns**. Holding fixed some inputs, as we add increasing amounts of the variable inputs, (such as labor), the extra output per unit of variable input falls. This "extra output per unit of variable input" may be measured as the slope of the production function. The decreasing slope of the function in Figure 6.1 illustrates the diminishing returns.

### Figure 6.1

Aggregate Production for a Given Capital Stock ($k_0$) and Variable Labor Input

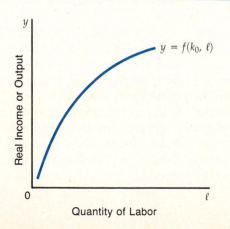

$y = f(k_0, \ell)$

Real Income or Output

Quantity of Labor

The increase in total output when one more unit of labor is added is called the **marginal product of labor**. Employers will wish to employ more labor whenever the value of the marginal product of labor exceeds labor's cost—the wage rate. Conversely, when the wage rate exceeds labor's marginal product value, employers will want to employ fewer workers. As firms increase the employment of labor, beyond some point, the value of marginal product will fall in accordance with the Law of Diminishing Returns. Hiring would continue until the value of marginal product just equals the wage. Thus the quantity of labor demanded at each real wage is that for which the value of labor's marginal product equals the real wage. Such a labor demand curve is illustrated in Figure 6.2.

Figure 6.2 relates wages and the quantity of labor demanded by plotting the slope of $y = f(k_0, \ell)$ from Figure 6.1 against the corresponding amounts of labor. In functional notation, we can write the labor demand function as:

$$\ell^d = \overset{- \; +}{\ell^d(w, k)} \tag{6.2}$$

As seen in Figure 6.2, the demand for labor is a decreasing function of the real wage $w$ since the greater the real wage, the smaller the labor input that can be profitably employed. With a given real wage, the demand for labor will generally increase with the amount of capital employed, as the greater stock of capital increases the productivity of labor. Remember that the Law of Diminishing Returns was applicable with a fixed quantity of one input. By increasing the capital stock, the production function of Figure 6.1 would shift up so that the output increases for each quantity of labor, the labor demand

> marginal product of labor
> Increase in total output due to the addition of one more unit of labor

> Labor demand depends on the capital stock and the wage rate.

---

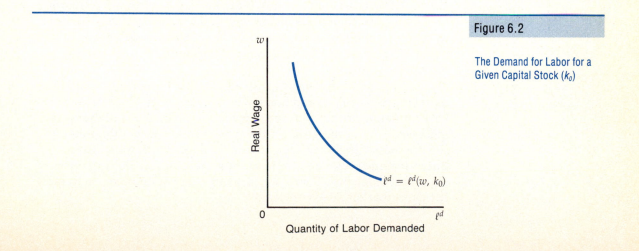

**Figure 6.2**

The Demand for Labor for a Given Capital Stock ($k_0$)

curve would shift to the right so that a greater quantity of labor is demanded at each wage rate.

## SUPPLY

**supply of labor**
Total amount of possible labor times the labor participation rate

Labor supply depends on the size of the age-eligible population and the labor participation rate.

The **supply of labor** depends upon the amount of labor available in the age-eligible population and the average rate of participation in the labor force. Since, at any time, the quality and size of the age-eligible population is fixed, the supply of labor largely reflects changes in the fraction of the population actually in the labor force. In practice, such labor-force participation varies because of holidays and seasonal work patterns. Since macroeconomists are concerned with fluctuations in employment due to business cycles and long-term growth, the recurring seasonal changes in employment are removed from the data by a process called *seasonal adjustment*. This allows us to concentrate on the basic employment trends aside from expected seasonal changes.

The key determinants of the labor participation rate, and therefore of the short-run labor supply, are the real wage rate $w$, the average quality of labor $q$, and the per capita income from capital $\rho k/n$:

$$\pi = \overset{\pm\ \pm\ \ -}{\pi\ (w, q,\ \rho k/n)} \tag{6.3}$$

**real rental rate on capital**
The return on capital owned by firms

where $n$ is the age-eligible population and $\rho$ is the **real rental rate on capital**. The real rental rate on capital is analogous to the real wage rate of labor. Firms normally own the capital equipment they use; $\rho$ is the return on capital that the firms receive. These returns are channeled into interest and dividends paid to the households holding the financial securities issued by the firms. In terms of the labor participation rate function (6.3), if the per capita income from capital $\rho k/n$ increases, then households will find leisure relatively more attractive and the labor force participation rate will fall, other things equal. The other things include the real wage $w$ and the average quality of labor $q$.

As was just pointed out, the alternative to work is leisure (remember that students and housewives, or those involved in nonmarket production are not counted in the labor force). Since higher wages increase income, the effect of the wage rate on $\pi$ is ambiguous. On the one hand, higher wages obviously make work more attractive. But as income increases, consumption increases, including the consumption of leisure. Therefore, the net effect of an increase in $w$ on the participation rate is unclear.

A similar ambiguous effect is found for the effect of the average quality of labor $q$ on the participation rate. Since an increase in the quality of labor means higher productivity, we expect incomes to rise with $q$. But as we just discussed with respect to $w$, higher labor incomes increase the attractiveness of both work and leisure so that the net effect is ambiguous.

The actual labor supply is equal to the participation rate times the average quality times population size, or:

$$\ell^s = \pi(\overset{\pm}{w},\overset{\pm}{q}, \overset{-}{\rho k/n}) \cdot \overset{++}{q \cdot n} \qquad (6.4)$$

Since the theoretical effect of $w$ on $\ell^s$ is ambiguous, it would be helpful if we could appeal to empirical research that indicates the actual response of the labor supply to changing wages. However, researchers have found conflicting results. Studies of male labor supply behavior tend to indicate a **backward-bending supply curve of labor** as in Figure 6.3a, where increases in the real wage ultimately lead to a reduction in the quantity of labor supplied. George Borjas and James Heckman reviewed the research in this area and suggested that, on average, if a man's wage increases by 10 percent, there would be a 1–2 percent reduction in the quantity of his labor supplied.[1] The re-

**backward bending supply curve of labor**
A curve where beyond some point increasing wages leads to fewer workers in the labor force

---

[1]George Borjas and James Heckman, "Labor Supply Estimates for Public Policy Evaluation," *Proceedings of the Industrial Relations Research Association*, 1978, 320–31.

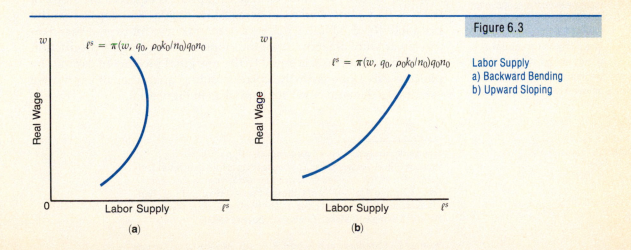

**Figure 6.3**

Labor Supply
a) Backward Bending
b) Upward Sloping

search on female labor supply is less definitive, but suggestive of a positively sloped supply curve of labor as depicted in Figure 6.3b.[2] What is the net effect of a change in the real wage on labor supply? To be correct, the state of the evidence will not allow any strong conclusions. As pointed out by Ronald Ehrenberg and Robert Smith of Cornell University, there are many potential problems associated with the interpretation of the data, so that it may not be correct to assume that the results found for men will dominate those found for women (or vice versa) and carry over to the overall labor supply.[3]

While we must be careful in assigning a specific effect of the real wage on labor supply, it seems quite probable that an increase in the quality of labor will increase labor supply as will an increase in population. With labor participation rates unchanged, an increase in labor quality will mean an increase in labor supply as the *effective* labor units increase with higher quality workers. An increase in labor supply would cause the labor supply curves of Figure 6.3 to shift to the right. If the real rental rate on capital or the stock of capital increased so that household nonlabor income increased, labor supply would decrease so that the curves of Figure 6.3 shift to the left.

## 6.2 THE CAPITAL MARKET

### DEMAND

marginal product of capital
Increase in total output due to the addition of one more unit of capital

The demand for capital depends on the quantity of labor and the real rental rate on capital.

The arguments used to derive the demand for labor can be repeated for the demand for capital. We start with Figure 6.4, which shows the output associated with different stocks of capital for a given amount of labor $\ell_0$. The **marginal product of capital**, the increase in output resulting form a one unit increase in capital, is equal to the slope of the $y = f(k, \ell_0)$ line. Since the demand for capital will depend on the productivity of capital, we draw a demand curve for capital based on a given amount of labor. Since the slope of the aggregate production function in Figure 6.4 is equal to the marginal product of capital, by plotting this slope with the corresponding quantities of capital we can draw a demand curve for capital as in Figure 6.5.

---

[2]See Jacob Mincer, ''Labor Force Participation of Married Women,'' in *Aspects of Labor Economics* (Princeton: Princeton University Press, 1962), Glen G. Cain, *Married Women in the Labor Force* (Chicago: University of Chicago Press, 1966); and Lois Banfill Shaw (ed.), *Unplanned Careers: The Working Lives of Middle-Aged Women* (Lexington, Mass.: Lexington Books, 1983).

[3]Ronald G. Ehrenberg and Robert S. Smith, *Modern Labor Economics* (Glenview, Ill: Scott, Foresman and Co., 1982), pp. 164–66.

Figure 6.4

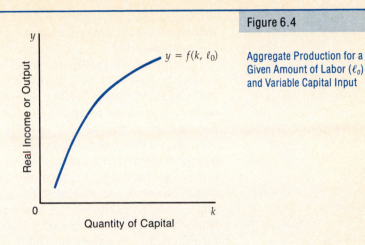

Aggregate Production for a
Given Amount of Labor ($\ell_0$)
and Variable Capital Input

In general, the demand for capital is a decreasing function of the real rental rate $\rho$ and an increasing function of the amount of labor used:

$$k^d = k^d(\overset{-}{\rho}, \overset{+}{\ell}) \qquad (6.5)$$

Since firms would be willing to hire capital goods up to the point where the real rental rate $\rho$ equals the marginal product of capital, we can see why the demand for capital is a decreasing function of $\rho$. As $\rho$ increases, the marginal product of capital must increase correspondingly. But with technology and the quantity of labor constant in the short run, this means that less capital will be employed. As employment of capital falls, the marginal product of the capital stock

Figure 6.5

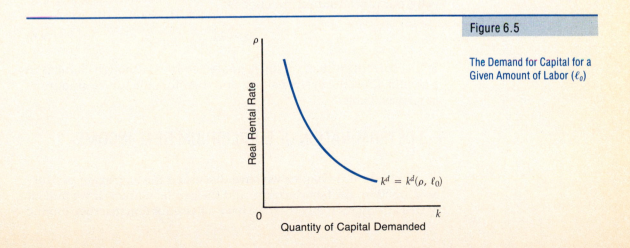

The Demand for Capital for a
Given Amount of Labor ($\ell_0$)

still being used will increase so that the marginal product equals ρ. Thus we have the inverse relationship between ρ and the amount of capital demanded.

The real rental rate ρ of capital is analogous to the real wage rate *w* of labor. Just as firms will hire labor up to the point where *w* equals the marginal product of labor, so will they hire capital up to the point where ρ equals the marginal product of capital. However, firms cannot own labor, but they do typically own the capital which they use. Therefore ρ is not something physically paid by the firm as is *w*, but instead indicates the returns to capital received by the firm. These returns are then used to pay interest and dividends to the households which finance the capital stock by holding securities issued by firms. Sometimes economists refer to the real rental rate as the *shadow price of capital*—a price not actually observed, yet firms behave as if they actually paid ρ to use their capital.

## SUPPLY

Capital is measured as those capital goods actually used in production, and its amount can be changed over time only by investment and depreciation. In a sense, the same argument could be made about labor supply by considering education as investment, except that with labor there is the substitutability between leisure and work that can change the supply of labor in the short run. For capital, there is a desired amount at any point in time, and the difference between the actual and desired level of capital will determine the rate of investment. While we will consider changes in the capital stock along with changes in population in our analysis of economic growth, for purposes of analyzing the level of income, as in this chapter, we assume that the supply of capital is represented by a vertical line at some existing capital stock $k_0$, as illustrated in Figure 6.6. Algebraically, our capital supply function is:

$$k^s = k_0 \tag{6.6}$$

So the current stock of capital is unafected by ρ, although changes in ρ should affect the desired stock, and therefore the future amount of capital available.

## 6.3 DETERMINATION OF EQUILIBRIUM REAL INCOME

So far in this chapter we have discussed the aggregate production function, the labor market, and the capital market. If we pull all of this information together, we have a five equation macroeconomic

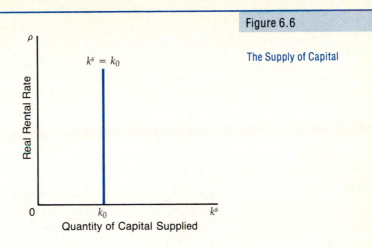

Figure 6.6

The Supply of Capital

model which can be used to solve for the values of five unknowns: $y$, $k$, $\ell$, $\rho$, and $w$. The five equations we will gather together are:

$$y = f(k,\ell) \tag{6.1}$$
$$\ell^d = {}^d(w,k) \tag{6.2}$$
$$\ell^s = \pi(w,q,\rho k/n) \cdot qn \tag{6.4}$$
$$k^d = k^d\,(\rho,\ell) \tag{6.5}$$
$$k^s = k_0 \tag{6.6}$$

For equilibrium, the quantities of capital and labor demanded must equal the amounts supplied, or $\ell^d = \ell^s = \ell$ and $k^d = k^s = k$. Furthermore, the quality of labor $q$ is fixed at $q_0$ and the size of the age-eligible population is fixed at $n_0$. We will illustrate the solution to this model graphically in the following sections.

## LABOR MARKET EQUILIBRIUM

Let us begin with an illustration of labor market equilibrium. Our labor demand and labor supply equations are graphed in Figure 6.7, with the real wage $w$ and the quantity of labor $\ell$ on the two axes. The labor demand curve is identical to Figure 6.2. For a given capital stock $k_0$, labor demand simply relates the real wage to the quantity of labor. Labor supply, however, is a bit more complex, as the quantity of labor supplied is given by the real wage and the real rental rate on capital $\rho$, as well as by $q_0$ and $n_0$. To draw a labor supply curve in $w\ell$ space we must plot our function for a given $\rho$, say $\rho_1$. In Figure 6.7 we see that if $\rho$ equals $\rho_1$, then the labor market is in equilibrium at the real wage $w_1$ and quantity of labor $\ell_1$. If $\rho$ were some higher value $\rho_2$, then the labor supply function would lie to the left of the one for $\rho_1$, since

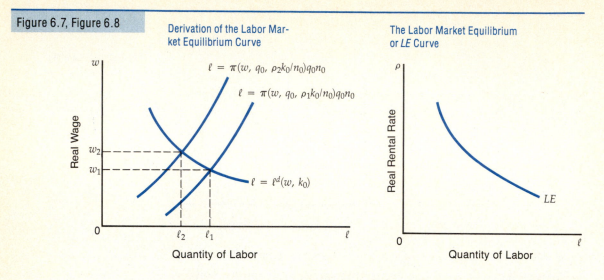

Derivation of the Labor Market Equilibrium Curve

The Labor Market Equilibrium or *LE* Curve

$\ell = \pi(w, q_0, \rho_2 k_0/n_0)q_0 n_0$

$\ell = \pi(w, q_0, \rho_1 k_0/n_0)q_0 n_0$

$\ell = \ell^d(w, k_0)$

workers can afford more leisure when nonwage income increases (such as income from securities held). With $\rho_2$, we see that the labor market equilibrium occurs at $w_2$ and $\ell_2$. By varying $\rho$, we find the alternative values of $w$ and $\ell$ which are consistent with equilibrium. A labor market equilibrium (*LE*) curve may be drawn as in Figure 6.8 to see the combinations of $\rho$ and $\ell$ for which the labor market is in equilibrium. As was seen in Figure 6.7, higher values of $\rho$ are associated with smaller values of $\ell$, so that the *LE* curve has the negative slope seen in Figure 6.8.

**The LE curve gives the combinations of the real rental rate and the quantity of labor for which the labor market is in equilibrium.**

## CAPITAL MARKET EQUILIBRIUM

Just as we looked at labor demand and supply to derive our labor market equilibrium (*LE*) curve, we will also look at the demand and supply of capital to find a capital market equilibrium (*KE*) curve. Figure 6.9 contains the demand and supply curves for capital. As was seen in Figure 6.6, the supply curve is a vertical line, indicating that the quantity of capital remains at the current amount $k_0$ regardless of $\rho$. The capital demand function is drawn as in Figure 6.5 for a given quantity of labor. If the quantity of labor is $\ell_1$, then the equilibrium rental rate is $\rho_1$. For a higher quantity $\ell_2$, the rental rate increases to $\rho_2$ as the demand for capital increases (shifts to the right) with increases in the quantity of labor. By choosing different values of $\ell$, we find the alternative values for $\rho$ and $k$ that give capital market equilibrium. The capital market equilibrium (*KE*) curve depicted in Figure 6.10 plots the combinations of $\rho$ and $\ell$ for which the capital market is in equilibrium. The *KE* curve has a positive slope since higher $\ell$ is associated with higher $\rho$, as was seen in Figure 6.9.

**The KE curve gives the combinations of the real rental rate and quantity of labor for which the capital market is in equilibrium.**

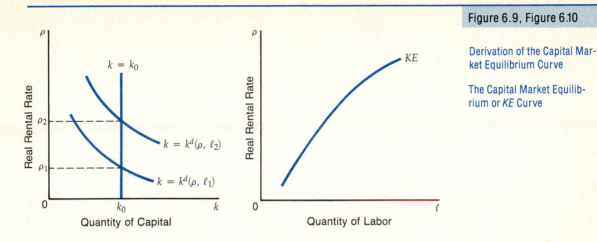

Figure 6.9, Figure 6.10

Derivation of the Capital Market Equilibrium Curve

The Capital Market Equilibrium or *KE* Curve

## EQUILIBRIUM IN THE LABOR AND CAPITAL MARKETS JOINTLY

The *LE* curve shows all combinations of $\rho$ and $\ell$ for which the labor market is in equilibrium. The *KE* curve shows all possible values for which the capital market is in equilibrium. By plotting the *LE* and *KE* curves on one graph, as shown in Figure 6.11, the intersection of the two curves gives the only combination of $\rho$ and $\ell$ for which both the labor and capital markets are in equilibrium at the same time. The important point is that the equilibrium values $\rho_e$ and $\ell_e$ are not determined in the capital market or in the labor market separately, but by the joint actions of the two markets.

We already know that the equilibrium value of capital will be the existing stock $k_0$. So of our five original unknown variables—$y, w, k, \ell$, and $\rho$—we now know $k$, $\ell$, and $\rho$ and have only to solve for $y$ and $w$.

The intersection of the LE and KE curves determine the equilibrium values of the real rental rate and quantity of labor.

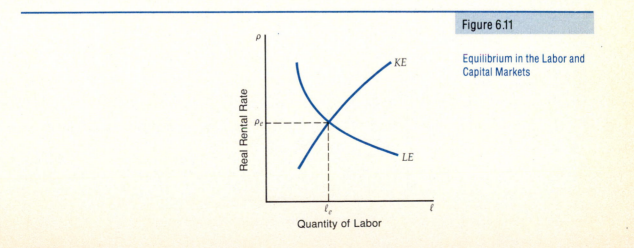

Figure 6.11

Equilibrium in the Labor and Capital Markets

The real wage $w$ is found in the labor demand function. Figure 6.12 illustrates the labor demand function consistent with the given capital stock $k_0$. Since we know the equilibrium quantity of labor $\ell_e$ from Figure 6.11, there is but one real wage $w_e$ that corresponds to $\ell_e$.

## EQUILIBRIUM REAL OUTPUT

The equilibrium k and l are related to the equilibrium level of y through the production function.

There remains but one unknown variable, equilibrium real income or output $y_e$. For the given state of technology reflected in the current production function, and the given quantity of capital $k_0$, there is but one equilibrium output level consistent with the quantity of labor $\ell_e$. Figure 6.13 illustrates the production function given $k_0$. for $\ell_e$, the production function locates $y_e$ as the amount of goods and services produced by $\ell_e$ and $k_0$.

## RELATIONSHIP TO *IS–LM* MODEL

Now we have illustrated graphical solutions to the five-equation macroeconomic model presented at the beginning of this section. How does this equilibrium level of output $y_e$ relate to the *IS–LM* equilibrium of Chapter 5? Remember that we used the *IS–LM* approach to determine the short-run impact of some macroeconomic change. If the world was unchanging, then the long-run equilibrium $y_e$ of this chapter would be identical to the $y_e$ found by the intersection of the static *IS* and *LM* curves. Once there is a shift in either the *IS* or *LM* curve, then the short-run $y_e$ of *IS–LM* derivation will not be identical to the new long-run $y_e$ that is determined by the five-equation model of this chapter. The dynamic analysis of later chapters will detail how we go from the short run to the long run.

**Figure 6.12**

Determination of the Equilibrium Real Wage $w_e$ Given the Equilibrium Quantity of Labor $\ell_e$

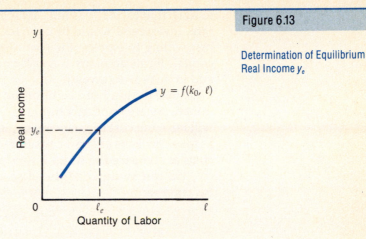

Figure 6.13

Determination of Equilibrium Real Income $y_e$

## 6.4 THE EQUILIBRIUM INTEREST RATE

While we have now solved for the values of the endogenous variables in our five-equation model, there are still two important variables which did not appear in the model: the equilibrium interest rate $R_e$ and price level $P_e$. While section 6.5 will address the determinants of $P_e$, here our concern is with $R_e$. Since the interest rate works to equate saving and investment, we can solve for $R_e$ using the saving and investment functions.

The investment function was discussed earlier, in section 4.3 of Chapter 4. Remember that investment refers to the demand for additional capital goods. Earlier in this chapter we examined the demand for capital. At that time we argued that the desired stock of capital was a function of the quantity of labor employed $\ell$ and the real rental rate of capital $\rho$. The real rental rate on capital adjusts so that firms are willing to employ just the existing stock of capital. In this sense, the desired and actual stocks of capital to employ are always the same. Suppose, however, that the real rental rate $\rho$ (which measures the return to capital owned by firms) was high relative to the cost of financing additional capital, which is measured by the nominal interest rate $R$.[4] Then firms would want to add to the existing stock of capital at more rapid rates than before. If $\rho$ were low relative

---

[4]As discussed in Chapter 4, the cost of financing capital is actually the real interest rate $r$, which differs from the nominal rate by expected inflation ($r = R - \hat{P}$). With given $\hat{P}$, $R$ changes with changes in $r$, so that nothing is lost at this point by using the nominal rate $R$ as the cost of financing capital.

to $R$, so that capital was not earning enough to pay the going interest rate, investment would be cut back. Thus $\rho$ adjusts so that firms are just willing to employ the *flow of services* from the existing stock of capital. Firms compare $\rho$ and $R$ to decide how rapidly they want to add to this stock (invest).

Since the long-run equilibrium value of $\rho$ has already been determined, we are implicitly thinking of movements in $R$. Increases in $R$ will raise the cost of financing capital and lead to a fall in investment as fewer projects are now considered profitable with higher financing costs as compared to when $R$ was lower.

We can summarize this discussion by writing our investment function as:

$$i = i \overset{- \ +}{(R, \rho)} \cdot \qquad (6.7)$$

Investment is a decreasing function of the interest rate $R$, and an increasing function of the real rental rate $\rho$. We graph the investment function in $Ri$ space in Figure 6.14, using the value $\rho_e$ as previously determined in Figure 6.11.

This investment demand function differs from the earlier Keynesian one, $i = i(R,y)$. When real income rises, demand for investment rises because firms will find the rental rate on capital increasing with the growth in employment and productivity that generally accompanies rising real income. So in Chapter 4 we used real income $y$ as an observable proxy variable for the real rental rate, taking note of the fact that the real rental rate grows with real output. As a result, the Keynesian investment function does not explicitly include $\rho$, since this effect is captured by $y$.

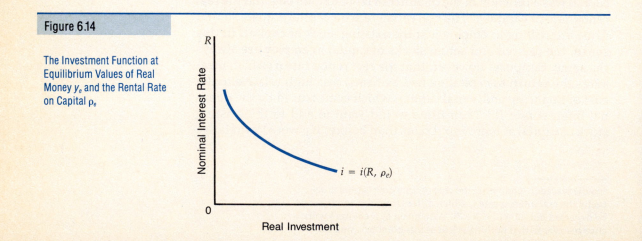

**Figure 6.14**

The Investment Function at Equilibrium Values of Real Money $y_e$ and the Rental Rate on Capital $\rho_e$

$R$

Nominal Interest Rate

$i = i(R, \rho_e)$

0

Real Investment

We have not yet seen a saving function, but saving refers to not consuming. That part of income which is not consumed is saved. Where does this saving go? It becomes investment spending, so we have a crucial relation for macroeconomic equilibrium that *planned saving equals planned investment*. Of course, there is no necessary reason why the saving desired by households must be equal to the investment spending planned by business firms. Yet after the fact, regardless of plans, net purchases of securities by individuals (saving) must exactly equal the net issuance of securities by firms to finance investment.[5]

We already know what determines investment, but what about saving? Individuals want to save because a positive interest rate allows them to exchange a dollar's worth of real goods and services now for a greater amount of real goods and services in the future. So the rate of interest $R$ has a positive effect on saving.[6] However, by saving, you must give up some current consumption. We learned in Chapter 4, that consumption rises with income by the marginal propensity to consume (*MPC*) times the change in income.[7] That increase in income not consumed is saved. So (1 - *MPC*) determines the *marginal propensity to save* (*MPS*)—the change in saving given a change in income. If the *MPC* equals ¾, then the *MPS* equals ¼, so that saving increases by 25 percent of any increase in income. Table

[5]We are simplifying the analysis by consolidating government activity with private consumption and investment. For instance, saving could realistically be used to finance government borrowing as well as business borrowing. We similarly take net exports to be zero since saving can also finance investment abroad.

[6]There are models of consumer behavior in which an increase in $R$ can decrease saving by reducing the present amount that must be saved to provide a given amount of income in retirement. Although most economists expect the positive effect indicated in the text, convincing empirical evidence for that position does not yet exist. None of the analysis would be affected if the effect on saving of an increase in $R$ were mildly negative or zero as assumed in the strict Keynesian consumption function (4.4).

[7]The *MPC* of Chapter 4 may be considered a short–run *MPC* consistent with the short-run Keynesian analysis of that chapter. In the long run, the *MPC* will be higher than in the short run as consumption spending adjusts in line with permanent income. Current income may deviate from permanent income in the short run, but households will not alter spending in response to current income fluctuations to the extent they will adjust to permanent income changes.

Table 6.1

U.S. Saving Behavior (billions of dollars)

|  | (1)<br>Gross Private Income | (2)<br>Gross Private Saving | (3)<br>Gross Private Saving<br>Gross Private Income |
|---|---|---|---|
| 1940 | 84.5 | 14.2 | .168 |
| 1945 | 165.4 | 44.7 | .270 |
| 1950 | 224.6 | 42.7 | .190 |
| 1955 | 310.4 | 64.4 | .207 |
| 1960 | 388.0 | 78.0 | .201 |
| 1965 | 532.7 | 119.7 | .225 |
| 1970 | 748.4 | 158.6 | .212 |
| 1975 | 1,189.6 | 282.7 | .238 |
| 1980 | 1.999.1 | 435.4 | .218 |
| 1984 | 2,833.5 | 675.3 | .228 |

Source: *Economic Report of the President*, 1985.

Note: Gross private income and gross private saving both include the capital consumption allowance. The ratio of (net) private saving to (net) private income is typically about .12 lower than the gross ratio.

6.1 indicates that private saving has been a fairly constant fraction of private income. Aside from dramatic increases in saving needed to finance wartime spending, the relation between saving and income has been quite stable through time, with private saving averaging a little more than 20 percent of private income in Table 6.1.

*Saving depends on the level of income and the interest rate.*

To summarize, saving is a function of real income and the interest rate, or:

$$s = s(\overset{+}{y},\overset{-}{R}) \tag{6.8}$$

Figure 6.15 illustrates a hypothetical saving function in $Rs$ space. Based on the equilibrium level of income $y_e$, we see the upward sloping saving function indicates that saving is an increasing function of $R$.

*The equilibrium interest rate is determined by the intersection of the saving and investment functions.*

If we put our saving and investment functions together, as in Figure 6.16, we find the equilibrium interest rate $R_e$ at the intersection point of the $s$ and $i$ curves. Only at this level of interest will the amount of saving desired by households be equal to the investment spending desired by business firms.

Now we have found the equilibrium values for all but one key variable, the price level. To investigate the determinants of $P_e$, we will turn to the money market and see how money supply and money demand work to establish an equilibrium price level.

The Saving Function at the
Equilibrium Level of Income
$(y_e)$

Equilibrium Interest Rate as
Determined by Saving and
Investment

## 6.5 DETERMINATION OF EQUILIBRIUM PRICES

### MONEY SUPPLY AND DEMAND

In Chapter 4 we introduced the concepts of money supply and money
demand in the context of the fixed-price Keynesian model. Now we
want to analyze the role that the money market plays in determining
the equilibrium price level. Again we assume that the nominal supply of money is fixed at some value $M_0$ by central bank policy. Graphically, this given amount $M_0$ appears as a vertical line in Figure 6.17.
As with any nominal variable, the real quantity of money is found by
dividing by the price level, $P$, or:

$$m^s = \frac{M_0}{P} \tag{6.9}$$

With given $M_0$, variations in $P$ will result in real money $m$ having the
shape illustrated in Figure 6.18. This sort of curved line is known as
a rectangular hyperbola. At any point on a rectangular hyperbola,
the product of the two variables being measured will be the same.
Since the nominal money supply is fixed at $M_0$, and equation (6.9)
can be rewritten as $M_0 = Pm^s$, Figure 6.18 indicates that for any
combination of $P$ and $m^s$ lying along the curve, the product of $Pm^s$ is
a constant amount equal to $M_0$.

**Figure 6.17**

The Nominal Supply of Money as Given by Central Bank Policy

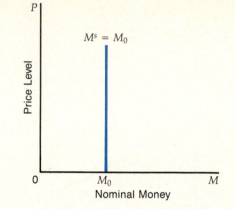

Now that we have reviewed money supply, we must consider the role of money demand in determining the price level. In Chapter 4, the real money demand function was written as:

$$m^d = m^d(\overset{+}{y}, \overset{-}{R - R_M})$$

(6.10)

Real money demand is a positive function of income, as the greater volume of transactions associated with higher income requires higher money balances. Money demand is a negative function of the opportunity cost variable $R - R_M$, where $R$ is the interest rate on bonds (instead of holding money you would hold bonds) and $R_M$ is the interest rate on money balances. Note that the real demand for money $m^d$ is not determined by the price level $P$ in equation (6.10).

**Figure 6.18**

The Real Supply of Money When the Nominal Value Is Fixed at $M_0$

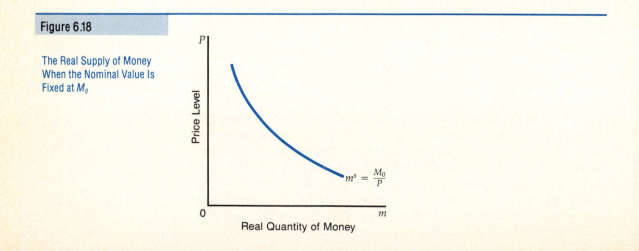

Graphically, in $Pm$ space, the real quantity of money demanded is drawn as a vertical line, indicating that real money demand is independent of the price level. In Figure 6.19 we see that the equilibrium real quantity of money is $m_e^d$ regardless of the price level. The level $m_e^d$ is determined by the equilibrium level of real income $y_e$ and the interest rate $R_e$. We have already determined $y_e$ and $R_e$ from our macroeconomic model considered earlier in this chapter, but what about $R_M$? It is reasonable to expect that the interest paid on money balances $R_M$ would change with $R$, the interest paid on bonds. However, since banks must hold non-interest-bearing reserves and incur other costs in providing deposit services, we should expect $R_M$ to be lower than $R$. While it is not always necessary that $R_M$ changes proportionally to $R$, it will simplify matters if we assume $R_M = aR$, where $a$ is some fraction less than 1. For instance, if $a$ equals ⅘, then if bonds are yielding a 10-percent rate of interest, bank deposits yield 8 percent. In this case $(R - R_M) = (R - aR) = (0.1 - 0.08) = 0.02$. If bonds yield 20 percent, then $R_M$ equals 16 percent so that $(R - R_M)$ also increases and the opportunity cost of holding money rises with $R$. Since any given $R$ implies a value of $R_M$ equal to $aR$, we can graph our money demand function as a function of $R$. As $R$ increases, $(R - R_M)$ increases, leading to a fall in the quantity of money demanded. Figure 6.19 shows that the real quantity of money demanded is determined by $y_e$ and $R_e$ apart from $P$.

Rather than write the demand for money in the general form of equation (6.10), it is useful to consider an alternative based on the Cambridge identity:

$$M \equiv KyP \qquad (6.11)$$

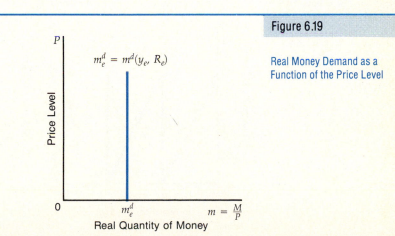

**Figure 6.19**

Real Money Demand as a Function of the Price Level

**Cambridge K**
The numerical value that relates nominal money stock to nominal income

This identity states that the nominal stock of money is some fraction K of nominal income yP. The fraction K is known as the **Cambridge K**. The "Cambridge" identifier comes from the use of this approach by the nineteenth century English economist Alfred Marshall and his followers at Cambridge University. (Tradition requires us to use K to denote this fraction; but K is, of course, nominal capital—be careful to avoid confusion, particularly since the Cambridge K can be interpreted as a real variable.) The identity (6.11) is converted to a theory by explaining the behavior of K.

What determines the size of the money stock relative to income? The Cambridge approach emphasized the role of the transactions demand for money. People hold money to link expenditures and receipts. In this regard, the amount of money demanded will depend upon the magnitude of the receipts and expenditures along with the payment practices followed. Nominal income or yP is our best, although crude, measure of the magnitude of receipts and expenditures in the economy. Other things being equal, the higher nominal income, the greater the demand for money balances. However, other things are not always equal. Figure 6.20 illustrates how the demand for money changes with changes in payments practices. If firms pay employees once a month, as in Figure 6.20 (a), monthly household receipts are $2\overline{M}$, which we assume will be spent evenly through the month. With one payday per month, after 2 weeks, money balances are down to $\overline{M}$, and then continue falling to zero at month's end, after which the next month's pay is received and money balances are once again at $2\overline{M}$. With one payday per month, the average money balances are $\overline{M}$.

Figure 6.20

Changes in Payment Practices and Changes in Average Money Balances for Transactions

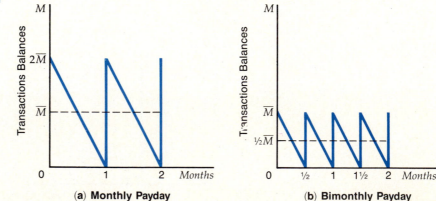

(a) **Monthly Payday**

(b) **Bimonthly Payday**

Suppose now firms pay employees every two weeks as illustrated in Figure 6.20(b). Households receive $\overline{M}$ in receipts on payday, which we assume they spend evenly over time, so that after one week their balances equal $\frac{1}{2}\overline{M}$ and then continue toward zero at the end of the two week period when the next payday occurs and money balances are again $\overline{M}$. Note the implications of the difference in payment practices for average money balances. In Figure 6.20(a), average money balances equal $\overline{M}$, while in Figure 6.20(b), average money balances equal $\frac{1}{2}\overline{M}$. The more frequently payments are made, the lower the average transactions balances for a given level of income.

While we assumed that expenditures occurred evenly over time in Figure 6.20, this certainly is not necessary. Changes in expenditure patterns will also affect average transactions balances. Consider Figure 6.21. If expenditures occur evenly over time, then the solid line reflects the path of actual money balances, so that average money holdings equal $\overline{M}$. If instead, individuals spend more heavily right after payday than at other times, actual money balances follow the broken line in Figure 6.21 so that average money balances are $\overline{M}'$. The more closely expenditures follow receipts, the lower the average transactions balances.

Aside from the transactions motive for holding money just reviewed, there also exists an asset demand for money balances. On this basis, money is demanded due to the uncertain nominal value of other financial assets like stocks and bonds, as well as a reserve for emergencies. Since any dollar can simultaneously serve both the transaction and the asset demand function, the actual distinction is blurred. Still it is useful to discuss both motives for holding money to

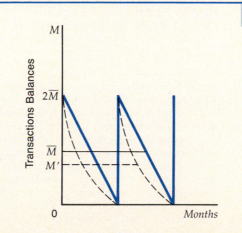

**Figure 6.21**

Changes in Expenditure Patterns and Changes in Average Money Balances for Transactions

organize coherently an argument for the desired magnitude of money balances. The asset demand for money is also related to income, although wealth or permanent income is a better concept when analyzing the scale of a financial portfolio. As nominal income increases, asset holdings generally increase along with the dollar value of potential emergencies for which money balances serve as insurance.

The gains from holding additional money balances must be weighed against the cost. The cost of holding money for a period of time is the lost interest earnings. The cost of holding money is our familiar $(R - R_M)$ variable. The demand for money is a decreasing function of the interest rate on money substitutes like bonds and an increasing function of the interest paid on money. There will be some optimal money–income ratio that balances the costs of additional money balances against the costs of more frequent payments and more careful planning to reduce money holdings. Deviations in $K$ from the desired value will lead individuals to adjust money receipts and expenditures to the desired levels consistent with the optimal $K$. To translate the Cambridge identity (6.11) into a theory, we express the Cambridge money demand as:

$$M^d = K^d(\overset{+}{y}, \overset{-}{R} - \overset{+}{R_M}) \cdot yP \tag{6.12}$$

This equation states that nominal money demand is a fraction $K^d$ of nominal income $yP$. The exact fraction is determined by the money demand determinants $y$ and $(R - R_M)$. Real income is included as a determinant of desired $K^d$ because people may want to allocate a larger or smaller fraction of their wealth to money holdings as they become wealthier in real terms. However, whether $K^d$ increases or decreases with higher $y$ is uncertain, both theoretically and empirically.[8] Of course, $K^d$ increases as $R_M$ increases and decreases as $R$

[8]It may be expected that as income increases, there would be some economies of scale associated with money held for transactions purposes. This means that each dollar would tend to do more work as income increases. On the other hand, as wages rise with income the opportunity cost of time increases (your time becomes more valuable as wages rise) so that individuals would tend to hold more money thereby spending less time coordinating receipts and expenditures. For a discussion of this ambiguity see Joel Fried, "Money, Exchange and Growth," *Western Economic Journal*, 11 (September 1973), 285–301; and the discussion in David E.W. Laidler, *The Demand for Money* (New York: Harper and Row, 1977), pp. 154–57.

increases. Since $R_M$ moves proportionally to $R$ in the long run as discussed above, we can write our Cambridge $K$ function as $K^d(y,R)$. Increases in $R$ will increase the opportunity cost variable $(R - R_M)$ and therefore lower money demand. The $K^d$ function in equation (6.12) implicitly incorporates the technology for making payments and expenditures in the economy. An example of a change in technology would be an increased use of credit cards as a substitute for carrying money balances—the increase in credit card usage would imply a reduction in money demand. While such technology may gradually change over time, it is assumed given for the instant of time considered here.

Our nominal demand-for-money equation (6.12) may be illustrated graphically in Figure 6.22. As the price level rises, the nominal quantity of money demanded rises proportionally, so that the money demand curve in Figure 6.22 has a slope of 1. This proportionality feature of nominal money demand arises from the fact that real money demand is independent of the price level as was illustrated in Figure 6.16. In terms of the Cambridge $K$ approach, we can divide both sides of equation (6.12) by $P$ to find our real money demand function:

$$m^d \equiv \frac{M^d}{P} = \overset{+\ -\ +}{K^d(y,R)}\, y \qquad (6.13)$$

Notice that $(R - R_M)$ has been simplified to $R$ consistent with our earlier discussion. While equilibrium real money demand $m_e^d$ is determined by $y_e$ and $R_e$, nominal money demand varies directly with the price level.

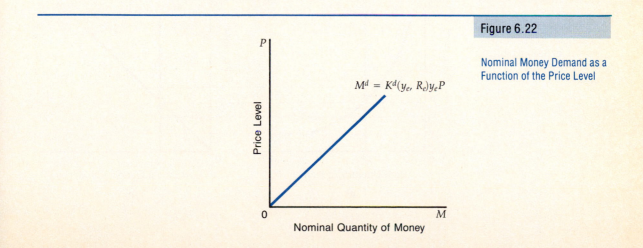

Figure 6.22

Nominal Money Demand as a Function of the Price Level

$P$

Price Level

$M^d = K^d(y_e,\ R_e)y_e P$

0      $M$

Nominal Quantity of Money

## EQUILIBRIUM PRICES AND NOMINAL OUTPUT

The equilibrium price level is determined by the *equilibrium condition* that money supply equal money demand:

$$M^s = M^d \text{ for equilibrium} \tag{6.14}$$

Alternatively, we can write this in real terms by dividing both sides of equation (6.14) by the price level $P$:

$$m^s = m^d \text{ for equilibrium} \tag{6.15}$$

*The equilibrium price level is set to equate the real money supply to real money demand.*

We can solve for the equilibrium values of money supply, money demand, and the price level graphically as in Figure 6.23. Figure 6.23(a) depicts the real money market equilibrium where the price level adjusts to equate the real value of the given nominal stock of money $M_0$ to the real quantity of money demanded. This equilibrium position occurs at price level $P_e$. In Figure 6.23(b), the price level adjusts to equate the nominal amount of money demanded to the fixed nominal amount supplied. Once again, $P_e$ is the equilibrium price level. Note that while the nominal supply of money is determined on the supply side by the monetary authorities, the real quantity of money is determined by money demanders. While the authorities can fix the nominal supply of money at any level they wish, the public will ultimately determine the real value of that money.

**Figure 6.23**

The Determination of the Equilibrium Price Level in Terms of (a) Real and (b) Nominal Monetary Equilibrium

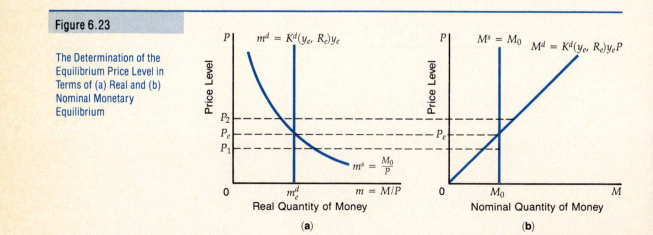

Why does the price level move to equate money supply and money demand? Suppose that price in Figure 6.23 is below the equilibrium level at $P_1$ so that the quantity of money supplied exceeds the amount demanded. This excess supply of money would be reflected in increased spending for goods and services as people act to reduce their money holdings. With a fixed quantity of goods and services available in the short run, the increased spending will generate higher prices and move the price level to equilibrium. Just the reverse occurs if the price level is higher than equilibrium like at $P_2$ in Figure 6.23. In this case there is an excess demand for money as the quantity of money demanded at this price exceeds the quantity supplied. People now cut back on their spending to build their money balances to desired levels. The decrease in spending causes prices to fall back toward equilibrium.

One implication of this approach is that the equilibrium price level $P_e$ is proportional to the nominal quantity of money supplied. This is easily seen by noting that the nominal quantity of money divided by the real quantity of money equals the price level, or:

$$P = \frac{M}{m} \tag{6.16}$$

Since the real quantity of money is fixed by the amount demanded and the nominal quantity is fixed by the amount supplied, equation (6.16) can only hold if any given increase in the amount of money supplied causes an equal percentage change in the price level. For instance, a 5 percent increase in the money supply must cause a 5 percent increase in the price level.

Once we have determined the equilibrium price level $P_e$, we can find the equilibrium level of nominal income $Y_e$ as the product of $y_e$ and $P_e$, or:

$$Y_e = y_e P_e \tag{6.17}$$

With given $y_e$, nominal income is proportionate to changes in the price level and therefore changes in the nominal money supply.

This chapter has described the determination of long-run macroeconomic equilibrium using several equations to find the values of three key variables: real income, the interest rate, and the price level. Table 6.2 summarizes the determination of these equilibrium values.

| Variable | Determined by |
|---|---|
| Real output or income | Labor market, capital market, and technology (equation (6.1)) |
| Interest rate | Saving and investment (equations (6.7) and (6.8)) |
| Price level | Money supply and money demand (equation (6.16)) |

## SUMMARY

**1** Long-run equilibrium is the position of the economy when the temporary effects of unexpected changes in macroeconomic conditions have been eliminated.

**2** An aggregate production function relates quantities of input to quantities of output.

**3** The increase in total output resulting from a one-unit increase in an input is the marginal product of that input.

**4** The demand for labor is a decreasing function of the wage rate and an increasing function of the capital stock.

**5** Labor supply is an increasing function of the age-eligible population, its average quality, and the average labor-force participation rate.

**6** The labor participation rate depends upon the real wage, the average quality of labor, and the per capita income from capital.

**7** The demand for capital is a decreasing function of the real rental rate and an increasing function of the quantity of labor.

**8** The labor market equilibrium curve shows the combinations of the real rental rate and quantity of labor for which the labor market is in equilibrium.

**9** The capital market equilibrium curve shows the combinations of the real rental rate and quantity of labor for which the capital market is in equilibrium.

**10** The intersection of the *KE* and *LE* curves will determine the equilibrium value of the real rental rate and the quantity of labor.

**11** Once the equilibrium quantity of labor is found, equilibrium real output or income is found by the $y_e$ on the aggregate production function consistent with $\ell_e$.

**12** Investment is a decreasing function of the interest rate $R$, and an increasing function of the real rental rate $\rho$.

**13** Saving is an increasing function of real income and the interest rate.

**14** The equilibrium interest rate is found by the intersection of the saving and investment functions.

**15** The nominal money supply is fixed by the central bank.

**16** The Cambridge $K$ measures the ratio of the money supply to income.

**17** The more frequently money is received and the more closely expenditures follow receipts, the lower the average transactions balances.

**18** The size of the Cambridge $K$ is a decreasing function of the interest rate on bonds, and an increasing function of the interest rate paid on money balances. The effect of real income is uncertain.

**19** The equilibrium price level is established to equate the real amount of money demanded with the real value of the nominal amount supplied.

## EXERCISES

1. It is difficult to add different kinds of machines and buildings to obtain a measure of capital. Is this problem conceptually any different from estimating real income or real labor input? Explain why or why not?

2. Part of the rental value of the capital stock accrues to individuals who do not work in any case, such as retired people. Does this eliminate or merely reduce the change in the quantity of labor supplied, other things being equal, if the rental rate on capital somehow increases? Would these people really not work even if the rental rate on capital fell to zero?

3. What is the difference between the labor market equilibrium ($LE$) curve and the demand curve for labor? What is the difference between the capital market equilibrium ($KE$) curve and the demand curve for capital?

4. Use the $KE$ and $LE$ curves to analyze the effects of the following situations on real income, real wage rate, real rental rate, and amount of labor used:

    a. A decrease in the age-eligible population.

**b.** An earthquake which destroys a substantial part of the capital stock without harming the population.

**c.** An increased taste for leisure as opposed to work.

5. An investment project is expected to yield returns of $10, $10, and $110 at the end of 1, 2, and 3 years, respectively, and nothing thereafter. If the investment costs $100 now, would it be profitable at a market interest rate of 8 percent per annum, compounded annually? 10 percent? 12 percent?

6. Suppose the exact saving and investment functions are:

$$s = -5 + 0.1y + 100R$$
$$i = 110 + 1000\, \rho - 1000R$$

   **a.** Find the equilibrium value of the interest rate (measured as a decimal fraction) if $y_e = \$1,000$ billion and $\rho_e = 0.04$.

   **b.** What is the equilibrium value of saving and investment?

7. If individuals were free to use money however they wanted, except that they had to hold exactly $100 at noon each Sunday, the economy would be a sort of barter economy. Explain why.

8. Suppose that the interest paid on deposits is a constant fraction of the interest rate on short-term bonds. Show that the gap between the interest rates on short-term bonds and deposits increases as the interest rate on short-term bonds increases. In what sense is this an increase in the cost of holding money instead of bonds?

9. Figure 6.23(a) in the text indicates that real money demand is determined by the interest rate $R$ and real income $y$. What about $R_M$, the interest paid on money? How can $R_M$ be excluded as a determinant of $K$ in the figure? Illustrate graphically and explain carefully how the equilibrium would be changed if $R_M$ is now a higher fraction of $R$.

10. Why do we discuss the real money supply adjusting to equal fixed real money demand, but talk about the nominal money demand adjusting to equal the fixed nominal money supply? Why are these statements not contradictory?

11. Consider two alternative states which differ only in the nominal supply of money. Each state is in long-run equilibrium. Denote values of variables which exist in state 1 by a subscript 1 and in state 2 by a subscript 2. In state 1, $M_1 = 200$, $P_1 = 1.25$, $y_1 = 800$. What is $Y_1$? $K_1$? In state 2, $M_2 = 300$. What are $P_2$, $y_2$, $Y_2$, $K_2$? What are $M_2/M_1$, $P_2/P_1$, $y_2/y_1$, $Y_2/Y_1$, $K_2/K_1$? What do you conclude?

## REFERENCES FOR FURTHER READING

Ehrenberg, Ronald G., and Robert S. Smith. *Modern Labor Economics*, Second Ed. Glenview, Ill: Scott, Foresman and Co., 1985.

Friedman, Milton. "A Theoretical Framework for Monetary Analysis." *Journal of Political Economy*, March/April 1970, 193–238.

Jorgensen, Dale W. "Econometric Studies of Investment Behavior: A Survey." *Journal of Economic Literature*, 9 (December 1971), 1111–47.

Laidler, David E. W. *The Demand for Money*. New York: Harper and Row, 1977.

## INTEREST PAYMENTS ON MONEY

One of the determinants of money demand is the interest rate on money balances $R_M$. In equation 6.12 we indicated that the opportunity cost of holding money was the difference between the interest paid on money substitutes like bonds $R$ and the interest paid on money $R_M$. This $R - R_M$ variable will have a negative effect on the demand for money. As $R$ rises relative to $R_M$, the cost of holding money rises; as a result, less money should be demanded.

While most of us have some idea of what $R$ is—either through experience investing or just hearing the financial news report interest rates on U.S. Treasury bills or corporate bonds—knowledge regarding $R_M$ is much scarcer. There are, of course, good reasons for this. First, there is no such thing as the interest rate on money. We are all aware that the money we carry around in our pocket, currency, yields no interest. So only a part of the money supply yields interest, and that is the part that is deposited in commercial banks. At this point the reader may be thinking, "I have a checking account and my bank doesn't pay me any interest on my balance. In fact, I must pay a service charge to the bank each month!" It is true that many bank accounts do not pay explicit interest on deposits. For small accounts, the costs associated with servicing the accounts are so high relative to the value of that account to the bank that service charges are needed to induce the bank to offer such small accounts. For large accounts, banks can now pay explicit interest. Beginning in January 1983, banks have been allowed to offer Super NOW accounts which pay market-determined competitive interest rates. Super NOW accounts have minimum balance requirements, and in March 1983, the average balance was about $13,500.[1] Banks nationwide have been able to offer regular NOW (negotiable order of withdrawal) accounts since December, 1980 for smaller balances. The regular NOW accounts have a maximum legal interest rate of 5-1/4 percent as of April, 1983, so the removal of interest-rate ceilings for the Super NOW opened the way for establishing competitively determined interest rates on bank deposits. These new accounts have greatly enhanced the competitive position of commercial banks relative to other financial institutions, since a tremendous inflow of funds to the banking system has resulted. What sort of explicit $R_M$ is associated with

---

[1]For a discussion of Super NOWs, see Frederick T. Furlong, "New Deposit Instruments," *Federal Reserve Bulletin*, May 1983, 319–26.

Super NOWS? Since the rate is unregulated, it differs somewhat across institutions; however, Table E6.1 reports some average data taken from the *Federal Reserve Bulletin*. Today we can observe market-determined, explicitly paid $R_M$, but Super NOWs are quite new.

What about before bank deregulation, when banks were prohibited from paying interest on demand deposits? Was there no $R_M$? Previous macroeconomics textbooks typically assumed $R_M$ equals zero, or else mentioned only in passing how $R_M$ might theoretically effect money demand. We believe that there is sufficient evidence regarding the existence of a positive $R_M$ prior to bank deposit deregulation to warrant its inclusion in the text as more than a new effect. But how could there be a positive $R_M$ when banks were prohibited from paying interest on demand deposits? The interest was paid implicitly, so that rather than depositors having their account credited with earned interest receipts, they were compensated in other ways. **Implicit** $R_M$ may be paid by the provision of free banking services.

Several economists have studied the question of implicit $R_M$. Benjamin Klein of UCLA estimated the "competitive" $R_M$ that would have existed if competition forced banks to "pass on to their depositors, in an open or covert manner, all marginal profit from their deposit accounts."[2] Alternatively, Robert Barro of the University of Rochester and Anthony Santomero of the University of Pennsylvania surveyed large commercial banks and estimated the remission of customer service charges as a measure of $R_M$.[3] More recently, Richard Startz of the University of Wash-

---

[2]Benjamin Klein, "Competitive Interest Payments on Bank Deposits and the Long–Run Demand for Money," *American Economic Review*, 64 (December 1974), 935.

[3]Robert J. Barro and Anthony M. Santomero, "Household Money Holdings and the Demand Deposit Rate," *Journal of Money, Credit, and Banking*, 4 (May 1972), 397–413.

Table E6.1

|  | Jan. 26, 1983 | Feb. 23, 1983 | Mar. 30, 1983 |
|---|---|---|---|
| $R_M$ | 7.6% | 7.3% | 7.3% |
| $R$ | 8.4 | 8.2 | 9.0 |

$R_M$: average interest rate paid by a sample of commercial banks.
$R$: three-month T-bill rate, coupon-equivalent yield.

Source: *Federal Reserve Bulletin*, May 1983, p. 321.

ington estimates the value of bank services provided to customers as implicit interest by measuring the costs to banks in providing such services.[4] Based on his careful analysis, Startz concludes that there was indeed positive $R_M$ paid implicitly on demand deposits, and this $R_M$ varied with $R$. However $R_M$ was less than the perfectly competitive rate envisioned by Klein, and was in fact approximately half the competitive rate. Table E6.2 reports the estimated implicit $R_M$ along with the three-month T-bill rate for $R$ in each period investigated by Startz.

Now we have a better idea of the nature of the $R_M$ variable appearing in our money demand functions. Today commercial banks are allowed to pay explicit interest on demand deposits so that $R_M$ is an observable variable. Prior to the regulatory changes that allowed explicit interest payments on money, implicit payments occurred, so that $R_M$ has always been a factor in determining money demand.

---

[4]Richard Startz, "Implicit Interest on Demand Deposits," *Journal of Monetary Economics*, 5 (October 1979), 515–34.

**Table E6.2**

**The Implicit Interest Rate on Money ($R_M$) Compared to the Treasury Bill Rate ($R$)**

| Year | Implicit $R_M$ | R |
|---|---|---|
| 1954 | .85116 | .95 |
| 1955 | .90555 | 1.74 |
| 1956 | .92859 | 2.66 |
| 1957 | 1.04196 | 3.26 |
| 1958 | 1.05996 | 1.84 |
| 1959 | 1.14471 | 3.42 |
| 1960 | 1.26637 | 2.94 |
| 1961 | 1.19594 | 2.38 |
| 1962 | 1.19036 | 2.78 |
| 1963 | 1.23182 | 3.16 |
| 1964 | 1.14878 | 3.55 |
| 1965 | 1.07157 | 3.95 |
| 1966 | 1.18285 | 4.88 |
| 1967 | 1.21917 | 4.33 |
| 1968 | 1.57511 | 5.35 |
| 1969 | 1.82214 | 6.69 |
| 1970 | 2.42028 | 6.44 |
| 1971 | 2.17040 | 4.34 |
| 1972 | 1.85507 | 4.07 |

Sources: $R_M$: Richard Startz, "Implicit Interest on Demand Deposits," *Journal of Monetary Economics*, 5 (October 1979), 527.
    $R$: *Federal Reserve Bulletin*

# CHAPTER SEVEN

# FOUNDATIONS OF AGGREGATE DEMAND AND SUPPLY

## 7.1 AN OVERVIEW OF ALTERNATIVE MODELS

### IS–LM

The *IS–LM* model presented in Chapter 5 offers a relatively simple way to determine the short-run impact of macroeconomic changes. Some economists have criticized the *IS–LM* model because of the restrictiveness of some of its underlying assumptions. One particularly controversial assumption is the exogenously given, constant price level. The controversy arises over whether it is reasonable to assume that the price level is relatively constant in the short run when interest rates and real income are affected by macroeconomic shocks. That is, if the price level does adjust in a short enough time, is *IS–LM* analysis unrealistic?

In this chapter, we begin to consider macro models that allow real income and prices to vary simultaneously. We will examine the determinants of the price level, and the extent to which prices respond in the short run to various macroeconomic shocks.

Before the reader is tempted to completely disregard Keynesian *IS–LM* analysis, it should be realized that researchers have generally found *that prices seem to adjust more slowly than both interest rates and real income*. It would then seem that if we are only concerned with the *immediate* impact of macro shocks, the Keynesian, exogenously given price level is a reasonable assumption. It is important to note, more-

Prices seem to adjust more slowly than interest rates and real income.

151

over, that the *IS–LM* model is not the only useful economic model in which prices and output are not both able to vary in a realistic manner. While *IS–LM* has real income changing while prices remain constant, the quantity theory of money is often viewed as a theory of price-level movements in which real income is constant. (Remember from our discussion in Chapter 1 that the quantity theory of money is summarized in the equation $MV = Py$.)

Before introducing an economic model in which both prices and output vary, let's consider in more detail the quantity theory of money. Following this discussion, the rest of the chapter will be devoted to developing an understanding of how macro changes cause both output and prices to vary. While it may seem that this abundance of models is designed solely to confuse the student, in fact professional economists choose among these various approximations of reality to provide the simplest approach consistent with the problem at hand. The macroeconomists' variety of models is like the carpenter's variety of tools. In a pinch, one tool might be substituted for another. But there is generally a specific tool best suited for each specific job.

## THE QUANTITY THEORY OF MONEY

The simple quantity theory of money has real income constant with a variable price.

As a theory of the price level, the quantity theory of money utilizes assumptions that are just the opposite of the assumptions underlying the *IS–LM* model! While the *IS–LM* approach assumes constant prices and varying real income, *the simple quantity theory of money assumes that real income is constant but that prices vary.* As a long-run theory of the price level, the quantity theory of money assumes that output and interest rates will be at their equilibrium levels $y_e$ and $R_e$ in the long run. The value of $y_e$ will be the output level derived in Chapter 6, which can be produced from the given capital stock and labor supply when unemployment is at its normal value (we will consider later just what is "normal"). The $R_e$ derived in Chapter 6 also may be thought of as the interest rate consistent with $y_e$ on the *IS* curve.

The simple quantity theory of money has the price level ($P_e$) being determined by the nominal money supply ($M$) and real money demand ($m_e$). The nominal supply of money demanded is set by the monetary authorities. The real quantity of money is determined in long-run equilibrium by the money demand equation:

$$m_e = K^d(y_e, R_e)y_e \qquad (7.1)$$

We have already discussed the rationale for such a money demand equation in Chapter 6. Here we simply are recognizing that the long-run equilibrium income and interest rate will be consistent with a particular real amount of money demanded $m_e$. Money market equilibrium requires that the real quantity of money supplied (which is $M/P$) be equal to the real quantity demanded, or:

$$M/P_e = m_e \qquad (7.2)$$

We can use equation (7.2) to solve for the equilibrium price level as:

$$P_e = M/m_e \qquad (7.3)$$

This equation indicates that the price level $P$ increases with increases in $M$. The exact increase in $P$ is $1/m_e$ times the increase in $M$. This relationship is illustrated in Figure 7.1.

This simple form of the quantity theory of money provides a good indication of the long-run effects of money on the price level. Suppose, for instance, that the Federal Reserve System provided a money supply of $600 billion when the equilibrium real quantity of money demanded was $300 billion. We would expect the average price level (or price index) to be about 2. This means that goods, on average, would cost about twice as much as they did in the base year. As we have already mentioned, macroeconomic shocks, or unexpected changes in an exogenous variable like the money supply, will initially affect real income more than prices. While we have not explicitly analyzed the impact of people's expectations (i.e., expected versus unexpected macro shocks), the evidence that will be discussed later indicates that if the money supply change is expected, prices will adjust in line with equation (7.3) as the money stock changes. If the change in the money supply is unexpected, then prices do not adjust at the same time that the money supply changes.

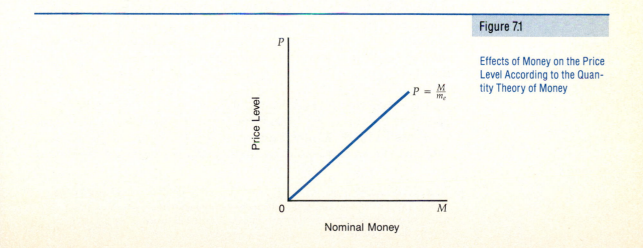

**Figure 7.1**

Effects of Money on the Price Level According to the Quantity Theory of Money

As a result, we will sometimes find the quantity theory of money most useful to find the effects on the price level of the expected (rather than actual) nominal quantity of money (since the actual quantity includes both expected and unexpected money).

Now we are familiar with an economic model that holds real income constant while analyzing changes in the price level—the quantity theory of money. We are also familiar with a model that holds prices constant while analyzing changes in real income—the *IS–LM* model. While these models both have their uses, it is time to consider a model that offers a method of analyzing both price and quantity changes—the aggregate demand/aggregate supply model. First we will discuss aggregate demand, then aggregate supply. Chapter 8 will then present some important issues in aggregate demand–aggregate supply analysis.

## 7.2 DERIVATION OF THE AGGREGATE DEMAND CURVE

### VARYING THE PRICE LEVEL IN THE *IS–LM* MODEL

The underlying rationale for the aggregate demand curve can be understood quite simply by using the *IS–LM* model. As covered in Chapter 5, the *IS–LM* model analyzes the determination of aggregate expenditures (or aggregate demand) in the short run, during which the price level is fixed. The aggregate demand curve plots different *IS–LM* equilibrium expenditures associated with different price levels. Since price is fixed for any single *IS–LM* graph, we can think of the aggregate demand curve as recording a succession of alternative *IS–LM* equilibria. The end product is a graphical representation of the amount of output people wish to purchase at each price level.

The aggregate demand curve plots alternative IS-LM equilibrium income associated with alternative price levels.

We can view the price level $P$ as entering the *IS–LM* model through the difference between the nominal money supply $M$, determined by the Federal Reserve, and the real quantity of money $m = M/P$. For any given nominal money supply $M$, a lower price level $P$ implies a larger quantity of real money $m$, because $M = mP$. For instance, suppose price level $P_0$ is greater than $P_1$. Then with a constant $M$, the real quantity of money ($m_1$) associated with $M = P_1(m_1)$ is larger than that ($m_0$) associated with $M = P_0(m_0)$. Thus the corresponding *LM* curve $LM(P_1)$ for $m_1$ lies to the right of $LM(P_0)$, the curve associated with $m_0$, as illustrated in Figure 7.2.[1] Note that the equilibrium income $y_1$, corresponding to the lower price level, exceeds that

---

[1]In Figure 7.2 we are assuming that the increase in real money balances does not affect aggregate expenditures or the *IS* curve, so only the *LM* curve shifts.

Figure 7.2

Effects of Alternative Price
Levels on Real Income in the
*IS–LM* Model

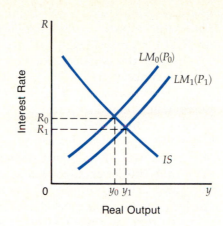

for the higher price level $y_0$. That is, the higher price level $P_0$ is associated with a lower output $y_0$. Since our focus is on income and the price level, we need not be concerned with the implied changes in the interest rate.

## THE AGGREGATE DEMAND CURVE

If we investigated the effect of additional price levels in Figure 7.2, we would find a relationship between output and prices as depicted in Figure 7.3. Figure 7.3(a) illustrates the *IS–LM* equilibrium income for three alternative price levels. Panel (b) of the figure places the price and income variable in the same graph. These are alternative *IS–LM* equilibria at which desired expenditures equal output *and* money demanded equals money supplied for each possible price level. The price–income relationship in (b) traces out an **aggregate demand curve.** Since lower values of $P$ are associated with higher values of $y$, this aggregate demand curve is downward sloping.

    The discussion to this point has been rather mechanical, so we should stop and interpret what all of this curve shifting means in terms of economic behavior. Our analysis has had the price effect working through the money market, so what is there about money demand that causes the LM curve to shift out when the price level falls? In Chapter 5 we learned that the real demand for money is considered to be a function of income and the interest rate. When the price level falls with a constant nominal money supply, the real quantity of money increases. With a constant level of $y$ and $R$, there will be an excess supply of money. As individuals spend these excess money balances, output and income rise and interest rates fall (as spending on bonds increases, bond prices rise and interest rates fall). Since money demand is a positive function of income and a negative

**aggregate demand curve**
The curve showing the combinations of *y* and *P* for which there is goods and money market equilibrium

function of the interest rate, $y$ will rise and $R$ will fall until the real quantity of money demanded and supplied are equal. This then explains the behavior underlying Figure 7.3(a), and consequently Figure 7.3(b), relating lower price levels to higher income.

Besides the negative slope of the aggregate demand curve, we are also concerned with the elasticity of the curve. Remember that elasticity measures the percentage change in quantity relative to a percentage change in price. Since nominal income is equal to the price level $P$ times the real quantity of output produced $y$, *the elasticity of aggregate demand will indicate how nominal income changes with changes in the price level.* If aggregate demand is unit elastic (an elasticity of $-1$), then the percentage change in quantity is equal to minus the percentage change in the price level and nominal income remains constant as the price level changes. Therefore, if the price level increases 1 percent, the quantity of output demanded falls 1 percent so that $Py$ is a constant amount. An elastic aggregate demand curve exists when the percentage change in output exceeds the percentage change in price. In this case, a lower price will result in a greater nominal income. When aggregate demand is inelastic, the percentage change in output demanded is less than the percentage change in price, so that decreases in price lead to a reduction in nominal income.[2]

Now that we know the implications of aggregate demand elasticity, which case describes the real world? There is indirect evidence that the aggregate demand curve is somewhat elastic.[3] However, this

---

[2]Relating elasticity of aggregate demand to the quantity theory of money ($MV = Py$), $Py$ is nominal income and we are treating $M$ as fixed, so the elasticity of aggregate demand will be related to the velocity of money. Since $Py$ is constant for a unit elastic aggregate demand, velocity is unchanged as the price level changes. With an elastic demand, $V$ increases as $P$ falls, while with an inelastic demand, $V$ falls as $P$ falls.

[3]See Douglas Purvis, "A Comment on The Use of the Aggregate Demand Curve," *Journal of Economic Literature*, 13 (June 1975), 474. Purvis demonstrates that the elasticity depends on three parameters: the short-run elasticities of money demand with respect to real income and the nominal interest rate, and the elasticity along the IS curve of the nominal interest rate with respect to real income. Some economists prefer to treat the aggregate demand curve as being unit elastic so that the determination of nominal income $Y$ can be separated from an analysis of the division of Y between changes in $P$ and $Y$. This is essentially a simplifying assumption and really plays no substantive role in the analysis (see, for example, Chapters 11 and 12 below or Milton Friedman, "A Monetary Theory of Nominal Income," *Journal of Political Economy*, 79 (March/April 1971), 323–37).

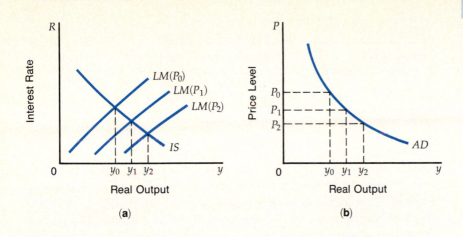

Figure 7.3

The Effect of a Lower Price Level on Aggregate Demand
a) The Effect of Shifting Price Levels in the *IS–LM* Model
b) Alternative *IS–LM* Equilibrium Income at Alternative Price Levels: The Aggregate Demand Curve

issue has not received much research because shifts in the aggregate demand curve are generally considered more important in explaining real world behavior than movements along a given aggregate demand curve in response to shifts in the aggregate supply curve.

    Anything that changes the equilibrium income of the *IS–LM* analysis will cause shifts in the aggregate demand curve. Holding the price level constant, if a particular macroeconomic change increases (decreases) the *IS–LM* equilibrium output by a certain amount, then it shifts the aggregate demand curve to the right (left) by the same amount. For example, suppose that the shift to the right in the *LM* curve from $LM(M_0)$ to $LM(M_1)$ in Figure 7.4(a) reflected not lower price levels (as we previously assumed), but an increase in the

Shifts in aggregate demand are more important in explaining real world behavior than movements along a given aggregate demand curve.

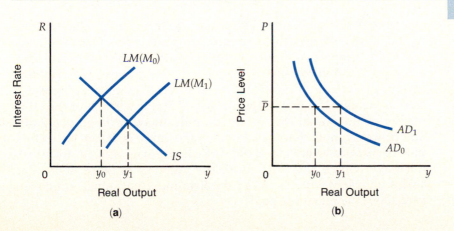

Figure 7.4

The Shift in the Aggregate Demand Curve
a) The Effect of Increasing the Money Supply in the *IS–LM* Model
b) The Shift in the Aggregate Demand Curve Caused by an Increase in the Money Supply

Table 7.1

| Increase in: | Aggregate Demand: |
| --- | --- |
| Money supply | Shifts right (increases) |
| Government spending | Shifts right (increases) |
| Taxes | Shifts left (decreases) |
| Consumption function | Shifts right (increases) |
| Investment function | Shifts right (increases) |

money supply from $M_0$ to a higher level $M_1$, holding prices constant at $\overline{P}$. Figure 7.4(b) shows the impact of this change on aggregate demand. The increase in aggregate demand from $AD_0$ to $AD_1$ is a result of the increase in money from $M_0$ to $M_1$. Curve $AD_0$ passes through the point representing the constant price level $\overline{P}$ and the original output level $y_0$, while $AD_1$ passes through the point with $\overline{P}$ and the higher output $y_1$.

We could apply any of the macroeconomic changes that were previously covered in the Chapter 5 introduction to *IS–LM* to shifts in aggregate demand. Table 7.1 summarizes the effects of increases in key macroeconomic variables on aggregate demand. Decreases in these variables would shift the aggregate demand curve in opposite directions.

When we combine our aggregate demand curve with the aggregate supply curve, we are able to analyze how such changes affect the equilibrium level of real income and the price level.

## 7.3 DERIVATION OF THE AGGREGATE SUPPLY CURVE

### AGGREGATE PRODUCTION AND THE LABOR MARKET

The aggregate supply curve can be derived from labor market behavior in combination with the aggregate production function introduced in Chapter 6. Figure 7.5(b) reproduces the aggregate production function originally introduced in Figure 6.1. Holding constant the stock of capital, increases in the quantity of labor will lead to increases in real output. Figure 7.5(a) is a graph of the labor market analogous to that originally introduced in Figures 6.2 and 6.3. However, note that the labor demand curve is drawn based on a particular price level $P_1$, and the vertical axis is labeled $W$, the nominal wage. Given any price level, the quantity of labor demanded varies inversely with the wage the firm must pay, since employers care about the real wage paid.

Figure 7.5

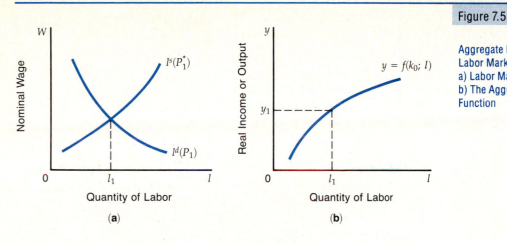

In Figure 7.5(a), the labor supply curve is based on the expected price level $P_1^*$ (an asterisk denotes expected values). It is reasonable to believe that the response of labor to any particular wage will be dependent upon the price level expected to prevail in the economy. Workers care about expected real wages. So for a given expected price level, the higher the nominal wage, the higher the expected real wage and thus the greater the quantity of labor supplied. Thus we have the upward sloping labor supply curve with respect to the nominal wage in Figure 7.5(a).

Relating the outcome of the labor market to the aggregate production function in Figure 7.5, we see that the equilibrium quantity of labor determined in the labor market is $\ell_1$. Plugging this quantity of labor into the aggregate production function indicates that with a given capital stock $k_0$, the economy will produce a real output of $y_1$.

What happens if the price level varies? Figure 7.6 indicates the shift occurring if the price level rises to $P_2$. The higher price level will cause a rightward shift in the labor demand curve, as firms are now willing to employ more labor at any given nominal wage. If workers still expect $P_1$ to prevail, then there is no shift in the labor supply curve, and the new equilibrium quantity of labor is $\ell_2$ with a corresponding level of output $y_2$. So if the change in price is not expected by labor, the result is an increase in output.

The role of expectations here is important. Suppose that workers anticipate a higher price level. Figure 7.7 illustrates the shifts in the labor market when the price level increases to $P_2$ and labor expects the higher price. When the price level rises to $P_2$, the demand for labor increases as before, but now the labor supply curve also shifts. A higher expected price level causes the labor supply curve to shift

## Figure 7.6

Aggregate Production and the
Labor Market: Effect of a
Higher Price Level
a)  Labor Market Equilibrium
When the Price Level Rises
Unexpectedly
b)  The Increase in Real Out-
put Caused by a Higher Price
Level

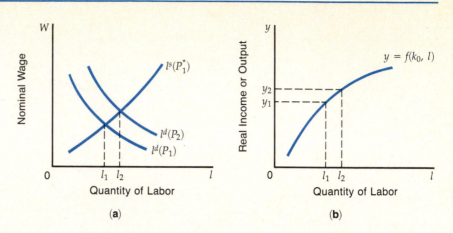

(a)                                    (b)

left to the curve labeled $\ell^s(P_2^*)$. When labor expects a higher price
level, then a constant nominal wage will mean a fall in real wages.
Therefore, the only way to employ $\ell_1$ workers, as before, is to raise
the nominal wage to compensate for the price increase from $P_1^*$ to
$P_2^*$. Obviously, if the nominal wage increase just compensates for the
higher expected price level, no real change occurs—labor expects to
receive the same real wage as before, so the quantity of labor employed remains at $\ell_1$, and the level of real output remains at $y_1$.

    The way in which expectations are actually formed is very im-
portant to economic policymaking, but we will delay a discussion of
this issue until after the complete derivation of the aggregate supply
curve. At that time, it will be easy to see the importance of the issue.

## Figure 7.7

Aggregate Production and the
Labor Market: When the
Higher Price Is Expected
a)  Labor Market Equilibrium
When the Price Level Increase
Is Expected
b)  Unchanged Real Output
When the Price Level Increase
Is Expected

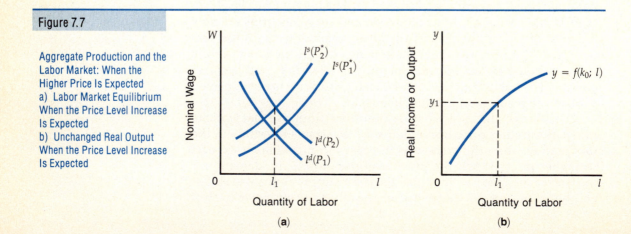

(a)                                    (b)

## THE AGGREGATE SUPPLY CURVE

The aggregate supply curve depicts the real output produced at alternative price levels. Figure 7.8(c) illustrates an aggregate supply curve (labeled *AS*) based on unexpected changes in price. As was seen in Figure 7.6, when the price level increases unexpectedly, the labor demand curve shifts up but labor supply is unchanged. The resulting increase in the equilibrium quantity of labor from $\ell_1$ to $\ell_2$ will be associated with an increase in real output from $y_1$ to $y_2$. The aggregate supply curve in Figure 7.8(c) measures the real output produced at each alternative price level. Since higher prices (that are not anticipated) cause higher output, the aggregate supply curve will be upward sloping. When price is $P_1$, we have the output $y_1$ which corresponds to point *A* on the aggregate supply curve. When price increases unexpectedly to $P_2$, output rises to $y_2$. This new output taken from the production function corresponds to point *B* on the aggregate supply curve.

What if the change in the price level is anticipated? Figure 7.9(a) shows that since a properly anticipated price level increase shifts the labor supply curve up by the same amount as the labor demand curve, the new labor market equilibrium will have the same equilibrium quantity as before the price increases ($\ell_1$). The only change is an increase in the nominal wage proportional to the price level increase. Therefore the aggregate supply curve in Figure 7.9(c) will be a vertical line at the output level $y_1$.

Notice that the aggregate supply curve in Figure 7.8(c) is drawn for a given anticipated price level $P_1^*$ and capital stock $k_0$. The capital stock is held fixed so that we may analyze the impact of a change in labor on the aggregate production function. The given price level

The aggregate supply curve shows real output produced at alternative price levels.

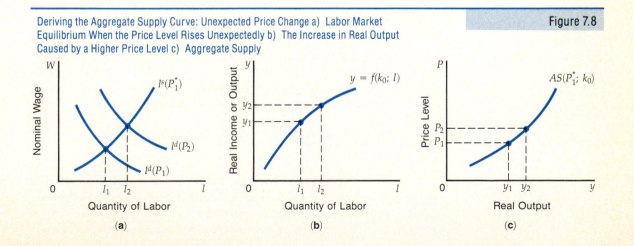

Deriving the Aggregate Supply Curve: Unexpected Price Change a) Labor Market Equilibrium When the Price Level Rises Unexpectedly b) The Increase in Real Output Caused by a Higher Price Level c) Aggregate Supply

Figure 7.8

(a)

(b)

(c)

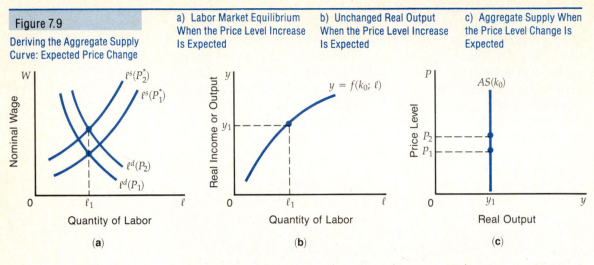

**Figure 7.9**

Deriving the Aggregate Supply Curve: Expected Price Change

a) Labor Market Equilibrium When the Price Level Increase Is Expected

b) Unchanged Real Output When the Price Level Increase Is Expected

c) Aggregate Supply When the Price Level Change Is Expected

expectation $P_1^*$ results in actual changes in price being unanticipated by labor so that there is no change in the nominal wage needed to attract a given quantity of labor. $\ell_1$. When the price level increases with a constant nominal wage, the real wage falls, inducing employers to hire more workers. As the quantity of labor employed increases, real output will increase and we will observe an upward sloping aggregate supply curve.

In Figure 7.9(c), the aggregate supply curve is drawn based on a constant capital stock $k_0$, but price level changes are properly anticipated. When labor expects a price level increase, it will be necessary to raise the nominal wage so that real wages are unchanged in order to employ $\ell_1$ workers. Since real wages do not change, employers will not increase the quantity of labor employed when the price level increases. Since the labor input is held constant, real output remains at $y_1$ and there is a vertical aggregate supply curve as output is unchanging as price varies. A vertical aggregate supply curve like in Figure 7.9(c) is referred to as a long-run aggregate supply curve. An upward-sloping curve as depicted in Figure 7.8(c) is often called a short-run aggregate supply curve. This time reference is based on the notion that people are more easily surprised in the short run than the long run, so that a change in the price level that may be unexpected in the short run will come to be expected as people learn over time.

The aggregate supply curve is flatter in the short-run than in the long-run.

## 7.4 EQUILIBRIUM OUTPUT AND PRICE LEVEL

Now that we have derived the aggregate demand curve and the aggregate supply curve, we can combine the two curves in one diagram to determine the equilibrium price level and output. Figure 7.10 depicts the aggregate demand-aggregate supply equilibrium. The

**Figure 7.10**

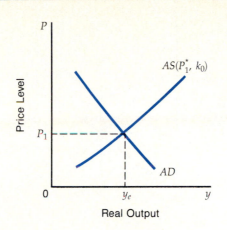

intersection of the aggregate demand and aggregate supply curves occurs at a price level of $P_1$. Note that the aggregate supply curve is based on an expected price level of $P_1^*$, which is equal in numeric value to the realized equilibrium value $P_1$. In this case, expectations are realized and the normal level of output $y_e$ is produced.

## EXPECTED VERSUS UNEXPECTED SHIFTS IN AGGREGATE DEMAND

Suppose there is a shift in aggregate demand. How will equilibrium price and quantity be affected? The answer depends on whether the shift in aggregate demand is expected or not. Figure 7.11 illustrates two possible results of a shift in aggregate demand. The initial equilibrium occurs at point *1*, where the demand curve $AD_1$ intersects the short-run aggregate supply curve based on an expected price $P_1^*$. At this point, the equilibrium price level is $P_1 = P_1^*$ and the equilibrium output is the normal output $y_e$.

 Now consider the effect of an unexpected increase in aggregate demand to $AD_2$. Since the demand shift was unexpected, the new equilibrium will occur at point *2* on the original aggregate supply curve based on an expected price level $P_1^*$. When aggregate demand increases unexpectedly, the actual price level rises to $P_2$ and real output increases beyond the normal level to $y_2$. As we learned in Figure 7.8, when the price level is higher than expected, the equilibrium quantity of labor increases so that with a fixed capital stock, real output will increase.

 Intuitively, the expected price level used in deriving the short-run aggregate supply curve must reflect the expected aggregate demand. Since unexpected prices largely reflect unexpected changes in demand, individuals must consider the expected level of aggregate demand when forming expectations of future prices. The expected

Figure 7.11

Expected Versus Unexpected
Aggregate Demand Shifts

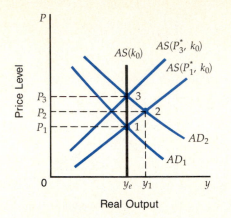

aggregate demand curve must pass through the expected price level $P_1^*$ and the normal level of output $y_e$, occuring at point *1* in Figure 7.11. If aggregate demand increases unexpectedly, the actual price level will rise (to $P_2$ in Figure 7.11) and real output will increase (to $y_2$ in Figure 7.11).

What happens if the shift in aggregate demand and consequent price level change is expected? The short-run aggregate supply curve shifts to the left reflecting the higher expected price. This shift occurs because firms must pay higher nominal wages to keep expected real wages constant when workers expect the price level to rise. Otherwise, the equilibrium quantity of labor, and thus output, would fall with the drop in real wages. Since firms must incur higher costs of producing output, the aggregate supply curve shifts left so that any given level of output will be associated with a higher price level.

When the change in the price level is correctly anticipated, the aggregate supply curve shifts up by enough to offset any effect on output of the shift in aggregate demand, like the shift from point *1* to point *3* in Figure 7.11. The only result of the anticipated increase in aggregate demand is a higher price level $P_3 = P_3^*$. Real output remains at the normal level $y_e$.

Notice that points *1* and *3* both lie on the long-run vertical aggregate supply curve. Remember that this vertical aggregate supply curve reflects aggregate supply when price changes are correctly anticipated. We refer to the vertical aggregate supply curve as the long-run aggregate supply curve because price level changes will ultimately be recognized, so that short-run aggregate supply shifts to reflect the correctly anticipated price. As long as the price level is correctly anticipated, the real output level will be $y_e$. Only unexpected shifts in aggregate demand will affect real output. The exis-

Only unexpected shifts in aggregate demand will affect real output in the short-run.

tence of $y_e$ regardless of the price level is illustrated by long-run aggregate supply curve.

The various equilibria in Figure 7.11 could occur in sequence over time. A likely sequence would begin at point *1*. Then aggregate demand increases unexpectedly to $AD_2$. Since $P_1^*$ is initially the expected price level, the new equilibrium will occur at point *2* on the initial aggregate supply curve. The result of the unexpected increase in aggregate demand is to increase both output (to $y_1$) and the price level (to $P_2$). If aggregate demand remains at $AD_2$, it eventually becomes the expected aggregate demand and the aggregate supply curve shifts up to reflect the higher price level expected. When the short-run aggregate supply curve shifts up, the new equilibrium occurs at point *3*. Output falls back to $y_e$ while the price level rises to $P_3$. In summary, the increase in aggregate demand has an initial effect of stimulating output as long as the increased demand is unanticipated. Once expectations adjust to the new level of aggregate demand and the corresponding higher price level, actual price rises and output returns to the normal output $y_e$.

While the Keynesian *IS–LM* analysis addressed the problem of finding the short-run equilibrium output for a given state of expectation, the aggregate demand–aggregate supply approach broadens the problem to include a changing price level but still assumes a given state of expectation for any particular equilibrium. Later on we shall see that in some cases, whether or not expectations are formed rationally (using all available information) is very important; for now we need not consider the exact nature of expectation formation.

## THE KEYNESIAN AGGREGATE SUPPLY CURVE

The IS–LM assumption of a given price level $\overline{P}$ has traditionally been thought by Keynesian economists to apply to an economy of less than full employment output, where full employment represents the maximum amount that can be produced from the economy's available resources. If $y_F$ represents **full employment output**, then $y_F$ is greater than the normal level of output consistent with long-run equilibrium $y_e$. The end-of-chapter essay to Chapter 8 will offer a discussion of the normal rate of unemployment and output. For now we simply need to realize that $y_e$ is less than $y_F$.

A typical derivation of the Keynesian aggregate supply curve is shown in Figure 7.12. Full employment is represented by $\ell_F$ and this is the largest amount of workers that can be obtained at any wage. So all labor supply curves must rise vertically at $\ell_F$. A key assumption in this approach is that nominal wages are flexible upward but rigid downward; in other words, labor is not willing to take any nominal wage cuts. Accordingly, in Figure 7.12(a) the effective labor supply

**full-employment output**
The total output that results when the labor force is fully employed

Figure 7.12    The Keynesian Aggregate Supply Curve a) Keynesian Labor Market b) Aggregate Production Function c) Keynesian Aggregate Supply Curve

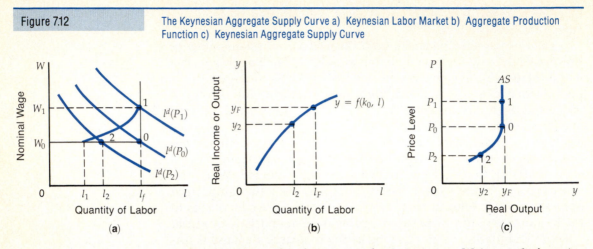

curve is horizontal at the assumed existing wage $W_0$ instead of continuing downward as in Figures 7.5 through 7.9. Consider the lowest price level $P_0$ at which everyone wants to work at $W_0$ or any higher wage. For this price level (or any lower one) the labor supply curve will look like the right angle running across at $W_0$ to $\ell_F$ and then up: workers won't accept a wage lower than $W_0$ but all of them want to work at a wage of $W_0$ or higher.

Now consider a higher price level $P_1$. At this price level, the real wage $W_0/P_1$ associated with the minimum acceptable wage $W_0$ is too low to induce employment of more than $\ell_1$ at $W_0$. As nominal wages rise, so does the amount of labor supplied until we reach full employment at $W_1$ where the real wage $W_1/P_1$ equals the minimum real wage $W_0/P_0$ at which everyone will work. So for a price level less than or equal to $P_0$ we have a right-angle labor supply curve, but for higher price levels like $P_1$ there will be an upward sloping segment joining the horizontal and vertical branches.

Suppose that the labor demand curve passes through point 0 at $P_0$. In that case, the minimal acceptable wage $W_0$ is consistent with full employment $\ell_F$ at a price level of $P_0$. With $\ell_F$, the production function in panel (b) indicates that the level of output will be the full employment level $y_F$. Therefore one point on the aggregate supply curve occurs at point 0, where the price level equals $P_0$ and output equals $y_F$.

Suppose the price level rises to $P_1$. Labor demand in Figure 7.12(a) will shift out to $\ell^d(P_1)$. At the original wage $W_0$, there would be an excess demand for labor. Since wages are flexible upward, the excess demand is eliminated by a rise in the wage rate to $W_1$. The wage increase to $W_1$ offsets the increase in price so that the real wage is unchanged and the equilibrium quantity of labor remains at $_F$. Therefore a second point on the aggregate supply curve in panel (c) is point 1, where the price level equals $P_1$ and real output is still $y_F$.

So the Keynesian aggregate supply curve becomes vertical at the full employment level of output.

    Let's begin at the initial equilibrium point $0$ in Figure 7.12(a). Now suppose the price level falls from $P_0$ to some lower price $P_2$. The labor demand curve shifts left to $\ell^d(P_2)$. Since wages are rigid downward, the nominal wage does not fall below $W_0$. This causes an excess supply of labor. At a wage of $W_0$, $\ell_2$ labor is demanded while $\ell_F$ is supplied—there is unemployment in the labor market. If $\ell_2$ is the quantity of labor employed, we see from Figure 7.12(b) that output will equal $y_2$. This leaves us with point $2$ on the aggregate supply curve in panel (c). The Keynesian aggregate supply curve has an upward slope for output levels less than full employment.

    Now we see why the Keynesian assumption of a given price level $\overline{P}$ has been thought to apply to an economy of less than full employment output. The flatter the Keynesian aggregate supply curve, the lower real output or the greater unemployment. While the aggregate supply curve in Figure 7.12 has an upward slope at less than full employment, an approximation to this $AS$ is often given as in Figure 7.13. This approximation is consistent with the familiar assumption of a constant price level $\overline{P}$ at less than full employment output $y_F$. Once the full employment level of output is reached, any increases in aggregate demand would simply bring higher price levels with no increase in output. For instance, suppose aggregate demand is initially at $AD_0$. This gives equilibrium output of $Y_F$ and an equilibrium price level of $\overline{P}$. If aggregate demand increases to $AD_1$, the only result is a higher equilibrium price level. Suppose from the initial equilibrium given by $AD_0$, aggregate demand falls to $AD_2$. The equilibrium price will remain at $\overline{P}$ but output will fall.

    Notice that whenever the aggregate demand–aggregate supply equilibrium occurs at less than the full employment level of output, increases in aggregate demand will lead to increases in real output with no increase in the price level. This occurs until aggregate demand just intersects aggregate supply at the full employment output, as occurs at $AD_0$ in Figure 7.13.

    The Keynesian aggregate supply curve really has no role for expectations and is generally not considered by modern macroeconomists to be a realistic view of an economy. The view of the previous section regarding the importance of aggregate demand changes being expected or unexpected is the popular view today. If the conditions underlying the aggregate demand curve are as expected, desired expenditures (viewed from the demand side) will just equal normal output $y_e$ (on the supply side) at the expected price level.

    While the location of equilibrium when expectations are realized is important, the really interesting (i.e., realistic) results of the aggregate demand and supply approach occur when expectations are not consistent with actual events. Let us turn to those cases now.

> The Keynesian aggregate supply curve becomes vertical at the full employment level of output.

> The flatter the Keynesian aggregate supply curve, the lower real output or greater unemployment.

| Figure 7.13 |
| --- |

An Approximate Keynesian
Aggregate Supply Curve

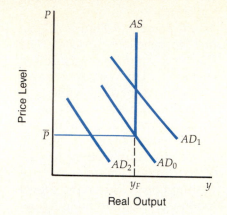

## 7.5 EFFECTS OF MONEY-MARKET SHOCKS

### MONEY-MARKET SHOCKS DEFINED

**money market shocks**
When expected results and actual results differ for either money supply or money demand

**Money-market shocks** may emanate from the supply or the demand side. In terms of *IS–LM* analysis, the *LM* curve may differ from its expected position either because the nominal quantity of money supplied is different from what was expected or because the real quantity of money demanded differs from the amount that was expected (at the expected levels of income and the interest rate).

The *money-supply shock* is conveniently measured as the proportionate or *percentage difference* between the actual money supply $M$ and the expected money supply $M^*$, or $(M - M^*)/M^*$.[4] This provides

---

[4]It is convenient to measure such deviations in proportionate or percentage terms rather than absolute terms (i.e., $M - M^*$). This is because proportionate changes can be easily related to other variables and effects, and are independent of units of measurement. For instance, if the expected money supply is $500 billion and the actual money supply is $550 billion, there is a 10 percent money-supply shock $((550 - 500)/500)$. If at the same time in Japan, the expected money supply is ¥300,000 billion (Japanese currency is yen) compared to the actual money supply of ¥330,000 billion there is a Japanese money shock of 10 percent $((330,000 - 300,000)/300,000)$. In percentage terms both the U.S. and Japan have a 10 percent money-supply shock——the unexpected component of the money supply as a proportion of the expected component equals 10 percent. Had we measured in absolute terms rather than proportionate, we would have a $50 billion money-supply shock for the U.S. and a ¥30,000 billion money-supply shock for Japan.

a quantitative measure of the unexpected portion of monetary policy. A *money-demand shock* would be measured by the proportionate difference between actual ($m$) and expected ($m^*$) real quantities of money demand *at the expected values of income and the interest rate*, or $(m - m^*)/m^*$ evaluated at $y_e$, $R^*$. This provides a quantitative measure of any unpredictable shifts in the money demand function.

## ANALYSIS OF A MONEY-SUPPLY SHOCK

We can now use the aggregate demand and supply approach to find the effects on output and prices of a nominal money supply which is 5 percent higher than expected. Throughout this exercise we make what is a very common assumption in most economic analysis: "all other things equal." The implication of this assumption is that we will concentrate strictly on the effects of the money supply shock; other government policy, private sector behavior (like the consumption and investment function), and the state of nature (supply shocks) are held constant.[5]

Suppose that $LM(P^*)$ in Figure 7.14 (a) represents the expected position of the $LM$ curve with $M = M^*$ and $P = P^*$. Based on $LM(P^*)$, the short-run equilibrium level of output $y^*$ would correspond to the normal output $y_e$. The actual $LM$ curve, labeled $LM$, reflects the fact that the actual nominal money supply is 5 percent higher than expected ($M = 1.05M^*$). The actual $LM$ curve is, however, drawn based on the expected price level $P^*$. So the equilibrium actual output *if* the price level were $P^*$ is $y^{(P^*)}$, which is greater than $y_e$. However, the actual price level will not be $P^*$. Since the $IS$–$LM$ model holds price fixed, we can now see an advantage of the aggregate demand–aggregate supply approach. Panel (b) of Figure 7.14 illustrates the rightward shift of the aggregate demand curve to $AD$ caused by the positive money supply shock. If the price had remained at $P^*$, the new aggregate demand curve indicates that output would equal $y^{(P^*)}$. This is not an equilibrium since the aggregate supply curve is upward sloping. In other words, the only way to increase output above $y_e$ is to have an unexpected price level increase. The positive money shock will lead to a new equilibrium at $P_1$, so that more labor will be employed and aggregate production rises—this is, of course, what accounts for the movement along the $AS(P^*)$ curve in Figure 7.14(b). Let's consider a numerical example to help clarify the analysis. Sup-

An unexpected increase in money supply would cause the aggregate demand curve to increase unexpectedly leading to a higher equilibrium price and output.

---

[5]That is, $g = g^*$, $t = t^*$, there are no unexpected shifts in the behavioral relations in the economy, and no disturbances shifting the aggregate supply curve.

Figure 7.14

Analysis of an Unexpectedly
High Nominal Money Supply
Based on the Expected Price
Level P*
a) *IS–LM* Effects
b) Aggregate Supply and Demand Effects

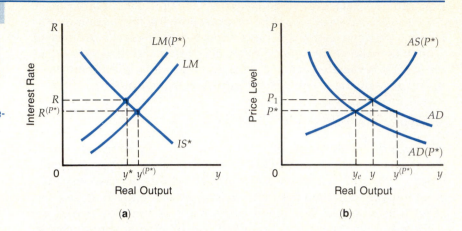

(a)                                                              (b)

pose, for example, that a 5 percent money-supply shock would increase real output by 3 percent if the price level were unchanged at
$P^*$; that is, $y^{(P^*)} = 1.03y_e$. For simplicity, let's assume that the aggregate demand curve is unit elastic. Recall that this means a given
percentage change in the price level will be associated with an equal
percentage change in real income in the opposite direction, so that
nominal income is the same along any point on the aggregate demand
curve. We then have a diagram like Figure 7.15 that can be used to
find the actual values of $y$ and $P$.[6]

The intersection of the $AD$ and $AS(P^*)$ curves indicates that the
short-run equilibrium output and price level are approximately $1.02y_e$
and $1.01P^*$, respectively. So the 5 percent unexpected increase in
nominal money brings about a 3 percent increase in *nominal output*,
which is divided between a 2 percent, above-normal *real output* and a
*price level* 1 percent above expectations. As mentioned before, $y_e$ is the
normal level of real output in the economy and $P^*$ is based on the
expectations of individuals. Given values for $y_e$ and $P^*$, we can determine the exact value of $1.02y_e$ and $1.01P^*$.

If the nominal money supply were unexpectedly reduced instead of increased, we would find the actual aggregate demand curve

---

[6]Given the scale used for each axis of Figure 7.15, the aggregate
demand curve appears as almost a straight line. This should not
be considered a general characteristic of unit elastic aggregate
demand curves.

Figure 7.15

A Numerical Example of the
Effects of an Unexpectedly
High Nominal Money Supply

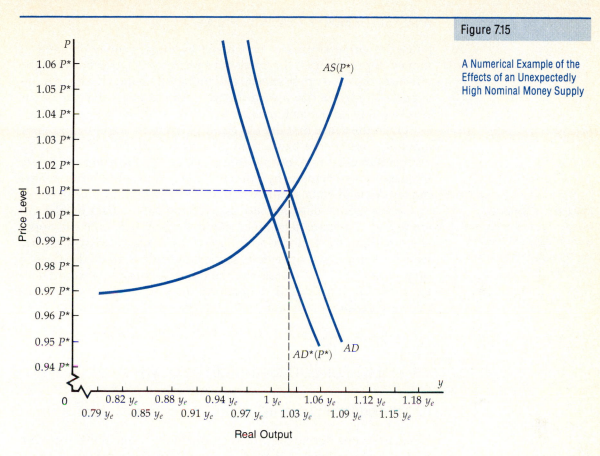

$AD$ lying to the left of the expected aggregate demand curve $AD(P^*)$, so that output would be below normal and prices would be less than expected.[7]

---

[7]We could think in terms of inflation rates rather than price levels. If people expected a 5-percent rate of inflation per period and the short-run equilibrium price level turns out to be $0.99P^*$ rather than $P^*$, then the actual inflation rate will be 4 percent. Prices will still rise, but less rapidly than expected. We could even have periods where the inflation rate is accelerating (suppose it was 3 percent last period) yet still the actual inflation rate is less than expected.

## ANALYSIS OF MONEY-DEMAND SHOCKS

Since *LM* curve shifts can be caused by either money-demand or money-supply shocks, there exists a symmetric relation between the effects of money-supply shocks and money-demand shocks. An unexpected 5 percent downward shift in the money demand function is equivalent to a 5 percent unexpected increase in the nominal money supply in the sense that the *LM* curve shifts to the right by the same amount. This is true because in either case, at the expected price level and interest rate, output must increase by the same amount to increase money demand by 5 percent and restore equilibrium where money demand equals money supply.

Unexpected money demand decreases (increases) work just like unexpected money supply increases (decreases).

Since money-demand shocks have the same effect on the *LM* curve and aggregate demand as money-supply shocks in the opposite direction, we do not need to repeat the graphical analysis. If we went back through the previous section and substituted "decrease in money demand" for "increase in the money supply," we would have the identical graphs used to illustrate the effects of an unexpected decrease in money demand.

## 7.6 EFFECTS OF GOODS-MARKET SHOCKS

### GOODS-MARKET SHOCKS DEFINED

goods market shocks
When expected results and actual results differ for *G* or *I* or *C* or *X*

When first considering the *IS–LM* model, we saw that there are many potential **goods-market shocks**. These include unexpected changes in government spending or taxes and unpredictable shifts in the investment, consumption, or net export function. We shall formally consider only the three shocks which have most interested macroeconomists (because of their empirical significance), since the other shocks have analogous effects.

Government spending shocks are measured by the difference between expected and actual values as a fraction of normal output, or $(g - g^*)/y_e$. The investment shock would be measured by the same fractional difference between actual and expected values of desired investment evaluated at the expected levels of output, the price level, and the interest rate, or $(i - i^*)/y_e$ for given $y_e$, $P^*$, and $R^*$.

We measure the shocks relative to normal output $y_e$, rather than in the proportionate terms used for money shocks, because an unexpected increase or upward shift of $50 billion a year in the investment function (at $y_e$, $R^*$) has the same effect on the *IS* curve and hence output at $P^*$ as a $50 billion unexpected increase in government spending. In either case, total spending increases by $50 billion. If government spending was expected to be $1,000 billion/year and investment spending $500 billion/year, the proportionate measures of the shocks are 5 percent (50/1000) for $g$ and 10 percent (50/500) for $i$. Yet since total spending went up by $50 billion in both cases, we should measure the shocks as being equal. If normal real output is $4,000 billion/year, then our measure of shocks relative to $y_e$ is ($50 billion/year $\div$ $4,000 billion/year) = 0.0125 or 1.25 percent in both cases. This is the appropriate measure of the shock for equal increases in the spending components. Since the effects on the *IS* curve and output are identical, the magnitude of the shocks should be reported as being identical.

However, since taxes do not change spending directly by an amount equal to the tax change, but instead indirectly via consumption spending, we do not measure tax shocks directly as a proportion of $y_e$. Recall from Chapter 4 that for any given change in taxes, we must multiply this change by the negative of the marginal propensity to consume to find the spending change associated with the tax change. An unexpected increase in taxes will lower the aggregate demand curve unexpectedly, causing lower equilibrium price and output. With an *MPC* of 0.9, an increase in taxes of $100 billion would lower consumption spending by $90 billion. The tax shock is multiplied by $-MPC$ and then divided by $y_e$ to be conformable to a government spending or investment shock. With $y_e$ of $4,000 billion/year, the unexpected increase in taxes of $100 billion/year produces a shock of $((-0.9 \times 100)/4{,}000) = -90/4{,}000 = -0.0225$ or $-2.25$ percent.[8]

An unexpected increase in taxes will lower the aggregate demand curve unexpectedly, leading to lower equilibrium price and output.

## EFFECTS ON OUTPUT AND PRICES

Once we have defined goods-market shocks, analysis of their effects is relatively easy. Consider, for example, a government spending or investment shock of 4 percent, or alternatively, an equivalent tax

---

[8]Some economists prefer to analyze the short run for given tax rates rather than for given <u>levels</u> of real taxes. While we have always referred to $t$ as the level of taxes (the dollar amount collected), there would be no substantive difference to anlayze changes in the tax rate as our tax shock since we could think of $t$ and $t^*$ as values of the tax function evaluated at $y_e$ and $P^*$. So a higher tax rate with a constant nominal income level would lead to a higher level of tax revenue $t$.

**Figure 7.16**

Effects of a Stimulative
Goods-Market Shock in the
IS–LM Model

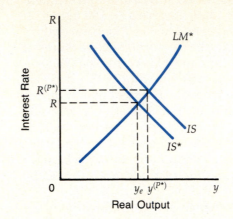

shock.[9] The unexpected increase in spending will shift the *IS* curve to the right as illustrated in Figure 7.16. As we did in Figure 7.14, we denote the equilibrium level of output if the price level equalled its expected value as $y^{(P^*)}$. Since $y^{(P^*)}$ lies to the right of $y_e$, the actual aggregate demand curve *AD* lies to the right of the expected aggregate demand curve $AD(P^*)$ and passes through the point $(y^{(P^*)}, P^*)$ just as in Figure 7.14(b). To reiterate, we know that *AD* lies to the right of $AD(P^*)$ since $P^*$ is associated with $y_e$ on the expected aggregate

---

[9]To find the tax shock equivalent to a 4 percent *g* or *i* shock, we must know the *MPC*. As was learned in the previous section, the tax shock times $-MPC$ gives us the spending change which is then divided by $y_e$ to be comparable to the measurement of a *g* or *i* shock. To have consumption spending change by an amount equal to 4 percent of normal income $y_e$, we know that taxes will change by more than 4 percent. The 4-percent change in consumption may be written as:

$$\frac{-MPC \times \Delta t}{y_e} = 4\%.$$

Rewriting this expression to solve for $\Delta t$ gives:

$$\Delta t = \frac{4\%}{-MPC} y_e.$$

If the *MPC* is equal to 0.4 in the short run, then $t = -.1y_e$, or the required drop in taxes is 10 percent of GNP, in order for the tax shock to be equivalent to a *g* or *i* shock of 4 percent. Realistically, it would be very difficult to find an example of an unexpected decrease in taxes equal to 10 percent of GNP!

demand curve $AD(P^*)$, but is associated with a higher level of income $y^{(P^*)}$ after the increase in spending. The new aggregate supply–aggregate demand equilibrium will result in a higher than normal equilibrium income $y$, and a price level $P$ that exceeds the expected price level $P^*$.[10]

If we had a negative goods-market shock, where spending fell unexpectedly, the result would be below-normal output and prices below their expected level. We see then that unexpected spending decreases have short-run effects on real output and prices analogous to restrictive money-market shocks.

Unexpected increases in government or investment spending will shift the aggregate demand curve unexpectedly, leading to higher equilibrium price and output.

## CONCLUSIONS ON AGGREGATE DEMAND SHOCKS

We can analyze shocks to the aggregate demand curve directly in terms of the *IS–LM* model. First we analyze how a particular money-market or goods-market shock—or combination of both types of shock—affects output in the *IS–LM* model if the price level were at its expected value of $P^*$. The resulting change in the *IS–LM* equilibrium level of income indicates by how much the actual aggregate demand curve $AD$ is shifted to the left or right relative to the expected aggregate demand curve $AD(P^*)$. The new short-run equilibrium level of output will change in the same direction as that predicted by the *IS–LM* change. The actual change in output, however, will be less than that predicted by the *IS–LM* model——price does not remain at $P^*$ (unless the aggregate supply curve is horizontal at $P^*$), but rises because part of the increased spending brings about higher prices rather than more goods.

Considering the shape of the usual aggregate supply curve, as aggregate demand shifts farther right, the marginal effect on real output declines—the steeper aggregate supply provides that more of the additional spending go for higher prices. This, of course, reflects the supply constraints of limited-factor (labor and capital) supplies in the short run. On the other hand, as the aggregate demand curve shifts farther to the left, the marginal effect on real output increases while the effect on prices decreases.

---

[10]If we could identify $y^{(P^*)}$ as being equal to $1.03y_e$, then the numerical analysis of Figure 7.15 would also apply to this case of a goods-market shock. Note that $y^{(P^*)} = 1.03y_e$ would indicate that with no price level rise above P*, a 4 percent spending shock would raise income only 3 percent above normal. In introductory economics classes, the change in equilibrium income given a change in spending is referred to as the *multiplier*. In this short-run case, the multiplier equals 0.75 or 3/4 as the final change in $y$ given a change in $g$, i, or $c$ is but 75 percent of the spending change.

Regarding the actual shape of the aggregate supply curve, most economists tend to believe that it has the pronounced curvature depicted in this chapter. Still we have generally found that changes in aggregate demand have different effects in the short run than in the long run (when shifts in the aggregate supply curve, due to changing expectations, technology, and factor supplies, can occur). We must postpone until later the discussion of short-run versus long-run effects. For now, we simply realize that the increasing slope of aggregate supply means that a change in nominal income will be divided into price and output changes differently according to where we are on the current aggregate supply curve. The end-of-chapter essay will briefly address the issue of the actual shape of the aggregate supply curve for the U.S.

## 7.7 THE EFFECTS OF AGGREGATE SUPPLY SHOCKS

### PRICE AND OUTPUT EFFECTS

An unexpected decrease in aggregate supply would lower equilibrium output and raise equilibrium price.

Suppose that the world price of crude oil unexpectedly rose as it did in 1973–74 and 1979–80. Such an adverse change in production costs would shift the aggregate supply curve up and to the left as in the shift from $AS(P^*)$ to $AS$ in Figure 7.17. The new equilibrium will have a higher price than expected and a lower level of output. The increase in imported oil input costs leads firms to raise prices or cut back production at any given price so that with a given aggregate demand, the firms find they cannot sell as much real output as expected.

While the case of oil price rises is perhaps the best known aggregate supply shock in recent years, one can think of many additional possibilities that could shift the aggregate supply curve unexpectedly. Natural disasters like earthquakes or hurricanes, which destroy some of the nation's productive capacity, would cause the aggregate supply curve to shift up and to the left. Unexpected labor strikes which lower industrial production could similarly shift the aggregate supply curve. What about positive aggregate supply shocks? If the weather is better than forecasted in agricultural areas so that harvests are larger than expected, we would realize an unexpected shift in aggregate supply down and to the right.

While we could discuss additional examples of aggregate supply shocks, the lesson is hopefully clear by now. It is important to realize, however, that we are analyzing the aggregate supply of the economy as a whole. A shock that occurs in one sector of the economy or in one industry could be very important for that sector, but relatively unimportant for the nation as a whole so that the aggregate supply curve is only slightly affected. For instance, an unexpected freeze in the Florida citrus groves could prove very damaging for the orange juice industry, but is not likely to significantly affect the overall level

Figure 7.17

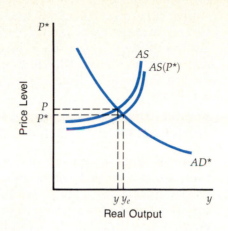

of national output. Even for well-publicized shocks, like the oil price shocks, we find experts not at all confident of their overall empirical significance. While the direction of the effect of the oil shocks is clear in principle as Figure 7.17 illustrated, the actual evidence regarding the magnitude of the effect is not so clear. Some economists argue that after controlling for aggregate demand, the effect of price controls, and other factors operative during the period of oil shocks, the depressing effects on real output lie in the range of 0 to 1 percent. Other economists have argued that the oil shocks may have decreased U.S. output by 5 percent or more in the short run.[11] This does not mean that the aggregate supply–aggregate demand analysis is useless, or even worse, misleading. If the only change occurring is an unexpected increase in oil prices, we are correct in expecting the results pictured in Figure 7.17, i.e. an unexpected decrease in aggregate supply and a higher price and lower output than expected. The evidence considered by researchers includes the multitude of "other

---

[11]In the first group are: J.R. Norsworthy, Michael J. Harper, and Kent Kunze, "The Slowdown in Productivity Growth: Analysis of Some Contributing Factors," *Brookings Papers on Economic Activity*, 1979(2), 387–421; Michael R. Darby, "The Price of Oil and World Inflation and Recession," *American Economic Review*, 72 (September 1982), 738–51; and Michael R. Darby, "The U.S. Productivity Slowdown: A Case of Statistical Myopia," *American Economic Review*, 74 (June 1984), 301–22. The argument that the oil shocks may have decreased output by a much larger amount is made by Robert H. Rasche and John A. Tatom, "Energy Price Shocks, Aggregate Supply and Monetary Policy: The Theory and the International Evidence," *Carnegie-Rochester Conference Series on Public Policy*, 14 (Spring 1981), 9–94.

factors'' that are, in fact, not constant. The aggregate demand and supply curves are constantly being buffeted by new developments, and researchers must account for these other factors in order to isolate the effect of a single shock like oil prices. While some economists may disagree, it seems likely that after accounting for these other factors, the shift in aggregate supply caused by the oil price shock was small.

## THE IMPORTANCE OF EXPECTATIONS

Expectations play a crucial role in the analysis of short-run equilibrium: we measure effects on the price level by reference to the expected price level; shocks are measured in terms of deviations between actual and expected values of policy variables such as government spending, or of behavioral functions like investment spending. In principle we could measure these expectations by appropriate surveys of the relevant people; so there is no logical flaw in our analyzing a single short period given the predetermined state of expectation. However, we want to go beyond the short run to predict the effects of present policies in future periods—periods in which the formation of expectations may be affected by present policies.

Our ability to determine the effects of current policies on future expectations depends upon the manner in which expectations are formed. If expectations were formed arbitrarily, without reference to economic fundamentals, then it would be hopeless to try to work through the effects of current policies on future expectations. The Keynesian investment function assumes that expectations are so arbitrary that any forward looking analysis is made very difficult.[12]

---

[12]According to Keynes ''Most . . . of our decisions to do something positive, the full consequences of which will be drawn out over many days to come, can only be taken as a result of animal spirits——of a spontaneous urge to action rather than inaction, and not as the outcome of a weighted average of quantitative benefits multiplied by quantitative probabilities.'' (John Maynard Keynes, *The General Theory of Employment, Interest, and Money* (Harbinger Edition), New York: Harcourt Brace, 1964, p. 161). Such arbitrary ''animal spirits'' underlie the Keynesian idea that shifts in the investment function are an important cause of fluctuations in real output. Suppose, for instance, that the expected inflation rate were subject to large, arbitrary changes and investment demand depended upon real output and the *real* interest rate $r$. Then an investment demand function written as a function of real output and the *nominal* interest rate $R$ would shift about in an arbitrary way with the shifts in inflation expectations which cause shifts in expected $r$.

Perhaps this is one reason why Keynes emphasized the short run. Today most economists believe that the public does form its expectations in a predictable way based upon the information which is available. There does remain, however, much debate as to the exact nature of the formation of expectations. Chapter 8 will address this issue along with other important topics related to our aggregate demand–aggregate supply analysis.

**SUMMARY**

1   While the *IS–LM* model provides a theory of real income determination holding prices constant, the quantity theory of money determines the price level holding real income constant.

2   Aggregate demand relates output demanded to the price level.

3   Changes in the price level can be related to changes in the nominal value of output or income by the elasticity of aggregate demand.

4   Aggregate supply relates output supplied to the price level.

5   The aggregate supply curve may be derived by relating labor market behavior to the aggregate production function.

6   The short-run aggregate supply curve indicates that when the price level is higher (lower) than expected, output will exeed (be below) normal output.

7   The Keynesian aggregate supply curve is based upon the notion that as long as there are unemployed resources, output could increase without any rise in prices. Once full employment is reached, output is at its maximum so that any increases in demand would simply raise prices.

8   If the conditions underlying the aggregate demand curve are as expected, then desired aggregate expenditures will equal normal output at the expected price level.

9   A money-market shock may arise from either the supply or demand side of the market.

10   Positive money-market shocks shift the aggregate demand curve to the right of its expected location so that equilibrium output and the price level are higher than expected. Negative shocks (when there is an unexpected excess demand for money) have just the opposite effects.

**11**   Goods-market shocks arise from unexpected changes in the underlying nonmonetary components of aggregate expenditures.

**12**   Should an element of aggregate expenditures be higher than expected, then the aggregate demand curve will lie to the right of its expected value so that the equilibrium levels of output and prices are higher than expected. Negative shocks have just the opposite effects.

**13**   The slope of the aggregate supply curve will determine how a nominal income change resulting from an aggregate demand shift is broken down into real output and price level changes.

**14**   Unexpected events that lead to changes in input prices or the ability of the economy to produce cause aggregate supply shocks.

**15**   An unexpected decrease in aggregate supply will tend to lower output $y$ and raise the price level $P$ above its expected value, the exact changes in $P$ and $y$ being determined by the slope of the aggregate demand curve. An unexpected increase in aggregate supply has just the opposite effects.

## EXERCISES

1. Compare and contrast *IS–LM* analysis with the simple quantity theory of money. What are the advantages and disadvantages of each?

2. Draw and explain the L-shaped Keynesian aggregate supply curve. Why does it have this shape? Draw and explain how shifts in this curve could occur from supply shocks. Will output necessarily increase if there is a new technology that shifts the aggregate production function?

3. Starting with an *IS–LM* diagram, explain and illustrate graphically how to derive an aggregate demand curve.

4. Briefly discuss and illustrate the determinants of aggregate supply; then combine the aggregate demand curve derived in question 3 with an aggregate supply curve to locate the equilibrium level of income and price.

5. Construct an example of a unit elastic aggregate demand curve. In other words, the price and real output combinations found along your curve should result in the nominal value of output remaining constant as price varies. Be sure to indicate clearly on your graph the actual price–output values for at least 5 points on your aggregate demand curve.

**6.** Indicate how the following shocks affect the *IS–LM* equilibrium and the aggregate demand–aggregate supply equilibrium (indicate graphically the change from the initial equilibrium resulting from the shock):

**a.** an unexpected increase in money demand,

**b.** an unexpected decrease in money supply,

**c.** an unexpected increase in taxes,

**d.** an unexpected decrease in government spending,

**e.** an earthquake destroys 10 percent of the productive capacity of the country.

**7.** Use the following information to answer the questions below:

Actual money supply ($M$) = $800 billion
Expected money supply ($M^*$) = $900 billion
Normal real output ($y_e$) = $4,000 billion
Actual investment ($i$) = $400 billion
Expected investment ($i^*$) = $380 billion
Actual government spending ($g$) = $1,000 billion
Expected government spending ($g^*$) = $1,250 billion
Marginal propensity to consume (MPC) = 0.8
Actual taxes ($t$) = $900 billion
Expected taxes ($t^*$) = $850 billion

What is the magnitude of the (a) money-supply shock? (b) investment shock? (c) government spending shock? (d) tax shock?

**8.** Construct an aggregate supply shock example.

**a.** Tell a story about an unexpected event that will shift the aggregate supply curve.

**b.** Illustrate the effect of your shock in an aggregate demand–aggregate supply diagram.

**c.** Explain carefully the determinants of the breakdown of the induced nominal income change into price versus real output changes.

## REFERENCES FOR FURTHER READING

Barro, Robert J. "Unanticipated Money, Output, and the Price Level in the United States" *Journal of Political Economy*, 86 (Aug. 1978), 549–80.

Gordon, Robert J. "The Impact of Aggregate Demand on Prices." *Brookings Papers on Economic Activity*, 3, 1975, 613–62.

Lucas, Robert E. "Some International Evidence on Output-Inflation Tradeoffs." *American Economic Review*, June 1973, 326–41.

Nordhaus, William. "Recent Developments in Price Dynamics." In O. Eckstein, ed., *The Econometrics of Price Determination*. Federal Reserve System, 1972.

Weintraub, Sidney. "The Micro-Foundations of Aggregate Demand and Supply." *Economic Journal*, 67 (Sept. 1957), 455–70.

# THE EFFECTS OF UNANTICIPATED MONEY ON REAL OUTPUT AND THE PRICE LEVEL

Chapter 7 discussed the measurement of unexpected changes in the money supply and their effects on the aggregate demand–aggregate supply equilibrium. When the money supply is higher than expected, the aggregate demand curve shifts to the right of the expected aggregate demand curve causing both the price level $P$ and real output $y$ to exceed their expected values. It was pointed out, however, that the relative magnitudes of the changes in $P$ and $y$ will depend upon the slope of the aggregate supply curve. The steeper aggregate supply, the greater the change in $P$ relative to $y$.

Since the end result hinges on the slope of aggregate supply, what does the actual aggregate supply curve look like? As our discussion on Keynesian aggregate supply and expectations-adjusted aggregate supply indicated, we may expect the aggregate supply curve to have different shapes at different times in the business cycle. Still there are empirical studies that offer insights into the effects of monetary shocks. Perhaps the best-known study is by Robert Barro.[1] Barro estimated the effect of money shocks on real output and price over the period 1948–76. Based on his findings, he constructed a simulation experiment indicating the likely effects of a money supply 1 percent greater than expected. Table E7.1 shows the effects on $y$ and $P$ of this shock.

---

[1]Robert J. Barro, "Unanticipated Money, Output, and the Price Level in the United States," *Journal of Political Economy*, 86 (August 1978), 549–80.

Table E7.1

Simulated Effects of a 1-Percent Money Shock on the Price Level and Real Output

| Year | Value of $y$ relative to normal $y_e$ | Value of $P$ relative to expected $P*$ |
|------|---------------------------------------|----------------------------------------|
| 0 | $1.0102y_e$ | $1.0018P*$ |
| 1 | $1.0118y_e$ | $.9981P*$ |
| 2 | $1.0068y_e$ | $.9985P*$ |
| 3 | $1.0025y_e$ | $1.0012P*$ |
| 4 | $y_e$ | $1.0049P*$ |
| 5 | $y_e$ | $1.0071P*$ |
| 6 | $y_e$ | $1.0083P*$ |
| 7 | $y_e$ | $1.0091P*$ |
| 8 | $y_e$ | $1.0096P*$ |
| 9 | $y_e$ | $1.0098P*$ |
| 10 | $y_e$ | $1.0099P*$ |

Source: Adapted from Barro, 1978.

The money shock occurs in year 0. Initially, the effect of the shock is largely reflected in an increase in real output. While real output increases more than 1 percent above its normal level $y_e$, the price level is only about 0.2 percent above the expected level $P^*$. This year 0 impact effect on $P$ and $y$ is the effect addressed in the aggregate demand–aggregate supply analysis of Chapter 7. Barro's evidence suggests that the short-run aggregate supply curve is quite flat—shifts in aggregate demand lead primarily to output changes rather than price changes. Note, however, that the long-run effect is quite different from the short-run effect. The increase in output resulting from the unexpectedly large money change is short lived, disappearing completely by year 4. For the price level, we see that the very small short-run impact eventually grows large, as the long-run impact is a permanent increase in the price level of approximately 1 percent ($P = 1.0099P^*$ by year 10).

Such long-run effects are very important, and we will be developing the tools needed for their dynamic analysis beginning in Chapter 9. At this point, however, we focus on the (year 0) short run, and see that the immediate short-run effects of an expansive money shock are suggestive of a Keynesian aggregate supply curve at less than full employment, as discussed in Chapter 7. Remember the flat region of the Keynesian aggregate supply curve at less than full employment? While we expect price to rise above $P^*$ as output surpasses $y_e$, so that the curve is not perfectly flat, the evidence suggests that the short-run increase in $P$ is much smaller than the realized increase in $y$.

This is not meant to suggest that there is a nice policy choice open to the monetary authorities whereby money surprises stimulate output with very small inflationary consequences. Remember that such results only hold in the short run. In the long run, the output gains vanish but we face a legacy of a rising price level. So, in effect, the short-run gain in real output is purchased at the cost of a permanently higher price level. Some economists have pointed out the motivation for a *political business cycle*, as there could be an incentive to stimulate the economy shortly before an election. Since in the short run, output increases with little rise in inflation, the political officials in power look good. The inflationary costs of such stimulative policies are realized only after the election, so the political temptation to manipulate the economy in this manner is obvious.

Robert E. Lucas, Roger C. Kormendi, and Philip G. Meguire[2] have offered evidence suggesting that even the favorable short-run benefits

[2]Robert E. Lucas, Jr., "Some International Evidence on Output-Inflation Tradeoffs," *American Economic Review*, 63 (June 1973), 326–34. Roger C. Kormendi and Philip G. Meguire, "Cross-Regime Evidence of Macroeconomic Rationality," *Journal of Political Economy*, 92 (October 1984), 875–908.

of an unexpected increase in aggregate demand may disappear if government policymakers persist in exploiting these benefits. In essence, the aggregate supply curve will be steeper for countries that have frequent significant shifts in aggregate demand. The citizens of such countries learn that policymakers have repeatedly surprised them with expansionary aggregate demand policies, so they respond to current aggregate demand shocks in a manner that results in most of the initial increase in nominal output coming from price increases rather than real output. This suggests that the real output effects of government policy aimed at cre ating expansionary money-market or goods-market shocks can occur only if such policies are seldom used.

# CHAPTER EIGHT

# AGGREGATE SUPPLY ISSUES

Chapter 7 developed the basic aggregate demand and supply framework. Now we can build upon that foundation to analyze some important issues of macroeconomic policy and theory that are essentially related to aggregate supply.

## 8.1 THE PHILLIPS CURVE AND AGGREGATE SUPPLY

### DERIVING AGGREGATE SUPPLY FROM THE PHILLIPS CURVE

**Phillips curve**
Graphic relationship between the rate of unemployment and the rate of inflation

Introduced in the late 1950s, the **Phillips curve**, a graphical device, was developed to relate changes in the price level to the level of unemployment in the economy. Undoubtedly, the popularity of the Phillips curve was related to its compatibility with the Keynesian aggregate supply curve. Specifically, the Phillips curve, as popularly used, relates the rate of inflation to the unemployment rate in a particular period.[1]

Throughout the 1960s, the Phillips curve was thought to indicate a stable relationship between inflation and unemployment as illustrated in Figure 8.1. The downward slope of the curve indicates a negative tradeoff—you can have lower inflation by accepting higher unemployment, or lower unemployment at the cost of higher inflation. For instance, Figure 8.1 indicates that on our particular Phillips

Figure 8.1

A Hypothetical Phillips Curve

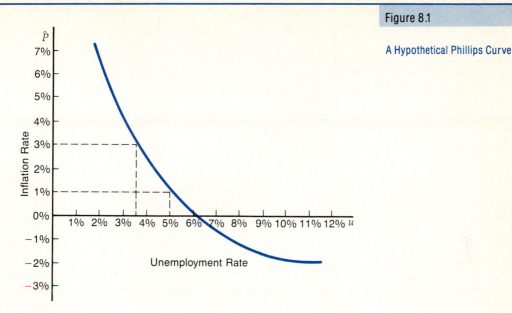

curve, an inflation rate of 1 percent per year is associated with a 5 percent unemployment rate, while an inflation rate of 3 percent is associated with an unemployment rate of 3.5 percent.

Comparing the Phillips curve of Figure 8.1 with the Keynesian aggregate supply curve of Figure 8.2, we note some differences. The Keynesian aggregate supply has prices and output varying until full employment is reached. With full employment, only the price level varies as output is constant at $y_F$. The Phillips curve indicates that regardless of the unemployment rate, decreases in the rate can be purchased at the cost of higher inflation. The bend in the Phillips

---

[1]As introduced in A. W. Phillips, "The Relation between Unemployment and the Rate of Change in Money Wage Rates in the United Kingdom, 1861–1957," *Econometrica*, 25 (Nov. 1958), 283–99, the curve plotted the unemployment rate against the growth rate of nominal wages. There was, however, a neglected article that appeared much earlier, dealing with the relationship between unemployment and inflation: Irving Fisher, "A Statistical Relation between Unemployment and Price Changes," *International Labor Review*, 13 (June 1926), 785–92; reprinted posthumously as "I Discovered the Phillips Curve," *Journal of Political Economy*, 81 (Mar./Apr. 1973), 496–502.

Figure 8.2

The Keynesian Aggregate Supply Curve

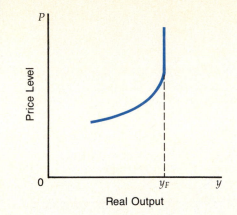

The Phillips curve and the Keynesian aggregate supply curve indicate that a trade-off exists between unemployment and inflation.

curve takes us closer to the spirit of Keynesian aggregate supply—we see that the lower the unemployment rate, the greater the increase in inflation associated with any further reduction in unemployment. Without defining the *full employment rate of unemployment* as some particular number, we can see that as the unemployment rate drops, the implied aggregate supply curve would become more nearly vertical, approaching the extreme case of Figure 8.2.

We can, in fact, use the statistical relationship given by the Phillips curve to derive the underlying aggregate supply curve. Since the aggregate supply curve relates prices and real income or output, we must consider the relationship between the unemployment rate and real income in order to link the Phillips curve to an aggregate supply curve. In 1962 the late Arthur M. Okun of the Brookings Institution published a paper that persuasively argued the existence of a stable relationship between unemployment and real output that has come to be called **Okun's Law**: for each 1 percentage point the unemployment rate is above (below) normal, real output will be approximately 3 percentage points below (above) normal.[2] To see this relationship better, we can measure the unemployment rate $u$ as a decimal num-

**Okun's Law**
For every 1 percent that unemployment varies from full employment, real GNP will vary by 3 percent in the opposite direction

---

[2]Arthur M. Okun, "Potential GNP: Its Measurement and Significance," *1962 Proceedings of the Business and Economic Statistics Section of the American Statistical Association*, 98–104. More recent estimates suggest that the relationship between output and unemployment is closer to 2 to 1 than Okun's 3 to 1. Since the nature of the relationship rather than its precise measurement is what is important here, we use the traditional value for illustrative purposes.

ber (5 percent $= 0.05$) and denote the normal level of unemployment as $u_N$. Okun's Law can then be used to find real income or output as:

$$y = [1 - 3(u - u_N)]y_e \qquad (8.1)$$

where equilibrium income $y_e$ is the level of real output corresponding to the normal rate of unemployment and $u - u_N$ is the deviation of the unemployment rate from its normal value, or the **cyclical unemployment rate**.

It is best to think of Okun's Law—like the Phillips curve—as an average statistical relationship. This means that equation (8.1) does not hold in all instances. Okun's Law is not a hard and fast relationship that can be rigorously derived from the underlying determinants of the economy's output. But it does hold as a general relationship between the cyclical unemployment rate and real output, and therefore can be used to approximate the aggregate supply function underlying a Phillips curve.

The final step toward our aggregate supply function is relating the current price level $P$ to last year's price level $P_{-1}$ and the rate of inflation $\hat{P}$. This relationship may be expressed as:

$$P = (1 + \hat{P})P_{-1} \qquad (8.2)$$

So if $\hat{P}$, the inflation rate, is 1 percent per year (or 0.01 in decimal terms), given last year's price level $P_{-1}$, we find the current price level as $P = (1 + 0.01)P_{-1} = 1.01P_{-1}$.[3]

Now let's use equation (8.1) and our Phillips curve depicted in Figure 8.1 to derive the aggregate supply curve. Let's suppose that the normal unemployment rate $u_N$ is 5 percent. If the actual unemployment rate is also 5 percent, then $y$ would equal $y_e$ and the inflation rate would be 1 percent according to Figure 8.1. By equation (8.2), this implies $P = 1.01P_{-1}$. If $u$ were 6 percent, then the cyclical unemployment rate would be $0.06 - 0.05 = 0.01$, or 1 percent; and by Okun's Law or equation (8.1), $y$ would equal $.97y_e$. The Phillips curve of Figure 8.1 indicates that 6 percent unemployment is consistent with zero inflation so that $P = P_{-1}$. Table 8.1 lists alternative combinations of the cyclical unemployment rate and the corresponding $y$ and $\hat{P}$. Plotting these various combinations yields the aggregate supply curve pictured in Figure 8.3.

**cyclical unemployment rate**
Unemployment resulting from movements of the business cycle

---

[3]If the period from $P_{-1}$ to $P$ is not a calendar year, $\hat{P}$ must be multiplied by the length of the period in years to convert it to the percentage growth in one period (this is just the reverse of the way we converted the interest rate on a bond maturing in less than a year into an annual rate of interest in Chapter 3).

**Table 8.1**

Calculating Points on the
Aggregate Supply Curve

| If $u$ is: | Then u − $u_N$ is: (assuming $u_N = .05$) | By Okun's Law $y$ is: | And from the Phillips Curve (Fig. 8.1) $\hat{P}$ is: |
|---|---|---|---|
| 3-1/2% | −1-1/2% | 1.045 $y_e$ | 3% |
| 5% | 0 | $y_e$ | 1% |
| 6% | 1% | .97 $y_e$ | 0 |
| 7-1/3% | 2-1/3% | .93 $y_e$ | −1% |
| 12% | 7% | .79 $y_e$ | −2% |

**Figure 8.3**

The Aggregate Supply Curve
Implied by the Phillips Curve
of Figure 8.1

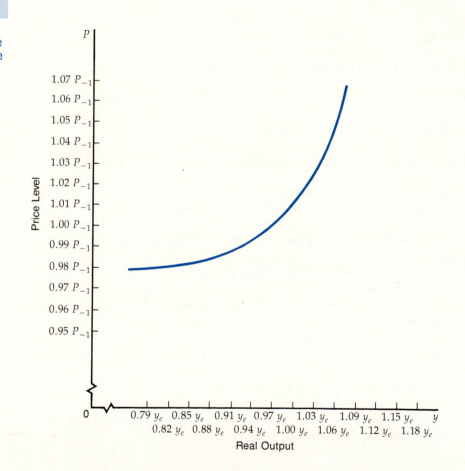

This aggregate supply curve is consistent with Keynesian macroeconomics. Note that as the economy passes beyond the normal
level of output $y_e$, equal increments in output are associated with
larger and larger price increases as the curve grows steeper. On the
other hand, when the economy is in a recession with high unemploy-

ment, increases in output are associated with very small changes in prices. This consistency of the Phillips curve with Keynesian macroeconomics resulted in the widespread popularity of the Phillips curve for analysis in the 1960s.

Before discussing the weaknesses of the Phillips curve, we should note that to locate exactly the aggregate supply curve in $Py$ space we must know the values of $P_{-1}$ and $y_e$. The past price level $P_{-1}$ was determined in the past period by the same sorts of factors that determine the current price level $P$ this period. In Chapter 6 we discussed the determinants of the long-run equilibrium price level. For our analysis of the current period, we can take $P_{-1}$ to have whatever value it in fact had. Thus the current price level is strongly related to past events, although not as tightly as in the approximate Keynesian aggregate supply curve of Figure 7.13, where price is unchanging at less than full employment. Long-run equilibrium output $y_e$ is given by the interaction of the economy's resources with the aggregate production function as discussed in Chapter 6.

## THE EXPECTATIONS-ADJUSTED PHILLIPS CURVE

In the 1970s it became apparent that there was no stable Phillips curve relationship between inflation and unemployment as we depicted in Figure 8.1. Although the Phillips curve appears to be stable for certain periods of time for some countries, the curve shifts around so much that for the post-World War II period as a whole, there is essentially no statistical relationship between unemployment and inflation rates as Figure 8.4 illustrates.[4]

The analysis can be modified to give the Phillips curve more stability and more applicability to the data by replacing $\hat{P}$ on the vertical axis with $\hat{P} - \hat{P}^*$, where $\hat{P}^*$ is the expected inflation rate.[5] We shall find, as we progress further into the text, that the role of expectations of macroeconomic variables has become a crucial element of modern macro analysis. $\hat{P}^*$ is the rate of inflation that indi-

---

[4]Milton Friedman, an early critic of the Phillips curve analysis, discusses the shifting nature of the Phillips curve in "Nobel Lecture: Inflation and Unemployment," *Journal of Political Economy*, 85 (June 1977), 451–72.

[5]We still do not expect such a relationship between unemployment and unexpected inflation ($\hat{P} - \hat{P}^*$) to be precise. As was mentioned earlier, the Phillips curve, Okun's Law, and the aggregate supply curve discussed here all provide reasonable approximations to more complex relationships among inflation, output, and other variables which will be addressed in Chapters 11 through 13. It is not possible to find simple relationships of the sort examined here that will be perfectly stable and precise.

**Figure 8.4**

Plot of Observed Inflation and Unemployment Rate Combinations, 1947–83: The Shifting Phillips Curve

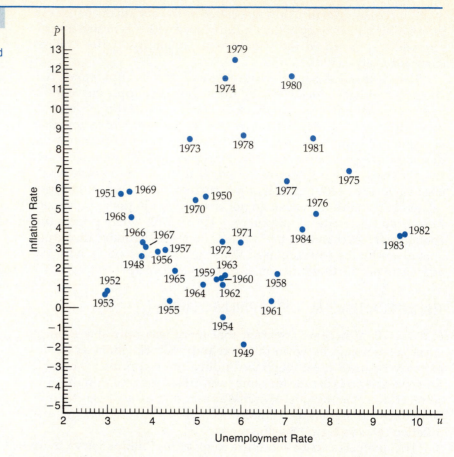

viduals expected for the current period based on what they knew in the previous period.

An *expectations-adjusted Phillips curve* is presented in Figure 8.5. We maintain the earlier assumption of 5 percent being the normal level of unemployment, but note that the unemployment rate is equal to 5 percent only if the inflation rate is correctly anticipated or $\hat{P} - \hat{P}^* = 0$. If the inflation rate is higher than expected, then the unemployment rate will fall below 5 percent, while unexpectedly low inflation will be associated with higher than normal unemployment rates.[6]

---

[6]In Chapter 12 we will again see a Phillips curve similar to this one associated with a Lucas aggregate supply function (named after the University of Chicago economist, Robert E. Lucas). While the analysis developed here is quite close to the Lucas function, we will put off a discussion of this well known approach to aggregate supply until Chapter 12.

Figure 8.5

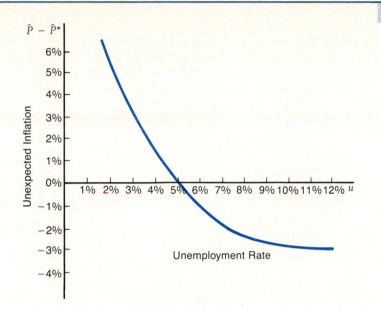

For any given rate of expected inflation, we could hold $\hat{P}^*$ constant and draw a simple Phillips curve diagram relating $\hat{P}$ to $u$. For instance, if we substituted 1 percent for $\hat{P}^*$ in Figure 8.5, we could then examine how $(\hat{P} - .01)$ related to $u$ and draw a simple Phillips curve, with the vertical axis labeled $\hat{P}$, applicable only with an expected inflation rate of 1 percent. In fact, the aggregate supply curve of Figure 8.3 is consistent with just such an expectations-adjusted Phillips curve with $\hat{P}^*$ equal to 1 percent. When the actual inflation rate is 1 percent, this is equal to the expected rate and so the unemployment rate equals the normal rate of 5 percent and the equilibrium income $y_e$ will be realized.

The expectations-adjusted Phillips curve is consistent with the aggregate supply curve analysis discussed in Section 7.3. Remember the short-run *AS* curve indicated that when the price level is higher (lower) than expected, output will exceed (be below) the normal output. Why does $(P - P^*)$ have the effect on $u$ illustrated in Figure 8.5, or the effect on $y$ illustrated by the aggregate supply curve of Chapter 7? In Chapter 7, we considered the effects on income of $(P - P^*)$ to arise in the labor market as labor supply was based on $P^*$. Now we will proceed beyond this simple labor market analysis to a more detailed discussion of sources of the $(P - P^*)$ effect on $u$ and $y$ suggested by modern macroeconomists.

$P^*$ is the price level expected by households and business firms. Such expectations regarding the current price level are formed last period after considering any available factors that may aid the forecast. While macroeconomists are still debating exactly how expectations are formed (we will consider further the issue of price expectations in future chapters), for our present purposes it is sufficient to say that the current expected price $P^*$ is given by the joint decisions of households and business firms. Why do unexpectedly high prices increase real income and unexpectedly low prices decrease $y$? As is often the case in macroeconomics, there are some debatable issues here, so we will consider a number of factors which researchers have suggested as important. It is good to remember that different economists will emphasize different factors. As a result, it is important to be open-minded toward the various arguments and yet retain a healthy degree of skepticism toward those who would reject out of hand any approach which differs from their own.

## 8.2 SEARCH UNEMPLOYMENT

In Chapter 7, we derived the aggregate supply curve from labor market behavior. There is a good reason for using this approach. The most obvious way for output to be changed in the short run is through changes in the fraction of the labor force employed—or its complement, the unemployment rate. The labor input must vary since the other factor of production, capital, is fixed in the short run. For most industries it is easier to hire or lay off workers than to alter the quantity of machines and factories employed.

One of the ways in which unexpected prices affect real output or production is through the behavior of the unemployed. As we learned in Chapter 3, there are two types of individuals counted as unemployed: those actively searching for a job and those not searching because they are waiting to be recalled from temporary layoffs. In this section we will concentrate on the behavior of the searchers while section 8.3 will consider the determinants of layoff unemployment.

The unemployment of productive resources occurs whenever the owner of these resources takes time to search for a higher valued use rather than accept just any offer, no matter how low. While we primarily measure the unemployment of workers, we could just as easily think about the unemployment of factories, houses, apartments, machines, or automobiles which are held out of use while their owner searches for an acceptable offer or for someone willing to meet the owner's asking price. If it were costless to match resources with their highest valued uses, then no such search would occur; but since free information is as rare as free lunches, search unemployment is common for productive resources. You would never spend any time searching for a new job if you knew immediately which employer valued your services most highly. You would immediately go to work for this employer because no one else would pay you more. But this is not the way the world works. Since you do not have perfect knowledge of all potential job offers, it pays to spend some time in a job search where you investigate your alternatives.

A spell of search unemployment can begin because someone has just entered the labor force or because he or she has left another job. There are many reasons why individuals leave a previous job, and such change can be initiated by either the employee or the employer. In normal times, both the new entrants and the job leavers will provide a steady stream of people beginning to search for a job. The normal **search unemployment rate**—the number of actively searching unemployed people measured as a fraction of the labor force—will reflect two basic factors: (1) the fraction of the labor force beginning to search in any given month, the **search flow**, and (2) the number of months it takes on average to find and begin a new job, the **search duration**. Suppose, for example, that 2 percent of the labor force begins searching each month and that, on average, it takes about 2 1/2 months to find a job. The normal level of the search unemployment rate would be (2 percent/month) × (2 1/2 months) = 5 percent. Figure 8.6 summarizes the determinants of the search unemployment rate. Changes in either the search flow, from 2 percent, or the search duration, from 2 1/2 months, would cause changes in the search unemployment rate. Let's consider in more detail, then, these two determinants of the rate of search unemployment.

> The search unemployment rate is the product of the search flow and search duration.
>
> **search unemployment rate**
> The number of unemployed actively looking for work measured as a fraction of the labor force
>
> **search flow**
> The newly unemployed beginning their job search each month, measured as a fraction of the labor force
>
> **search duration**
> The number of months, on average, it takes the unemployed to find work

## NORMAL SEARCH FLOW

The normal level of the search flow reflects demographic factors—characteristics of the working population like age, sex, and experience. These demographic characteristics determine both the rate at which people first enter the labor force as well as the normal amount of shifting around from job to job. We would expect, for instance, young workers to be more likely to leave a job in any given month than more experienced workers, since the more experienced worker is more likely to have found a suitable job (from the viewpoint of the employer as well as the employee).

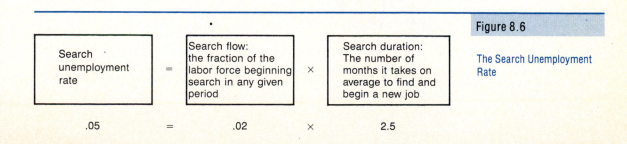

**Figure 8.6**

The Search Unemployment Rate

| Search unemployment rate | = | Search flow: the fraction of the labor force beginning search in any given period | × | Search duration: The number of months it takes on average to find and begin a new job |
|---|---|---|---|---|
| .05 | = | .02 | × | 2.5 |

Figure 8.7 presents estimates of the number of people who become unemployed each year as a percentage of the labor force. Note that someone who had two or more spells of unemployment would be counted more than once in this measure.[7] The general upward trend present in Figure 8.7 provides evidence of the impact of both the ''baby boom'' generation and the rising labor-force participation of women on the normal level of search unemployment. These younger, new entrants into the labor force will have a higher associated search flow than more experienced workers. During the early 1950s and the middle and latter 1960s, the Korean and Vietnamese wars reduced the fraction beginning search, especially among young males. The recessions occurring at the end of these wars increased the number of searchers temporarily.

**Figure 8.7**

Percentage of the Labor Force That Experienced Unemployment—The Search Flow

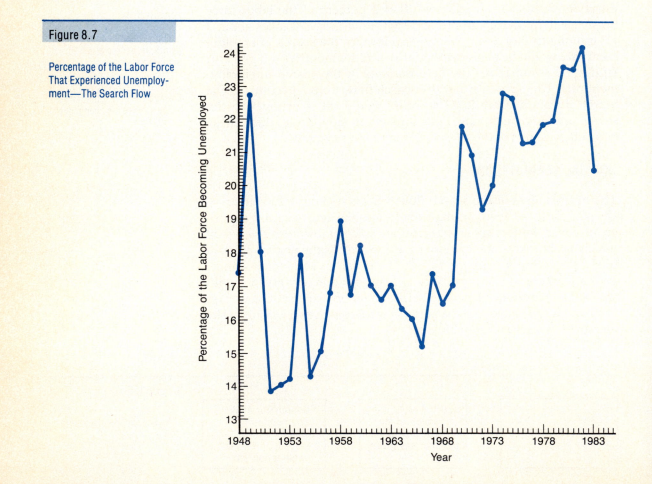

## NORMAL SEARCH DURATION

In a sense, use of the term "unemployment" in the context of job search is misleading. While someone searching for a job is called unemployed, economists think of the unemployed as employing their resources in the productive activity of producing information about higher valued uses of their talents. As in other economic decision making activities, we analyze the decision to continue searching in terms of the marginal benefits versus the marginal costs of continued search.

John J. McCall has shown that the optimal strategy for looking for a new job is **sequential search**.[8] Sequential search is a strategy that people have applied to many activities, including the search for a job or a spouse, since long before economists learned to express it formally. Sequential job search involves choosing a minimal acceptable wage offer and then visiting potential employers until an offer is received which equals or exceeds this **reservation wage** $W^r$.[9]

The basic idea of sequential search is to continue the job search until the expected gain from further search (the marginal benefit) is less than the cost of that search (the marginal cost). The reservation wage is chosen so that the expected marginal value of further search is just equal to the expected marginal cost of further search. Regard-

**sequential search**
Balancing further search (i.e., higher wages) against search costs (time and aggravation)

**reservation wage**
Minimally acceptable wage offer in a sequential search

---

[7]Also note that if we measure search flow in per-year units, we should measure search duration as a fraction of a year. For instance, our previous example of 2 percent per month and 2 1/2 months would correspond to annual figures of (24%/year) × (0.208 year) = 5%.

[8]See J. J. McCall, "Economics of Information and Job Search," *Quarterly Journal of Economics*, 84 (February 1970), 113–26; and S. A. Lippman and J. J. McCall, "The Economics of Job Search: A Survey," *Economic Inquiry* (in two parts), 14 (June and September 1976), 155–89, 347–68.

[9]The reservation wage may be adjusted somewhat over time as searching provides new information about the wage distribution being offered and the searcher uses up his or her resources. We are using wages as the single measure of job desirability. In practice they would have to be adjusted for the value of any differences in working conditions. All other things equal, a worker would prefer a higher to a lower wage. When all other things are not equal, the wage must be adjusted to compensate for the differences. A firm offering good working conditions and fringe benefits can pay a lower wage than a firm offering poor working conditions and fringe benefits.

ing the marginal value of further search, the present value of the increase in wage obtained is the specific gain. But the increase expected from further search should fall as the searcher rejects higher and higher wage offers. The most important cost of further search is the wages foregone by searching instead of working. This will increase as the searcher rejects higher and higher offers.

Search continues until a wage is offered which exceeds or equals the reservation wage ($W \geq W^r$). By following this procedure, a worker who is lucky enough to find a good job quickly will not waste time on further search. Nor will an unlucky worker give up looking for a good job just because of a string of bad luck.

Figure 8.8 illustrates the frequency with which a particular searching worker expects to receive a particular wage offer by visiting a large number of firms. The height of the bell-shaped curve at any given wage measures the probability of receiving an offer of that wage. The shape of the curve then represents the searcher's beliefs about the likelihood of receiving various wages on any particular visit to an employer. The shaded area to the right of the reservation wage $W^r$ represents the probability, which the searcher believes, of receiving an acceptable offer where $W \geq W^r$.[10] If this area to the right of the reservation wage equalled half of the bell, and there was no probability of receiving no offer at all, then there would be a 50 percent probability of receiving an acceptable offer on a single visit. The shaded area to the right of $W^r$ is obviously less than half the area under the curve so that the worker assigns a probability less than 50 percent to being offered the reservation wage on a single visit.[11] The higher the reservation wage, the further to the right is $W^r$ in Figure 8.8 and, of course, the lower the probability of receiving an offer of $W^r$ or better.

A well known formula from statistics tells us that the expected number of visits until an acceptable offer is received is $l/h$ if $h$ is the probability of an acceptable offer on any one visit. Suppose that on average the reservation wage is chosen so that the probability of an acceptable offer on any one visit is only 1 in 50 or 0.02. Then the

---

[10]The thick vertical axis allows for a positive probability that no offer will be received at all. The sum of this probability and the area under the curve must sum to 100 percent or 1.

[11]If the probability of no offer is zero, half of the area under the curve is 0.5, or 50 percent. If there is a positive probability of no offer, even half the area under the curve would correspond to a probability less than 50 percent.

Figure 8.8

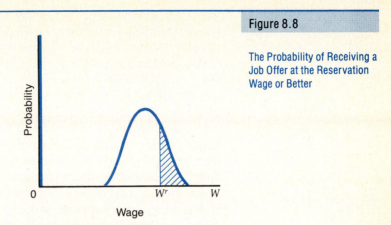

expected number of visits is 50.[12] If the average searcher can visit 20 firms per month, then the normal duration of search would be $(1/0.02) \times (1/20 \text{ month}) = 2.5$ months, as we had previously assumed. Sequential search theory, then, helps us understand why people on average will be unemployed for a significant amount of time (although the time for each individual may vary greatly).

It is interesting to note that search unemployment theory provides a solid economic basis for income-maximizing individuals to choose periods of unemployment. Rather than being shiftless or lazy, individuals who remain unemployed do so because they are able to search for the highest valued use of their services. If we want to ensure that the economy utilizes its resources most efficiently, we must recognize the search aspects of unemployment and allow individuals to search as long as the marginal benefits exceed costs.

## CYCLICAL FLUCTUATIONS IN SEARCH DURATION

In the previous section, our calculations of the normal search duration assumed that people had a good idea about the kinds of wage offers firms were making. During normal times this is not a bad assumption, but during times dominated by unexpected events,

---

[12]This is just a bit higher than the probability of drawing a particular card from a deck on any one try when the card is replaced and the deck is shuffled after each try. In our job search example, it may be that most people would be lucky enough to find a job in fewer than 50 visits, but the average is increased by the very unlucky, who take much longer.

searchers may be surprised by actual wage offers. Suppose, for instance, that the money supply was greater than expected. The shift outward in the *LM* curve would cause the equilibrium income level to rise, and as a result, firms would demand more labor to increase production. Since the money supply increase was unexpected, so too will be the resulting increase in the demand for labor. Figure 8.9 illustrates this unexpectedly good labor market with the actual distribution of wage offers larger and to the right of the expected distribution. In other words, the average unemployed worker searching for a job will choose a reservation wage $W^r$ based on the expected distribution of wage offers reflected in the lower distribution. Yet the actual distribution differs from that expected so that the probability of receiving an acceptable wage offer is actually higher than the worker realizes. In fact, we see that for the case illustrated, $W^r$ occurs at approximately the highest point on the new distribution, so that $W^r$ is, in fact, the most likely wage to be offered on any single visit to an employer.

Since the expected search duration is the inverse of this probability of an acceptable offer times the average time spent on one visit, a higher than normal probability implies a lower than normal search duration. How would things differ if spending and labor demand are less than expected? We could just reverse the labels on the two bell-shaped curves of Figure 8.9 to illustrate this case. The searcher would now find that the probability of an acceptable offer is actually lower than expected (or realized by the searcher). Since the worker bases the reservation wage on the expected distribution of wage offers, the now lower actual distribution will result in a longer than normal time for a searcher to find an acceptable job.

**Figure 8.9**

The Difference Between the Actual and Expected Wage Distribution When the Demand for Labor Is Higher than Expected

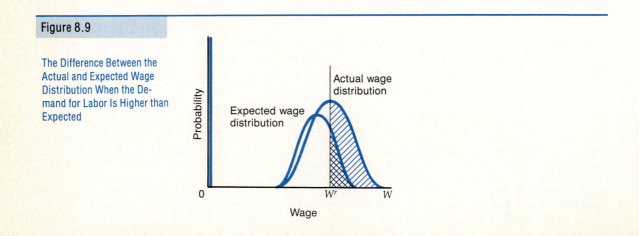

In summary, for a given search flow, the search duration, and hence the search unemployment rate, falls (rises) when total spending is unexpectedly high (low).[13] Such unexpectedly high spending will be reflected in unexpectedly high wages, producers' prices, and ultimately the prices of goods and services sold to final users. We now have an explanation of the relationship between unexpected inflation and unemployment pictured in the expectations-adjusted Phillips curve and unexpected price level and real output in the aggregate supply curve: unexpectedly high inflation is associated with a below normal (search) unemployment rate.

## CYCLICAL FLUCTUATIONS IN SEARCH FLOW

The story behind the expectations-adjusted Phillips curve and aggregate supply curve can be developed beyond the search duration effects just covered. Cyclical fluctuations are also seen in the fraction of the labor force who begin looking for a job, the search flow. At the same time as the expected duration of search decreases (increases), so too does the search flow decrease (increase). Thus changes in search flow reinforce the effects of search duration on the search unemployment rate following an unexpected change in aggregate spending. This cyclical movement in the search flow occurs primarily because of the response of business firms to changing goods-market conditions. When demand for goods is lower than expected so that demand for labor is correspondingly lower, firms tend to weed out less satisfactory workers. These displaced workers then start searching. When total spending is higher than expected, demand for labor is correspondingly higher so that firms tend to hold on to their current employees in order to meet the increased demand. Overall then, when total spending and labor demand are higher than expected, both search duration and search flow fall, causing the search unemployment rate to fall; when aggregate expenditures are lower than expected, just the opposite occurs.

> When aggregate expenditures are higher (lower) than expected, the search unemployment rate falls (rises) and output increases (decreases).

Realistically, matters are not quite so clear cut and clean as we have depicted so far. The increase in "involuntary" separations (firings and layoffs) during a recession is offset somewhat by a decrease in "voluntary" separations (quits). A more important offset to the tendency for the search flow to increase in a recession is termed the **discouraged worker** phenomenon. During recessions, the labor force

> **discouraged worker**
> A worker who is no longer looking for work and thus no longer a member of the labor force

---

[13]The dynamics of this adjustment process is considered in detail in Chapter 12. For now, it is enough to know the direction of change.

grows less rapidly than usual due to the withdrawal of those workers who are very pessimistic about their chances of finding an acceptable wage offer. During booms, the labor force grows more rapidly than usual as these previously discouraged workers enter the labor force with the increased likelihood of finding an acceptable job.

Because of offsetting movements in quits and labor force participation, the predominant cyclical effect on the search flow is variation in involuntary separations. Taken as a whole, cyclical movements in search flow reinforce the effects of search duration in changing the search unemployment rate. We see, then, that the cyclical influence of unexpected changes in aggregate expenditures on the search unemployment rate can be used to explain the short-run aggregate supply curve. When spending is higher than expected, prices and wages are higher than expected. The unexpected increase in wage offers leads to a lower unemployment rate and higher levels of output. While this seems like a reasonable explanation of the positive relation between unexpected prices and real income, it is most certainly not the only explanation.

## 8.3 INVENTORIES AND TEMPORARY LAYOFFS

### AN OVERVIEW

By holding inventories and allowing inventories to vary, business firms are able to follow the most efficient or cost-effective production strategy. The role of inventories is particularly critical for durable-goods producers. While sales may fluctuate both seasonally and randomly, a firm may find a constant rate of production to be preferred. In this case, inventories will fluctuate around the constant rate of production. When sales are relatively low, inventories will rise and when sales are high, inventories fall. These inventory fluctuations are necessary when prices are set—as they often are—for a period of some months at a level which will, on average, balance sales and production over the long run. Then instead of prices adjusting to every short-run fluctuation in sales relative to production, falling as sales fall and rising as sales rise to equate sales to the more stable flow of production, inventories serve as buffers between sales and output. In fact, the inventory holdings of business firms are not unlike the cash balances held by households. The household uses its holdings of cash to balance out the difference between income receipts and expenditures while the firm uses its holdings of inventories so that production need not correspond exactly to sales.

Sometimes a firm will find that its inventory level builds up to greater than desirable levels, usually because sales were overestimated at prevailing prices. When this occurs, firms will generally do two things: cut back production and lower price. Both of these moves will tend to lower inventories to a desirable level.

When firms cut production, there must be adjustments in the labor force. Some workers may be switched from production to maintenance work, others may find their hours worked reduced, while still others may be forced to take temporary layoffs. A *temporary layoff* may mean that the workers will be without work for a specified number of weeks, or it may mean that they will be recalled only after conditions improve. The laid-off workers will usually find it to their advantage to await the recall to their old jobs rather than to search for a new employer. This is because both the workers and firms may have a substantial investment in training and skills that can only be useful if the employment relationship continues in the long run. Since workers on temporary layoff do not generally begin searching, we did not include temporary layoff unemployment in the discussion of search unemployment in Section 8.2 above.

The sequence of events is this: Demand is less than expected so inventories build up. Then firms cut prices and use temporary layoffs as one of the means to reduce production. Now we can relate this behavior to the expectations-adjusted aggregate supply curve. As inventories build up, unemployment rises, output falls, and the inflation rate falls so that prices are lower than normal or expected. These facts are consistent with the analysis of the downward sloped expectations-adjusted Phillips curve and an upward sloped short-run aggregate supply curve as portrayed in Figures 8.5 and 7.8, respectively.

When aggregate expenditures are higher (lower) than expected, inventories are unexpectedly low (high) so production increases (decreases).

## CYCLICAL BEHAVIOR OF INVENTORIES

In normal times then, some firms will have higher than desired inventories and some will have inventories lower than desired, but these deviations from desired levels will average out. A restrictive monetary policy that unexpectedly reduces the growth of the money supply will bring about unexpectedly low average sales at the expected equilibrium price. This will result in a build-up of inventories throughout the economy. As discussed in the last section, we expect the layoff unemployment rate to rise as a result of the inventory build-up. Figure 8.10 illustrates this link between inventories and unemployment by comparing how the ratio of inventories to sales changes over time relative to the layoff unemployment rate. Figure 8.10 emphasizes the importance of inventories as a transmission mechanism between changes in aggregate demand and the unemployment rate (and ultimately prices and output).

**Figure 8.10**

Comparing the Ratio of Inventories to Sales and the Layoff Unemployment Rate

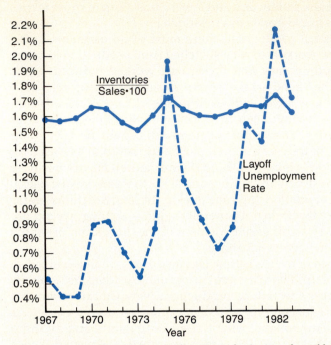

**Sources:** Inventory-sales ratio for manufacturing trade. Average of monthly data, Series no. 77, *Business Conditions Digest*. Layoff unemployment rate from Mark W. Plant, "On the Measurement of Disequilibrium in the Labor Force," U.C.L.A. Institute of Industrial Relations, June 1983.

## TEMPORARY LAYOFFS AND EQUILIBRIUM CONTRACT THEORY

Researchers have recently argued that temporary layoffs are similar to a mass vacation when a firm's demand for labor is relatively low due either to seasonal factors or to excessive inventories of finished goods. The research addressing this issue has focused on the economic rationale underlying long-term labor contracts and is referred to as **equilibrium contract theory**.[14]

equilibrium contract theory
The role of long-term labor contracts in explaining temporary layoffs.

Layoffs result from decreases in sales and increases in inventories. Since inventories involve costs of storage, interest, and deterioration, the firm has an incentive to minimize inventory excesses. When inventories are high relative to sales, the value of labor to the firm may be less than the value to workers of their time on layoff. There is some point beyond which it is preferable to not work at all rather than to work part-time. For example, not working avoids commuting costs and makes one eligible for unemployment benefits. The firm will have an incentive to consider these factors since employees are concerned with the long-run benefits of working for any particular employer. Of course the firm that uses temporary layoffs must make up the difference between the value of leisure while on layoff and the wages lost if it is to keep old employees and attract new. Unemployment benefits,[15] along with higher wages while working, can make up the difference.

The underlying concept for equilibrium contract theorists is that it makes sense for workers to concentrate their work hours in periods when they are most valuable and take more of their leisure at other times. As a result, normal shifts in demand for the output of individual firms will be associated with fluctuations in average hours worked and some temporary layoffs at individual firms. Cyclical variations in the layoff unemployment rate and average hours worked in the whole economy occur only if there are unexpected changes in aggregate expenditures. These economywide fluctuations are the effects we relate to the aggregate supply curve, not the layoffs at individual firms that occur during normal times as some firms prosper while others wane.

Finally, it should be realized that temporary layoffs differ from permanent layoffs. Temporary layoffs occur in response to undesirably high inventories. For instance, if General Motors has unacceptably high inventories of Cadillacs, a production line may be shut down for 2 weeks. When these inventories are drawn down to an acceptable level, workers will be recalled. Permanent layoffs result from a desire to permanently reduce the size of a firm's labor force in the face of a perceived permanent reduction in demand. If the demand for Cadil-

---

[14]Optimal long-run labor contracts as an explanation of temporary layoffs have been used by Costas Azariadis, "Implicit Contracts and Underemployment Equilibria," *Journal of Political Economy*, 83 (December 1975), 1183–1202; Martin N. Baily, "On the Theory of Layoffs and Unemployment," *Econometrica*, 45 (July 1977), 1043–63; and Martin Feldstein, "Temporary Layoffs in the Theory of Unemployment," *Journal of Political Economy*, 84 (October 1976), 937–57. For a recent survey of this literature, see Costas Azariadis, "Implicit Contracts and Related Topics: A Survey," in Z. Hornstein, *et al.*, (eds.) *The Economics of the Labour Market* (London: Her Majesty's Stationery Office, 1981); and Sherwin Rosen, "Implicit Contracts: A Survey," *Journal of Economic Literature*, 23 (September 1985), 1144–75.

[15]Unemployment benefits are largely paid by the individual firm. To the extent that the cost is shifted to other taxpayers, this provides an additional incentive to the individual firm to use temporary layoffs. On the importance of this incentive, see Robert H. Topel, "On Layoffs and Unemployment Insurance," *American Economic Review*, 73 (September 1983), 541–59.

lacs is too low to warrant the continued offering of the autos, a plant may be permanently closed. The analysis of such permanently laid-off workers was considered with those who are actively searching for new jobs in Section 8.2.

## STAGGERED WAGE CONTRACTS AND AGGREGATE SUPPLY

The equilibrium contract theory just presented implies that workers will undergo temporary layoffs only if the value to them of their time and government-paid unemployment benefits exceeds the value to the firm of their marginal product if working.[16] Some economists believe instead that since wages are often set by long-term contracts, firms compare the value of labor's marginal product with the previously contracted wage rate so that unexpected variations in aggregate expenditures, and hence ultimately in the derived demand for labor, can cause layoffs and a reduction in employment as illustrated in Figure 8.11. In Figure 8.11 the vertical axis measures the wage paid to labor while the horizontal axis measures the quantity of labor. The horizontal supply curve indicates that the firm can hire all the workers it wants at the nominal wage $W^*$, where the expected labor demand curve is $D_1$ at which $\ell_1$ workers would be employed, giving normal employment of the labor force (assume that $\ell_1$ is the normal level of employment). If the actual demand curve turned out to be $D_2$, then only $\ell_2$ workers would be demanded, and the difference ($\ell_1 - \ell_2$) would be reflected in temporary layoffs, shortened working hours, or both.

The basic idea underlying Figure 8.11 is that when demand for the firm's output is less than expected, the firm will demand less labor at any given wage. Since the wage $W^*$ is set by long-term labor contracts, the firm will lay off workers until goods demand has returned to a level warranting the employment of $\ell_1$ workers at $W^*$. How does this analysis relate to the positive correlation between unexpected price changes and changes in output observed in the short-run aggregate supply curve? In each period, some fraction of the firms will sign new wage contracts consistent with current expectations of the equilibrium levels of wages and prices over the term of the contract. In the face of unexpected decreases in demand for their

---

[16]The value of a worker's marginal product is found by multiplying the extra output produced as a result of the worker's employment times the selling price of the output. Here we should reduce the selling price by expected expenses of holding the additional output in inventory until sold.

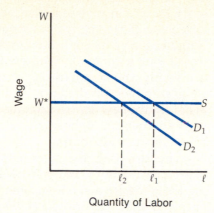

products, firms with expiring contracts will negotiate lower wages and reduce their prices while those firms with unexpired contracts will reduce their employment via temporary layoffs. Of course eventually, with an absence of any new surprises, all firms will adjust their wages and prices to the previously unexpected change in demand conditions.

Since labor contracts set wages for long periods of time, firms will respond to surprisingly low sales by laying off employees.

The early to mid-1980s provide a good example of the adjustment of the economy through a period of unexpectedly low inflation to a period of relatively low expected inflation. After years of rapid increases in nominal wages, the disinflation of the early 1980s was clearly built into expectations by 1984. For example, 21 percent of the union workers covered by new labor contracts negotiated in the first nine months of 1984 received no pay raise in the first year of their contract. An even more telling result is that 6 percent of the workers covered by new contracts took a cut in pay. The adjustment of the labor market to the decline in the U.S. inflation rate occurred steadily in the early 1980s. According to Robert S. Gay, "Average wage adjustments exclusive of cost-of-living payments during the first year of new union contracts dropped from about 10 percent in 1982 to 2 1/2 percent during 1983 and the first months of 1984."[17] Since different firms and industries negotiate labor contracts at different points in time, not all industries were able to adjust their wage increases in line with the drop in the U.S. inflation rate.

[17]Robert S. Gay, "Union Settlements and Aggregate Wage Behavior in the 1980s," *Federal Reserve Bulletin*, December 1984, p. 843.

We see then that since wage contracts are not all set simultaneously but are instead *staggered*, we get the positive correlation between unexpected prices and output changes.[18] If aggregate demand is higher than expected, then those firms with unexpired contracts would want to hire more workers at the preset wage $W^*$, while those firms with expiring contracts will have to bid up the wages they offer along with their product prices to maintain their existing labor force in light of the new demand conditions. Taken together, the staggered wage contracts produce unexpectedly high prices and a higher level of employment and output.

The supposed reason these long-term contracts exist in the first place is that senior workers, who do not anticipate any layoffs affecting them, desire a stable income. Since the wage rate is fixed, the only way that the firm can alter its labor costs is by altering the quantity of labor employed as the demand for labor shifts. In effect, the variability of employment of junior workers insures the senior workers against changes in either wages or employment.

The equilibrium contract theorists discussed above criticize this staggered contract view as ignoring the long-term nature of the employment relationship. The firm will have to pay an average wage over many periods which compensates for all conditions of employment, including frequency of temporary layoffs.[19] So although staggered contracts provide one possible explanation of the short-run aggregate supply curve, it does require us to believe that firms and workers are constrained somehow from pursuing their individual best interests.

---

[18]Important papers in the staggered contract approach include Stanley Fischer, "Long Term Contracts, Rational Expectations, and the Optimal Money Supply Rule," *Journal of Political Economy*, 85 (February 1977), 191–205, and John B. Taylor, "Aggregate Dynamics and Staggered Contracts," *Journal of Political Economy*, 88 (February 1980), 1–23.

[19]Suppose that the quality of labor normally employed is worth $5 per hour to a firm except during July when it is worth $3 per hour. If July leisure is worth less than $3 per hour to the employees, they should be employed year around. It is a matter of indifference to the firm whether it pays $5 per hour for 11 months and $3 per hour in July or $4.83 per hour all year [($5) (11/12) + ($3) (1/12) = $4.83]. If stable wages are otherwise preferable, they could be paid. But the firm should remember that $1.83 of the July wage is not the cost of July labor but rather of labor during the other 11 months.

# 8.4 FURTHER ISSUES FOR THE AGGREGATE SUPPLY CURVE

## VARIATIONS IN HOURS WORKED

The average number of hours worked has very gradually declined (at a trend rate of $-0.3$ percent per year) throughout the twentieth century. Around this gentle downward trend, there are pronounced cyclical fluctuations with average hours increasing in booms and declining in recessions.[20] Such variations in *average hours worked* reduce the extent to which temporary layoffs are used to vary output. In fact, variation in hours worked is a reason for Okun's Law associating changes in output with much smaller percentage movements in unemployment: the movements in total hours worked will be larger in percentage terms than the movements in the percent unemployed.[21]

The equilibrium contract theory emphasized that workers are willing to vary their average hours worked over the cycle because it permits them to maximize their work effort at times when their services are most valuable, while devoting their maximum leisure time to periods when the cost of foregone work is least. We would expect workers to plan vacations and time off during periods of lower than usual hours worked so that when opportunities for additional work or overtime come up they will be available to work. This suggests that some variation in hours worked, like temporary layoffs, can be understood as a rational response to temporary fluctuations in the value of the marginal product of labor. With regard to the aggregate supply curve, we now realize that output may fall with surprisingly low prices due to a reduction in hours worked as well as temporary layoffs.

---

[20]Annual data on average hours worked are available on a consistent basis back to 1889 in Michael R. Darby, *Labor Force, Employment, and Productivity in Historical Perspective*, (Los Angeles: U.C.L.A. Institute of Industrial Relations, 1984). The classic work on cyclical variations in average hours worked is by Gerhard Bry, *The Average Workweek as an Economic Indicator*, National Bureau of Economic Research Occasional Paper No. 69 (New York: National Bureau of Economic Research, 1959).

[21]Other factors reinforcing the effect of changes in unemployment on output include the tendency for the labor force to rise a bit above normal in a boom and fall in a recession, and fluctuations in the intensity with which the capital stock is used over the business cycle.

## RATIONAL EXPECTATIONS AND ERRORS

So far we have associated changes in output with two kinds of incorrect expectations: (1) If the actual distribution of wage offers from firms differs from that expected by workers, the search unemployment rate and hence output is affected. (2) If the firms err in their estimate of the equilibrium price level, inventories will move away from desired levels and this will lead to changes in the value of labor's marginal product and hence changes in average hours worked, the layoff unemployment rate, and the search unemployment rate.[22]

The fact that people lack perfect foresight implies that errors will occur, but this is no way suggests that they are mistaken or irrational in the way that they form their expectations. In fact, if people use all available information efficiently, we say that they have formed **rational expectations**.[23] But even if they use all the available information as well as any economist or statistician could to formulate their expectations about wages and prices, truly unpredictable changes in government policy and other macroeconomic shocks can make reality different from expectations.

Rational expectations, as conventionally defined, may seem to imply considerable sophistication and effort on the part of the person forming the expectation. Realistically, a person weighs the cost of gathering and using additional information against the benefits of

**rational expectations**
Expectations about economic events based on all available relevant information

Rational expectations are formed on the basis of all available information that is profitable to consider.

---

[22]The effect on the search unemployment rate would come from effects on both search duration and search flow. Some economists would add a third sort of expectational error: An increase (decrease) in the nominal wage rate is mistakenly believed to be a temporary increase (decrease) in the real wage because workers are unaware of a general unexpected increase (decrease) in wages and prices. In other words, workers are fooled in the short run, thinking they are better off because of the nominal wage increase than in fact they are. Since this can be thought of as a short version of the inventory story of Section 8.3, where unexpected shifts in the wage distribution lead to changes in unemployment, it will not be discussed further.

[23]The term was introduced by John F. Muth in "Rational Expectations and the Theory of Price Movements," *Econometrica*, 29 (July 1961), 315–35. The literature following Muth shall be discussed repeatedly in future chapters. A convenient compendium of major contributions is found in Robert E. Lucas, Jr., and Thomas J. Sargent, eds., *Rational Expectations and Econometric Practice*, (Minneapolis: The University of Minnesota Press, 1981). For a lighthearted critical review, see Rodney Maddock and Michael Carter, "A Child's Guide to Rational Expectations," *Journal of Economic Literature*, 20 (March 1982), 39–51.

the increased accuracy of predictions based on the information. Thus **economically rational expectations** use information only to the extent that the expected value of the marginal gain in accuracy exceeds the expected cost of obtaining and processing additional information.[24] Expectational errors may then rationally result either from irreducible uncertainty about future events or from people economizing on the use of available, but costly, information. We should be aware that, in general, the longer into the future we try to predict, the greater is the irreducible uncertainty.

> **economically rational expectations**
> Expectations formed by balancing information benefits against costs

Researchers examining the formation of expectations in financial markets have generally found evidence that such expectations are formed rationally. In the finance literature, tests of rational expectations are often termed tests of "market efficiency," the idea being that an **efficient market** is one where prices reflect all available, relevant information. While there exist some subtle differences between the implications of rational expectations and market efficiency, for our purposes it is only necessary to realize that researchers generally find evidence that financial markets are efficient and/or expectations are formed rationally.[25] Since investors in financial markets control billions of dollars, it would be surprising if they did not use all relevant and available information in forming their expectations of future variables like stock prices and interest rates.

> **efficient market**
> A market whose prices reflect all available relevant information

In the case of business firms setting prices for goods and services, tests of the rationality of expectations are not so easily done. However, if we consider how costly undesirable changes in invento-

---

[24]See Michael R. Darby, "Rational Expectations under Conditions of Costly Information," *Journal of Finance*, 31 (June 1976), 889–95, and Edgar L. Feige and Douglas K. Pearce, "Economically Rational Expectations: Are Innovations in the Rate of Inflation Independent of Innovations in Measures of Monetary and Fiscal Policy?" *Journal of Political Economy*, 84 (June 1976), 499–522.

[25]Such research generally considers whether an expectational variable like a forward or futures price (a price set now for delivery of something in the future) reflects all known information. For an application to the foreign exchange market see Jacob A. Frenkel, "The Forward Exchange Rate, Expectations, and the Demand for Money: The German Hyperinflation," *American Economic Review*, 67 (September 1977), 653–70. An interesting discussion of rational expectations, market efficiency, and investor behavior is found in John F. O. Bilson, "The 'Speculative Efficiency' Hypothesis," *Journal of Business*, 54 (July 1981), 433–51. For a detailed textbook analysis of market efficiency, see Eugene Fama, *Foundations of Finance* (New York: Basic Books, 1976), or Thomas E. Copeland and J. Fred Weston, *Financial Theory and Corporate Policy*, 2nd edition (Reading, Mass.: Addison-Wesley, 1983).

ries must be, it would seem that economically rational expectations for large business firms would incorporate a great deal of available information. Although, since firms often set prices for long periods of time, we would expect the firm to face a considerable amount of irreducible uncertainty regarding the level of aggregate demand over the fixed-price period. How often does Sears issue a new catalog? Each new catalog commits the firm to the advertised prices until the next catalog is issued.

Finally, searching workers are probably subject to large forecasting errors regarding the distribution of wages. In principle they could continuously adjust their reservation wage to the latest information on the state of the economy. However, for unemployed workers the cost of acquiring and processing information may be substantial relative to the value of improved forecasting accuracy. As a result, substantial errors between the forecasted and realized wage distribution may result. The economically rational expectations of searching workers are considerably less accurate than would be rational expectations using all available data.

In summary, we should expect substantial expectational errors to occur in the goods market, since prices are set for significant periods, and in the labor market, because workers economize on the use of costly information.

## SUPPLY SHOCKS

We have been concentrating on reasons for output and prices to vary together relative to their normal or expected levels. Expected prices and normal output have been taken as fixed amounts about which the economy fluctuates in the short run. While the emphasis has been on unexpected changes in aggregate expenditures or demand-side shocks, occasionally aggregate supply changes unexpectedly as discussed in section 7.7, leading to a change in the level of output associated with the expected price level. We will now consider in more detail the nature of such shocks. Such disturbances, or **supply shocks**, may occur in two different forms. First we may have a disturbance to the **aggregate production function**. Remember the derivation of the aggregate supply curve in section 7.3? A production function summarizes the relationship between inputs and output.

How can disturbances to the aggregate production function lead to supply shocks? Anything that unexpectedly changes the quantity of output produced at any level of unexpected prices will shift the expectations-adjusted aggregate supply curve. For instance, new technology would alter the relation between inputs and output, and

**supply shock**
Anything that unexpectedly changes the quantity of output produced at the expected price level

**aggregate production function**
The relationship between inputs and outputs

the entire production function would shift. However, technological innovation would be unlikely to occur on a scale that would substantially shift the aggregate production function in the short run. A natural disaster like an earthquake could wipe out a substantial amount of capital, shifting the production function down, so that less output is produced by any particular level of labor input. As a result, the aggregate supply curve would shift to the left as in the move from $AS_0$ to $AS_1$ in Figure 8.12. In the past, and in some countries today, major crop failures are a source of similar movements in the aggregate supply curve.

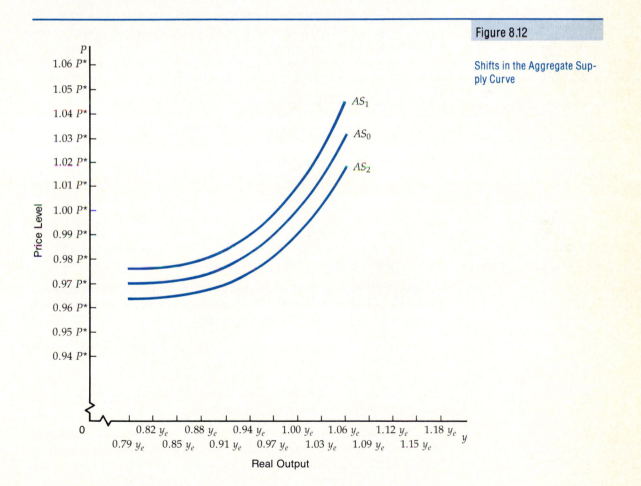

**Figure 8.12**

Shifts in the Aggregate Supply Curve

**terms of trade**
The rate at which domestic goods exchange for foreign goods

Besides shifts in the aggregate production function, aggregate supply shocks may also arise from a change in our **terms of trade** with the rest of the world. A country's terms of trade refers to the amount of domestic goods which must be given up in exchange for a certain amount of foreign goods. An unexpected change in the terms of trade could be caused by an international oil cartel unexpectedly raising the price of oil to an oil-importing nation. Since oil is an input in the production of so many goods, we would expect domestic producers to respond to this higher oil price by raising the prices of their output. This would raise domestic prices relative to wages, so that if wages, search unemployment, and output are at their expected levels, then prices must be higher than would have been expected; so once again we would expect the supply curve to shift up as in the move from $AS_0$ to $AS_1$ in Figure 8.12. This, in fact, is what we observed following the OPEC cartel's price increases in 1973–74.

A shift in the aggregate production function or a change in imported input prices can cause a change in the aggregate supply curve.

We see then that either increases in the cost of imported inputs or decreases in the aggregate production function will shift the aggregate supply curve upward and to the left relative to the normal curve that passes through point $(y_e, P^*)$. If the aggregate production function shifted up, or the cost of imported inputs fell, then the aggregate supply curve would shift down and to the right as in the move from $AS_0$ to $AS_2$ in Figure 8.12.

## SUMMARY

**1** The simple Phillips curve indicates the existence of a negative trade-off between unemployment and inflation.

**2** Okun's Law says that for each 1 percentage point the unemployment rate is above (below) normal, real output will be approximately 3 percentage points below (above) normal.

**3** While the simple Phillips curve relation between unemployment and inflation has not held up well over time, one can usefully modify the relationship to one between the unemployment rate and unexpected inflation. This expectations-adjusted Phillips curve seems to be more consistent with real world behavior.

**4** The relationship between unexpected price and changes in output is due to: temporary layoffs due to unexpected inventory fluctuations, and/or unemployed job searchers holding incorrect expectations of the actual distribution of wages, and/or staggered wage contracts giving some workers and firms an opportunity to set wages based on current conditions while others must adjust to current conditions at a pre-set wage.

**5** The search unemployment rate is determined by the search flow—the fraction of the labor force beginning to search in any given month, and the search duration—the average number of months required to find and begin a new job.

**6** When total spending and consequently labor demand are higher than expected, both search duration and search flow fall; when total spending is lower than expected they both rise.

**7** When total spending is lower (higher) than expected, inventories rise (fall), temporary layoffs rise (fall), output falls (rises), and prices are lower (higher) than expected.

**8** Equilibrium contract theory suggests that workers should concentrate their work effort in periods when they are most valuable, taking more leisure at other times.

**9** Since new wage contracts are staggered across time and not all signed at the same time, those firms with contracts currently negotiated will set wages and prices in line with current demand conditions, while those firms still living under an existing contract may use temporary layoffs to respond to changing demand conditions.

**10** The effect of changes in unemployment on output will be reinforced by changes in the average hours worked by those still working.

**11** If people form their expectations based on all the relevant information currently available, they form rational expectations.

**12** Expectations are economically rational if information is used to the extent that it profitably improves the forecast.

**13** Even if expectations are formed rationally, we still expect forecasting errors as the world is characterized by unexpected changes or shocks.

**14** Aggregate supply shocks could occur because of a shock to the aggregate production function or an unexpected change in an imported input price.

## EXERCISES

**1.** It is sometimes said that the Phillips curve relationship is unstable in the long run but is useful in the short run. Plot the inflation-unemployment rate combinations existing for monthly data over the past two years. (Use the Federal Reserve Bulletin or some other data source). Does your graph indicate a negative trade-off between inflation and unemployment?

2. Make up a simple Phillips curve diagram relating inflation to the unemployment rate. Using your Phillips curve information and Okun's Law, derive and plot graphically an aggregate supply curve (assume the normal rate of unemployment is 4 percent).

3. Modify your example of question 2 to include an expectations-adjusted Phillips curve. Assume the expected rate of inflation is 3 percent. Your Phillips curve should now relate unexpected inflation to the unemployment rate. How should the aggregate supply curve be changed if $P^*$ (the expected price) is 1.00, and $y_e$ (the normal or equilibrium output) is \$100 million.

4. Explain the economic rationale underlying the short-run aggregate supply curve. (In other words, why is output only different from normal output when actual prices differ from expected?)

5. Make a list of the factors determining the reservation wage of an unemployed job searcher. How could government policy directly affect this reservation wage?

6. Analyze the following quotation in light of the economic analysis of this chapter:

   *"The unemployed are generally shiftless, lazy bums. Why else would someone remain out of work when the newspaper is advertising many available openings?"*

7. Discuss and contrast "rational expectations" and "economically rational expectations."

8. Review the sources of supply shocks and give a specific example of a shock which you consider most likely to occur.

## REFERENCES FOR FURTHER READING

Friedman, Milton. "Nobel Lecture: Inflation and Unemployment." *Journal of Political Economy*, 84 (June 1977), 451–72.

McCallum, Bennett T. "The Significance of Rational Expectations Theory." *Challenge*, January/February 1980.

Okun, Arthur M. "Potential GNP: Its Measurement and Significance." *Proceedings of the Business and Economic Statistics Section of the American Statistical Association*, 1962, 98–104.

Solow, Robert M. "The Citizen's Guide: The Trade-Off View," *The Public Interest*, Winter 1975, 30–66.

## THE NATURAL RATE VERSUS THE FULL EMPLOYMENT RATE OF UNEMPLOYMENT

The *normal rate of unemployment* discussed in Chapters 7 and 8 is often referred to as the **natural rate of unemployment**. This is the unemployment rate which the economy tends toward in the absence of any macroeconomic shocks. Similarly, normal real income may be called the natural-employment real income. The natural rate of unemployment is given by the search behavior of unemployed workers—the search duration, as well as by the number who become unemployed—the search flow.

Note that the natural rate of unemployment does not occur at zero unemployment. In any dynamic market economy it is only natural that workers move between jobs or enter the labor market and spend some time searching for the job best suited for them. In fact, it is highly unlikely that a free market economy would ever come close to zero unemployment. As covered in the chapter, workers remain voluntarily unemployed because it is in their best interest to efficiently utilize the time spent searching for the best available job. Figure E8.1 and Table E8.1 illustrate the unemployment rate for the United States. It can be seen that the unemployment rate has approached a low of 1 percent but briefly, and has generally been considerably greater than 1 percent.

In the past, it was popular to talk about the **full-employment rate of unemployment**. While the exact notion and definition of such an unemployment rate varied across economists and time, no one ever argued that the full employment unemployment rate was zero. In fact, the various notions of what constitutes full employment often sounded quite like our normal or natural unemployment rate definition. Generally, the economy was at full employment if everyone who wanted to work was working. Some allowance was made for those moving between jobs (our search unemployment) and those displaced by changing technology, so that some positive unemployment was expected. With such a loose definition of full unemployment, one could always change the definition to suit the times so that full employment always exists. As the unemployment rate rose over time, there was a tendency to alter the definition of what constitutes full employment. In the 1950s, economists frequently asserted that 3 percent was the unemployment rate consistent with full employment. By the 1960s, 4 percent was a popular figure, which then rose to 5 percent by the early 1970s. In the 1983 *Economic Report of the President*, the President's Council of Economic Advisers suggested that the "inflation threshold" level of the unemployment rate was 6 to 7 percent. While the Council is very careful not to refer to any full-employment rate of unemployment, the arguments surrounding their "inflation threshold" rate sound suspiciously close to the

**natural rate of unemployment**
The level of unemployment the economy tends toward in the absence of macro shocks

**full-employment rate of unemployment**
The rate of unemployment when everyone who wishes to work is employed

217

The Unemployment Rate in the U.S.: 1900–83

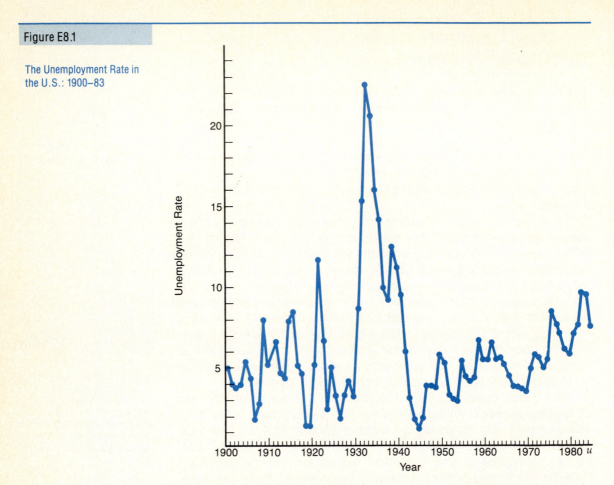

**Source:** Data for 1931–1943 are from Michael R. Darby, "Three-and-a-Half Million U.S. Employees Have Been Mislaid: Or an Explanation of Unemployment, 1934–41," *Journal of Political Economy*, 84 (February 1976), 1–16. Other data are from *Historical Statistics of the United States, Colonial Times–1970*, and the *Economic Report of the President*, February 1985.

arguments that have, in the past, been associated with the full-employment unemployment rate.

Since no one expects zero unemployment to be achieved or even desirable, the use of the term "full-employment" seems potentially misleading and quite inferior to the term, the normal or natural rate of unemployment. In fact, since "full employment" is such a misleading term, government economists now use the term "high employment" to describe the economy when not suffering from the economywide unemployment that exists during recessions or downturns in the business cycle. Most economists would agree that what we are concerned with

All civilian workers— unemployment rate

| Year | Rate | Year | Rate | Year | Rate | Year | Rate | Year | Rate | Year | Rate |
|------|------|------|------|------|------|------|------|------|------|------|------|
| 1900 | 5.0 | 1915 | 8.5 | 1930 | 8.7 | 1945 | 1.9 | 1960 | 5.5 | 1975 | 8.5 |
| 1901 | 4.0 | 1916 | 5.1 | 1931 | 15.3 | 1946 | 3.9 | 1961 | 6.7 | 1976 | 7.7 |
| 1902 | 3.7 | 1917 | 4.6 | 1932 | 22.5 | 1947 | 3.9 | 1962 | 5.5 | 1977 | 7.1 |
| 1903 | 3.9 | 1918 | 1.4 | 1933 | 20.6 | 1948 | 3.8 | 1963 | 5.7 | 1978 | 6.1 |
| 1904 | 5.4 | 1919 | 1.4 | 1934 | 16.0 | 1949 | 5.9 | 1964 | 5.2 | 1979 | 5.8 |
| 1905 | 4.3 | 1920 | 5.2 | 1935 | 14.2 | 1950 | 5.3 | 1965 | 4.5 | 1980 | 7.1 |
| 1906 | 1.7 | 1921 | 11.7 | 1936 | 9.9 | 1951 | 3.3 | 1966 | 3.8 | 1981 | 7.6 |
| 1907 | 2.8 | 1922 | 6.7 | 1937 | 9.1 | 1952 | 3.0 | 1967 | 3.8 | 1982 | 9.7 |
| 1908 | 8.0 | 1923 | 2.4 | 1938 | 12.5 | 1953 | 2.9 | 1968 | 3.6 | 1983 | 9.6 |
| 1909 | 5.1 | 1924 | 5.0 | 1939 | 11.3 | 1954 | 5.5 | 1969 | 3.5 | 1984 | 7.5 |
| 1910 | 5.9 | 1925 | 3.2 | 1940 | 9.5 | 1955 | 4.4 | 1970 | 4.9 | | |
| 1911 | 6.7 | 1926 | 1.8 | 1941 | 6.0 | 1956 | 4.1 | 1971 | 5.9 | | |
| 1912 | 4.6 | 1927 | 3.3 | 1942 | 3.1 | 1957 | 4.3 | 1972 | 5.6 | | |
| 1913 | 4.3 | 1928 | 4.2 | 1943 | 1.8 | 1958 | 6.8 | 1973 | 4.9 | | |
| 1914 | 7.9 | 1929 | 3.2 | 1944 | 1.2 | 1959 | 5.5 | 1974 | 5.6 | | |

Sources: U.S. Bureau of the Census (*Historical Statistics of the United States, Colonial Times to 1970*) and U.S. Bureau of Labor Statistics.

Data for 1931–43 from Michael R. Darby, "Three-and-a-Half Million U.S. Employees Have Been Mislaid: Or, an Explanation of Unemployment, 1934–41," *Journal of Political Economy*, 84 (February 1976), 1–16.

is distinguishing cyclical fluctuations in unemployment from the underlying natural rate of unemployment that exists in the absence of cyclical fluctuations in output and income. As the forces described in Chapter 8 alter the normal search unemployment rate, we can usefully analyze how the natural rate of unemployment and income change.

One must be careful not to consider the attainment of the natural rate as a desirable goal. Insofar as unemployment is costly, we want to avoid cyclical increases in the unemployment rate above the natural rate. Yet just remaining at the natural rate may also be undesirable. Since the natural rate of unemployment is determined by the search behavior of individuals, and since such behavior is influenced by the wage distribution and search costs, we may at times believe that the natural rate of unemployment involves either too much or too little unemployment considering the benefits and costs of searching. For instance, unemployment benefits tend to reduce the cost of search to the individual—but not to the economy—in terms of foregone income. This might then encourage too long a search. While there are many other policy issues one could raise with regard to the appropriate natural rate of unemployment, we should simply remember that the concept of the natural rate is inherently neither good nor bad (in contrast to the "full-employment" concept), but simply related to the unemployment rate existing during normal periods.

# CHAPTER NINE

# REAL GROWTH TRENDS

## 9.1 INTRODUCTION

The world's economies are generally characterized by rising prices, income, and standards of living. Such changes do not occur evenly through time. There are cyclical fluctuations around the long-run trend of economic growth. In other chapters we will focus on the determinants of the fluctuations—the booms and busts of the business cycle—about the long-term growth trend. In this chapter, the emphasis is on understanding the gradual changes in the determinants of the trend or **secular growth rate** of real income over time. Once we understand the causes of real income growth as explained in Chapter 9, Chapter 10 will consider the role of money and the growth of the price level. Macroeconomists put so much of their effort into addressing the issue of business cycles that it is easy for students to forget that over time these ups and downs in economic activity average out into real growth. While we certainly are interested in prolonging the expansions and moderating the recessions, it is difficult—as this chapter will show—to offer useful prescriptions without understanding the basic determinants of economic growth.

**secular growth rate**
The trend in economic growth

### MEASURING GROWTH

How is growth measured? Two separate but related concepts are useful. First, the *rate of change* of a variable measures the growth per year in terms of the units by which the variable is measured. For example, the civilian labor force was 109,034,000 persons at the beginning of 1982 and 111,129,000 persons at the end of the year. The rate of change of the labor force for 1982 was 2,095,000 persons per year. Second, the *growth rate* of a variable expresses growth as a proportion or fraction of the amount of the variable. For example, the 2,095,000 persons per year change in the labor force as a proportion of the beginning level of 109,034,000 indicates a growth rate of 0.019 per year. Growth rates are usually stated in percentage terms, so we would say that the labor force grew by 1.9 percent per annum.

Growth rates are usually calculated at annual rates or *percent per annum*. While the previous example of labor force growth from the beginning to the end of 1982 measures the growth of the labor force over a year, had we instead considered the growth from July to December, then we would have to make an adjustment to calculate the growth over such a 6-month period in terms of percent per annum. In general, we can calculate the rate of change at annual rates by subtracting the beginning level from the ending level of a variable and dividing by the length of the period to convert the change into annual rates. For example, in June of 1982, the labor force equaled 110,191,000 persons. Subtracting this figure from the December ending figure of 111,129,000 gives a change of 938,000. But this is just for 6 months or half a year. To convert the 6-month rate of change into annual terms we divide by 1/2, as 6 months is half a year. So from June to December of 1982, the labor force rate of change occurred at a 1,876,000 ($= 938,000 \div 1/2$) annual rate.

Throughout the remainder of the text we will denote the rate of change of a variable by the use of the symbol $\Delta$. So $\Delta\ell$ is the rate of change in the labor force calculated at an annual rate. We will always compute measures of growth at annual rates even if we are talking about the rate of change existing at an instant in time. Similarly, we will always measure growth rates in percent per annum terms. In the example of the change in the labor force over the 6-month period from June to December of 1982, the rate of growth is found by dividing the rate of change by beginning value of $\ell$ or, if we denote growth rates by placing a hat ($\hat{\ }$) over a variable:

$$\hat{\ell} = \frac{\Delta\ell}{\ell} = \frac{1,876,000}{110,191,000} = .0170 \tag{9.1}$$

So the growth rate equalled 1.70 percent per annum, a bit less than the average for the whole year.

There are two rules associated with the use of growth rates that we will find quite useful:

(1) The growth rate of a product of two or more variables equals the sum of the growth rates of the individual variables.

(2) The growth rate of a ratio of two variables equals the growth rate of the numerator variable minus the growth rate of the denominator variable.

To illustrate the first rule, suppose we consider the growth rate of nominal GNP $\hat{Y}$. Since nominal GNP is equal to the product of real GNP $y$ and the price index $P$, or $Y = Py$, the growth rate of nominal GNP may be found by summing the growth rates of $P$ and $y$. From 1981 to 1982, the price level grew at a 6 percent annual rate while real GNP actually fell by 1.8 percent. We find nominal GNP as the sum of these two growth rates, or:

$$\hat{Y} = \hat{P} + \hat{y} = 0.06 - 0.018 = 0.042$$

So nominal GNP grew by 4.2 percent during 1982.

To illustrate the second rule, we could use the same three variables just considered, but now find the growth rate of real income $\hat{y}$ given the rate of inflation $\hat{P}$ and the growth of nominal income $\hat{Y}$. Since real GNP is equal to nominal GNP divided by the price level, we find real GNP growth as:

$$\hat{y} = \hat{Y} - \hat{P} = 0.042 - 0.06 = -0.018$$

Since prices rose faster than nominal income, real income obviously fell, and the fall was equal to 1.8 percent over 1982.

We have discussed equilibrium in terms of levels of our key variables. In such cases where all growth rates are zero so that the values of variables are unchanging, we say that the economy is in a **stationary state**. A moving equilibrium, or **steady state**, refers to an economy in which all macroeconomic variables—like income, price level, population, and money supply—are growing at constant rates. We will be using the steady-state growth path of the economy as a standard against which actual economic performance can be measured.

**stationary state**
An economy in which all growth rate variables are zero

**steady state**
An economy in which all growth rate variables are growing at constant rates

## HISTORICAL TRENDS

What is the record of long-run growth in the U.S. for the key variables: real income, the price level, population, and the money supply? Figures 9.1 through 9.4 plot the values of these variables over time. While it is apparent that each series has its ups and downs, and some are more stable than others, we can compute the average annual rates of growth as a measure of the long-run trend growth rate. Real income over the 1929–84 period has grown at an annual 2.9 percent rate on average. This very important indicator of the

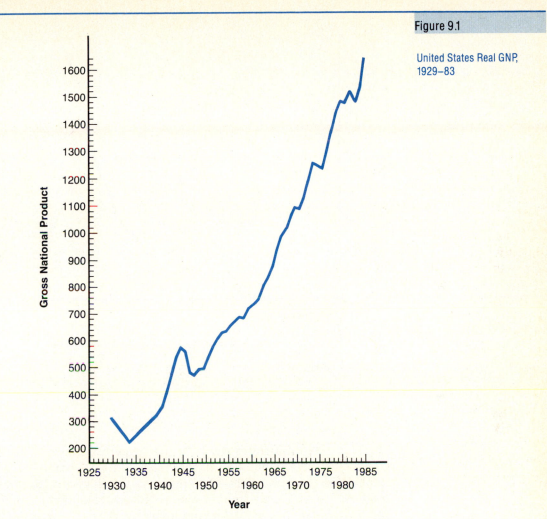

Figure 9.1

United States Real GNP, 1929–83

health of the economy has fallen during recessions and risen rapidly over booms so that any short-run view will only pick up the cyclical pattern. By analyzing more than 50 years of the record, we see a trend of real economic growth that has averaged approximately 3 percent.

Figure 9.2 reports the historical record of the price level in the U.S. Over the 1929–84 period, the implicit GNP deflator has grown at a 3.4 percent average annual rate. This serves to remind us that the double-digit inflation rates of the late 1970s and early 1980s were very high by historical standards in this country. In later chapters we will analyze the events that led to the growth of prices deviating so much from the long-run trend.

Figure 9.2

U.S. Price Level as Measured
by the Implicit GNP Deflator,
1929–83

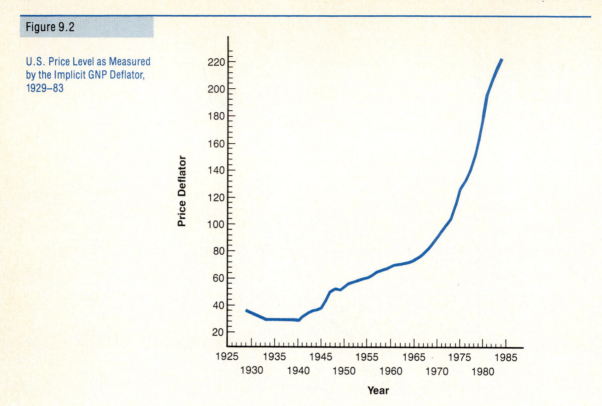

Figure 9.3 illustrates the long-run growth pattern of the U.S. population. The population has increased at a 1.2 percent average annual rate over the 1929–83 period. As we shall see, this rather moderate rate of population growth relative to the higher growth in real income implies a rising standard of living for the average U.S. citizen.

Finally, we see the time path of the U.S. money supply illustrated in Figure 9.4. Due to several changes in the appropriate definition of money, we have reported the money supply only over the 1959–84 period. As we shall see later on, fluctuations in this key variable of macroeconomic policy have been implicated in the fluctuations in real income and prices that characterize the U.S. business cycle. While money growth rates have fluctuated considerably from year to year, the average annual rate of growth of $M_1$ over the 1959–83 period was 5.3 percent.

Now that we know how to measure growth and have an idea of historical growth rates in the U.S., it is time to discover the underlying determinants of real economic growth. The rest of Chapter 9 will

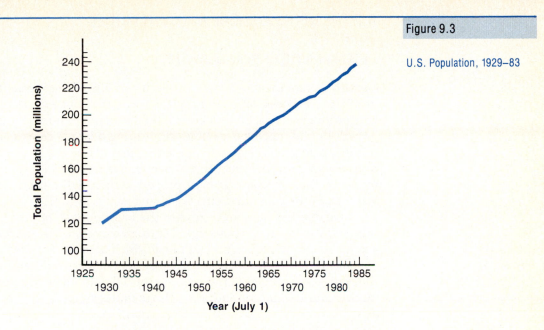

Figure 9.3

U.S. Population, 1929–83

be devoted to a discussion of real income growth. In Chapter 10 we will expand our view and consider how money growth and prices add to the analysis.

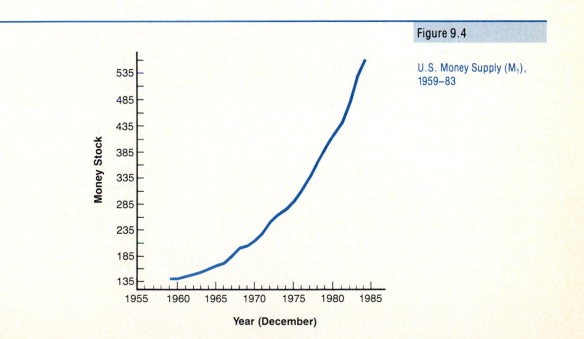

Figure 9.4

U.S. Money Supply ($M_1$), 1959–83

## 9.2 THE NEOCLASSICAL GROWTH MODEL

### DETERMINANTS OF REAL GROWTH

Growth in real income occurs through growth in the inputs to the productive process, labor and capital, through changes in the aggregate production function, or both. While we tend to think of upward growth in real income over time, continuing adverse changes, such as those due to a widespread epidemic, may cause negative growth rates over a period of time. In this section we will develop a popular model of the economic growth process which will aid our understanding of the cause and effect of changes in real GNP.

In analyzing economic growth, the basic determinants are usefully separated into two groups: (1) those affected in a predictable way by economic factors and (2) those which are not. The first group contains the *endogenous* variables whose values will be determined by the *exogenous* variables of the second group. It should be realized that modern models of economic growth are quite complex and are often described by the use of sophisticated mathematics. We will consider only the most basic results here.

In most simple growth models the growth rate of labor is assumed to be fixed by noneconomic factors at a constant rate. If the growth rate of labor $\hat{\ell}$ is constant and the amount of labor at any point in time is known, it is possible to compute the amount of labor at every other instant. While more elaborate models have been developed in which the growth rate of labor is endogenous, these more complex models give similar results to the exogenously fixed growth rate of labor models and we will use the simplifying assumption of a constant $\hat{\ell}$. Using a bar over a variable to denote a constant, our constant growth rate of labor assumption produces a labor growth equation like:

$$\hat{\ell} = \bar{\hat{\ell}} \tag{9.2}$$

The growth rate of capital is, of course, measured as the rate of change in the capital stock $\Delta k$ divided by the capital stock:

$$\hat{k} = \Delta k / k \tag{9.3}$$

Since the capital stock is measured in real terms, the rate of change in the capital stock will be equal to the rate of real investment $i$, so

$$\hat{k} = i / k \tag{9.4}$$

That is, the growth rate of capital equals the rate at which the capital stock is increased by investment in percent per annum terms.

By consolidating the government with the private sector and assuming international trade is balanced, we can use a simplified national income accounting system where real saving $s$ equals real investment $i$:

$$s \equiv i \qquad (9.5)$$

Also, since the fraction of income saved tends to be fairly constant over time, we can approximate real saving as a constant fraction, let's call it $a$, times real income $y$:[1]

$$s \equiv ay \qquad (9.6)$$

Combining (9.4), (9.5), and (9.6), we can solve for $\hat{k}$ as:

$$\hat{k} = a\,\frac{y}{k} \qquad (9.7)$$

That is, the growth rate of capital equals the saving–income ratio $a$ times the ratio of income to capital. Equation (9.7) endogenously determines the growth rate of capital given saving behavior as captured by $a$, real income, and the existing capital stock.

Now that we have discussed input growth, we must relate these inputs to output. Remember our aggregate production function:

$$\overset{++}{y = f(k,\ell)} \qquad (9.8)$$

To simplify the analysis, we will assume that this production function exhibits *constant returns to scale*. This means that if capital and labor change in the same proportion, then output changes by that same proportion also. For instance, if both capital and labor were doubled, income would also double. This kind of production function can also be written as:

$$y = k \cdot f(1,\ \ell/k) \qquad (9.9)$$

The functional expression in parentheses determines the amount of output per unit of capital, and by multiplying this amount times the quantity of capital we find total output. If we wanted to find the

> The output-capital ratio is an increasing function of the labor-capital ratio.

---

[1]Earlier in the text we used $a$ as our symbol for aggregate expenditures. In equilibrium, income $y$ and aggregate expenditures are equal, so we can use $y$ for our output and total spending variable. Since we have used the other letters of the alphabet to stand for other variables, it is desirable to now choose $a$ to stand for the saving–income ratio.

amount of output per unit of capital, we divide both sides of equation (9.9) by $k$ giving:

$$\frac{y}{k} = f(1, \ell/k) \tag{9.10}$$

This $y/k$ ratio is usually depicted as in Figure 9.5 as a function of the labor–capital ratio. Note that as $\ell/k$ increases, $y/k$ increases, but at a decreasing rate. This decreasing slope of the curve reflects the law of diminishing returns as was found earlier where we introduced the concept of the aggregate production function in Chapter 7. If the quantity of one input (in this case labor) rises relative to another input (capital), smaller increases in output will be forthcoming from each additional unit of labor.

## STEADY-STATE REAL EQUILIBRIUM

In the absence of any changes in the economy, what is the long-run or steady-state rate of economic growth? This is the question we will now address. In equation (9.7) it was shown that the growth rate of capital is equal to the *saving–income ratio a* times the *output–capital ratio* $(y/k)$. Combining this result with equation (9.10) allows us to express the growth rate of capital as an increasing function of the *labor–capital ratio*:

$$\hat{k} = a\overset{+}{f}(1, \ell/k) \tag{9.11}$$

This relationship is graphed in Figure 9.6. For any given saving–income ratio $a$, increases in the output–capital ratio will cause in-

**Figure 9.5**

The Output–Capital Ratio as a Function of the Labor–Capital Ratio

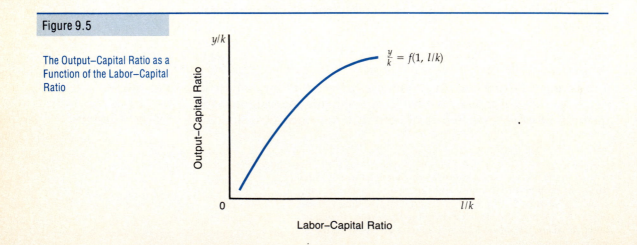

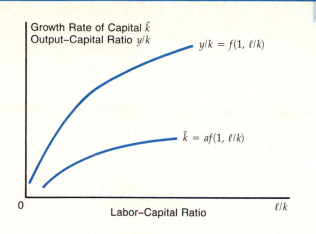

**Figure 9.6**

Relation of the Growth Rate of Capital to the Output–Capital Ratio

creases in the growth rate of capital. How can we graph the $\hat{k}$ function in the same space as the $y/k$ function Obviously $\hat{k}$ will be measured in percent per annum terms, but what about $y/k$? Since $y$ is measured as a flow amount of output per year and capital is a stock amount of output, the ratio $y/k$ is in percent per annum units as is $\hat{k}$. In Figure 9.6 we see that the growth rate of capital increases with increases in $\ell/k$, but at a decreasing rate. Since $\hat{k}$ equals a constant fraction $a$ times $y/k$, as $y/k$ increases with $\ell/k$ but at a diminishing rate, so must increases in $\hat{k}$ diminish with higher $y/k$.

We can add the growth rate of labor to the same diagram as a horizontal line at $\bar{\hat{\ell}}$, which is measured in percent per annum units. This is done in Figure 9.7. Now we can use the three curves in Figure 9.7 to find the real growth equilibrium. Recalling our second rule on computing growth rates, the growth rate of the labor–capital ratio is the difference between the growth rates of labor and capital:

$$(\widehat{\ell k}) = \hat{\ell} - \hat{k} \tag{9.12}$$

Whenever the growth rate of labor exceeds the growth rate of capital, the labor–capital ratio will be increasing. The growth of $\ell/k$ is negative when the growth of labor is less than the growth of capital. Figure 9.7 illustrates this effect. At the ratio $\ell_e/k_e$, the growth rate of labor equals the growth rate of capital. For any $\ell/k$ less than $\ell_e/k_e$, the labor force is growing faster than the capital stock so that $\ell/k$ increases. Similarly for any $\ell/k$ greater than $\ell_e/k_e$, the labor force grows at a slower rate than the capital stock, so $\ell/k$ falls. Thus we see that $\ell_e/k_e$ is the equilibrium labor–capital ratio as any move away from $\ell_e/k_e$ will result in forces pushing us back to that particular equilibrium value where the labor–capital ratio remains constant.

Figure 9.7

Determination of the Equilibrium Real Growth Rate

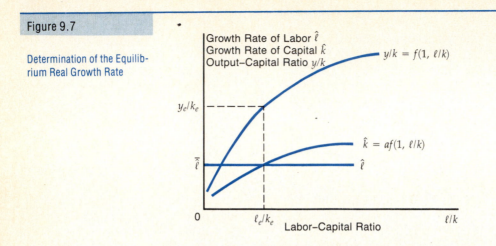

Now we know that a stable equilibrium labor–capital ratio ($\ell_e/k_e$) exists. This ratio is maintained when saving is just sufficient to finance new units of capital for use with new units of labor in the same proportion as exists for the previous amounts of labor. Since this is a stable equilibrium, if any macroeconomic shock moves the economy away from this equilibrium, over time equilibrium will be restored.

With a constant labor–capital ratio, output per unit of capital will also be constant at

$$\frac{y_e}{k_e} = f(1, \hat{\ell}_e/\hat{k}_e) \tag{9.13}$$

This equilibrium output–capital ratio is shown in Figure 9.7. How can the ratio of output to the capital stock remain equal in a growing economy? Only by having real output grow at the same rate as the capital stock, which we already know grows at the same rate as the labor force. So in steady-state equilibrium, it must be true that:

$$\hat{y} = \bar{\hat{k}} = \bar{\hat{\ell}} \tag{9.14}$$

In the steady-state, the growth rates of capital, labor, and output are all equal.

The endogenously determined growth rates of real income and capital adjust to equal the exogenously given constant growth rate of labor.

## THE EFFECTS OF SAVING SHIFTS

A surprising result of the steady-state equilibrium analysis is that changes in the saving–income ratio $a$ will not affect the equilibrium growth rate of real income. Remember, the growth rate of real income adjusts to equal the growth rate of labor. However, the saving–income ratio will generally affect the level of real income at any particular point in time.

To analyze the effects of alternative values of $a$, let's consider two alternatives $a_0$ and $a_1$, where $a_1$ is greater than $a_0$. All other conditions are assumed equal, so the aggregate production function and the growth rate of labor are held constant. In Figure 9.8 we see two $\hat{k}$ curves. As always, equilibrium occurs where the growth rate of capital equals the growth rate of labor. We use the subscripts 0 and 1 to denote the equilibrium values of variables associated with $a_0$ and $a_1$ respectively. The equilibrium labor–capital ratios are $\ell_0/k_0$ and $\ell_1/k_1$ with corresponding income–capital ratios $y_0/k_0$ and $y_1/k_1$. We can see that $\ell_1/k_1$ is less than $\ell_0/k_0$, so a higher saving–income ratio implies a lower labor–capital ratio. But since the quantity of labor is exogenously given at any point in time, a lower $\ell/k$ implies that there is more capital with $a_1$ than with $a_0$. Furthermore, a larger amount of capital with the same quantity of labor will yield more output at any point in time. Over time the growth of real output will be unchanged since $\hat{\ell}$ is constant; so the level of $y$ increases while the growth rate is constant.

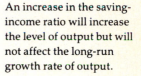

An increase in the saving-income ratio will increase the level of output but will not affect the long-run growth rate of output.

At first, it may sound like a contradiction to say that the level of output increases yet the growth rate is constant. We can say this only because we are comparing two *alternative*, hypothetical economies. At any time, say $t_0$, $y_1$ will be higher than $y_0$ as in Figure 9.9(a), but income is growing in both cases at the same rate $\hat{y}_0 = \hat{y}_1 = \hat{\ell}$. This is illustrated in Figure 9.9(b). If we were instead supposing that one particular economy had saving–income ratio $a_0$ until $t_0$ and thereafter

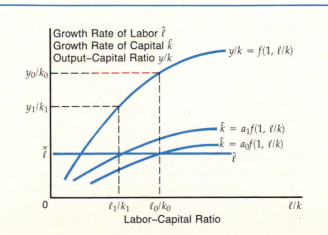

Figure 9.9

The Effect of Alternative Saving–Income Ratios on Real Income
a) The Level of Real Income for Alternative Saving–Income Ratios
b) The Growth Rate of Real Income for Alternative Saving–Income Ratios

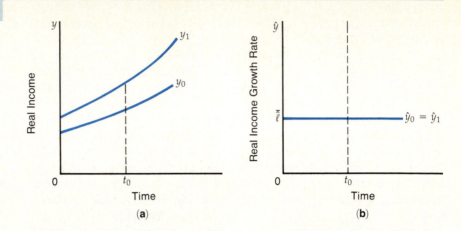

had the saving–income ratio $a_1$, things would be different: There would be a period of time after $t_0$ during which the economy would accumulate more capital, the labor–capital ratio would fall toward $\ell_e/k_e$, and real income would move up from $y_0$ to $y_1$. During this adjustment period, the actual growth rate of real income $\hat{y}$ would exceed the unchanged steady-state growth rate of $\hat{\ell}$. In this chapter and the next, we will be concerned with the simpler problem of comparing alternative hypothetical economies in steady-state equilibrium. Beginning with Chapter 11 we will analyze adjustment periods following a change in steady-state equilibrium.

## GROWTH IN THE STANDARD OF LIVING

**standard of living**
The material well-being of a country

The **standard of living** is measured by per capita real income, or $y/n$. Remembering our rules regarding growth rates, the growth rate of per capita real income may be computed as the difference between the growth rates of real income and population:

$$\widehat{(y/n)} = \hat{y} - \hat{n} \tag{9.15}$$

Assuming a constant growth rate of population $\bar{n}$, and recalling that the steady-state $\hat{y}$ equals the constant growth rate of labor $\bar{\ell}$, the steady-state growth rate of per capita real income is:

$$\widehat{(y/n)} = \bar{\ell} - \bar{n} \tag{9.16}$$

Consequently, per capita real income grows at the rate by which the growth of labor exceeds the growth of population.

The quantity of labor is the product of the participation rate $\pi$, the quality index $q$, and the age eligible population $n$; so the growth rate of labor is the sum of the growth rates of these three factors:

$$\hat{\ell} = \hat{\pi} + \hat{q} + \hat{n} \tag{9.17}$$

If all of these growth rates are constants ($\bar{\hat{\pi}}$, $\bar{\hat{q}}$, and $\bar{\hat{n}}$, respectively) we can subtract $\hat{n}$ from each side of equation (9.17) yielding

$$\hat{\ell} - \hat{n} = \hat{\pi} + \hat{q} \tag{9.18}$$

Substituting equation (9.18) into (9.16) yields:

$$(\widehat{y/n}) = \bar{\hat{\pi}} + \bar{\hat{q}} \tag{9.19}$$

So growth in the standard of living ultimately reflects growth in the labor participation rate and in the average quality of labor.

> Standard of living will increase as the labor participation rate and average quality of labor increases.

Growth in the labor participation rate reflects trends in the average work week and work life as well as in participation by sex and race. The growth rate of average labor quality reflects the impact of such forces as steadily increasing education and on-the-job training. Growth in average labor quality also allows for *technical progress*—the fact that advances in knowledge make individuals with a given amount of education and experience more productive as time goes on. The end-of-chapter essay discusses some attempts to measure average labor quality.

The growth rate of the labor participation rate has been slightly negative in the United States as shown in Figure 9.10. Declining male participation and average hours worked more than offset rising female participation. So the distinctly positive trend in the growth rate of the quality of the labor force has been the source of growth in *both* per capita real income and leisure. Figure 9.11 illustrates the long-term rate of growth in the U.S. standard of living. Over the period 1929–83, per capita real GNP in the U.S. grew at an average annual rate of 1.7 percent. We should remember that per capita real income is an imperfect measure of standard of living. As was discussed in the end-of-chapter essay to Chapter 2, much activity escapes the national income accounts. Furthermore, in some countries per capita real income rises because of increases in the labor participation rate, but since people enjoy leisure time, it is not clear that more work is always desired. Lastly, changes in the institutions of society (unem-

Figure 9.10

Labor Participation Rate in
the United States

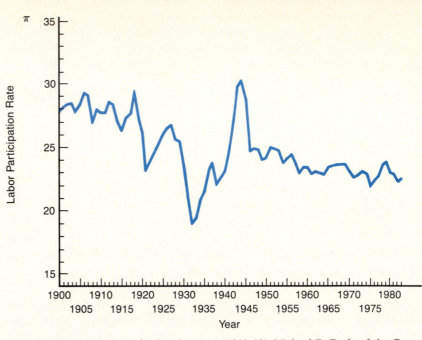

**Sources:** Bureau of Labor Statistics (1948–83); Michael R. Darby, *Labor Force,
Employment, and Productivity in Historical Perspective* (Los Angeles:
U.C.L.A. Institute of Industrial Relations, 1983) (1900–47).

ployment insurance, welfare, etc.) make comparisons of well being
based on per capita income, both over time and across economies,
somewhat difficult.

Beyond the determination of the steady-state growth rate of per
capita income, we can infer the distribution of income between labor
and capital. Any given labor–capital ratio will imply a constant marginal product of labor and capital, and hence a constant real wage of
labor and real rental rate on capital. Since a constant amount is
earned per unit of capital and per unit of labor, and since capital and
labor will grow in constant proportions to maintain a given labor—
capital ratio, the ratio of people's total earnings from capital to their
total earnings from labor will be constant in steady-state equilibrium.
This, in fact, has been found to hold fairly well over long periods of
time in the U.S. Table 9.1 displays data on United States national
income by source. We see that labor income accounts for approximately 80 percent of national income, while roughly 20 percent of
national income is derived from capital.

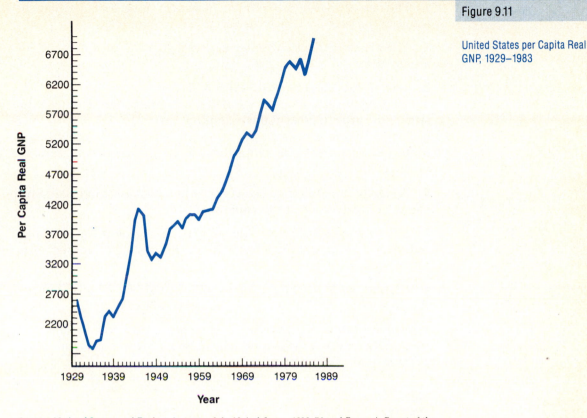

Figure 9.11

United States per Capita Real GNP, 1929–1983

**Source**: *National Income and Product Accounts of the United States, 1929–76* and *Economic Report of the President*, February 1985.

Table 9.1

The Derivation of National Income From Labor and Capital

| Year | Total National Income (Billion $) | Derived from Labor[1] | Derived from Capital[2] |
|------|-----------------------------------|----------------------|------------------------|
| 1940 | 79.7 | 82% | 18% |
| 1950 | 237.6 | 81% | 19% |
| 1960 | 415.7 | 82% | 18% |
| 1970 | 810.7 | 84% | 16% |
| 1980 | 2,116.6 | 81% | 19% |
| 1984 | 2,959.4 | 79% | 21% |

[1]Found as compensation of employees plus proprietors' income.

[2]Found as rental income of persons plus corporate profits plus net interest.

Source: *Economic Report of the President*, February 1985.

## SUMMARY

1   The rate of change of a variable measures the growth per year in terms of the units by which the variable is measured.

2   The growth rate of a variable expresses growth as a percent per annum rate.

3   Two useful rules of growth arithmetic are:
a The growth rate of a product of two or more variables equals the sum of the growth rates of the individual variables.
b The growth rate of a ratio of two variables equals the growth rate of the numerator variable minus the growth rate of the denominator variable.

4   A steady state refers to an economy in which all macroeconomic variables are growing at constant rates.

5   Steady-state equilibrium occurs when the growth rates of real output and the capital stock equal the exogenously given growth rate of labor.

6   Changes in the saving–income ratio will affect the level but not the growth rate of real income in the steady state.

7   Standard of living is measured by per capita real income and ultimately reflects growth in the labor participation rate and in the average quality of labor.

### EXERCISES

1.  Suppose we consider an explicit example of an aggregate production function: $y = 3\sqrt{k\ell}$.

    a.  Compute two alternative values of $y$, where $y_0$ is produced by $k_0 = 1$ and $\ell_0 = 4$ and $y_1$ is produced by $k_1 = 40,000$ and $\ell_1 = 160,000$.

    b.  Compute the values of $y_1/y_0$, $k_1/k_0$, and $\ell_1/\ell_0$, then explain how this illustrates constant returns to scale.

2.  Divide the production function in question 1 by $k$ and show that output per unit of capital is dependent on the ratio of labor to capital, but not on their levels.

3.  Two economies are alike in their aggregate production function and saving–income ratio, but differ in their growth rates of labor which are $\hat{\ell}_0$ in country $0$ and $\hat{\ell}_1$ in country $1$. Assume $\hat{\ell}_0$ is less than $\hat{\ell}_1$. Use a graph to derive and compare the equilibrium labor–capital ratios in the two countries. Can you tell which country will have the highest income per unit of capital? The highest per capita income? Explain.

4. Does a high level of education imply a higher growth rate of per capita income? Does a rising level of education imply a higher growth rate of per capita income?

5. Calculate the annual rate of change and percent per annum growth rates for the following:

   a. The U.S. money supply ($M_1$) increased from $440.9 billion to $478.5 billion between December 1981 and December 1982.

   b. The Dow Jones Industrial Average of stock prices went from 1,028 in November 1982 to 1,033 in December 1982.

   c. Between the second and third quarters of 1982, U.S. agricultural exports changed from $10,673 million to $8,496 million.

6. Suppose that instead of relating the labor–capital ratio to the output–capital ratio, as was done in Chapter 9, we instead want to relate the capital–labor ($k/$ ) ratio to the output–labor ($y/$ ) ratio. Starting with the general form of the production function: $y = f(k, )$, *explain how this is done and provide a graphical example.*

7. What is the steady-state growth rate of real income in an economy where the age-eligible population is growing at 2 percent per year, labor force participation is declining at a rate of 0.5 percent per year, and the index of labor quality is increasing at a 1.5 percent per annum rate? What is happening to per capita income over time in this economy?

8. What qualifications might one consider when using per capita income as a measure of standard of living?

## REFERENCES FOR FURTHER READING

Hahn, Frank H., and R. C. O. Matthews. "The Theory of Economic Growth: A Survey." *Economic Journal*, 74 (December 1964), 779–902.

Solow, Robert M. *Growth Theory: An Exposition*. New York: Oxford University Press, 1970.

# HAS PRODUCTIVITY IN THE U.S. FALLEN?

One of the most popular topics for discussion in the early 1980s was the alleged slowdown in the growth of labor productivity in the U.S. Labor productivity is commonly measured as output per employee or output per hour worked. According to data published in the 1980 *Economic Report of the President*, private nonfarm output per labor hour grew at an average annual rate of 2.6 percent from 1948 to 1965, 1.9 percent from 1965 to 1973, and only 0.5 percent from 1973 to 1979. Since wages paid are based on productivity, we can readily understand labor's interest in the productivity issue. Yet much of the discussion surrounding the apparent decline in U.S. labor productivity is devoted to comparisons with other nations, particularly Japan where productivity growth is still quite rapid. Such cross-cultural comparisons encouraged the development of several alternative hypotheses regarding the cause of the decline in U.S. productivity. Factors suggested as contributing to the decline of U.S. productivity include government regulation and taxation policy, a decline in the quality of the U.S. educational system, obsolete management policies in U.S. firms, a fall in the capital–labor ratio, and even a decline in the moral fiber of the U.S. population. We will review the evidence and consider whether there is indeed cause for alarm.

First it must be made clear that we are concerned with the long-run growth rate of productivity. It is well known that productivity changes in a regular, systematic fashion over the business cycle—rising early in the expansion and then declining as the economy approaches the peak of the cycle. Such recurring cyclical patterns are not our concern. We want to know what has happened to the underlying trend apart from the cyclical fluctuations. Many researchers have claimed that there were two distinct breaks since World War II in the growth of productivity, with major slowdowns occurring in the mid-1960s and again in 1973–74. On the other hand, William Nordhaus, Arthur Blakemore and Don Schlagenhauf have argued that there has been a continuous gradual slowdown which is better explained by a gradual change in the underlying factors determining productivity.[1] Those suggesting distinct breaks in the growth of productivity have offered special circumstances, such as oil price shocks, to explain the shift in productivity growth. Blakemore and Schlagenhauf estimate that the trend growth rate of output per labor hour has fallen

---

[1]Arthur E. Blakemore and Don E. Schlagenhauf, "A Test for Structural Instability in the Secular Growth Rate of Productivity," *Economics Letters*, 13 (1983), 153–59; William D. Nordhaus, "Economic Policy in the Face of Declining Productivity Growth," *European Economic Review*, 18 (May 1982), 131–57.

steadily from a 2.9 percent annual rate in 1960 to a 0.9 percent rate in 1980. Such a precipitous decline in productivity would seem to signal a need for national concern and in fact, President Reagan and the U.S. Congress sponsored a White House Conference on Productivity in 1983 which drew economists, politicians, and business leaders from all parts of the nation. The outcome of the conference was a list of recommendations including tax reforms aimed at stimulating productivity, more educational resources for gifted students, and a reduction of the impact of government borrowing so that more investment funds are available to U.S. industry.

While it appears that most in the economics profession are in general agreement regarding the decline in U.S. productivity, it is not a unanimous sentiment. Michael Darby claims that if we adjust the quantity of labor for quality changes, hourly labor productivity has grown at a constant rate of about 1.7 percent over the twentieth century. Darby adjusts for changes in the quality of labor because using output per hour of labor as a measure of productivity implicitly assumes that the kind of labor being studied is unchanging. Darby adjusts the measure of hours worked for demographic factors such as the age and sex composition of the labor force, average level of education, and immigration. Making allowance for these measurable effects on average quality and for variations in the labor–capital ratio associated with the Great Depression and World War II, he finds a constant underlying trend rate of technical progress. Darby summarizes his findings by saying, "it appears that there is no substantial variation in trend private productivity growth over the twentieth century to be explained by variations in regulation growth, oil prices, the failure of American management, labor, or any of the other popular whipping boys."[2]

Controversy is nothing new to macroeconomics. Since policy decisions are based on prevailing beliefs, it is important that the prevailing wisdom be challenged by those who think they have convincing evidence. The "productivity problem" is one such area of controversy that will be subjected to continuing scrutiny as long as economists continue to produce differing evidence.

---

[2]Michael R. Darby, "The U.S. Productivity Slowdown: A Case of Statistical Myopia," *American Economic Review*, 74 (June 1984), 301–22.

# CHAPTER TEN

# INFLATION AND MONEY GROWTH TRENDS

In Chapter 9 we discussed economic growth in real terms. The focus was on the determinants of the long-run trend rate of growth in real income. But just as the world is generally characterized by rising real income and output over time, so is it generally characterized by rising prices or inflation. As with income, prices do not grow steadily through time, but differ over time and across countries, depending upon short-run cyclical changes as well as the underlying determinants of the long-run trend inflation rate. While later chapters address the short-run cyclical changes, in this chapter we are concerned with the factors that influence the long-run trend rate of inflation.

## 10.1 MONEY AND GROWTH

### THE DYNAMIC CAMBRIDGE IDENTITY

Chapter 10 is concerned with the growth of nominal variables. Such growth is most easily analyzed in terms of the Cambridge identity seen earlier as equation (6.11) which is rewritten here:

$$M \equiv KyP \qquad (10.1)$$

Nominal money ($M$) is equal to the product of the price level ($P$), real income ($y$), and the "Cambridge $K$"—the fraction of nominal income people choose to hold as money. $K$ is the ratio of money to income. Recalling from Chapter 9 that the growth rate of a product of variables is equal to the sum of the growth rates of the individual variables, we can transform equation (10.1) into growth rates to yield the **dynamic Cambridge identity**.

$$\hat{M} \equiv \hat{K} + \hat{y} + \hat{P} \qquad (10.2)$$

The dynamic version of the Cambridge identity indicates that the growth rate of the money supply is equal to the sum of the growth rates of the money–income ratio, real income, and the price level.

We usually refer to the growth rate of the price level as the **inflation rate**. To say that the rate of inflation was 6 percent over the last year means that the price level is 6 percent higher today than it was a year ago. By subtracting $\hat{K}$ and $\hat{y}$ from each side of equation (10.2), we can solve for the inflation rate as:

$$\hat{P} \equiv \hat{M} - \hat{K} - \hat{y} \qquad (10.3)$$

So inflation can be explained by the growth rates of nominal money, the Cambridge $K$, and real income.

Alternatively, since real money $m$ is equal to nominal money divided by the price level ($m \equiv M/P$), the price level is equal to the ratio of nominal to real money ($P \equiv M/m$). In terms of growth rates, an alternative expression for inflation is:

$$\hat{P} \equiv \hat{M} - \hat{m} \qquad (10.4)$$

Equation (10.4) explains inflation as the difference between the growth rates of nominal and real money. A comparison of equations (10.3) and (10.4) reminds us that $\hat{m} \equiv \hat{K} + \hat{y}$, or in terms of the levels of the variables, real money is equal to the product of $K$ and real income.[1]

## THE EQUILIBRIUM INFLATION RATE

Equation (10.3) indicates that the inflation rate is determined by the growth rates of nominal money, the money–income ratio, and real income. The growth rate of nominal money is assumed exogenous, being determined by government monetary policy. The chosen value

---

[1]Since $K = \dfrac{M}{Y} = \dfrac{m}{y}$, multiplying $K$ by $y$ cancels the $y$ term and leaves

$m \colon \left(\dfrac{m}{y}\right) y = m.$

of the money growth rate will be denoted as $\overline{M}$. Different values of $\overline{M}$ will imply different rates of inflation. Remember, however, that at this point we are considering the steady-state values of our growth rates, or the trend growth of money and inflation. Later chapters will consider the short-run fluctuations around the trend.

The growth rate of real income is determined by the factors considered in Chapter 9. In the neoclassical growth model, real income was growing at the steady-state rate $\bar{y}$ determined by the exogenously given growth rate of labor. We can use this value for $\bar{y}$ to find our steady-state inflation rate.

Finally, we must know $\hat{K}$ or the growth of the desired ratio of money to income. In long-run equilibrium, the actual value of $K$ will equal its desired value. This is equivalent to saying that money demand and supply will be equal. So the growth rate of $K$ can be explained by changes in the factors which determine the desired $K$. In Chapter 6 we learned that at any point in time, desired $K$ ($K^d$) was a function of real income and the difference between the return on bonds ($R$) and the return of money ($R_M$):

$$K^d = K^d\,(y, R - R_M) \tag{10.5}$$

In terms of the desired growth in $K$, real income growth will cause desired $K$ to increase or decrease over time if people want to hold an increasing or decreasing fraction of their wealth as money as they become wealthier.[2] As was pointed out in Chapter 6, the effect of $y$ on $K$ is uncertain both theoretically and empirically, as the existing evidence will not allow definitive judgments. Regarding the $(R - R_M)$ interest differential, we know that the level of nominal interest rates will be constant in steady-state equilibrium; therefore, there are no steady-state changes in the opportunity cost variable to contribute to the growth rate of $K^d$. So while $(R - R_M)$ will affect the level of desired $K$, it will not influence the steady-state growth rate. There are additional factors which are not explicitly listed in equation (10.5) that could affect the growth rate of $K$. Changes in technical and institutional conditions affecting the way we use money in transacting, like the use of credit cards, are potentially very important sources of

---

[2]If K increases with real income growth, money is often said to be a luxury (something you consume relatively more of as income increases). If $K$ decreases with real income growth, then money is often said to be a necessity (something you consume relatively less of as income increases). See Chapter 6, footnote 8 for additional discussion.

change in $\hat{K}^d$.[3] Such factors are not easily measured and are best thought of as shifting the relation between $K^d$ and $y$ and $(R - R_M)$. Taken as a whole, we may assume that the combined effects of real income growth, institutional changes, and technological progress produce a constant trend growth rate of $K^d$ denoted as $\bar{\hat{K}}^d$. This is not at all an unreasonable assumption, as the trend growth of $K$ has appeared to be nearly constant for long periods of time. Figure 10.1 illustrates the downward trend in $K$ since the early 1950s. For the period 1952–83, $\hat{K}$ averaged $-2.87$ percent per annum, over the 1952–67 period, $K$ growth averaged $-2.87$ percent, and for 1967–83 the rate of growth was $-2.87$ percent. The assumption of a constant $\hat{K}$ is seen to be quite reasonable.

The steady-state equilibrium inflation rate is found by substituting the steady-state growth rates of $M$, $K$, and $y$ into equation (10.3):

$$\bar{\hat{P}} = \bar{\hat{M}} - (\bar{\hat{K}} + \bar{\hat{y}}) \tag{10.6}$$

Since $(\hat{K} + \hat{y})$ determines real money demand growth, equation (10.6) may be interpreted as saying that the inflation rate is given by the difference between the growth rates of the nominal money supply and real money demand. This is the inflation rate that will maintain the continuous equality of the supply and demand for money.

Inflation is equal to the difference between nominal money supply growth and real money demand growth.

The terminology relating to inflation and the price level is often confusing. *Inflation* properly refers to a condition of *rising* prices or a positive rate of inflation. *Deflation* is a condition of *falling* prices, or a negative rate of inflation. To say that prices are high is not the same thing as saying that there is a high rate of inflation. It must be understood that inflation refers to the growth rate of prices and not the price level at a particular point in time.

While equation (10.6) indicates that the rate of inflation depends upon the growth rates of real income and $K$, inflation is generally considered to be a monetary phenomenon. This is because money

---

[3]According to Michael David Bordo of the University of South Carolina and Lars Jonung of Lund University, institutional factors can explain much of the long-run behavior of the money-income ratio in the United States, Canada, Great Britain, Norway, and Sweden. Across countries, they argue that the differences between the level of the money-income ratio at a given point in time "could primarily be explained by the financial and monetary development of the economy." (Bordo and Jonung, "The Long Run Behavior of the Income Velocity of Money in Five Advanced Countries, 1870–1975: An Institutional Approach," *Economic Inquiry*, 19 (January 1981), 96–116).

**Figure 10.1**

The Value of *K*, the Ratio of
Money to Income, 1952–83

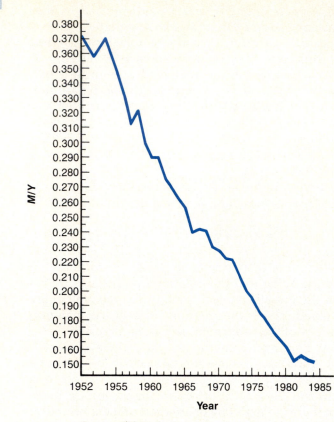

**Source:** *IFS Yearbook.*

supply growth, being subject to government policy, can change
widely compared to the growth rates of the real variables. Equation
(10.6) reminds us that inflation occurs when the nominal money supply grows faster than real money demand. It is generally true that
the impetus behind inflation comes from the supply side of the
money market when the monetary authorities increase money supply growth in excess of the growth in demand.

This theory of inflation summarized by equation (10.6) has been
very thoroughly documented and tested by numerous researchers.
Even though the experience across time and across countries generally conforms to the theory, there is a tendency by economists and
politicans to attempt to explain each inflationary episode as being
due to special circumstances rather than some general rule. In a
sense such rationalizations might be expected from the authorities
responsible for economic policy, who may not want to incur the costs
of lowering inflation or receive the blame for an unpopular inflation.

While macroeconomic policymaking will be discussed in Chapter 14, we will consider some of the special factors often cited as causing inflation in the essay at the end of the chapter.

## 10.2 INFLATION, INTEREST RATES, AND THE CAMBRIDGE *K*

### INFLATION AND INTEREST RATES

The essay at the end of Chapter 4 introduced the tax-adjusted **Fisher equation**:

$$R = r + \hat{P} + \frac{t}{1-t}\hat{P} \qquad (10.7)$$

Tax-adjusted Fisher equation

$$R = r + \hat{P} + \frac{t}{1-t}\hat{P}$$

The nominal interest rate ($R$) is equal to the real rate of interest $r$ plus the rate of inflation $\rho$ plus the additional increase in $R$ required to compensate for the effect of taxes $\frac{t}{1-t}\hat{P}$. The average real interest rate in the economy must equal the marginal product of capital—the increase in real output given an additional unit of capital. While actual individual returns may differ, this is the average real return earned by holders of financial securities. In the steady-state equilibrium, the marginal product of capital, and hence the real interest rate, is a constant $\bar{r}$ determined by the real factors discussed in Chapter 9. We have just determined the steady-state inflation rate in the last section, so we know $\hat{P}$. As for the tax effect, $t$ is the tax rate set by the government and applied to income. Since nominal interest receipts are taxed as income, the nominal interest rate must rise by more than the rate of inflation to keep the after-tax real rate of interest constant (see the End-of-chapter essay for Chapter 4).

Given $\bar{r}$, $t$, and $\hat{\bar{P}}$, we can determine the steady-state nominal interest rate:

$$\bar{R} = \bar{r} + \hat{\bar{P}} + \frac{t}{1-t}\hat{\bar{P}} \qquad (10.8)$$

Now we can see the constancy of the nominal interest rate in steady-state equilibrium.

### IMPLICATIONS FOR THE CAMBRIDGE *K* AND REAL OUTPUT

If the steady-state equilibrium has an unchanged interest rate, then changes in nominal interest rates are not a source of steady-state growth in $K$. However, the level of nominal interest rates will affect the level of $K$ at any point in time as equation (10.5) indicates. We know from equation (10.6) that higher rates of money supply growth are associated with higher rates of inflation, while the Fisher equation shows that higher inflation leads to higher nominal interest rates. We can then put together a causal chain of events leading to a change in the level (but not the growth rate) of $K$: An increase in money supply growth causes greater inflation and therefore a higher nominal interest rate; the higher interest rate causes a fall in the level of $K$. Figure 10.2 illustrates this effect using a **comparative dynamics** approach where we consider two alternative steady-state growth rates of money.

**comparative dynamics**
Comparison of different steady-state growth rates

Suppose $\bar{\hat{M}}_1$ exceeds $\bar{\hat{M}}_0$, where the subscripts 1 and 0 denote the two alternative steady states. With the higher money growth of state 1, there will be a higher inflation rate and consequently a higher nominal interest rate $\bar{R}_1$ than in state 0. Since $K$ is a decreasing function of the nominal interest rate, $K$ or the ratio of money to income will be lower in state 1 than in state 0 at any point in time. The faster money growth of state 1 is shown in Figure 10.2(a) by the steeper $M_1$ line, relative to $M_0$. Figure 10.2(b) illustrates the growth rate curves. The higher line for $\bar{\hat{M}}_1$ than $\bar{\hat{M}}_0$ indicates that the steady-state money growth rate in state 1 will exceed that of state 0. But what about the money-income ratio? Figure 10.2(a) indicates that the curve giving the level of $K$ is lower in the higher money growth state 1. With the $K_1$ line below the $K_0$ line, at any point in time the level of the money-income ratio will be lower along $K_1$ than $K_0$. However the $K_0$ and $K_1$ lines both show $K$ growing at the same rate at any point in time. This is indicated in Figure 10.2(b) by the fact that the growth rate curves for $\hat{K}_0$ and $\hat{K}_1$ are identical. Whether $\bar{\hat{M}}_1$ or $\bar{\hat{M}}_0$ is realized, the steady-state growth rate of the Cambridge $K$ is unchanged although the level of $K$ is altered.

**Figure 10.2**

Effects of the Growth Rate of Nominal Money on the Growth Path of the Money–Income Ratio
a) Levels
b) Growth Rates

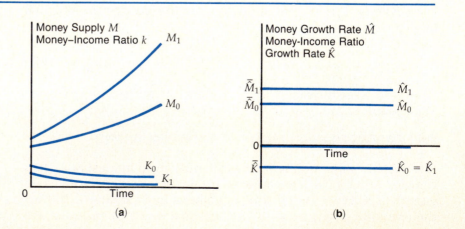

(a)

(b)

An important question is whether there are any real economic changes as a result of the change in the steady-state path of the level of *K*. If the use of money increases economic efficiency compared to a barter economy, then the fact that high interest rates lower the ratio of money to income may impose real costs on the economy. If high interest rates cause people to use more real resources to economize on money holdings, then taking into consideration the costs of making transactions, real income will fall for any given level of labor and capital. The level of real money balances to facilitate monetary exchange is a factor underlying the aggregate production function. Therefore, the higher growth rate of the money supply would lower real money balances, and hence the level of real income, at any point in time due to the downward shift in the production function. Yet the growth rate of real income remains equal to the growth of labor (in line with the growth model of Chapter 9) after the one-time fall in *y*.

We should not expect this once-and-for-all drop in the level of real income to be very substantial. The lower level of income at each point in time reflects the substitution of real resources—computing payrolls more often, making more trips to the bank, making more detailed cash flow plans and the like—for the services of real money balances. Furthermore, empirical estimates of the size of the negative impacts of money-induced increases in interest rates on the desired money-income ratio (*K*) and real income are unsettled.[4] The major impact of interest rates on money demand should apply to currency since banks may pay interest, either explicitly or implicitly, on deposits.

These indirect effects of the rate of growth of the nominal money supply on the desired money-income ratio and real income blur the strict distinction between the real sector of the economy and the nominal money supply that economists often assume in analyses of long-run equilibrium. In Chapters 7–9 we assumed that money had no impact on the real value of output or its determinants. In Chapter 8 it was stated that the level of the nominal money supply affects only

Nominal money growth can affect the level of real output.

_____

[4]The difficulty in evaluating the empirical data occurs because the money-income ratio is expected to vary over the business cycle for reasons other than just variations in interest rates. Economists who include some or all of these other reasons in their analyses report a much smaller, or no influence of interest rates on the long-run desired level of *K* than do those who leave the alternative forces out of their statistical analyses. For a particularly agnostic view on the effect of interest on money demand, see Thomas F. Cooley and Stephen F. LeRoy, "Identification and Estimation of Money Demand," *American Economic Review*, 71 (December 1981), 825–44.

**neutrality**
The level of the nominal money supply affects only the nominal variables, not the real economy in the long run

**superneutrality**
The growth rate of the nominal money supply affects only nominal variables, not the real economy in the long run

the price level and not the real economy in long-run equilibrium. This is often referred to as the **neutrality** of money. In the present section we have suggested that *the growth rate of the nominal money supply can affect the real value of output and the equilibrium money-income ratio*. If this is not true, so that even the growth rate of nominal money will not affect real income and $K$ in long-run equilibrium, then money is said to be **superneutral**. To illustrate the difference between an economy characterized by the superneutrality of money and an economy where money growth has real effects, we will consider two examples using **comparative dynamics**—comparing the steady-state equilibrium growth rates under two alternative money growth rates.

## 10.3 COMPARATIVE DYNAMICS EXAMPLES

### SUPERNEUTRAL MONEY

We will compare and contrast the steady-state equilibria implied by two alternative nominal money supply growth rates. The implications of such alternatives would influence the government's choice of a monetary policy. We assume here that the desired value of $K$, the money-income ratio, and real income are independent of the growth rate of nominal money. Thus we are assuming money is superneutral.

Suppose that the two proposed nominal money growth rates are 3 percent and 7 percent per annum. We will use a subscript 0 for steady-state equilibrium values corresponding to the 3 percent per annum growth rate and a subscript 1 for those corresponding to the 7 percent rate. We will measure growth rates in percentage points (sometimes they are measured as decimal numbers, like 0.03 or 0.07) so that $\hat{M}_0 = 3\%$ and $\hat{M}_1 = 7\%$.

Before considering specific numerical examples, we can summarize the important relationships covered by Chapters 9 and 10 in Table 10.1. By substituting actual numerical values into the definitions of Table 10.1 we can obtain solutions. Some values—such as the level and growth rate of money—are given as the basis of the problem. Other values—like the growth rate and level of the money-income ratio and real income and the level of the real interest rate—will reflect the real resources, tastes, technology, and institutions of the economy, and are unaffected by changes in $\hat{M}$ in the superneutral case. The remaining values can be derived from the given variables.

Table 10.2 gives actual numerical values for our key variables assuming $\hat{M}_0 = 3\%$, $\hat{M}_1 = 7\%$, $\hat{K} = -2\%$, $\bar{\hat{y}} = 4\%$, $\bar{r} = 3\%$, $M = 200$, $K = 0.2$, and $y = 800$. Working down through the table, the values of $\hat{M}$ are given as are the values of $\hat{K}$. The growth rate of nominal income

Table 10.1

| | | |
|---|---|---|
| Growth rate of nominal money | $\hat{M}$ | |
| Growth rate of the money-income ratio | $\hat{K}$ | |
| Growth rate of nominal income | $\hat{Y} = \hat{M} - \hat{K}$ | |
| Growth rate of real income | $\hat{y}$ | |
| Inflation rate | $\hat{P} = \hat{Y} - \hat{y}$ | |
| Real interest rate | $r$ | |
| Nominal interest rate | $R = r + \hat{P} + \dfrac{t}{1-t}\hat{P}$ | |
| | | |
| Nominal money | $M$ | |
| Money-income ratio | $K$ | |
| Nominal income | $Y = M/K$ | |
| Real Income | $y$ | |
| Price level | $P = Y/y$ | |

A Summary of Key Macroeconomic Variable Definitions

is computed as the difference between the growth rates of nominal money and the money-income ratio:

$$\hat{\bar{Y}}_0 = \hat{\bar{M}}_0 - \hat{\bar{K}}_0 = 3\% - (-2\%) = 5\%$$
$$\hat{\bar{Y}}_1 = \hat{\bar{M}}_1 - \hat{\bar{K}}_1 = 7\% - (-2\%) = 9\%$$

Notice that the difference in the two states' nominal-income growth rates equals the difference in their nominal money growth rates, 4 percent. Continuing down through the table, the growth rate of real income is given at 4 percent. The inflation rate is computed as the difference between the growth rates of nominal and real income:

$$\hat{\bar{P}}_0 = \hat{\bar{Y}}_0 - \hat{\bar{y}}_0 = 5\% - 4\% = 1\%$$
$$\hat{\bar{P}}_1 = \hat{\bar{Y}}_1 - \hat{\bar{y}}_1 = 9\% - 4\% = 5\%$$

Note that the difference between the two steady-state inflation rates also equals the money growth differential of 4 percent. The real interest rate is given at 3 percent, and the nominal interest rate is equal to the sum of the real rate, the rate of inflation, plus a tax adjustment. Assuming the marginal tax rate is 1/3:

$$\bar{R}_0 = \bar{r} + \hat{\bar{P}}_0 + \frac{t}{1-t}\hat{\bar{P}}_0 = 3\% + 1\% + \frac{(1/3)}{(2/3)}1\% = 4.5\%$$

$$\bar{R}_1 = \bar{r} + \hat{\bar{P}}_1 + \frac{t}{1-t}\hat{\bar{P}}_1 = 3\% + 5\% + \frac{(1/3)}{(2/3)}5\% = 10.5\%$$

Note that the nominal interest differential between the two states is 6 percent, which exceeds the money growth differential. When two

Table 10.2

| Variable | State 0 | State 1 |
|---|---|---|
| Growth rate of nominal money ($\hat{M}$) | 3% | 7% |
| Growth rate of the money-income ratio ($\hat{K}$) | −2% | −2% |
| Growth rate of nominal income ($\hat{Y}$) | 5% | 9% |
| Growth rate of real income ($\hat{y}$) | 4% | 4% |
| Inflation rate ($\hat{P}$) | 1% | 5% |
| Real interest rate ($\bar{r}$) | 3% | 3% |
| Nominal interest rate ($\bar{R}$, assuming t = 1/3) | 4.5% | 10.5% |
| Nominal money ($M$) | 200 | 200 |
| Money-income ratio ($K$) | 0.2 | 0.2 |
| Nominal income ($Y$) | 1000 | 1000 |
| Real income ($y$) | 800 | 800 |
| Price level ($P$) | 1.25 | 1.25 |

steady-state money growth rates are considered, the difference in the steady-state nominal interest rates will always exceed the difference in money growth rates unless the tax rate *t* is zero.[5] Remember that this increase in the interest rate is required to be larger than the difference in inflation rates to keep the after tax real rate of interest unchanged.

To complete the rest of Table 10.2, it is convenient to investigate the values of the levels of the variables when the nominal money supplies are equal, say at $M_0 = M_1 = 200$. Assuming that at this point in time, the desired money-income ratio equals 0.2, the level of nominal income may be found by dividing the nominal money supply by the money-income ratio:

$$Y_0 = M_0/K_0 = 200/0.2 = 1000$$
$$Y_1 = M_1/K_1 = 200/0.2 = 1000$$

At this point in time, nominal income will be the same in either case. Yet over time, with the higher growth rate of case 1, we would expect nominal income in case 1 to diverge farther and farther from that of case 0. Assuming that at this point in time real income equals 800 in

[5]The interest differential may be written as:

$$\bar{R} - \bar{R}_0 = \bar{\hat{P}}_1 - \bar{\hat{P}}_0 + \frac{t}{1 - t}(\bar{\hat{P}}_1 - \bar{\hat{P}}_0) = \frac{1}{1 - t}(\bar{\hat{M}}_1 - \bar{\hat{M}}_0)$$

As long as *t* exceeds zero, $\bar{R}_1 - \bar{R}_0$ will exceed the inflation increase.

either case, the price level may be found by the ratio of nominal to real income:

$$P_0 = Y_0/y_0 = 1000/800 = 1.25$$
$$P_1 = Y_1/y_1 = 1000/800 = 1.25$$

Since we know that the inflation rate is higher in state 1, the state 1 price level will rise faster and diverge from that of state 0 as we progress beyond this particular point in time.

To sum up the superneutral case, different growth rates of the nominal money supply do not affect the growth rates of the money-income ratio, real income, or the real interest rate; they do, however, cause identical differences in the rates of growth of nominal income and prices, and differences in nominal interest rates $1/(1 - t)$ times as large as the difference in nominal money growth rates. The levels of real variables, such as real income and the money-income ratio, are independent of *both* the level and growth rate of nominal money. Nominal income and the price level in the two states are in proportion to the nominal money supplies. While the real world never provides such neat, clear-cut examples as Table 10.2, such a table does allow us to better understand what superneutral money implies.

## NONSUPERNEUTRAL MONEY

Let us now turn to the case in which money is not superneutral. While the interest rates and growth rates of the variables are unchanged in this case and therefore equal to their values shown in Table 10.2, the levels will be affected by the steady-state change in money growth. Table 10.3 provides a numerical example of new equilibrium values of our key variables. The top part of the table down to nominal money is identical to Table 10.2. However, if money is not superneutral, then changes in money growth can have real effects, as we see with the money-income ratio. Suppose that when nominal interest rates increase from 4.5 percent to 10.5 percent, money demand falls so that the desired level of the money-income ratio is reduced by 25 percent, others things equal.[6] This is reflected in the new level of $K$ equal to 0.15 in state 1 of Table 10.3. While nominal

---

[6]This would correspond to an interest elasticity of money demand equal to about $-0.3$. If this elasticity were $-0.1$, the decrease in $K$ would be only about 8 percent. See Chapter 5, section 1, for a discussion of money demand elasticity.

Table 10.3

Numerical Solution for Nonsuperneutral Money Example

| Variable | State 0 | State 1 |
|---|---|---|
| Growth rate of nominal money ($\bar{\hat{M}}$) | 3% | 7% |
| Growth rate of the money-income ratio ($\hat{K}$) | −2% | −2% |
| Growth rate of nominal income ($\hat{Y}$) | 5% | 9% |
| Growth rate of real income ($\hat{y}$) | 4% | 4% |
| Inflation rate ($\hat{P}$) | 1% | 5% |
| Real interest rate ($\bar{r}$) | 3% | 3% |
| Nominal interest rate ($\bar{R}$, assuming $t = 1/3$) | 4.5% | 10.5% |
| Nominal money ($M$) | 200 | 200 |
| Money-income ratio ($K$) *Nonsuperneutral* | 0.2 | 0.15 |
| Nominal income ($Y$) = ($M/K$) | 1000 | 1333 |
| Real income ($y$) *Nonsuperneutral* | 800 | 784 |
| Price level ($P$) = ($Y/y$) | 1.25 | 1.70 |

income is the same in state 0 as before, in state 1 we find the new nominal income as the given money supply divided by the new value for the money-income ratio:

$$Y_1 = M_1/K_1 = 200/0.15 = 1333$$

While real income is given in state 0 as being equal to 800, we will assume that the increased transactions costs associated with holding less money lowers real income in state 1. Let's asume that real income is decreased by 2 percent in state 1 so that $y_1 = 0.98 \times y_0 = 0.98 \times 800 = 784$. We can then find the price levels by dividing nominal income by real income:

$$P_0 = Y_0/y_0 = 1000/800 = 1.25$$
$$P_1 = Y_1/y_1 = 1333/784 = 1.70$$

Note that the ratio of the price levels of 1.70/1.25 = 1.36 differs from the ratio of nominal money in the two states: 200/200 = 1. This differ-ence is determined by the fall in real income of 2 percent and the fall in the money-income ratio of 25 percent. In fact, the ratio of the price levels differs from the nominal money ratio by a factor of $1/[(K_1/K_0) \times (y_1/y_0)]$:[7]

$$\frac{1}{(K_1/K_0 \times y_1/y_0)} = \frac{1}{0.75 \times 0.98} = \frac{1}{0.735} = 1.36$$

The greater the fall in $K$ and $y$ in state 1, the higher the price level.

If money is not superneutral, then the steady-state levels—but not growth rates—of real variables will be affected by a higher growth rate of nominal money. In particular, there will be a smaller amount of real goods and services available for consumption and investment. Is this likely, or is superneutrality more probable? While the strict conditions for the superneutrality of money almost surely do not hold, many economists nevertheless analyze a particular problem as if money were superneutral on the grounds that the shifts in the levels of real variables are negligible compared to the changes in growth rates.[8]

The effects of money growth on real output are likely to be small so that superneutrality may be a useful assumption.

---

[7]Since $P = Y/y$ and $Y = M/K$, we can write our price ratio as
$$\frac{P_1}{P_0} = \frac{(M_1/K_1)/y_1}{(M_0/K_0)/y_0} = \frac{(M_1/M_0)}{(K_1/K_0 \times (y_1/y_0))}.$$ So $P_1/P_0$ will differ from the ratio of nominal money in the two states by $\dfrac{1}{(K_1/K_0) \times (y_1/y_0)}$.

[8]This is similar to the use of the perfectly competitive model in microeconomics to analyze problems for which it is not strictly applicable. Frequently a simple understandable analysis which gives an answer correct to within, say, 5 percent is preferable to a more accurate, but much more complicated, analysis.

---

**SUMMARY**

1   Desired growth of the money-income ratio will be determined by growth in real income and the interest rate.

2   The steady-state equilibrium inflation rate is found by subtracting the steady-state growth rates of the money-income ratio and real income from the steady-state money growth rate, or inflation occurs when the nominal money supply grows faster than real money demand.

3   The steady-state nominal interest rate is equal to the steady-state real rate of interest plus the steady-state rate of inflation plus the additional increase in interest required to compensate for the effect of taxes.

4   The steady-state equilibrium interest rate is constant.

5   Higher steady-state nominal money growth will lower the level of the money-income ratio, but not its growth rate.

6   Since the use of money makes transacting more efficient, a fall in the money-income ratio could lower the level of real income by making transactions more costly.

7   Money is neutral if the level of the nominal money supply does not affect the values of real variables in equilibrium.

8   Money is superneutral if the growth rate of the nominal money supply will not affect real income in long-run equilibrium.

## EXERCISES

1. Comment on the following quotation: "Inflation arises from too much money chasing too few goods."

2. During the post-World War I German hyperinflation, German central bankers claimed that the inflation could not be blamed on them because they were just meeting the increased demand for money due to increased income. Indeed, they claimed, monetary policy was restrictive because interest rates were high and money was a smaller fraction of income. What is wrong with this argument?

3. Compare the effects of alternative rates of monetary growth by filling in the blanks in the following table:

| Variable | State 0 | State 1 |
|---|---|---|
| Growth rate of money supply | 6% | 11% |
| Growth rate of the money-income ratio | | |
| Growth rate of nominal income | 5% | |
| Growth rate of real income | | |
| Growth rate of the price level | 2% | |
| Real interest rate | | |
| Nominal interest rate (tax rate = 1/2) | 8% | |

4. Test your understanding of the relationships among key macroeconomic variables by filling in the following table:

| Variable | State 0 | State 1 |
|---|---|---|
| Nominal money | 600 | 600 |
| Money-income ratio | .4 | .3 |
| Nominal income | | |
| Real income | | |
| Price level | 1.25 | 1.67 |

5. If the steady-state nominal growth rate of money increases from 10 percent to 12 percent, how much should the nominal interest rate rise if the marginal tax rate on interest income is 0.25? Why do you expect the interest rate to rise by this particular amount?

6. If money is not superneutral, how much will the price level rise from the initial steady state to the new steady state if: $M_0 = 100$, $M_1 = 110$, $K_0 = .3$, $K_1 = .2$, $y_0 = 2000$, $y_1 = 1800$?

## REFERENCES FOR FURTHER READING

Bordo, Michael David, and Lars Jonung. "The Long-Run Behavior of the Income Velocity of Money in Five Advanced Countries, 1870–1975: An Institutional Approach." *Economic Inquiry*, 19 (January 1981), 96–116.

Johnson, Harry G. "Money in a Neo-Classical One-Sector Growth Model." In *Essays in Monetary Economics*. London: George Allen and Unwin, 1967.

Meltzer, Allan H. "Money, Intermediation, and Growth." *Journal of Economic Literature*, 7 (March 1969), 27–56.

Tobin, James. "Money and Economic Growth." *Econometrica*, 33 (October 1965), 671–84.

## WHO CAUSES INFLATION?

When asked "Who causes inflation?" the average citizen often puts the blame on a perceived adversary. Labor groups have argued that what we experience is "profit-push" inflation, caused by greedy business leaders raising prices to increase profit margins. Business spokesmen have argued that our inflation is "wage-push" inflation, caused by greedy workers demanding wage increases in excess of productivity increases. Still another group, politicians, often point to special circumstances like bad weather or foreign powers as causing our inflationary problems. Is there any truth to be distilled from this outpouring of blame or do the root causes of inflation lie elsewhere?

Consider the first two charges of "profit push" and "wage push" inflation. There is no doubt that both labor and management want to live as well as possible—we all do. But this is nothing new. People have always wanted to maximize their incomes to better provide for their families. If business and labor have always been "greedy," then how do we explain the fact that the inflation rate has risen and fallen, and while U.S. inflation rates were quite high in the late 1970s, in the 1950s we experienced a long period of price stability? It would be stretching matters to suggest that during periods of rapid inflation, people are greedier than at other times, so we must look for other explanations.

The "special circumstances" school of thought would explain each inflationary episode by a unique event. Thus the inflation of the 1970s would be labeled "energy-related," as the dramatic increase in oil prices of that period would be tied to the overall inflationary climate. The problem with such explanations is that each "event" would cause a rise in the price level and not the long-run growth rate of prices. If by inflation, we mean a prolonged rise in the price level, then a single event like a price rise by an oil cartel, a bad harvest, or a major flood could not explain such inflation. While each event could certainly cause a shift in the price level, this would be a once-and-for-all shift that would not involve a change in the steady-state inflation rate. So where can we find an acceptable explanation of inflation?

We know from Chapter 10 that solving the dynamic Cambridge identity for the inflation rate (equation 10.3) yields:

$$\hat{P} \equiv \hat{M} - \hat{K} - \hat{y}$$

As an identity, this will always be true and accepted by all. We can view this equation as saying inflation is given by the difference between nominal money supply and real money demand. So to say that inflation is a monetary phenomenon is a tautology. A sustained rise in the price level would be the result of a sustained fall in the growth of real money demand relative to the growth of nominal money supply or a sustained rise in the growth of the nominal money supply relative to the growth of real money demand. When we consider the growth of the determinants of real money demand, it would seem that real money demand should grow over time with the growth of real income. But if real money demand is rising at the same time the inflation rate is rising, it must be true that the nominal money supply is growing faster than demand. Most macroeconomists today would agree that inflation is caused by the monetary authorities following a policy of excessive monetary growth rates. If money demand grows in a fairly stable fashion, as studies indicate, then fluctuations in the rate of inflation will be caused by fluctuations in the growth rate of money. Table E10.1 shows the growth rates of nominal money (M1 definition) for Germany, Israel, Mexico, and the U.S. While conditions differ in each country, we see that higher money growth rates are associated with higher inflation rates.

While there may be important policy issues related to the timing of the relationship between money and inflation that cannot be shown in Table E10.1, the obvious feature is the link between high inflation and high money growth. This is not a startling result, as virtually no studies of inflation find rapid inflation apart from rapid money growth.

Putting the blame for inflation on the government officials in charge of the money supply seems reasonable in light of the historical evidence. The obvious question is why have governments chosen to follow a policy of inflation? While we will address macroeconomic policy in detail in Chapters 14 and 15, we can offer some simple answers here. In many countries, government-issued money is an important source of funding government spending. The resources the government gains from money creation is known as *seigniorage*. Stanley Fischer of M.I.T. has estimated that seigniorage was approximately 2.1 percent of total U.S. government revenue over the 1960–78 period.[1] While this figure is quite small, indi-

---

[1]Stanley Fischer, "Seigniorage and the Case for a National Money," *Journal of Political Economy*, 90 (April 1982), 295–313.

Money Growth and Inflation, 1978–1983

| Country | Money Growth* | Inflation Rate† |
|---------|---------------|-----------------|
| Germany | 4.3% | 4.4% |
| Israel | 77.0% | 91.0% |
| Mexico | 36.0% | 39.0% |
| U.S. | 7.1% | 7.8% |

*Average annual growth rate of M1.
†Average annual growth rate of the consumer price index.

cating that seigniorage is not an important source of government revenue in the U.S., for other countries we see a different story. Fischer estimates that seigniorage was approximately 10 percent of government revenue in Italy and 46 percent of government revenue in Argentina.

Aside from the seigniorage issue, governments manipulate the money supply to help finance government bond sales, affect the level of interest rates, and achieve a myriad of other goals suggested by economists. Monetary economists have spent a considerable research effort trying to understand central bank behavior. While it seems fair to say that inflation is essentially created by those in charge of the money supply, economists disagree when assessing the motives for inflationary money growth. The discussion in Chapter 14 will allow a better understanding of the issues.

# CHAPTER ELEVEN

# DYNAMIC ADJUSTMENT OF NOMINAL INCOME TO A MONETARY SHOCK

## 11.1 TYPES OF MONETARY SHOCK

In Chapters 9 and 10 we focused on the process of steady-state economic growth. Realistically, our steady-state growth paths are continually interrupted by macroeconomic shocks, unexpected events that either force the economy away from equilibrium or change the equilibrium itself. Much of the dynamics of business cycles can be seen as the adjustment response to a shock. In this sense, the analysis of adjustments to macroeconomic shocks is the heart of macroeconomics.

Macroeconomic shocks are unexpected events.

Shocks to the economy could be real, like unexpected tax or government spending changes. We will concentrate on monetary shocks here, however, as these can be easily related to discretionary policy decisions and have been shown by researchers to be empirically important sources of economic disturbances. Chapter 13 will address the effects of real shocks.

There are two kinds of monetary shocks. First, there may be an unexpected change in the level of the money supply. In this case money growth is different from the steady-state growth rate only for the one period in which the shock occurs, and then returns to the steady-state growth rate in following periods. Second, the steady-state growth rate of the money supply could be changed unexpectedly. In this case, rather than a one-period unexpected change in the growth rate, the new steady-state growth rate will persist into the future. The element of surprise is crucial here. We refer to unexpected changes as shocks because they catch everyone by surprise. Predictable change—such as the central bank following an announced policy—will be incorporated in the steady-state equilibrium. We will see later that unpredictability is essential to the nature of shocks because people's actions are based on their expectations, yet things often do not turn out as expected.

We can highlight the effects of unexpected changes in nominal money supply growth by starting from an equilibrium based on one growth rate of the nominal money supply, changing that growth rate, and tracing the adjustment of the economy until the new steady-state equilibrium is achieved. In Chapter 10 we analyzed the difference between the initial steady-state equilibrium and the new steady-state. Now we want to analyze what happens in the period of transition from the initial steady-state to the new steady-state. A formal statement of the problem is: Starting from a steady-state with a nominal money supply growth rate of $\hat{M}_0$, what would be the effects of an unexpected change at time $z$ to a new, different growth rate $\hat{M}_1$, which is maintained indefinitely thereafter? Actually, the problem as stated is somewhat artificial since a change in the nominal money supply growth rate usually occurs long before the economy has adjusted to the preceding growth rate change. Money supply growth has been quite volatile. (Chapter 14 will provide evidence of this volatility.) Since we are constantly facing a barrage of macroeconomic shocks, analysis of the important effects in a useful manner is aided if we organize our thoughts assuming that the latest shock disturbed an economy in steady-state equilibrium. Our historical review in Chapter 15 will offer some insight into the potential for different forces to be at work simultaneously, so that the conditions when the shock occurs may yield either reinforcing or offsetting effects to those basic effects discussed here.

The problem as stated suggests that the Federal Reserve System increases or decreases the growth rate of the money supply while all other macroeconomic shocks are excluded. We cannot, however, discuss such monetary changes in isolation. The government (with the accounts of the Federal Reserve System and Treasury consolidated) is subject to the budget identity

$$G \equiv T + \Delta B + \Delta D \tag{11.1}$$

That is, the rate of government spending $G$ is equal to the total of the rate of net taxes $T$ and the rates of change in base money $\Delta B$ and in the government debt held by the public $\Delta D$, where each of the variables is measured in nominal terms. This **government budget constraint** identity reminds us that if the government wishes to spend

government budget
constraint
$G = T + \Delta B + \Delta D$

more than it receives in taxes, it must increase changes in base money and/or the national debt. Conversely, decreases in the rate of change of base money or debt are the alternative possible uses of a government budget surplus where tax revenues exceed government spending. How does the money supply fit into equation (11.1)? In Chapter 3 we learned that the money supply is equal to the money multiplier times base money: $M = \mu B$. So the growth rate of the nominal money supply is equal to the sum of the growth rate of base money and the money multiplier: $\hat{M} = \hat{\mu} + \hat{B}$. On the reasonable assumption that the growth rate of the money multiplier is unchanged, the change in the growth rate of the money supply will require an equal change in the growth rate of base money:

$$\hat{M} = \hat{B} \text{ if } \hat{\mu} = 0. \qquad (11.2)$$

For a given amount $B$ of base money outstanding, the change in $\hat{B}$ is accomplished by a change in $\Delta B$, the rate of change in base money. But from equation (11.1) we see that for $\Delta B$ to change, there must be an offset in $G$, $T$, or $\Delta D$ changes.

In this chapter we will assume that changes in $\Delta B$ are offset by an opposite change in the rate of increase in government debt ($\Delta D$), so $\Delta D = - \Delta B$. This corresponds to the Fed increasing the growth rate of nominal base money by buying government bonds from the public at a faster rate. In Chapter 13, effects of changes in the rate of government spending and taxation, offset by changes in the rate of increase in the national debt, will be discussed. The results of the two chapters can be combined to analyze the effects of an increased growth rate of money which finances an increased rate of government spending or decreased rate of taxation.[1]

---

[1]Remember from Chapter 2 that interest payments on the government debt, as well as transfer payments, are subtracted from gross taxes to obtain net taxes $T$. For this reason, if we hold $T$ constant while $D$ rises, gross taxes must rise or transfer payments fall to offset rising government interest payments. An alternative form of the government budget identity is

$$G \equiv t \cdot Y - R \cdot D + \Delta B + \Delta D$$

where $t$ is used for the tax rate (not real taxes) and $t \cdot Y$ represents gross taxes minus transfers and $R \cdot D$ represents government interest payments. If the tax rate $t$ is constant, then changes in $\Delta D$ will have cumulative effects on $R \cdot D$. Thomas J. Sargent and Neil Wallace of the University of Minnesota have expressed concern (in "Some Unpleasant Monetarist Arithmetic," *Federal Reserve Bank of Minneapolis Quarterly Review*, 5 (Fall 1981), 1–17) that these cumulative effects will be ultimately overwhelming so that we can only analyze steady-state changes in money growth if we make the sort of tax rate changes implicit in the text's assumption of a given $T$. The cumulative effects of changes in borrowing can be shown not to be explosive, even with a given tax rate $t$, for countries like the United States where the after-tax real interest rate on government debt is less than the growth rate of real income. (See Michael R. Darby, "Some Pleasant Monetarist Arithmetic," *Federal Reserve Bank of Minneapolis Quarterly Review*, Spring 1984, 15–20.) So we need not quibble over whether net taxes or tax rates are taken as given for the analysis.

**easy money policy**
Stimulating the economy by increasing the money supply faster than expected

**tight money policy**
Contracting the economy by increasing the money supply slower than expected

An increase in the growth rate of nominal money is termed a *stimulative monetary policy* or **easy money policy** for reasons which will soon be obvious. A decrease in the nominal money growth rate is a *restrictive monetary policy* or a **tight money policy**. Sometimes people use interest rates as a guide to interpreting current policy, the idea being that falling interest rates signal an easy money policy while rising rates signal tight money. Section 12.4 will show why the cyclical adjustment of nominal interest rates makes them an unreliable indicator of the direction of monetary policy.

## 11.2 CYCLICAL ADJUSTMENT OF THE MONEY–INCOME RATIO

In analyzing the effects of a higher money growth rate, it is useful to first examine the impact on the money-income ratio $K$, and then nominal income $Y$. In Chapter 12 we will consider how fluctuations in nominal income are divided between real income and price level fluctuations.

Suppose the money shock is an increase in the growth rate of money from $\hat{M}_0$ to $\hat{M}_1$. Figure 11.1 illustrates this shift in the growth rate of money occurring at time period $z$ (at this point, $z$ could be a particular day, month, or year depending upon how time is being measured). Up to $z$, the growth paths of our key macroeconomic variables will be consistent with steady-state $0$ defined by money growth rate $\hat{M}_0$. After $z$, the economy will seek new growth paths

**Figure 11.1**

An Increase in the Money Supply Growth Rate at Time $z$

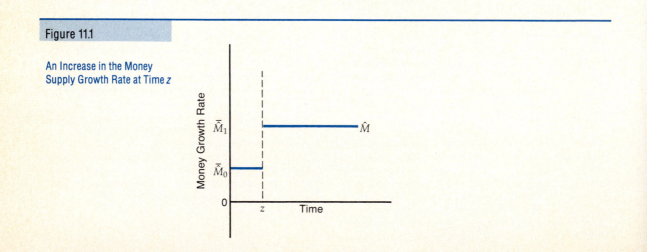

Figure 11.2

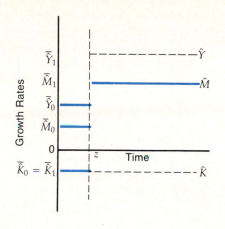

consistent with state l defined by $\hat{M}_1$. To see the cyclical response of our key variables to the monetary change, it is easier if we assume superneutrality of money. We will suppose that money yields a rate of interest $R_M$ such that money demanders are insensitive to changes in the return on money substitutes $R$. If the higher interest rate associated with higher money growth does not reduce the quantity of money demanded, then we may assume that changes in money growth have no real effect (see section 10.3), or money is superneutral. Be aware that we are not claiming $(R - R_M)$ is quite small in the real world, or that money is really superneutral; this is simply a convenient assumption which will allow us to see more easily the essential effects we consider.

Figure 11.2 illustrates the old and new steady-state growth rates of nominal income $\hat{Y}$ and the money-income ratio $\hat{K}$, along with the old and new money growth rates $\tilde{M}_0$ and $\tilde{M}_1$. Since the steady-state value of $\hat{K}$ is unaffected by the money growth rate change, maintaining this desired constant money-income ratio in the steady-state requires income to rise in proportion to the rise in money growth. Therefore the rise in the money growth rate in Figure 11.2 is equal to the rise in the nominal income growth rate. Why must this be true? Remember the dynamic Cambridge identity:

$$\tilde{M} \equiv \tilde{K} + \hat{Y} \qquad (11.13)$$

If $\tilde{K}$ is a constant, then $\tilde{Y}$ must rise to match the increase in $\hat{M}$. Why are the new steady-state growth paths, $\tilde{K}$ and $\tilde{Y}$, drawn with dashed rather than solid lines? This is because these new growth paths are not attained immediately following time $z$—the economy adjusts to the new money growth rate slowly over time. During this period of adjustment, the *actual* values of nominal income $Y$ and the money-income ratio $K$ deviate from their steady-state values. First we will consider the adjustment path of the money-income ratio, then we will turn to nominal income.

## THE SHOCK–ABSORBER ROLE OF MONEY

The analysis of Chapters 11 and 12 emphasizes that we should expect our key variables, following a shock, to behave differently in the short run than in the long run, when adjustment to the new steady-state equilibrium is complete. Underlying this dynamic pattern of adjustment is the money demand function. Specifically, there are two money demand functions worth noting: one in the short run and one in the long run. The long run demand for money underlies the steady-state equilibrium and determines the average money balances desired by individuals and firms. Such desired average money holdings are chosen considering the level of income and expenditures, wealth, and the interest rates paid on money and money substitutes. Yet for any particular individual or firm, actual money holdings would rarely be at this desired average level. In part, this reflects a normal pattern in which money holdings are above average just after receipt of a paycheck and are then drawn down until replenished by the next paycheck.

Money balances act as a shock absorber that cushions unexpected income and expenditure changes.

Most people also use money as a sort of "shock absorber," so that if something unexpected comes up they do not have to alter all their other plans. As a shock absorber, money balances rise above normal when money receipts are higher or expenditures lower than expected; when expenditures are higher or receipts lower than expected, money balances would fall. In this way, changes in money balances can absorb much of the income/expenditure shifts associated with unplanned events that would otherwise require an alteration in desired spending.

Obviously, the shock-absorber role of money is a short-run role. If receipts are consistently lower than expected, then money holdings will be drawn down to a point where desired spending must change. This could require postponing some purchases or simply "doing without." On the other hand, if receipts are consistently higher than expected, then money balances will grow to undesirably large levels so that either desired spending changes or some money is converted to higher-interest earning financial assets. This could involve buying some goods sooner than originally planned or buying stocks, bonds, or other financial assets in larger quantities than usual.

Short-run variations in money holdings are analogous to the shock-absorber of a car. If one drives over a bump (dip), the shock absorber compresses (extends) so that the passengers can continue level without much effect from the temporary disturbance. The shock absorber spreads the adjustment over time as it gradually returns to its normal level, where it will be ready to cushion future shocks.

What happens when the Federal Reserve creates more money than expected? Money receipts are higher than expected, government borrowing is less than expected (remember the government budget constraint identity), so financial institutions increase their loans to individuals and firms. The unexpected money growth creates excess money balances because individuals are holding a greater fraction of their wealth as money than they desire. These excess money balances are like a "hot potato"—they cannot disappear, but are passed from hand to hand. With the total supply of money determined by government policy, one person reducing his or her money balances by spending more causes someone else's money balances to be increased. This attempt to get rid of the excess money balances by spending them on other assets is essential to the adjustment process following a money shock.

The increased spending by individuals and firms (who find borrowing to finance investment easier) increases spending on final goods and services, and hence nominal income. The higher nominal income will increase money demand. So the newly created money must be held by someone and therefore cannot be eliminated. The excess *supply* of this money is eliminated, in a circular fashion, via an increase in money demand caused by the nominal income increase generated by the higher spending fueled by the unexpected increase in money. The end result is a higher average level of money balances and higher nominal income.

## IMPLICATIONS FOR THE MONEY–INCOME RATIO

In Chapter 6 we saw that the *desired* money-income ratio $K^d$ was defined as the ratio of money demanded $M^d$ (in a long-run sense) to income $Y$:

$$K^d \equiv M^d/Y \qquad (11.3)$$

The actual value of the ratio at any point in time is equal to the ratio of the nominal quantity of money supplied $M$ to nominal income $Y$:

$$K \equiv M/Y \qquad (11.4)$$

If we use our growth rate rule applying to a ratio and subtract the growth rate of $K^d$ from the actual growth rate of $K$ we have:

$$\hat{K} - \hat{K}^d \equiv (\hat{M} - \hat{Y}) - (\hat{M}^d - \hat{Y}) \equiv \hat{M} - \hat{M}^d \qquad (11.5)$$

This says that excess growth of the money-income ratio beyond its desired growth is identically equal to the growth rate of the supply of money in excess of money demand. Such fluctuations about the long-run quantity of money demanded indicate the shock absorber function of money is operating. Note that as the excess supply of money fluctuates from positive to zero or negative to zero, cushioning the impact of macroeconomic shocks, so too will the **excess money-income ratio** fluctuate in the same manner.

excess money–income ratio
$$\frac{K}{K^d} - 1$$

To see the time pattern of the money-income ratio following a shock, we will consider the various influences we have, so far, discussed. First, in Chapter 10 we learned that there will be some steady-state growth rate of the money-income ratio $\bar{\hat{K}}$. In addition, we just learned that the actual ratio will grow faster than its steady-state value if money grows faster than expected—a positive money shock; while a negative money shock would cause the money-income ratio to grow slower than its steady-state value. Finally, we know that as people spend the excess money balances over time, the excess supply of money eventually is eliminated and the money-income ratio once again grows at the steady-state rate. This means that the money-income ratio will grow slower (faster) than normal if actual $K$ exceeds (is less than) desired $K$. The three forces acting on the money-income ratio can be combined in a single equation describing the rate of growth of K over time:

$$\hat{K} = \bar{\hat{K}} + (\hat{M} - \hat{M}^*) - \lambda \left( \frac{K}{K^d} - 1 \right) \qquad (11.6)$$

The first term on the right-hand-side of the equation is the normal steady-state growth rate of the money–income ratio, $\bar{\hat{K}}$. The second term is the difference between the actual and expected growth rates of money, where an asterisk denotes the expected growth rate. This is the money shock term. When money growth is higher than expected, there is an initial excess supply of money and hence the money–income ratio grows at a faster rate.[2] The third term reflects the response of the money–income ratio, over time, to movements away from the long-run desired level. As long as actual $K$ exceeds the

---

[2]Remember that the steady-state $\bar{\hat{K}}$ is set based on planned spending and receipts.

desired value $K^d$, individuals will attempt to convert the excess money balances into other assets or services. This increased spending will lead to higher income and consequently a lower value of $K$ for the higher, given value of the money supply. Therefore, there will be an inverse relation between the ratio of the actual to desired money–income ratio and the growth rate of $K$. Once the adjustment period is over and actual and desired $K$ are equal, then $K/K^d = 1$; so the third term in equation (11.6) is zero $(\frac{K}{K^d} - 1 = 0)$ and $\hat{K}$ will be equal to $\bar{\hat{K}}$ in the absence of any new money shocks. The $\lambda$ term indicates the rate at which the excess money–income ratio is eliminated. The higher $\lambda$, the faster the adjustment of actual $K$ to its desired value.[3]

To better understand equation (11.6), let's look at a graphical analysis of the response of the money–income ratio to a money shock. To simplify matters, we can assume that the desired value of the money–income ratio $K^d$ is equal to its steady-state value. Prior to time period $z$, we assume that the economy is in steady-state equilibrium, so $\hat{K} = \bar{\hat{K}}$, and $K = K^d$. At time $z$, there is a money shock as the Fed unexpectedly increases the growth rate of the money supply. This increase in money growth raises the money–income growth rate above its steady-state level. Assuming that the higher money growth rate has no real effects, or that money is superneutral, the steady-state growth rate of the money–income ratio is unchanged at $\bar{\hat{K}}$. This is shown in Figure 11.3 as the broken line after time $z$. While the actual path of $\hat{K}$, illustrated by the heavy line, will diverge for a while from its steady-state value, it eventually returns to its steady-state path.

At time $z$, the actual growth rate of $K$ exceeds the steady-state growth rate by the full amount of the unexpected increase in nominal money supply growth ($\hat{M} - \hat{M}^*$). Now the adjustment process begins. The increase in the money-income ratio will mean that the

---

[3]Since our growth rates like $\hat{K}$ are measured in percent per annum terms, $\lambda$ is also in per annum units. A value of $\lambda = 1$ would indicate that the adjustment requires approximately one year. Some students may note that equation (11.6) is not strictly correct. We have been discussing growth rates as continuously compounded rates, but to avoid the use of logarithms we write the last term in equation (11.6) as the approximation ($K/K^d - 1$) rather than the exact term ($\log K - \log K^d$). For our purposes, it is the spirit of the adjustment response that is important to understand and not the exact mathematical calculations.

**Figure 11.3**

The Shock-Absorber Response of the Money–Income Ratio to a Money Shock

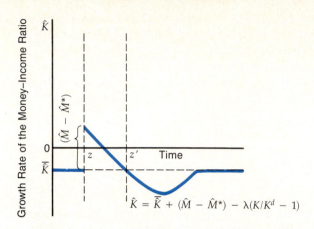

$$\hat{K} = \bar{\hat{K}} + (\hat{M} - \hat{M}^*) - \lambda(K/K^d - 1)$$

actual level of $K$ exceeds the steady-state level $K^d$. As indicated by the third term in equation (11.6), the growth rate of $K$ will begin to fall from the high point reached at time $z$ as individuals increase their spending in an attempt to get rid of excess money balances. At time $z$, $\hat{K}$ has reached the steady-state rate $\bar{\hat{K}}$, so by equation (11.6) it must be true that $(\hat{M} - \hat{M}^*) = \lambda \left(\dfrac{K}{K^d} - 1\right)$. Yet this cannot be the end of the adjustment. Since the money-income ratio has been growing above its steady-state rate since time $z$, the actual value of $K$ must exceed the desired steady-state value $K^d$. In order for $K$ to fall back to $K^d$, there must be a period where the money-income ratio grows at a slower-than-steady-state rate. As expectations adjust to the higher money growth rate, unexpected money growth falls to zero. The money-income ratio will continue to grow at less than the steady-state rate as long as the actual money-income ratio $K$ exceeds the steady-state ratio $K^d$. Eventually, $K$ will converge to $K^d$ and the adjustment process will end so that the money-income ratio once again grows at the steady-state rate $\bar{\hat{K}}$. To further illustrate the process of adjustment to a money shock, the following example provides numerical values for a hypothetical case.

**EXAMPLE 11.1 ▶**

In our hypothetical case, let's suppose that $\lambda = 0.5$ per annum and $\bar{\hat{K}} = -0.03$ per annum, so that equation (11.6) can be written as:

$$\hat{K} = -0.03/\text{year} + (\hat{M} - \hat{M}^*) - 0.5/\text{year} \left(\frac{K}{K^d} - 1\right)$$

Now the Fed increases the money growth rate from 2 to 4 percent per annum unexpectedly. The table illustrates the time pattern of adjustment. In the first quarter of the new monetary

| 1. Quarter | 2. Expected Nominal Money Growth $\hat{M}^*$ | 3. Money Growth Shock $(\hat{M} - \hat{M}^*)$ | 4. Desired Money–Income Ratio $(K^d)$ | 5. Actual Money–Income Ratio $K$ | 6. Excess Money–Income Ratio $(K/K^d - 1)$ | 7. Actual Growth of Money–Income Ratio $\hat{K}$ |
|---|---|---|---|---|---|---|
| 0 | 0.0200 | 0 | .2500 | .2500 | 0 | −.0300 |
| 1 | 0.0200 | 0.0200 | .2481 | .2494 | 0 | −.0100 |
| 2 | 0.0225 | 0.0175 | .2463 | .2484 | .0050 | −.0150 |
| 3 | 0.0250 | 0.0150 | .2444 | .2472 | .0088 | −.0194 |
| 4 | 0.0275 | 0.0125 | .2426 | .2458 | .0115 | −.0233 |
| 5 | 0.0300 | 0.0100 | .2408 | .2442 | .0132 | −.0266 |
| 6 | 0.0325 | 0.0075 | .2390 | .2424 | .0141 | −.0296 |
| 7 | 0.0350 | 0.0050 | .2372 | .2404 | .0142 | −.0321 |
| 8 | 0.0375 | 0.0025 | .2354 | .2384 | .0137 | −.0343 |
| 9 | 0.0400 | 0 | .2337 | .2362 | .0126 | −.0363 |
| 10 | 0.0400 | 0 | .2319 | .2341 | .0110 | −.0355 |
| " | " | " | " |  | " | " |
| ∞ | 0.0400 | 0 |  |  | 0 | −.0300 |

policy, the growth of the money-income ratio increases by the full amount of the money growth surprise. Instead of growing at the desired steady-state rate of −3 percent per annum, $K$ decreases at an annual rate of −1 percent as shown in Column 7. In the following quarters we assume that people steadily adjust their expectations regarding money growth upwards by 0.25 percentage points each quarter until they expect 4 percent money growth. If expectations adjusted more quickly than the two-year period assumed (at 0.25 percent each quarter, it will take 8 quarters for expected money growth to rise from 2 to 4 percent), the adjustment process would proceed more quickly.

The second column of the table gives the expected nominal money growth while the third column measures the money shock—the 4-percent money growth rate beginning quarter 1 less the expected value from column 2. Column 6 measures the excess money-income ratio calculated from the previous quarter's values of $K$ and $K^d$ in columns 4 and 5. When solving these models arithmetically period-by-period, we must use last period's (or the beginning of next period's) values for such disequilibrium concepts. The level of the desired money-income ratio is found by assuming an initial value of 0.25 and then reducing $K^d$ by the steady-state growth rate of −3 percent per annum. The actual money-income ratio is found by applying the column 7 value for $\hat{K}$ to the assumed initial value of 0.25. For instance, from the period 0 value of 0.25, we see in column 7 that $K$ grows at an annual rate of −0.0100 in period 1. One percent of 0.25 is

0.0025, but since this is only a one-quarter change and not a full year, we must divide .0025 by 4 to find the quarterly change of 0.000625. When we subtract 0.000625 from the period-0 $K$ of 0.25, we find the period-1 $K$ of 0.2494 when rounded to four digits. Where do we get the actual growth rates of the money-income ratio for column 7? We simply plug the required values into our formula. For instance, in the second quarter:

$$\hat{K} = \text{-0.03} + 0.0175 - 0.5(0.0050) = -0.0150$$

This is the sum of the desired steady-state growth rate of $-0.03$ and the money shock of 0.0175 minus the excess money-income ratio adjustment term of $-0.5(0.0050)$. This adjustment term is determined by the first quarter value of $K$ relative to $K^d$.

We then use our growth rate of $-0.0150$ to calculate the actual value of $K$ in the second quarter. Since $-0.0150$ is an annual rate of growth, it is multiplied by 0.25 to convert to a quarterly rate of growth as we did in computing $\hat{K}$ for the first quarter. The table repeats the calculations for the first 10 quarters. Notice that by the seventh quarter the actual $\hat{K}$ has fallen below the steady-state growth rate of $-0.03$. Over time the actual value of $K$ converges to the steady-state value and the adjustment process ends. The table indicates that it would take infinitely long for complete adjustment, because of the particular form of the adjustment equation we use. However, the economy comes quite close to complete adjustment within five years. Furthermore, it is likely that the economy will experience many more shocks, so that complete adjustment to this particular shock is irrelevant. The table nevertheless provides a more detailed view of the adjustment process than is given in Figure 11.3. Knowledge of the exact calculations underlying the table is not nearly so important as understanding the basic forces at work which shape our beliefs regarding this likely pattern of adjustment. ■

## 11.3 CYCLICAL ADJUSTMENT OF NOMINAL INCOME

### IMPLICATIONS FOR NOMINAL INCOME OF CHANGES IN THE MONEY–INCOME RATIO

Why do we emphasize the behavior of the money-income ratio? The adjustment pattern of nominal income to a monetary shock can be inferred directly from the adjustment of the money-income ratio. We know that central bank monetary policy determines the nominal money supply $M$, so the Cambridge identity $M \equiv KY$ can be solved for nominal income if we know the value of $K$.

To illustrate graphically the pattern of nominal income, it is handy to relate the actual values to steady-state values. We know that the actual growth rate of nominal income will be determined by solving the Cambridge identity for nominal income:

$$\hat{Y} \equiv \hat{M} - \hat{K} \tag{11.7}$$

The steady-state growth rate of nominal income is

$$\bar{\hat{Y}} \equiv \hat{M} - \bar{\hat{K}} \tag{11.8}$$

Subtracting (11.8) from (11.7) we have

$$\hat{Y} - \bar{\hat{Y}} \equiv -(\hat{K} - \bar{\hat{K}}) \tag{11.9}$$

So the differences in the growth rates between actual and steady-state nominal income will be equal to, but opposite in sign from, the difference between actual and steady-state growth in the money-income ratio. Therefore a graph of the adjustment path of nominal income growth following a money shock will mirror the adjustment path of the money-income ratio.

Figure 11.4 illustrates the growth rate of nominal income along with money growth and the money-income ratio growth rate. Since the desired steady-state growth rate of the money-income ratio is unaffected by the higher money growth rate, the rise in the steady-state growth rate of nominal income must mirror the rise in the growth rate of money. Note however that the initial jump in $\hat{K}$ is not matched by any immediate change in $\hat{Y}$. This is the shock-absorber role of $K$. The incipient increase in $\hat{M}$ is initially reflected in an increase in $\hat{K}$. Then as people start spending their larger than desired money balances, $\hat{Y}$ starts to rise. So nominal income growth rises gradually following a money shock, and continues to rise until it is above the new steady-state growth rate. This rise in $\hat{Y}$ above $\bar{\hat{Y}}_1$ is referred to as **overshooting** in the growth rate of nominal income. Such overshooting is required since nominal income grows at less than the steady-state rate for a while. In order for actual nominal income to reach the new steady-state level, there must be a period of "catching up," where $\hat{Y}$ grows at a rate faster than $\bar{\hat{Y}}_1$ to make up for the previous period of slower than $\bar{\hat{Y}}_1$ growth. The necessity for overshooting may be illustrated by the use of a simple analogy. Suppose two drivers desire to reach a destination 40 miles away in 1 hour. The first driver travels steadily at 40 miles per hour, reaching the destination at the appointed time. The second driver travels at 20 miles

If money growth is higher than expected, nominal income growth will rise slowly at first, then will overshoot the new steady-state growth rate until ultimately approaching the steady-state.

**overshooting**
When a growth rate variable moves above its steady-state rate

Growth Rate of:
Nominal Income $\hat{Y}$
Money Supply $\hat{M}$
Money–Income Ratio $\hat{K}$

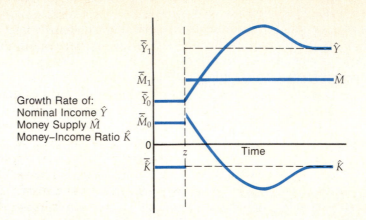

per hour for the first 30 minutes, and so must make up for this less than desired distance traveled in the first half hour by traveling at 60 miles per hour for the second half hour. By "overshooting" the steady-state rate of 40, the second driver is able to catch up to the first. Similar cyclical adjustment patterns may be expected for key macroeconomic variables like nominal income and the money-income ratio.

## DIRECT ANALYSIS OF NOMINAL INCOME ADJUSTMENT

While we can infer the adjustment pattern of nominal income from the adjustment of the money–income ratio, it is useful to consider further how spending changes affect this pattern. Spending plans for the entire economy will normally grow at the same rate as nominal income is expected to grow. This is necessary for plans to be consistent with the expectations on which they are based, since income and expenditures are identically equal in the aggregate. According to the Cambridge identity, this normal planned growth would equal $\hat{M}^* - \bar{\bar{K}}$, where $\hat{M}^*$ is the expected money supply growth implicit in expenditure and receipt plans.

During the adjustment period, people will attempt to reduce their money balances, which are growing faster than the quantity of money demanded at current levels of income and interest rates. Each individual attempts to do this by spending more money than he or she is receiving. Of course the total supply of money is set by government policy and cannot be reduced by passing it from hand to hand. Individuals will primarily want to convert the excess money balances into other assets with higher yields of interest payments or services.

To the extent that they purchase consumers' durable goods, expenditures for final goods and services are directly increased. To the extent that they increase their purchases of financial assets, market interest rates are lowered and the incentives for firms to invest in capital goods are increased, and so expenditures on final goods and services are indirectly increased. Then as final expenditures and income increase, this will encourage further increased expenditures by consumers and increased investment by firms. As for the timing of output and income increases, if firms at first meet the increased demand out of inventories, they will then increase production over time as the higher sales persist. So any extra spending need not immediately be translated into output and income increases.[4]

The growth rate of nominal income can be related to normal planned growth and attempts to spend excess money balances. We may express such a relation formally as

$$\hat{Y} = (\hat{M}^* - \bar{\hat{K}}) + \lambda(K/K^d - 1) \qquad (11.10)$$

This equation says that nominal income growth is equal to the amount[5] by which expected nominal money supply growth exceeds the trend growth rate of $K$, plus an adjustment term reflecting how individuals will rid themselves of any excess money balances. Note that this means that an unexpected increase in the nominal money supply growth rate will not affect nominal income growth until either the expected growth rate of the money supply changes or the public considers current money balances to be excessive ($K$ exceeds $K^d$). Equation (11.10) can be easily derived using equations (11.6) and (11.7) to substitute for $\hat{K}$ in the identity $\hat{Y} \equiv \hat{M} - \hat{K}$, so equations

---

[4]The slower the response of output and income, the longer the period for which the money–income ratio growth rate is increased by the full amount of the money–growth shock, or the more important the role of $K$ as a shock absorber. Note that for simplicity, we are referring to any difference between actual and steady-state money balances as excess money balances. More elaborate analyses would distinguish among actual, long-run desired (given current interest rates and income), and steady-state money balances, so that separate interest-rate and excess money balance effects on output can be considered. (See Jack Carr and Michael R. Darby, "The Role of Money Supply Shocks in the Short-Run Demand for Money," *Journal of Monetary Economics*, 8 September 1981, 183–99.)

[5]The amount $\hat{M}^* - \bar{K}$ is the normal planned growth in nominal income.

(11.10) and (11.6) are really just two different ways of summarizing the same dynamic forces at work in the economy.[6]

Reconsidering Figure 11.4 in terms of equation (11.10), at time $z$ there is no immediate jump in the growth of nominal income associated with the initial unexpectedly high money growth. As expected money growth rises due to learning about the new higher growth of the money supply, nominal income growth rises. As individuals come to perceive actual money balances as excessive, attempts to spend such balances will also increase nominal income growth. Just as we used a numerical example to supplement the graphical analysis of the growth rate of the money–income ratio, so can we use a numerical example to illustrate the cyclical adjustment of nominal income to higher money growth.

**EXAMPLE 11.2 ▶**

Suppose we use the same assumptions as in the earlier example of the adjustment of $K$: $\lambda = 0.5$ per annum and $\hat{\bar{K}} = -0.03$ per annum. Then equation (11.10) can be written as

$$\hat{Y} = (\hat{M}^* + 0.03/\text{year}) + 0.5/\text{year}(K/K^d - 1)$$

We will also follow our earlier example in assuming that money growth increases unexpectedly from 2 to 4 percent per annum, and expected money growth shifts up by 0.25 percentage points each quarter until it reaches 4 percent per annum.

The table shows the solved values for this example. The first column keeps track of the quarters since the change in monetary policy. In the first quarter, the increase in money growth is completely unanticipated, and as a result the actual growth of nominal income, as measured in column 5, is equal to its old steady-state rate of 5 percent. Column 3 indicates that this was the planned rate of growth, and column 4 indicates that in this first quarter there are no perceived excess money balances. The data of columns 2 and 4 are identical to the earlier table, only now we use them to infer nominal income growth.

––––––––––––––––

[6]To derive equation (11.10) we start with the nominal income identity:

$$\hat{Y} \equiv \hat{M} - \hat{K}$$

Using the equation (11.6) expression for $\hat{K}$ we have:

$$\hat{Y} = \hat{M} - \hat{\bar{K}} - (\hat{M} - \hat{M}^*) + \lambda(K/K^d - 1)$$

or, since $\hat{M} - \hat{M}$ equals zero, we can simplify this to:

$$\hat{Y} = \hat{M}^* - \hat{\bar{K}} + \lambda(K/K^d - 1)$$

| 1. Quarter | 2. Expected Nominal Money Growth $\hat{M}^*$ | 3. Planned Nominal Income Growth $\hat{M}^* - \hat{K}$ | 4. Excess Money–Income Ratio $(K/K^d - 1)$ | 5. Actual Growth of Nominal Income $\hat{Y}$ |
|---|---|---|---|---|
| 0 | 0.0200 | 0.0500 | 0 | 0.0500 |
| 1 | 0.0200 | 0.0500 | 0 | 0.0500 |
| 2 | 0.0225 | 0.0525 | 0.0050 | 0.0550 |
| 3 | 0.0250 | 0.0550 | 0.0088 | 0.0594 |
| 4 | 0.0275 | 0.0575 | 0.0115 | 0.0633 |
| 5 | 0.0300 | 0.0600 | 0.0132 | 0.0666 |
| 6 | 0.0325 | 0.0625 | 0.0141 | 0.0696 |
| 7 | 0.0350 | 0.0650 | 0.0142 | 0.0721 |
| 8 | 0.0375 | 0.0675 | 0.0137 | 0.0743 |
| 9 | 0.0400 | 0.0700 | 0.0126 | 0.0763 |
| 10 | 0.0400 | 0.0700 | 0.0110 | 0.0755 |
| " | " | " | " | " |
| $\infty$ | 0.0400 | 0.0700 | 0 | 0.0700 |

As we move past the first quarter, expected nominal money growth increases, so that planned nominal income growth also increases given the fixed growth of the steady-state money–income ratio. The increase in planned nominal income growth coupled with positive values of the excess money–income ratio in column 4 leads to higher growth of nominal income in column 5. Looking down column 5, we see that nominal income growth overshoots the new steady-state rate of 7 percent, reaching a maximum value of 7.63 percent in the ninth quarter, and then begins to fall to the new steady-state growth rate of 7 percent.

As we said earlier the table from the previous example is closely related to this table. We could, in fact, use the table from this example to find the growth rate of the money–income ratio as $\hat{K} = \hat{M} - \hat{Y}$. Conversely, we could have used the data from the earlier table to find nominal income growth as $\hat{Y} = \hat{M} - \hat{K}$. ■

Now that we have considered both graphical and numerical hypothetical examples of the dynamic adjustment of the money–income ratio and nominal income to a money shock, it is natural to wonder about the actual timing of the adjustment process. In other words, how many quarters will the actual pattern of adjustment be spread over? The exact timing remains an open empirical issue. There exist many studies, but the studies are often conflicting so that it is difficult to distill any definitive statement from this literature. The statistical problems encountered in such studies are beyond the scope of this text, but one obvious problem is that shocks do not occur in isolation. In a controlled experiment, we would increase the money supply unexpectedly, and then holding all other exogenous variables constant, would observe the adjustment of the economy to this monetary shock. Unfortunately, such controlled experiments are not possible in economics because the real world experiences a steady deluge of unexpected events. The researcher's challenge is to attempt to isolate the timing of the adjustment of nominal income to a particular money shock.

The effects of a money shock on nominal income can occur anywhere from 6 months to 5 years following the shock.

While researchers differ, it seems reasonable to say that the effects of a change in monetary policy on nominal income become apparent between two and four quarters following the policy change. Some researchers conclude that the adjustment process is essentially completed within three years, while others argue that the process requires five or more years.[7]

It is safe to say that the greater the change in monetary policy, the more quickly nominal income growth is affected and the larger the adjustment. The initial lag in the effect of money on income also can be explained by unplanned inventory changes. As the monetary surprise is reflected in spending on goods, the initial spending is largely met by sales from inventories rather than increased output or prices. As inventories fall below desired levels, firms increase production and we see real ouput start to rise. That is, the shock-absorber natures of the inventories of both money and goods can explain the delay (lag) between unexpected increases in money growth and nominal income or output growth. The next chapter will offer greater detail on the breakdown of nominal income into its real output and price level components.

While we have used examples of positive monetary shocks in this chapter, it should be understood that the examples for negative shocks—a money growth rate lower than expected—would simply work in reverse of the shocks we considered. An unexpected decrease in money growth would not affect the growth of nominal income at first. As nominal income initially proceeds along its old growth path, actual money balances fall relative to the quantity de-

---

[7]Compounding the problem for researchers is the fact that the lag in the effect of monetary policy on income is variable—sometimes income responds more quickly to money changes than at other times. This was pointed out in 1961 by Milton Friedman, "The Lag in the Effect of Monetary Policy," *Journal of Political Economy*, 69 (October 1961), 447–66, and was shown to still be true for more recent data by J. Ernest Tanner in "Are the Lags in the Effects of Monetary Policy Variable?," *Journal of Monetary Economics*, 5 (January 1979), 105–21.

manded and, as a result, the money–income ratio falls below its steady-state level. As people decrease their spending in an attempt to rebuild their money holdings, the growth rate of nominal income begins to fall. At this point the money–income ratio begins to grow at a faster rate. Whereas in the case of a positive money shock there is overshooting of the nominal income growth rate, in the adjustment to unexpectedly slow money growth there will be **undershooting** of nominal income growth. Since nominal income initially grows at too high a rate, the undershooting is needed to close the gap between actual and steady-state nominal income.

**undershooting**
When a growth rate variable moves below its steady-state rate

## SUMMARY

1   Macroeconomic shocks are disturbances which either force the economy away from equilibrium or change the equilibrium.

2   The rate of government spending is equal to the total of the rate of net taxes and the rates of change in base money and the government debt held by the public.

3   If changes in money growth have no real effects in the long run, money is said to be superneutral.

4   Money serves as a kind of macroeconomic shock absorber, spreading the impact of unexpected events over time.

5   Following an unexpected increase in the money growth rate, the growth of the money–income ratio initially rises by the full amount of the money shock. It then falls, eventually undershooting the steady-state money–income growth rate, and then rises back to the steady-state growth rate.

6   Following a positive money shock, nominal income growth rises gradually and continues to rise temporarily above the new steady-state growth rate. This overshooting of the steady-state requires a period of falling nominal income growth until the new steady-state is reached.

### EXERCISES

1. Figures 11.3 and 11.4 illustrate the adjustment of the money–income ratio and nominal income growth rates to an unexpected increase in nominal money growth. Draw similar diagrams for an unexpected decrease in money growth, carefully explaining why the key variables follow the patterns that they do.

**2. a.** If the money-multiplier growth rate averaged $-2$ percent per annum, the Fed would have to increase base money at a _____ growth rate to achieve a 4 percent per annum growth rate of the nominal money supply.

**b.** Suppose the Fed wished to increase the growth rate of the nominal money supply from 4 percent to 8 percent per annum for a year. If base money equals $100 billion initially and the money multiplier is 2.5, what would be the required increase in value of government securities purchased during the year for Fed open market operations to achieve the desired increase in money growth?

**3. a.** Suppose that at the end of 1990, the economy were in long-run equilibrium with a 4 percent per annum nominal money supply growth rate and a $-1$ percent per annum growth rate of the money–income ratio. What is the corresponding growth rate of nominal income?

**b.** If an unexpected change in monetary policy increased the money growth rate to 8 percent per annum, what would be the new steady-state nominal income growth rate?

**c.** Suppose that from the end of 1990 to the end of 1992, the average growth rate of nominal income were 7 percent per annum. To achieve long-run equilibrium by the end of the next 2 years, the average growth rate of nominal income from the end of 1992 to the end of 1994 would have to be how much? What is the implied average growth rate of nominal income from the end of 1990 to the end of 1994?

**4.** Why doesn't the growth rate of nominal income immediately reflect the higher growth rate of the money supply when there is an unexpected increase in money growth?

**5.** Suppose the government deficit equals $100 billion per year, government bonds outstanding equal $800 billion, and base money is $200 billion.

**a.** What will the rate of change in government bonds plus base money be this year?

**b.** If the deficit is financed entirely through money creation, what will the growth rate of base money be?

## REFERENCES FOR FURTHER READING

Darby, Michael R. "The Allocation of Transitory Income Among Consumers' Assets." *American Economic Review*, 62 (December 1972), 928–41.

Friedman, Milton. "The Lag in the Effect of Monetary Policy." *Journal of Political Economy,* 69 (October 1961), 447–66.

Goldberg, Matthew S., and Thom B. Thurston. "Monetarism, Overshooting, and the Procyclical Movement of Velocity." *Economic Inquiry,* 15 (January 1977), 26–32.

Tanner, J. Ernest, "Are the Lags in the Effects of Monetary Policy Variable?" *Journal of Monetary Economics,* 5 (January 1979), 105–21.

Taylor, Dean. "Friedman's Dynamic Models: Empirical Tests." *Journal of Monetary Economics,* 2 (November 1976), 531–38.

# MONETARY POLICY AND THE FEDERAL RESERVE

Throughout the text we have discussed the implications of changes in monetary policy. Chapter 11 specifically addressed the issue of the adjustment of the economy to an unexpected change in monetary policy. While the effects of monetary policy are of great importance, it is also useful to understand what goes on behind the scenes. We already know that the central bank of the U.S., the Federal Reserve, determines monetary policy for the United States, but how does the Fed go about this activity?

Decision-making at the Fed centers in the Federal Open Market Committee (FOMC). This committee consists of the seven members of the system's Board of Governors along with five of the 12 presidents of the regional Federal Reserve Banks, who rotate FOMC responsibilities. The chairman of the Board of Governors (as of this writing, Paul Volcker) presides over the FOMC. Meeting eight times a year, the FOMC engages in discussions of the current state of the economy as well as the outlook for the future, and then reaches a consensus regarding the appropriate course of money supply growth to achieve the policy goals of price stability with economic growth. In setting the current desirable growth rate targets of money and credit aggregates, the FOMC relies heavily on the forecasts and analyses of the economists employed by the Federal Reserve Board.

Once the FOMC decides upon the preferred course of money growth, a directive is sent to the domestic trading desk of the Federal Reserve Bank of New York where the policy is actually carried out. For instance, at the July 1983 meeting of the FOMC, the New York Fed was directed to support growth rates in the range of:

> . . . from the fourth quarter of 1983 to the fourth quarter of 1984 of 6½ to 9½ percent for M2 and 6 to 9 percent for M3. The Committee considered that growth in M1 in a range of 5 to 9 percent from the second quarter of 1983 to the fourth quarter of 1984 would be consistent with the ranges for the broader aggregates. . . . (*Federal Reserve Bulletin*, October 1983, p. 791)

While the directed ranges of money growth may seem quite broad, we shall see later on in Chapters 14 and 15 that the Fed has had a difficult time controlling money growth, so such ranges reflect practical considerations. The domestic trading desk in New York is a room where skilled bond traders buy and sell government securities to achieve the desired money growth rates. The buying and selling of government bonds is referred to as Federal Reserve open market operations.

The trading desk focuses on commercial bank reserves. By law, commercial banks are required to hold reserves against deposits. A bank holding excess reserves (more than legally required) will use these reserves to make loans. As is covered in macroeconomics principles classes, when commercial banks make loans they create money. If the trading desk is buying bonds, then private bond dealers exchange government bonds for money; this money is deposited in commercial banks so that bank reserves rise and then bank loans rise in turn, leading to an increase in the money supply. By monitoring bank reserves—buying bonds when reserves are growing too slowly, thereby injecting money into the system, or selling bonds when reserves grow too fast, thereby withdrawing money from the system—the trading desk is able to affect the rate of growth of the money supply.

Open market operations are not the only potential tool of monetary policy. The Fed also controls reserve requirements and the discount rate. If the Fed lowered the fraction of deposits required as reserves, banks would be able to increase lending as previously legally required reserves would now be freed as excess reserves. The reserve requirement is seldom changed and does not serve as an active tool of monetary policy. The discount rate is the rate of interest charged by the Fed when commercial banks borrow from the Federal Reserve system. While the discount rate changes with changes in credit conditions, banks may choose not to borrow from the Fed, and in fact actual borrowing from the Fed is very small as a fraction of total commercial bank debt. Thus the discount rate is not a very important tool of the day-to-day management of money growth.

The open market operations, broadly outlined by the FOMC and executed at the New York Fed trading desk, are the active way that the Fed manages the money supply. While the internal operations of the Fed and the institutions of the money market are properly considered in money and banking courses, macroeconomic shocks have often resulted from Federal Reserve policy decisions, making it helpful to have some knowledge of the source of such shocks. Later chapters will consider in depth past monetary policy actions and their implications.

# CHAPTER TWELVE

# DYNAMIC ADJUSTMENTS OF REAL INCOME, PRICES, AND INTEREST RATES TO A MONETARY SHOCK

## 12.1 AGGREGATE DEMAND AND SUPPLY APPROACH

In Chapter 11 we studied the adjustment of nominal income to a money shock. While there are times when nominal income may be of interest, economists often find it preferable to consider the decomposition of nominal income into its price level and real income components. Remember that nominal income is the product of real income and the price level: $Y = Py$. We already know the likely adjustment pattern of nominal income following a money shock, but we now want to know the individual adjustment pattern of the price level and real income. When nominal income begins to rise following a positive money shock, is this rise due to higher prices, greater real output, or both? Does overshooting in the growth rate of nominal income reflect overshooting in both prices and output?

To a certain extent, we have already considered the breakdown of nominal income change into a price level and output change in the aggregate demand and aggregate supply material of Chapter 7. There we considered how both money-demand and money-supply shocks determine the equilibrium *level* of real output and prices. At that time we were strictly concerned with short-run effects: if the aggregate demand curve shifts unexpectedly due to an unexpected increase in the money supply, how will the resulting rise in nominal income break down into a rise in the price level versus a rise in real income?

The answer hinges on the slope of the aggregate supply curve. The steeper aggregate supply, the greater the rise in price and the smaller the rise in real income. The essay at the end of Chapter 7 reported some empirical findings that support the notion of a relatively flat short-run aggregate supply curve consistent with a Keynesian view of aggregate supply—shifts in aggregate demand lead primarily to output changes rather than price level changes. However, the evidence also indicates that the increase in output resulting from the unexpectedly large money change is short-lived and soon disappears. While there is little change in the price level in the short run, in the long run it tends to rise by an amount proportional to the rise in the money stock.

The aggregate demand and supply approach was useful for understanding the short-run effects of money shocks but is not a good tool for portraying the long-run effects required by a dynamic view of the economy. As a result, we now turn to our dynamic analysis of the adjustment pattern of nominal income growth as covered in Chapter 11 and consider the division of the nominal income change into real income and price level growth.

## 12.2 CYCLICAL ADJUSTMENT OF REAL INCOME AND THE PRICE LEVEL

### THE DYNAMIC PATTERN

Suppose we once again consider the example used in Chapter 11—the Fed increases the money growth rate unexpectedly from $\hat{M}_0$ to $\hat{M}_1$ at time $z$. In Chapter 11 we examined the pattern of adjustment of nominal income. However, we know that nominal income $Y$ is equal to the product of real income $y$ and the price level $P$, or

$$Y = yP \tag{12.1}$$

Using our growth rate rule for products, we can write the growth rate of nominal income as

$$\hat{Y} = \hat{y} + \hat{P} \tag{12.2}$$

In Chapter 11 we examined the case of superneutral money, where nominal money supply growth does not affect the steady-state growth rates of real variables. In this case the entire change in the steady-state growth rate of nominal income is attributable to the increased steady-state inflation rate. Figure 12.1 indicates the change in the steady-state growth rates by the dashed lines showing the new

Figure 12.1

The Adjustment of Nominal
Income, Real Income, and the
Price Level to an Unexpected
Increase in Money Growth

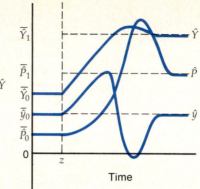

steady-state growth rates after the monetary policy change at time $z$. Note that the steady-state growth rate of real income is unchanged, but at $z$ the steady-state growth rates of nominal income and the price level both increase by the same amount (the same vertical distance). But what about the pattern of adjustment to the new steady-state?

In Figure 12.1 we see the adjustment path of nominal income growth is drawn as in Chapter 11. The growth rate of nominal income does not move instantaneously with the jump in money growth, but rises steadily after $z$, eventually overshooting the steady-state rate and then gradually returning to the steady-state.

The adjustment patterns for $y$ and $P$ are based on the general empirical observation that following a money shock, the resulting fluctuations in the growth of nominal income are initially reflected in real income growth and then later in prices. Initially, real income grows faster than its steady-state rate and then falls toward the steady-state. However, since real income originally grew faster than the steady-state, it must undergo a period of undershooting where the real income growth rate is below the steady-state rate in order for the level of real income to reach its steady-state level. Note that in Figure 12.1 we show $\hat{y}$ with a negative value for a brief time during the undershooting phase. It is not necessary that real income growth be negative, but a period of falling real income could well be consistent with the required adjustment. Remember that over the whole adjustment period the *average* actual real income growth will equal the steady-state rate $\bar{\bar{y}}$. The early period of relatively high growth is offset by a subsequent period of relatively low growth.

We can think of Figure 12.1 as recording the outcome of a series of aggregate demand and supply equilibria, where initially the aggregate demand curve shifts up relative to the short-run aggregate sup-

Following an unexpected
increase in money growth,
there is a period of relatively high real income
growth followed by a pe-
riod of relatively low
growth.

ply curve, which then catches up as individuals come to expect higher levels and growth of money and prices. Since the initial aggregate supply curve is likely to be quite flat, there is little initial impact on prices. In Figure 12.1 we see that right after period $z$, the rate of inflation is continuing at the old steady-state rate $\bar{\hat{P}}_0$. Gradually the inflation rate adjusts upward toward the new steady-state, but since actual inflation is initially less than new steady-state rate $\bar{\hat{P}}_1$, it must overshoot $\bar{\hat{P}}_1$ for a period of catch-up so that the actual price level will equal the steady-state price level.

Equation (12.2) pointed out the relationship between $\hat{Y}$, $\hat{y}$, and $\hat{P}$. Graphically or algebraically, if we know the adjustment paths of any two of these variables, we can infer the path of the third. So the path of adjustment of the inflation rate may be determined as the difference between the nominal income and real income adjustment paths. To summarize, the basic pattern is that an unexpected increase in nominal money supply growth leads to an unexpected increase in nominal income growth. At first, almost the entire unexpected increase in nominal income represents an increase in real income and the inflation rate is relatively constant. As time goes on, the difference between actual and expected nominal money growth will diminish, real income will grow at less than the steady-state rate, and the inflation rate will rise to make up for the initially sluggish price increases. Eventually, real income growth returns to the steady-state path of before the money shock (remember that money is assumed to be superneutral), while the new steady-state paths of nominal income growth and inflation rise in proportion to the new steady-state money growth rate.

At this point it is appropriate to find out if we are missing any important effects by assuming that money is superneutral, i.e., changes in money growth leave the steady-state values of real variables unchanged. If money is not superneutral, then higher money growth rates will lower the level of the steady-state money–income ratio through the negative interest elasticity of money demand. Higher money growth means higher nominal interest rates, which means a smaller equilibrium quantity of money demanded in the nonsuperneutral case. But the steady-state growth rate of the money–income ratio is unchanged, so while there is a one-time shift in the level of the ratio, the growth rate of $K$ after the change in monetary policy is the same as before. The adjustment pattern of real income growth and inflation are practically identical to Figure 12.1. The slight differences that exist, which we need not go into, reinforce the inflationary (deflationary) effects of a stimulative (restrictive) monetary policy. For our purposes, the simpler example of superneutrality does a good job of representing the expected dynamic pattern of adjustment following a monetary shock.

Following an unexpected increase in money growth, the inflation rate rises to overshoot the new steady-state before finally approaching the new growth rate.

## RATIONALE OF THE ADJUSTMENT PROCESS

Now let us be sure we understand the story behind the graphs. Figure 12.1 shows the adjustment of the economy to an expansionary monetary policy as something that evolves over time. In the real world there is an ongoing process of new information that must be interpreted by business firms. Realistically, most sellers will set their price for extended periods of time, selling all they can at that price. Periodically, selling prices are revised based on actual past costs and expected changes in costs, as well as on inventories and expected product demand. Current nominal income growth will have little effect on these factors in the present period, but will influence the future values of these factors. As a result, the current inflation rate will be influenced little by current nominal income growth, but the future inflation rate certainly could be. The expected demand in the current period will be shaped by the growth of nominal income last period. This is one reason why prices adjust slowly over time. Another reason is that costs may be incorrectly anticipated. Sellers of goods may find their costs rising unexpectedly, but they are already committed to selling at a previously announced price. So they must raise prices next period to make up for the current mistake regarding costs as well as to take account of future expected cost increases. Similarly sellers of labor make mistakes regarding the current cost of living and demand for labor, but can seldom adjust wages instantaneously. Over time, labor will seek wage increases based on past errors which shape expectations of the future. The general process of adjusting prices slowly over time gives us the initial inertia in the inflation rate which is overcome with time to move to the new steady-state.

An implication of sellers setting prices and then selling to meet demand is that the lack of immediate price adjustment to unanticipated growth in nominal income means that real output must be increased to meet the demand. The quicker that prices adjust to unanticipated changes in aggregate demand, the less will be the short-run effect on real income.[1]

We can summarize the forces operating on the growth rates of real income and the price level in equation form, similar to the equa-

---

[1]In terms of the aggregate demand and supply framework, this would mean that the aggregate supply curve shifts quickly following unexpected changes in aggregate demand. The essay at the end of this chapter will consider some factors that determine the speed with which prices adjust following an unexpected change in aggregate demand.

tions used to determine the growth rates of the money–income ratio and nominal income in Chapter 11. The growth rate of real income may be written as:

$$\hat{y} = \bar{\bar{y}} + (\hat{Y} - \hat{Y}^*) - \beta(y/y_s - 1) \qquad (12.3)$$

This equation says that the real income growth rate equals its steady-state growth rate $\bar{\bar{y}}$ plus any unexpected nominal income growth $(\hat{Y} - \hat{Y}^*)$, less an adjustment term reflecting the difference between actual and steady-state real income $\beta(y/y_s - 1)$, where the magnitude of $\beta$ indicates the speed of adjustment analogous to the $\lambda$ term of the nominal income growth equation in Chapter 11. Equation (12.3) indicates that real income will grow at its normal rate except when nominal income changes unexpectedly. Unanticipated changes in expenditures will be met by adjusting output, and thus unexpected nominal income growth is reflected in real income growth. Over time, the effects of such shocks on real income are eliminated as prices adjust to bring aggregate demand into line with the steady-state real income growth rate. The higher $\beta$, the quicker the adjustment, as any given change in the level of $y$ away from its steady-state level is reflected in a larger change in $\hat{y}$.

A related equation can be written for the inflation rate:[2]

$$\hat{P} = (\hat{Y}^* - \bar{\bar{y}}) + \beta(y/y_s - 1) \qquad (12.4)$$

The rate of inflation is equal to the difference between expected nominal income growth and steady-state real income growth plus a multiple $\beta$ of the excess of actual real income above steady-state real income. The first term in parentheses on the right-hand side of equation (12.4) is the inflation rate that is expected to be consistent with normal growth in real output. Sellers would adjust their prices around this rate to make up for past errors that caused the level of real output to deviate from its normal or steady-state level.[3] To ac-

---

[2]Starting with the identity $\hat{P} \equiv \hat{Y} - \hat{y}$, we can substitute equation (12.3) for $\hat{y}$ yielding $\hat{P} = \hat{Y} - \bar{\bar{y}} - (\hat{Y} - \hat{Y}^*) + \beta(y/y_s - 1)$ or $\hat{P} = (\hat{Y}^* - \bar{\bar{y}}) + \beta(y/y_s - 1)$.

[3]Michael Mussa of the University of Chicago has shown that a sensible price adjustment rule includes two components: the expected change in the equilibrium price level and a catch-up of part of the effects of past mistakes. See his "Sticky Prices and Disequilibrium Adjustment in a Rational Model of the Inflationary Process," *American Economic Review*, 71 (December 1981), 1020–27.

tually solve equations (12.3) or (12.4), we must know actual and expected nominal income growth. To reinforce the graphical
presentation, let's consider a numerical example of some hypothetical adjustment pattern.

EXAMPLE 12.1 ▶        Using equations (12.3) and (12.4), let's consider the effects
of a stimulative monetary policy on real income and price level
growth. We will return to the example of Chapter 11, where
money growth increases unexpectedly from 2 to 4 percent per
annum. We will take our nominal income growth rates from the
example of Chapter 11 and enter them in the second column of
the table here. Let's also assume that β equals 1 (100 percent
per annum) and $\bar{y} = 0.03$ per annum. With these assumptions,
equation (12.3) can be written as

$$\hat{y} = 0.03/\text{year} + (\hat{Y} - \hat{Y}^*) - (1/\text{year})\,(y/y_s - 1)$$

To find the actual growth rate of real income at any point in
time, as in column 5 we must know the difference between the
actual growth rate of nominal income from column 2 and the
expected rate of nominal income growth, as seen in column 3.
Let's assume that $\hat{Y};^*$ is determined as the simple average of the
actual and expected nominal income growth rates from the previous quarter. This way, the expected growth rate adapts to the

| 1. Quarter | 2. Actual Nominal Income Growth | 3. Expected Nominal Income Growth | 4. Excess Real Income | 5. Actual Real Income Growth | 6. Actual Real Income | 7. Steady-State Real Income | 8. Actual Inflation Rate |
|---|---|---|---|---|---|---|---|
| | $\hat{Y}$ | $\hat{Y}^*$ | $y/y_s - 1$ | $\hat{y}$ | $y$ | $y_s$ | $\hat{P}$ |
| 1 | 0.0500 | 0.0500 | 0 | 0.0300 | 1 | 1 | 0.0200 |
| 2 | 0.0550 | 0.0500 | 0 | 0.0350 | 1.0088 | 1.0075 | 0.0200 |
| 3 | 0.0594 | 0.0525 | 0.0012 | 0.0357 | 1.0177 | 1.0151 | 0.0238 |
| 4 | 0.0633 | 0.0560 | 0.0027 | 0.0346 | 1.0266 | 1.0227 | 0.0286 |
| 5 | 0.0666 | 0.0596 | 0.0038 | 0.0332 | 1.0351 | 1.0303 | 0.0334 |
| 6 | 0.0696 | 0.0631 | 0.0046 | 0.0318 | 1.0433 | 1.0381 | 0.0377 |
| 7 | 0.0721 | 0.0663 | 0.0051 | 0.0307 | 1.0513 | 1.0459 | 0.0414 |
| 8 | 0.0743 | 0.0692 | 0.0052 | 0.0299 | 1.0592 | 1.0537 | 0.0445 |
| 9 | 0.0763 | 0.0718 | 0.0052 | 0.0293 | 1.0669 | 1.0616 | 0.0470 |
| 10 | 0.0755 | 0.0740 | 0.0050 | 0.0264 | 1.0740 | 1.0696 | 0.0491 |
| 11 | 0.0748 | 0.0748 | 0.0041 | 0.0259 | 1.0809 | 1.0776 | 0.0489 |
| 12 | 0.0742 | 0.0748 | 0.0031 | 0.0263 | 1.0880 | 1.0857 | 0.0479 |
| " | " | " | " | " | | | " |
| ∞ | 0.0700 | 0.0700 | 0 | 0.0300 | | | 0.0400 |

Columns 6 and 7 are based on the assumption real income initially equals 1, where this could be interpreted as 1 billion or trillion, or any arbitrary unit of account.

actual growth rate steadily over time without being dominated completely by the last quarter. We assume that the first quarter has an expected nominal income growth rate of 5 percent per annum to be consistent with the initial steady-state. This is shown as .0500 in column 3.

In the first quarter, real income is growing at the steady-state rate of 3 percent as shown in column 5, since $(\hat{Y} - \hat{Y}^*)$ is zero and the previous quarter's actual level of $y$ was equal to $y_s$, the steady-state level, as indicated in columns 6 and 7. In the second quarter nominal income starts to grow at a faster rate, so real income growth rises accordingly. The rise is equal to the unexpected growth in nominal income, because last period's level of real income was equal to the steady-state level $y_s$ so that the excess real income ratio coming into the second quarter still equalled zero. If we continue to solve for each period's real income growth, we get the pattern indicated in column 5: $\hat{y}$ first rises above the steady-state rate, then falls below for a time before rising back toward the steady-state rate of 3 percent.

The rate of inflation is solved in column 8—by using equation (12.4)— with $\bar{y}$ equal to 3 percent:

$$\hat{P} = (\hat{Y}^* - 0.03) + 1(y/y_s - 1)$$

In the first two periods, the rate of inflation is equal to the expected nominal income growth of 0.05 less the steady-state real income growth rate of 0.03, or 2 percent. Since $y$ differs from $y_s$ at the end of the second period, only in period 3 do we start to observe the excess real income effect adding to the inflation rate. Note that the inflation rate rises slowly at first, but then overshoots the new steady-state rate of 4 percent in the seventh quarter. By the eleventh quarter, the rate of inflation has begun to fall toward the new steady-state. While the adjustment process takes a very long time to fully complete, if we kept following the example period after period, we would find that by the thirtieth quarter the adjustment process is reasonably complete. ■

## EXPECTATIONS FORMATION

The formation of expected values such as $\hat{M}^*$ and $\hat{Y}^*$ is the subject of much current theoretical and empirical research. The problem for the researcher is that unlike actual values of the money supply or nominal income, expected values are unobservable.

Expected values of macro-economic variables are unobservable.

Modern macroeconomists make great use of expectational variables in theoretical models of how the economy works. To test these theories, we need data on expected values of the crucial variables, but where do we get such values for the variables? Economists have used many advanced statistical techniques to try to create plausible data series on expected values of macroeconomic variables, but all such studies are subject to criticism. Ideally, we would like to be able to know what people actually expect, and in this regard, there have been some interesting studies using survey data on expectations. In particular, there exists a well known survey series on expected inflation published by the *Philadelphia Inquirer* and there is a well known survey series on expected money collected by Money Market Services, Inc.[4] In analyzing dynamic adjustment processes, economists must be able to explain how expected values will change over time in response to the macroeconomic shock being studied. Survey data may help to formulate better explanations, although the subject is one of the most hotly debated in macroeconomics.

In the arithmetic example just worked and its counterpart in Chapter 11, two different rules for formulating expectations were assumed. The expected money growth $\hat{M}^*$ in Chapter 11 is implicitly derived as a simple average of the previous eight quarters' money growth.[5] This is a particular form of the general class of **univariate expectations**. Univariate expectation rules are based only on past data about the series for which we are forming expectations. So a weighted or unweighted average of the past growth of money would be a univariate expectation formulation rule for $\hat{M}^*$.

In the example just worked $\hat{Y}^*$ was based on a special class of univariate expectation rules known as **adaptive expectations** (also

**univariate expectations**
Expectation rules based on past data on a variable

**adaptive expectations**
Expectations adjusted by a fraction of past forecasting errors

---

[4]The inflation data come from a semiannual survey of economists by Joseph Livingston of the *Philadelphia Inquirer*. For a detailed description and analysis of the Livingston data see John A. Carlson, "A Study of Price Forecasts," *Annals of Economic and Social Measurement*, 6 (Winter 1977), 27–56. Expected money data are collected by Money Market Services, Inc., which surveys approximately sixty participants in the money market each week. The participants give their best guess of what the weekly announced money supply figures revealed by the Fed will be. For an analysis of the data see Jacob Grossman, "The 'Rationality' of Money Supply Expectations and the Short Run Response of Interest Rates to Monetary Surprises," *Journal of Money, Credit, and Banking*, 13 (November 1981), 409–25.

[5]We assumed that the money growth rate had been at 5% for some years before the change in $M$. So for the first two years after the change, we are dropping a 5% growth rate quarter and adding a 7% growth rate quarter to our period being averaged. One eighth of 2% is 0.25%, and this is the rate at which $\hat{M}^*$ increases until it reaches 7% at the end of two years' time.

known as error-learning expectations).[6] In this type of model, current expectations are based partly on past forecast errors. The general rule for this class is that the expected value ($X^*$) for this period of any variable $X$ is equal to last period's expected value ($X^*_{-1}$) plus a fraction, say $a$, of the difference between last period's actual and expected values.

$$X^* = X^*_{-1} + a(X_{-1} - X^*_{-1}) \qquad (12.5)$$

Algebraic manipulations show that $X^*$ can also be expressed as $aX_{-1} + (1 - a)X^*_{-1}$ or as a weighted average of all past values of $X$ where the weights decline geometrically toward zero. In our arithmetic example, our $X$ was $\hat{Y}$ and $a$ was 0.5.

It is difficult to discuss how expectations are formed in the models we have been studying because we have not explicitly included any sources of uncertainty within the models. To do so would greatly increase their complexity without changing the basic results on which we have focused. Depending on how monetary policy actually changes over time, some particular univariate expectation rule might also be rational and economically rational in the sense discussed in Chapter 7. But information on money growth would surely be used to formulate rational expectations of $\hat{Y}$ and probably would be used in economically rational expectations of $\hat{Y}$. That is, past money growth would help statistically to predict nominal spending growth, and it would probably be worthwhile for a firm to use past money growth as well as past $\hat{Y}$ in formulating $\hat{Y}^*$. In this way, rational and economically rational expectations often imply **multivariate expectations**, which are based on variables in addition to the one for which expectations are being formed. Thus, in summary, we can say that univariate expectations depend on past changes of a single variable under study, while multivariate expectations depend on past changes of other variables in addition to the one under study.

If we assume that rational or economically rational expectations characterize $\hat{M}^*$, then long sequences of $\hat{M} - \hat{M}^*$ all with the same sign (positive or negative) would be unusual, as people would not consistently over- or underpredict $\hat{M}$. However, over two, three, or even four quarters such sequences might occur when there is an unannounced change in the underlying trend growth in money, and quarterly money growth is quite variable around the underlying

**multivariate expectations**
Expectation rules based on past data for more than one variable

With rational expectations, it would be unusual for individuals to consistently overestimate or underestimate future money growth.

[6]Adaptive expectations were introduced in the economics literature by Phillip Cagan of Columbia University, in his article on ''The Monetary Dynamics of Hyperinflation,'' in Milton Friedman, ed., *Studies in the Quantity Theory of Money* (Chicago: University of Chicago Press, 1956).

trend. At first people are confused as to whether $\hat{M}$ is abnormally high (or low) relative to an unchanged trend or whether the trend has in fact been increased (decreased). Federal Reserve announcements are not very helpful in resolving this uncertainty, perhaps because of internal disagreements over whether a policy change is temporary or relatively permanent. It seems to be the case that a sequence of two or three quarters of sharply negative $\hat{M} - \hat{M}^*$ is sufficient to cause a recession, while if the sequence is positive, a boom results.

## 12.3 EXPLANATIONS FOR PERSISTENT REAL OUTPUT EFFECTS

The adjustment pattern detailed in the previous section indicates that unexpected money growth would only affect real income growth in the short run. In the long run, real income returns to the previous steady-state growth rate. How long is "the long run"? This is not a question that can be answered precisely. As mentioned in Chapter 11, the empirical work in this area does not allow a unanimity of opinion across studies. One problem is that the effects of different money shocks seem to vary as to the time required to complete adjustment. However, it is reasonable to say that the initial change in nominal income growth following a money shock is largely a reflection of increased real income growth, which becomes apparent two to four quarters following the money shock. The rate of inflation begins to rise somewhere between five to seven quarters following the shock. The length of time required for full adjustment to a shock is much less clear, with estimates ranging from two to six years.

Since the steady-state real income growth rate is unaffected by the money shock, it may seem odd that real income growth should be at all affected. However, by definition a shock is unexpected and this is a crucial element in the time pattern of real income growth. We have explained that firms tend to set prices for each period and then sell all they can at the given price. If the money supply unexpectedly increases, then the excess money balances lead individuals to exchange the money for goods, services, and financial assets. In the short run, prices change slowly, if at all, in response to the unexpected increase in demand, but sales of real goods and services do increase—hence the increase in real output. Over time, as prices rise in response to the higher nominal demand, real income returns to grow at the constant steady-state rate. In the long run the money shock has no real effect.

The effects of a money shock on real output may persist for some time because: expectations are slow to adjust, contracts exist that hold prices and wages fixed, or it takes time to replenish inventories and adjust unemployment.

An interesting question is why the effect of the money shock has real income effects that persist beyond one or two quarters. The empirical evidence suggests that the adjustment process takes years rather than a few quarters to complete. Macroeconomists have developed several theories aimed at explaining the persistent real effects of money shocks. It is useful to organize these theories into three basic types: *expectational error theories, contract theories, and equilibrium theories.*

## EXPECTATIONAL ERROR THEORIES

These theories argue that when we observe a number of quarters of below (or above) normal real output, people must be expecting higher (or lower) aggregate demand in each of these periods than actually occurs. This would certainly seem to be the implication of the aggregate demand and supply analysis presented in Chapter 7. Simple univariate expectation models—particularly adaptive expectations—would seem to imply long periods of expectational errors after a change in the underlying trend in money growth. However, many macroeconomists today assume that people form their expectations rationally, taking into consideration all factors which may be profitably used. But the fact that people have rational expectations does not prevent them from making erroneous predictions, although it does mean that they cannot be consistently fooled as they will quickly learn from past mistakes. Economists may find it plausible that sequences of expectational errors as long as three or four quarters occur, but they do not believe that errors could persist for two or more years as would be required to explain the long observed adjustment period.

Most macroeconomists now view expectational errors as characterizing the first few quarters of the adjustment to a monetary shock and look for other explanations of the persistent effect of these shocks on real output. On this view, the aggregate demand and supply analysis of Chapter 7 can only be applied when we begin with an economy in long-run equilibrium. During the adjustment process, the aggregate supply curve will not intersect the aggregate demand curve at normal output $y$ even if actual aggregate demand turns out to be as expected at the beginning of the period.

## CONTRACT THEORIES

These theories assume that although current expectations may adjust rapidly to what is happening in the economy, past expectations are embodied in the structure of long-term contracts in the economy. If individuals enter into contracts to deliver goods at a stated price or provide labor services for a given wage, then these contracts build wage and price rigidities into the economy. If the contract periods

**expectational error theories**
When real output varies from normal steady-state rates, this results from incorrect expectations by consumers and firms

**contract theories**
The effects of money shocks may persist through time as contracts slow the reaction to the shock

extend beyond the time it takes the monetary authority to change monetary policy, then money shocks can have persistent real output effects even though individuals have rational expectations. When the shock occurs, the contractually agreed upon rigidities will lead to a drawing out of the adjustment process. For instance, suppose there is an unexpected increase in the money supply growth rate. The initial excess money balances stimulate nominal aggregate demand. With contractually rigid wages and prices, the initial response is an increase in real income. Over time, as contracts are renegotiated, the real effects are eliminated and wages and prices rise to the new, higher steady-state growth rates. John Taylor has emphasized the importance of staggered wage contracts in generating persistent real effects following a money shock.[7] Contracts are not set on an economywide basis simultaneously. The actual structure of contracts has them expiring in an uneven fashion across time. So a money shock in the current period may be taken into consideration quickly in an industry where wages are being agreed upon in the near future, but in an industry where wages are fixed for several periods before the present contract expires, the required adjustment in wages and prices may be postponed until that future contract settlement is realized. As a result, the real income effects of the money shock may persist through time.

Note that these contract-based theories may have expectations adjusting to the money shock quite quickly, but with the rigidities enforced by long-term contracts, the adjustment to the shock will be drawn out much longer than would be realized simply on the basis of people initially being fooled by the money shock. Realistically, the structure of contracts can be altered over time. Therefore, if the authorities try to exploit the contracting structure to stimulate real output in the short run, they will encourage a new structure. Workers will react to the unexpected decline in real wages brought about by repeated positive money shocks by negotiating contracts for shorter periods or having contracts written to guarantee real wages rather than just nominal wages.

## EQUILIBRIUM THEORIES

**equilibrium theories**
The effects of money shocks may persist over time if some variables, such as inventories, adjust slowly to new desired levels

Economists supporting equilibrium theories of persistent real output effects find it implausible that, on the one hand, expectational errors could persist for years, or, on the other, that contracts would not be indexed to money or prices (written in real terms) so as to avoid the

---

[7] John B. Taylor, ''Aggregate Dynamics and Staggered Contracts,''
*Journal of Political Economy*, 88 (February 1980), 1–23.

inefficient effects suggested by the staggered contract theorists. Equilibrium theorists propose instead that the way the economy operates during the comparatively brief period of expectational error will bring about a change in some variable, which in turn causes a persistent effect on output until the changed variable returns to its normal level. So even with no further expectational errors, the short-run effects of the initial error imply a longer-run period of adjustment. Equilibrium theorists differ in identifying which key variable has been changed in a manner that requires a long-run adjustment.

Alan Blinder of Princeton University and Stanley Fischer of M.I.T. have emphasized the role of inventory changes in the persistence of real income effects.[8] When the firm experiences an increased nominal demand for its output and raises prices, it cannot determine whether the change is nominal or real, so it is likely to treat the change as a higher relative price, in which case there is an incentive to increase sales and output. It is costly to increase production in the current period to the new desired level, so inventories are partially depleted to meet current sales. As inventories fall below desired levels, firms increase output in the following periods to rebuild the level of inventories. The need to have inventories rebuilt to desired levels is one explanation, then, of the persistent effect of money shocks on real output. Even if expectations adjust quickly to a money shock, real income growth may persist for a while away from the steady-state due to the required inventory adjustment.

A number of other stock variables have been identified as the key variable leading to persistent real output effects. These variables include the stock of physical capital, of investment projects in process, and of human capital that is useful to a specific employer. Since all of these factors are expected to have effects similar to the effect of inventories, we need not consider each separately.

Michael Darby, John Haltiwanger, and Mark Plant of U.C.L.A. have recently argued that the stock of unemployed persons plays a major role in explaining persistent real output effects after macroeconomic shocks.[9] They show that the change in the unemployment rate ($\Delta u$) over a month can be described essentially by the following equation:

$$\Delta u = (f - \bar{f}) - (h - \bar{h})u - \bar{h}(u - \bar{u}) \qquad (12.6)$$

---

[8]Alan S. Blinder and Stanley Fischer, "Inventories, Rational Expectations, and the Business Cycle," *Journal of Monetary Economics*, 8 (November 1981), 277–304.

[9]In their "Search and Layoff Unemployment Rate Dynamics and Persistent Unemployment Under Rational Expectations," *American Economic Review*, 75 (September 1985), 614–37.

The $(f - \bar{f})$ term represents the deviation of the actual fraction $(f)$ of the labor force beginning unemployment this month from its normal value $\bar{f}$. The $(h - \bar{h})$ term represents the deviation of the actual value $h$ from the normal value $\bar{h}$ of the probability that someone who starts the month unemployed finds employment during the month. We have discussed such terms earlier in Section 8.2, where the normal values of search flow and the probability of employment and cyclical fluctuations around these normal values were covered. In Chapter 8, however, the probability of employment was discussed primarily in terms of its inverse $1/h$, the expected duration of unemployment.[10]

Equation (12.6) tells us that the unemployment rate $u$ rises if the search flow rises or the probability of employment falls relative to normal. These are the kinds of changes that occur at the beginning of a restrictive monetary policy when expected prices and wages are high relative to actual demand and, as a result, inventories rise. After a few quarters, however, expectations adjust so that $f$ and $h$ return to their normal values and the first two terms on the right hand side of equation (12.6) are zero.[11] What about the $\bar{h}(u - \bar{u})$ term? During the first few quarters following the money shock, the unemployment rate rose above its normal level $\bar{u}$ so that $(u - \bar{u})$ is positive. Once $f$ and $h$ return to their normal levels $\bar{f}$ and $\bar{h}$, we are left with $\Delta u$ being equal to a fraction $\bar{h}$ of excess unemployment. As $u$ is greater than $\bar{u}$ , $\Delta u$ will fall by $\bar{h}(u - \bar{u})$. This means that unemployment does not immediately return to its normal value $\bar{u}$. Only a fraction of the higher than normal unemployment is eliminated each month, that fraction determined by $\bar{h}$, the normal probability of finding a job within a month. So once people are thrown out of work, it takes time to reem-

---

[10]If there is a 10-percent probability of finding a job in a given month, then the expected duration of unemployment is 1/.1 or 10 months. More precisely, $h$ represents the probability of an unemployed person finding a job or leaving the labor force within the month.

[11]Darby, Haltiwanger, and Plant show that the observed values of $h$ return to $\bar{h}$ much too slowly to be consistent with rational expectations. They show that this can be explained, however, by a kind of equilibrium behavior: individuals differ by sex, age, race, occupation, industry, and other characteristics in their individual probabilities of finding a job (or leaving the labor force). In the recovery from a recession, high-probability individuals quickly find a job depressing the *average* value of $h$ by the remaining excess of low probability individuals. This slows the return of $u$ to $\bar{u}$ compared to that implied by the $\bar{h}(u - \bar{u})$ term alone. Otherwise, these authors relate movements in $f$ and $h$ primarily to fluctuations in inventories.

ploy them even if all expectations are accurate. This persistence in the unemployment rate can be seen via Okun's Law to imply persistence in real output. Remember the Chapter 8 discussion of Okun's Law: for each 1 percentage point the unemployment rate is above (below) normal, real output will be approximately 3 percentage points below (above) normal. So as the unemployment rate is slow to adjust back to the normal level, so too will the level of real income persist in deviating from its normal level.

## 12.4 CYCLICAL ADJUSTMENT OF INTEREST RATES

### STEADY-STATE INTEREST RATES

The tax-amended Fisher equation (see the essay at the end of Chapter 4) states that the nominal interest rate exceeds the real interest rate by $(1/(1 - t))$ times the expected rate of inflation $\hat{P}^*$, where $t$ is the marginal tax rate applicable to borrowers and lenders. In Chapter 10 we saw that the steady-state real interest rate $\bar{r}$ can be considered as unaffected by the nominal money supply growth rate. Figure 12.2 illustrates the steady-state effects of an increase in the money growth rate at time $z$ from $\bar{\hat{M}}_0$ to $\bar{\hat{M}}_1$. In steady-state equilibrium, actual and expected inflation rates are equal to the steady-state inflation rates of $\bar{\hat{P}}_0$ before $z$ and $\bar{\hat{P}}_1$ after $z$. In Figure 12.2 we see that the nominal interest rate equals $\bar{R}_0$ prior to $z$. In terms of the Fisher equation this may be written as:

$$\bar{R}_0 = \bar{r} + \bar{\hat{P}}_0 + \frac{t}{1 - t} \bar{\hat{P}}_0 \qquad (12.7)$$

Since changes in the money growth rate are assumed to have no real effects in the steady-state, the steady-state real rate of interest remains fixed at $\bar{r}$ both before and after $z$ as shown in Figure 12.2. However, the figure shows the steady-state nominal interest rate rising to $\bar{R}_1$ after $z$. The increase in the steady-state money growth rate of $(\bar{\hat{M}}_1 - \bar{\hat{M}}_0)$ brings an equivalent increase in the rate of inflation of $(\bar{\hat{P}}_1 - \bar{\hat{P}}_0)$, other things equal. The new, higher inflation rate will be associated with a higher nominal interest rate as

$$\bar{R}_1 = \bar{r} + \bar{\hat{P}}_1 + \frac{t}{1 - t} \bar{\hat{P}}_1 \qquad (12.8)$$

We can solve for the increase in the steady-state nominal interest rate at $z$ as

$$\bar{R}_1 - \bar{R}_0 = (\bar{\hat{P}}_1 - \bar{\hat{P}}_0) + \frac{t}{1 - t} (\bar{\hat{P}}_1 - \bar{\hat{P}}_0) \qquad (12.9)$$

**Figure 12.2**

Steady-State Interest Rates
With an Increase in the
Money Growth Rate at Time $z$

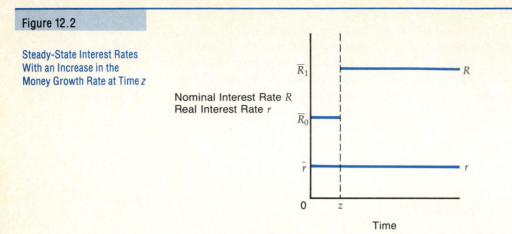

The first term on the right-hand side of equation (12.9) is the increase in the steady-state inflation rate. In a world without taxes, the nominal interest rate would rise by this amount to keep the real rate of interest (the nominal rate minus the inflation rate) constant. However, since interest payments are deductible while interest receipts are taxed as income, the nominal interest must rise by more than the simple increase in inflation to keep the after-tax real rate constant. The second term on the right-hand side of equation (12.9) captures this tax adjustment effect on the nominal rate of interest.

Relating the change in interest rates to the change in money growth, we said that $(\hat{\bar{M}}_1 - \hat{\bar{M}}_0)$ equals $(\hat{\bar{P}}_1 - \hat{\bar{P}}_0)$. So if we substituted $(\hat{\bar{M}}_1 - \hat{\bar{M}}_0)$ into equation (12.9) in place of $(\hat{\bar{P}}_1 - \hat{\bar{P}}_0)$, we would see that the rise in nominal interest rates would exceed the increase in the growth rate of money.[12] Let's consider a numerical example to correspond to Figure 12.2.

**Example 12.2** ▶

Suppose that the nominal money supply growth rate $(\hat{\bar{M}})$ were increased by 4 percentage points from 1 percent to 5 percent per annum at time $z$ and that the steady-state inflation rate $(\hat{\bar{P}})$ increased from 4 to 8 percent per annum as a result. Furthermore, let's assume that the marginal tax rate $(t)$ is 20 percent and the steady-state real rate of interest $(\bar{r})$ is 3 percent.

---

[12]These results, of course, are predicated on the marginal tax rate lying between 0 and 1, so that $t/(1-t)$ exceeds zero. Since no one pays 100 percent of any additional income earned as taxes, and we assume that there are taxes so that a rate of zero is ruled out, $0 < t < 1$ is expected.

The nominal interest rate prior to $z$ may be calculated, from equation (12.7), as

$$\bar{R}_0 = .03 + .04 + \frac{.2}{1 - .2}(.04) = .08$$

So the initial steady-state nominal interest rate is 8 percent per annum. After time $z$, when the inflation rate rises to 8 percent per annum, the new steady-state nominal interest rate is found, from equation (12.8), as:

$$\bar{R}_1 = .03 + .08 + \frac{.2}{1 - .2}(.08) = .13$$

So the new steady-state nominal interest rate is 13 percent per annum. While the money growth rate (and inflation rate) increased by 4 percentage points, the nominal interest rate rose 5 percentage points. ■

## ADJUSTMENT TO A STIMULATIVE MONETARY POLICY

Just as the economy does not immediately converge to the new steady-state growth rate of nominal income following a money shock, neither does it move immediately to $R_1$ at time $z$ in Figure 12.2. The process of adjustment of the nominal and real interest rate displays an interesting cyclical pattern which has been much studied.

When the growth rate of money increases, initially there is an excess supply of money at the existing income, interest rate, and price level.[13] As we have seen in earlier sections, prices and income are somewhat slow to change, so the interest rate must fall to equate money supply and demand. This initial fall in the nominal interest rate is known as the **liquidity effect**. Since the nominal interest rate is made up of a real rate and expected inflation, and expectations are not immediately altered by the money shock, fluctuations in the real rate of interest appear to dominate the early part of the adjustment process.

**liquidity effect**
The initial drop in nominal interest rates due to increased money supply

In addition to the liquidity effect depressing the interest rate, there also exists a credit or **financial effect**. When the growth rate of money increases, excess reserves of banks also increase. Banks use

**financial effect**
The change in nominal interest rates due to changed bank demand for short-term securities

---

[13]This section draws heavily from Michael Melvin, "The Vanishing Liquidity Effect of Money on Interest: Analysis and Implications For Policy," *Economic Inquiry*, 21 (April 1983), 188–202.

short-term marketable securities to adjust excess reserves to desired levels in the short run, and only adjust their loan portfolios over time. Thus as money growth increases, the financial effect will lead banks to purchase securities and thereby lower their rate of interest relative to loan interest rates in response to the increase in excess reserves. (Remember that an increase in securities prices means that interest rates fall.) Over time, as loan rates and portfolios adjust, the demand for marketable securities falls, tending to increase the interest rates. Thus, the time pattern of the financial effect suggests a decline and later rise in interest rates following an increase in money growth.

As nominal income starts to rise following the money shock, both spending and money demand rise, which leads to higher interest rates. This **income effect** on interest rates explains why some researchers looked at the monetary effects on interest rates to infer the lag in the effect of money on income.[14] The idea was to find the period when interest rates first turn from falling to rising, and identify this as the period when income rises following a money shock. We now know that this approach may be misleading, as other effects could cause interest rates to rise before any income effects occur.

**income effect**
The rise in interest rates due to increased money demand resulting from increased nominal income

Finally, there is the **Fisher or expectations effect** with which we are already familiar. As inflation expectations adjust to the new higher money growth rate, the nominal interest rate will rise. If the higher inflation and money growth rate have no effect on the real rate of interest in the steady-state, then the rise in nominal interest rates must be proportional to the increase in expected inflation (including the $t/(1 - t)$ tax adjustment factor).

**Fisher or expectations effect**
Inflation expectations increase nominal interest rates relative to real interest rates

Figure 12.3 summarizes these various effects on the pattern of adjustment. The initial drop in interest rates following the increased money growth rate at time $z$, labeled region A in the figure, reflects the operation of the liquidity effect. The offsetting income effect occurs in region B, while the financial effect is active in both A and B. Region C reflects growing influence of the expectations effect where the nominal interest rate increases due to the anticipation of a higher future inflation rate. In region D, full steady-state equilibrium is achieved.

---

[14]The classic study here is by Phillip Cagan of Columbia University and Arthur Gandolfi of Citibank, ''The Lag in Monetary Policy as Implied by the Time Pattern of Monetary Effects on Interest Rates,'' *American Economic Review*, May 1969, 277–84.

Figure 12.3

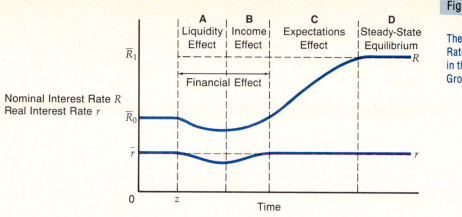

The Adjustment of Interest Rates Following an Increase in the Nominal Money Supply Growth Rate

## TIMING OF THE ADJUSTMENT

The period of time required for the interest rate adjustment of Figure 12.3 has undergone change in recent years. Early studies looking at postwar data through the 1960s found that following an increase in the growth rate of money, the initial drop in interest rates would last four to nine months before rising interest rates, consistent with inflation expectations, would be observed.[15] In terms of Figure 12.3, this suggests that region A covers roughly half a year. The nominal interest rate would then rise back to its original level approximately one year after the money growth increase, so region B accounts for roughly six more months. There is much uncertainty regarding when the new steady-state is attained, but the estimates generally run to at least several years. Our knowledge regarding the duration of period C was very weak in the past, and it remains so today.

The timing pattern just reviewed was based on studies that occurred around 1970. More recent research, using a similar methodology to the earlier authors, reveals an important change in the time pattern of interest rates following an increase in the money growth

---

[15]The best-known studies are Phillip Cagan, *The Channels of Monetary Effects on Interest Rates*, National Bureau of Economic Research, 1972, and William Gibson, "The Lag in the Effect of Monetary Policy on Income and Interest Rates," *Quarterly Journal of Economics*, May 1970, 288–300.

Following an unexpected increase in money growth, interest rates may fall for a brief period before rising to a new level consistent with inflation expectations.

rate.[16] It appears that in more recent times the initial liquidity effect of the faster money growth is likely to be offset within the month following the monetary policy change. In terms of Figure 12.3, this means that periods A and B have been compressed to approximately one month. Why has there been such a dramatic shortening of the negative effects of higher money growth on interest rates? The existing studies seem to indicate that inflationary expectations deserve most of the credit. Through the 1970s increasing attention has been given to the money supply data published by the Federal Reserve. As the rate of inflation became higher and more unstable in the 1970s compared to the period 1950–69, individuals were quicker to revise their inflation expectations. They may also have adopted multivariate expectations based on both past money growth and inflation, instead of looking only at past inflation. As a result, the expectations effect of region C in Figure 12.3 started to occur earlier than in the past.[17]

## CENTRAL BANK POLICY AND INTEREST RATE ADJUSTMENTS

Recently, several researchers have made use of the survey data on the expected weekly announcements of the money supply that were discussed in footnote 4 above. Every Thursday at approximately 4:15 P.M. EST, the Fed announces the magnitude of the money supply in existence for the week ending eight days earlier. The question of interest to researchers is how the interest rate responds to an unanticipated announcement on a Thursday afternoon. What may seem surprising is that these studies suggest that if the Fed announces an

---

[16]See Michael Melvin, "The Vanishing Liquidity Effect of Money on Interest: Analysis and Implications for Policy," *Economic Inquiry*, 21 (April 1983), 188–202, and W. W. Brown and G. J. Santoni in "Monetary Growth and the Timing of Interest Rate Movements," *Federal Reserve Bank of St. Louis Review*, August/September 1983, 16–25. H. H. Stokes and H. Neuburger also provide some interesting results in "The Effect of Monetary Changes on Interest Rates: A Box-Jenkins Approach," *Review of Economics and Statistics*, November 1979, 534–48.

[17]Several researchers have found evidence that the public's expectations have been altered in the manner suggested here. Some representative examples are Thomas F. Cargill and Robert A. Meyer in "Intertemporal Stability of the Relationship Between Interest Rates and Price Changes," *Journal of Finance*, 32 (September 1977), 1001–16, and Alexander Holmes and Myron Kwast, "Interest Rates and Inflationary Expectations: Tests for Structural Change 1952–1976," *Journal of Finance*, 34 (June 1979), 733–41.

unexpectedly high money supply on Thursday, interest rates rise.[18]
In the last section we reviewed a theory suggesting that increases in
the money supply should have an initial liquidity effect where the
rate of interest falls. What accounts for the positive effect of the
weekly money supply announcements? The answer lies in the policy
strategy of the Federal Reserve. As was detailed in the essay ending
Chapter 11, the Federal Open Market Committee establishes target
rates of money growth which the open market desk at the New York
Fed is directed to achieve. If the Fed announces that the money supply is larger than everyone expected, people will expect the Fed to
respond to this unexpected rise in money growth by lowering the
growth of the money supply in the future. Money market participants (banks, brokerage houses, and individuals) now expect that
this future monetary restraint by the Fed will lead to higher real
interest rates and so borrowers seek to obtain funds now at the current lower interest rate. Of course, all this aggressive bidding for
loanable funds now will drive up the interest rate. The positive effect
of the weekly money surprise on interest rates has been called the
**policy anticipation effect**. The distinguishing feature of this effect,
apart from the earlier analysis of the effect of actual changes in money
growth, is that the interest rate response on Thursday afternoon is a
response to an expected future change in money growth rather than
a response to an actual change.

**policy anticipation effect**
The effect of a money supply
announcement on interest rates
when based on market expectations of future Fed behavior

    Since the Fed has the power to move interest rates, it would seem
that there is an incentive to use monetary policy to maintain low
interest rates and thereby stimulate economic growth. In the Keynesian model of Chapter 5, lower interest rates stimulated investment
spending which in turn increased real income and output. Why don't
we use central bank policy to keep interest rates low? The answer lies
in the difference between nominal and real interest rates. What mat-

[18]Until 1984, the announcements were made Friday afternoon for
the week ending nine days earlier. Some contributors to this literature are V. Vance Roley in "The Response of Short-Term Interest
Rates to Weekly Money Announcements," *Journal of Money,
Credit, and Banking*, 15 (August 1983), 344–54; Thomas Urich and
Paul Wachtel in "Market Responses to Weekly Money Supply Announcements in the 1970s," *Journal of Finance*, 36 (December
1981), 1063–72, and Bradford Cornell in "Money Supply Announcements, Interest Rates, and Foreign Exchange," *Journal of
International Money and Finance*, 1 (August 1982); 201–208, and
"The Money Supply Announcements Puzzle: Review and Interpretation," *American Economic Review*, 83 (September 1983),
644–57.

ters for real economic decisionmaking, like investment spending, is the real rate of interest. Unfortunately, while it is clear that monetary policy can have a permanent impact on the steady-state nominal rate of interest, we have assumed, and this is not altogether unreasonable, that a change in the money growth rate will not affect the steady-state real interest rate. Only during the period of adjustment to a money shock might the real rate be changed. It appears that in the 1960s, the fact that a money shock could depress real interest rates for up to a year allowed a potentially attractive short-run policy. Of course the long-run cost is the new higher steady-state rate of inflation and nominal interest rate. However, in more recent times the liquidity effect has been so short-lived as to hardly be worth the increased inflation resulting from an expansionary monetary policy.

It is interesting to note that, perhaps partly as a result of the vanishing liquidity effect of money on interest, the Fed changed its basic operating procedure in October 1979. Prior to this time, the Fed had given great emphasis to keeping interest rates within a certain target range so monetary policy was aimed at affecting interest rates. In October 1979 the Fed adopted a new approach emphasizing target ranges for the money supply growth rates. We will consider the implications of this change in Chapter 14.

## SUMMARY

1   In the aggregate demand–aggregate supply analysis, money shocks shift the aggregate demand curve. The slope of aggregate supply determines the distribution of the change in nominal income into real income and price level change.

2   Following a money shock, the resulting fluctuations in nominal income are initially reflected in real income growth and then later in prices.

3   The steady-state growth rate of real income is unaffected by a change in the money growth rate, but the steady-state rate of inflation rises proportionally to the new money growth rate.

4   Expectational error theories of the effects of money shocks on real income emphasize that people make mistakes regarding future prices.

5   Contract-based theories of the effects of money shocks on real income emphasize that contractual arrangements build rigidities into the economy that limit the ability of individuals to respond to changes in money growth.

**6** Equilibrium theories attribute the persistent real output effects of a monetary shock after a brief period of expectational error to a stock variable, such as inventories or number unemployed, which slowly returns to normal.

**7** An increase in the growth rate of money has no effect on the steady-state real rate of interest, but raises the nominal interest rate by more than the increase in money growth due to the tax effect.

**8** Following an increase in money growth, there is an initial fall in interest rates before rates start to rise. While the real interest rate rises to return to its steady-state level, the nominal rate rises to a new steady-state level reflecting the new, higher rate of inflation.

**9** If the Fed announces a surprisingly large money supply figure on Thursday afternoon, interest rates rise due to a policy anticipation effect.

## EXERCISES

**1.** Draw a diagram similar to Figure 12.1 which indicates the pattern of adjustment of nominal income growth, real income growth, and the inflation rate following an unexpected fall in nominal money growth. Carefully explain the reasons behind your figure.

**2.** Draw a diagram similar to Figure 12.3 which indicates the pattern of adjustment of the nominal and real interest rate following an unexpected fall in nominal money growth. Carefully explain the reasons behind your figure.

**3.** Suppose that a restrictive monetary policy had reduced actual real income to 6 percent below its steady-state level and the price level was 4 percent above its steady-state level. If the steady-state growth rates of real income and inflation were 3 percent and 2 percent per annum, respectively, over the next 2 years, and steady-state equilibrium were reached at the end of those 2 years, what would be the average $\hat{y}$ and $\hat{P}$ during this recovery period?

**4.** Evaluate the following statement: Real income is temporarily increased by a stimulative monetary policy because sellers take actions that they would not take if they were aware of true conditions.

**5.** Explain why the initial effect on the nominal interest rate of a change in the nominal money supply growth rate is opposite to the long-run effect.

6. Compare the aggregate demand–aggregate supply approach to the dynamic representation of Figure 12.1. Is there a conflict between the aggregate demand–aggregate supply figure and Figure 12.1, or are the two graphical approaches related in some manner? Explain your answer carefully.

7. Evaluate the following statement: Since higher money growth stimulates the growth rate of real income temporarily, the authorities could contribute to a higher GNP by continuously raising the growth rate of the money supply unexpectedly.

8. How can a positive money shock have persistent effects on real income unless people adjust their expectations slowly?

## REFERENCES FOR FURTHER READING

Friedman, Milton, and Anna J. Schwartz. "Money and Business Cycles." *Review of Economics and Statistics*, 45 (February 1963), 32–64.

Lucas, Robert E., Jr. "Understanding Business Cycles." In K. Brunner and A. Meltzer, eds., *Carnegie-Rochester Conference Series*, 5, 1977, 7–29.

Santoni, G. J., and Courtenay C. Stone. "The Fed and the Real Rate of Interest." *Federal Reserve Bank of St. Louis Review*, 64 (December 1982), 8–18.

# UNEXPECTED MONEY INCREASES AND OUTPUT INCREASES: THE MORE IT'S TRIED, THE WORSE IT WORKS

In Chapter 12 we learned that a positive money shock can increase the growth rate of real income temporarily. The expected dynamic adjustment pattern of real income growth is an initial rise above the steady-state followed by a fall below the steady-state growth rate before the original steady-state growth path is once again attained. Since politicians typically have a short-run view of economic policy given the short intervals between elections, it would appear that there exists some incentive to increase money growth unexpectedly wherever there is a strong public sentiment that unemployment is too high. The initial good effects of a positive money shock would include a falling unemployment rate, and by the time the bad part of the adjustment pattern is experienced—falling real income growth and rising inflation and unemployment—the elections are past.

The evidence across countries indicates that even the short-run benefit may be elusive if a nation has tried to produce economic growth with money shocks in the past. In a well known study, Robert Lucas of the University of Chicago analyzed the data on inflation and output in 18 countries from 1951 to 1967.[1] Lucas formulates an information-based theory of the real effect of money shocks as was discussed in section 12.3. While economic decisions depend on relative prices, in the short run people cannot distinguish general price changes from relative price changes due to imperfect information. When aggregate demand increases unexpectedly due to a positive money shock, real output increases in the short run to the extent that suppliers are "fooled" into believing that this is a relative shift in demand favoring their firm rather than a general increase in demand affecting all firms similarly.

Lucas finds evidence that in relatively stable price countries like the United States and West Germany, policies which increase nominal income (like an unanticipated increase in money growth) tend to have a large initial effect on real output with little initial effect on inflation. In contrast, countries with relatively unstable inflation rates like Argentina or Paraguay, find that such policies have little or no effect on real output so that even the initial increases in nominal income are associated with rising prices. The differences between stable price countries and unstable price countries stem from the ability of government policies to catch people by surprise. When countries have followed erratic monetary policies

---

[1]Robert E. Lucas, Jr., "Some International Evidence on Output-Inflation Tradeoffs," *American Economic Review*, 63 (June 1973), 326–35.

leading to frequent money shocks, people learn to discern very quickly the increase in aggregate demand as a nominal change that affects everyone, rather than a relative change affecting only their industry or firm. In stable price countries, where monetary policy has been less erratic, an increase in aggregate demand is more likely to be interpreted as a relative demand shift rather than a general change. Since people have not been fooled often in the past, they are more susceptible to being fooled now. In summary then, the positive effect of unexpected money growth on real output, as detailed in Chapter 12, will exist as long as the authorities seldom create such shocks. The more frequent money shocks or the less predictable monetary policy, the smaller the real output effects of unanticipated money growth.[2]

---

[2]Since the time of Lucas's classic article, several other researchers have contributed to our knowledge in this area. Some of these are Jose Alberro in "The Lucas Hypothesis on the Phillips Curve: Further International Evidence," *Journal of Monetary Economics*, 7 (March 1981), 239–50, Clifford L. F. Attfield and Nigel W. Duck in "The Influence of Unanticipated Money Growth on Real Output," *Journal of Money, Credit, and Banking*, 15 (November 1983), 442–54, and Roger C. Kormendi and Phillip C. Meguire in "Cross-Regime Evidence of Macroeconomic Rationality," *Journal of Political Economy*, 92, 875–908.

# CHAPTER THIRTEEN

# DYNAMIC ADJUSTMENTS TO FISCAL AND OTHER SHOCKS

## 13.1 MACROECONOMIC SHOCKS

Macroeconomic shocks have their initial impact either on the aggregate demand for goods and services or on the aggregate supply. Thus they are termed either *demand shocks* or *supply shocks*. For large industrial economies, fluctuations in real income, unemployment, and inflation are almost exclusively related to demand shocks. While our discussion will concentrate on these shocks, supply shocks will be considered in Section 13.5.

Demand shocks are by definition unexpected. So too, then, will the related changes in aggregate demand be unexpected. We measure these changes by the change in the growth rate of nominal expenditures or nominal income. A demand shock changes the rate at which the aggregate demand curve shifts outward. A look at the dynamic Cambridge equation indicates that the growth rate of nominal expenditures is equal to the difference between the growth rates of the nominal money supply and the money–income ratio:

$$\hat{Y} \equiv \hat{M} - \hat{K} \qquad (13.1)$$

Therefore, a demand shock must operate by causing unexpected changes in the growth rate of the nominal money supply, the money–

Shocks are unexpected changes.

income ratio, or both. Without a change in $\hat{M}$ or $\hat{K}$, there can be no change in $\hat{Y}$. In Chapters 11 and 12 we considered demand shocks associated with changes in the nominal money supply growth rate, or *monetary shocks*. A demand shock occurring with an unchanged money growth path is termed a *nonmonetary demand shock*. While monetary shocks typically involve changes in the growth rates of *both* the nominal money supply and the money–income ratio, a nonmonetary demand shock acts only through changes in the growth rate of the money–income ratio, since the growth rate of nominal money is unchanged.

**policy shocks**
Demand shocks due to the exercise of government policy

**behavioral demand shocks**
Autonomous shocks due to shifts in basic macro functions

Demand shocks also can be the result of a government policy decision, and hence called **policy shocks**, or the result of an unexpected shift in macroeconomic behavioral functions, and therefore called **behavioral demand shocks**. Behavioral demand shocks are also referred to as autonomous demand shocks. Table 13.1 summarizes the demand shocks in the domestic economy which have been of major concern to macroeconomists.

Monetary policy, of course, refers to the actions of the central bank, that influence the growth rate of the nominal money supply. Nonmonetary macroeconomic policy is divided into fiscal policy and debt policy. Fiscal policy refers to decisions that determine taxes and aggregate expenditures on goods and services. *Debt policy* refers to decisions that determine the *maturity structure* of government debt. By maturity structure we mean the fraction of total outstanding government bonds existing at each term to maturity like 3 months, 6 months, 1 year, and so on. While government debt policy was once thought to be powerful, it appears that such policy is almost entirely neutralized by changes in the maturity structure of private borrow-

---

**Table 13.1**

Classification of Demand Shocks

| Source of Demand Shock | Monetary | Nonmonetary |
|---|---|---|
| Policy | Decisions that determine the growth rate of base money and influence the growth rate of the money multiplier | Decisions on government expenditures for (1) real goods and services, (2) the level of taxation, and (3) maturity structure of government debt. |
| Behavioral or autonomous | Banking panics | Shifts in (1) investment demand, (2) real money demand, and (3) consumer expenditures. |

ing and lending.[1] As a result, we will limit our discussion of non-monetary policy shocks to fiscal policy.

## 13.2 CHANGES IN GOVERNMENT SPENDING

### THE GOVERNMENT BUDGET IDENTITY AGAIN

Any analysis of fiscal policy must keep in mind the government budget identity:

$$G \equiv T + \Delta D + \Delta B \qquad (13.2)$$

That is, nominal government expenditures $G$ are identically equal to the sum of nominal taxes $T$, the rate of change in nominal government debt $\Delta D$, and the rate of change in nominal base money $\Delta B$. This identity relates total government expenditures for goods and services to the ways in which they may be financed. The difference between expenditures and taxes—the amount financed by money creation and debt issuance—is the government *deficit*: $G - T = \Delta D + \Delta B$. We assume that the activities of state and local governments are consolidated with those of the federal government.

Fiscal policy is defined in terms of decisions about government expenditures and taxes which leave the nominal money supply growth rate unchanged. In terms of equation (13.2), $\Delta B$ does not change with changes in $T$ or $G$. So our analysis of fiscal shocks assumes that any increase in government spending or decrease in taxes is financed by an equal increase in government borrowing $\Delta D$.

Government spending may be financed by taxes, debt, or base money.

---

[1]From 1961 until 1965, the Fed and the Treasury attempted to increase the interest rate on short-term bonds relative to that on long-term bonds in what was called "Operation Twist." This involved replacing long-term government bonds with short-term Treasury bills. While short-term rates did rise relative to long-term rates, it is not at all clear that the rise was due to Operation Twist, as other postwar business expansions had experienced similar changes in interest rates. Important unsuccessful attempts to find an effect of debt policy are Franco Modigliani and Richard Sutch, "Debt Management and the Term Structure of Interest Rates: An Empirical Analysis of Recent Experience," *Journal of Political Economy*, 75 (August 1967), 569–89; and Michael E. Echols and Jan Walter Elliott, "Rational Expectations in a Disequilibrium Model of the Term Structure," *American Economic Review*, 66 (March 1976), 28–44.

## LONG-RUN EFFECTS

Macroeconomic policymakers sometimes propose an unexpected increase in real government spending to increase the growth rate of nominal income. We will examine how this policy works by assuming that monetary and tax policies are unchanged, so that the increased spending is financed by increased borrowing. While it would be unusual in practice for policymakers to concentrate only on government spending, such a simplification allows us to more readily consider the essential effects at work. Once we understand the individual effects of fiscal policy actions, more complex policy measures can be considered.

As with a monetary shock, it is useful to start our analysis at the end rather than at the beginning. So we will first focus on the steady-state equilibrium effects of an increase in government spending and then discuss how we get there. The issues involved are best understood if related to the model of steady-state growth in Chapter 9. In Chapter 9 we saw that the steady-state growth path of real income is determined by the growth path of labor, the aggregate production function, and the ratio of real investment to real income. Unexpected changes in real government spending will temporarily affect the unemployment rate, and hence labor supply, during the period of adjustment. In the long run, the level of real government spending will not significantly affect the labor supply or its growth rate. The steady-state growth rate of real income is equal to the growth rate of labor, so it too is unchanged. Therefore, increased government spending may affect the level of real income but not its steady-state growth rate.

Some economists argue that increased government production will cause a decrease in overall productivity since the government is less efficient than the private sector. Others take just the opposite view. Since there is very little evidence in favor of either view, we will not consider this issue.

Whether or not a higher level of real government spending has effects on steady-state real income depends on whether or not total private and government investment is reduced relative to income. If the fraction of income invested changes, then real income will be affected. If higher government spending means that government investment is displacing an equal amount of private investment, then there is no change in total investment relative to income and there should be no effect on steady-state real income. This result would suggest that individuals see the government as simply an extension of the private sector. When government spending rises by some amount, private sector spending falls as private saving rises in anticipation of the future tax payments required to repay the higher government debt associated with the higher government spending. While one can imagine an economy in which people behaved in this fashion, few economists believe that such perfectly offsetting adjustments to government spending occur.[2] Economists do tend to believe that higher government spending will partially replace private investment with government consumption. If the investment–income ratio falls, then, as we learned in Chapter 9, the level of steady-state real income $y_s$ falls at each point in time, even though the growth rate is constant. This is illustrated in Figure 13.1. At time $z$, government spending increases, leading to a drop in total steady-state government and private investment. There is a drop in the level of $y_s$ as a result of this change, but the growth rate of $y_s$ after time $z$ is the same as the growth rate before the change.

There could be an additional effect on steady-state real income if money is not superneutral. The decrease in the fraction of income invested will make capital relatively scarce compared to labor. As a result, the marginal product of capital, and hence the real (and nominal) interest rate, increases. The higher interest rate then lowers the

---

[2]Such an economy is investigated by Robert Barro in "Are Government Bonds Net Wealth?" *Journal of Political Economy*, 82 (July/August 1974), 1095–1117; and Levis A. Kochin in "Are Future Taxes Anticipated by Consumers?" *Journal of Money, Credit, and Banking*, 6 (August 1974), 385–94. Perhaps the strongest evidence in favor of this view is found in an article by Paul A. David and John J. Scadding, "Private Savings: Ultrarationality, Aggregation, and 'Dension's Law,'" *Journal of Political Economy*, 82 (March/April 1974), 225–49; see the end-of-chapter essay for Chapter 5.

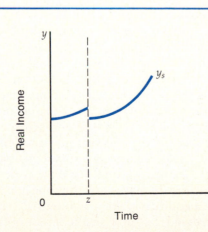

**Figure 13.1**

The Effect of Increased Government Spending on Steady-State Real Income When Private Investment Falls

steady-state level of the money–income ratio and real income if money is not superneutral as discussed in Chapter 10. This is in addition to the initial income effect of a lower investment–income ratio.

Real government spending changes will affect the steady-state equilibrium if total investment relative to income is changed.

In summary, then, higher real government spending will have real effects in steady-state equilibrium if total private and government investment is changed relative to income. If real income is affected, then with a constant monetary policy, prices must also change. While the steady-state inflation rate is unaffected since the steady-state growth rate of real income is unchanged, the percentage shift in the price level will equal the sum of the percentage shifts in real income and the money–income ratio, but in the opposite direction.

In the following analysis of the adjustment of the economy to a fiscal policy shock, we will assume that the steady-state equilibrium is unchanged. While it is likely that there may really be some change in the steady-state, it is not at all established that the magnitude of the steady-state effects are worth the additional complexity they add to our explanation. The simpler case is a good working approximation.

## CROWDING OUT

crowding out
When government spending leads to a reduction in private spending

If increases in government expenditures cause decreases in private spending which either partially or completely offset the government spending change, then we say that the government expenditures are **crowding out** private expenditures. This contrasts with *multiplier effects* that would occur if increased government spending caused increases in private spending, so that total income rose by more than the increase in government spending. The essay at the end of Chapter 5 provided an analysis of alternative ways in which crowding out could occur using the IS–LM framework.

It is useful to distinguish between nominal crowding out and real crowding out. Complete *nominal crowding out* occurs if the increase in nominal government expenditures leaves nominal income unchanged, i.e., every dollar that nominal government expenditures increases is matched by a dollar decrease in nominal private expenditures. Complete *real crowding out* occurs if the increase in real government expenditures leaves real income unchanged, i.e., each constant dollar increase in real government expenditures is matched by an equal decrease in real private spending.

*Partial* nominal (or real) crowding out occurs if nominal (real) income increases less than the increase in nominal (real) government expenditures, so that nominal (real) private expenditures are decreased, but by a smaller amount than in complete crowding out. In the analysis of the adjustment process that follows, it will seem likely that partial crowding out is more realistic than complete crowding out during the first year or two after an increase in government spending.

## AGGREGATE DEMAND AND SUPPLY ANALYSIS

An unexpected increase in the level of real government spending will involve both increased government employment and increased purchases of goods and services from private firms. Therefore, output and income will be directly increased, although at first the increased purchases will result largely in reduced inventories rather than increased production. Over time, production will increase to rebuild inventories to desired levels.

Using the aggregate demand–aggregate supply analysis developed in Chapters 7 and 8, we can illustrate the initial rise in spending and income as a rightward shift in the aggregate demand curve like the shift from $D$ to $D'$ in Figure 13.2. If the short-run aggregate supply curve is relatively flat, then output will increase with little or no price effects. In this case there is no need to distinguish between real and nominal crowding out. This is the impact effect of increased government spending discussed in Chapter 7 or, in the *IS–LM* analysis, in Chapter 5. To see how the economy moves from this initial impact to a steady-state equilibrium with (approximately) complete nominal and real crowding out, we might sketch a series of short-run aggregate demand–aggregate supply equilibria. An easier way of discussing the adjustment pattern is to examine the dynamic growth rate curves in terms of actual paths versus steady-state growth rates.

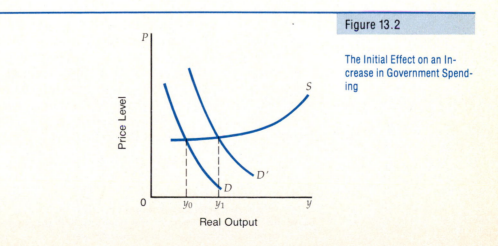

**Figure 13.2**

The Initial Effect on an Increase in Government Spending

## DYNAMIC ADJUSTMENT PATTERNS

Figure 13.3 presents a dynamic view of the adjustment process of nominal income, real income, and the money–income ratio. Note that the nominal income growth rate $\hat{Y}$ is initially increased sharply at time z when government spending increases. This is the impact effect captured in Figure 13.2. Growth continues above the steady-state rate for a while, as the increase in production of government goods is more rapid than the decrease in production of private goods. This rapid growth in nominal income is reflected in a below steady-state growth rate of the money–income ratio $\hat{K}$. Nominal income grows beyond the first quarter because some of the government purchases are originally taken out of inventories, which are subsequently rebuilt. However, at least five forces soon begin to reduce the effect of increased government spending on nominal income: (1) In Chapter 5 we saw that interest rates as well as income rise initially. Although fixed investment initially is not much reduced by rising interest rates because projects underway will normally be completed, fewer new projects will be started so that the investment function and aggregate demand curve shift back over time. (2) Besides the effects of higher interest rates on investment demand, some government spending—such as for a hydroelectric dam—may directly compete with private investment, also causing investment demand and aggregate demand to shift back. (3) As banks gradually adjust upward the interest rates paid on checking deposits, the quantity of money demanded at the higher $R$ will rise so that aggregate demand shifts back further. (4) Increased government spending may substitute for private consumption spending, so that again the aggregate demand curve shifts back. (5) People will quickly learn about the change in government spending and whatever residual effect it has on aggregate demand so that the aggregate supply curve will shift up as required to get back to normal unemployment.[3]

In this way, the positive initial effect of government spending on total income is offset. Ultimately, higher government spending shifts resources from production for private uses but does not increase those resources or the output that they can produce. During this catch-up period, the growth rate of nominal income falls below the steady-state growth rate so that actual nominal income can fall back to its steady state level. With given money growth, when $\hat{Y}$ is below its steady state, $\hat{K}$ will be above its steady state.

---

[3]In the case of long-run complete nominal and real crowding out, the second and fourth forces will return the aggregate demand curve and interest rate to their original positions, with the other forces operative only during the adjustment process.

Figure 13.3

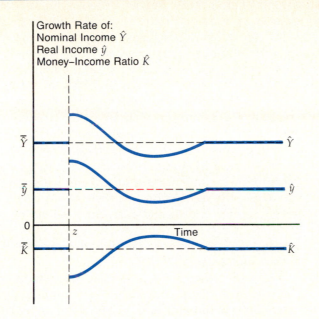

The adjustment pattern for real income growth follows that for nominal income. This is based on the assumption that price level effects are negligible. To the extent that there are price effects of higher government spending, the variations in nominal income growth around the steady-state growth rates will be reflected in temporary changes in both real income and prices: as nominal income rises above its steady-state growth rate, both real income and price level growth increase.

What is the timing of the government spending effects just discussed? While individual studies differ somewhat, it is possible to formulate a general impression of the time pattern of the effects based on the existing literature.[4] The effects on nominal and real

[4]See Franco Modigliani and Albert Ando, "Impacts of Fiscal Actions on Aggregate Income and the Monetarist Controversy: Theory and Evidence," in Jerome L. Stein, ed., *Monetarism* (Amsterdam: North-Holland, 1976); Ettore F. Infante and Jerome L. Stein, "Does Fiscal Policy Matter?," *Journal of Monetary Economics*, 2 (November 1976), 473–500; Benjamin M. Friedman, "Even the St. Louis Model Now Believes in Fiscal Policy," *Journal of Money, Credit, and Banking*, 9 (May 1977), 365–67; R. W. Hafer, "The Role of Fiscal Policy in the St. Louis Equation," *Federal Reserve Bank of St. Louis Review*, 64 (January 1982), 17–22; Dallas S. Batten and R. W. Hafer, "The Relative Impact of Monetary and Fiscal Actions on Economic Activity: A Cross-Country Comparison," *Federal Reserve Bank of St. Louis Review*, 65 (January 1983), 5–12.

income of an increase in government expenditures apparently build up over a period of 6 months to a year. At the peak, nominal income is increased about 1 dollar per dollar of increase in nominal government expenditures. However, all studies are not in complete agreement. Some studies indicate partial nominal crowding out, where a 1-dollar increase in $G$ results in a less than 1-dollar increase in $Y$. Other studies indicate a small multiplier effect, where a 1-dollar increase in $G$ generates more than a 1-dollar increase in $Y$.[5] Following the nominal (and real) income peak, the effects of increased government spending on income wear off about as rapidly as they build up. So the entire adjustment process is essentially complete one to two years following the increase in government spending.

It takes one to two years for income to adjust following a change in government spending.

While the discussion has focused on unexpected increases in government spending and borrowing, spending decreases will have opposite effects. Following an initial drop in income relative to the steady state, private spending will rise to offset the decrease in government spending.

To summarize this section, unexpected, borrowing-financed changes in the level of government spending cause movements in income in the same direction. The main effects on income are relatively short-lived; they build up and then wear off over a period of a year or two. Such fast effects could be very desirable in terms of eliminating a recession. If properly timed, an unexpected increase in real government spending would increase the growth rate of real income when income would otherwise be falling. Later, when private spending would tend to fall following the government spending shock, the normal recovery of the economy during the expansion phase of the business cycle would allow a continuation of real income growth. The problem with this antirecession fiscal policy is timing. Since no one can be sure exactly when the economy will hit the trough of the recession, it is very difficult to change policy in the manner described.

---

[5]In principles of economics courses, students learn that increased government spending increases nominal income by some multiple of the initial change in spending. The exact size of the multiplier is found by taking the reciprocal of the marginal propensity to save. Unfortunately, this simple multiplier effect ignores the increase in nominal money demand associated with higher nominal income. With a given money supply growth rate, the increase in money demand creates an excess demand for money, which must be eliminated by reducing private expenditures and raising interest rates. These latter effects are ignored in the introductory treatment of the multiplier.

## 13.3 CHANGES IN TAXATION

Now we turn to the other tool of fiscal policy, changes in taxation. As with changes in government spending and monetary policy, we assume that changes in taxes are offset by equal changes in borrowing so that the government budget identity holds. A reduction in taxes collected must be financed by equal increases in borrowing to support the given level of government spending. Tax increases finance equal reductions in borrowing, so we are analyzing the effects of alternative mixes of taxation and borrowing, holding both real government spending and money supply growth constant.

### AGGREGATE DEMAND AND SUPPLY ANALYSIS

The effect of a tax reduction on consumer expenditures is generally supposed to be the main channel by which tax changes influence the key macroeconomic variables. It is well established that over long periods of time, consumer expenditures are proportional to real net private income. So since tax reductions raise private income, it follows that increases in consumer expenditures will result.

Note that while changes in government expenditures increase aggregate expenditures directly, changes in taxes affect aggregate expenditures indirectly through private spending changes. In Chapter 4, we considered the effect of tax changes on consumption. Equation (4.6) indicated that the change in consumption given a change in taxes is:

$$c_1 - c_0 = -MPC \cdot (t_1 - t_0) \qquad (13.3)$$

> Tax changes change aggregate expenditures indirectly through private spending changes.

where $MPC$ stands for marginal propensity to consume, $c$ is real consumption spending, $t$ is the level of taxes, the subscript 1 refers to the new values of the variables following the tax change, and the subscript 0 refers to the initial values. Therefore, at any given level of income, the change in consumption given a change in taxes is determined by the MPC. Realistically, things are not quite as simple as the consumption function of Chapter 4 would have us believe. One problem lies in the differential effects of changes in permanent versus transitory income. **Transitory income** change refers to a short-run change or fluctuation, after which income returns to its steady-state level. A change in **permanent income** may be considered a change in the long-run, steady-state, real private income and is normally associated with a change in existing real wealth through saving and growth in human capital. However, a change in the normal fraction of total income which is left after taxes can also change permanent

> **transitory income**
> Short-term deviations from normal private income

> **permanent income**
> Normal real private income

income. As first identified in Section 3.6, transitory income $y_T$ is equal to actual real private income $y - t$ less permanent income $y_P$: $y_T = y - t - y_P$. Over the long run, growth in $y - t$ largely reflects growth in $y_P$. But in the short run, windfall gains and losses reflected in $y_T$ may account for most of the changes in $y - t$.

The crucial point for our analysis is that the proportional relationship between consumption and private income is based on permanent income. The effects of changes in transitory income on consumption are much smaller than the effects of changes in permanent income. When the tax reduction occurs, the role of consumer expectations is very important—is the rise in spendable income a permanent change so that consumption spending should adjust proportionally or a transitory change which will have but slight effects on consumption? Research in this area indicates that transitory income increases have about half the effect of permanent income increases on consumer expenditures.[6] The announced nature of the tax

*Permanent tax changes have a larger impact on spending than temporary changes.*

change could have an important effect on the spending change associated with the tax change. If the government announces that taxes will be reduced temporarily, then spending is likely to change by less than if the announced change was made permanent. Alan Blinder of Princeton University studied past tax cuts and concluded, "A temporary tax change is treated as a 50–50 blend of a normal income tax change and a pure windfall."[7] After examining the 1975–76 income tax cuts in the U.S., Blinder suggests that a permanent tax cut of about $9.5 billion would have had the same impact on consumer spending over the first four quarters as did the $20 billion temporary tax cuts of 1975–76. Any unexpected tax reduction will be treated as providing a transitory income change initially. Over time, as the tax reduction persists and is fully reflected in revised permanent income, consumer expenditures would tend to rise by the full amount suggested in equation (13.3). To summarize, an unexpected tax reduction would increase consumer expenditures for a given real in-

[6]See Michael R. Darby, "The Permanent Income Theory of Consumption—A Restatement," *Quarterly Journal of Economics*, 88 (May 1974), 228–50, "Postwar U.S. Consumption, Consumer Expenditures, and Saving," *American Economic Review*, 65 (May 1975), 217–22; and "The Consumer Expenditure Function," *Explorations in Economic Research*, 4 (Winter-Spring 1977–1978), 645–74.

[7]See Alan S. Blinder, "Temporary Income Taxes and Consumer Spending," *Journal of Political Economy*, 89 (February 1981), 26–53.

come by about one-third to one-half the amount of the tax reduction. The remainder of the tax reduction would be reflected in increased saving.

How do we depict these changes in our aggregate demand and supply diagram? Earlier we saw that the aggregate demand function was shifted to the right by the increase in government spending. Since government expenditures are a component of aggregate expenditures, it is readily apparent that there is a direct link between higher government spending and increases in aggregate demand. In the case of taxes, there is an indirect link to the aggregate demand curve. Tax reductions increase private income, which in turn leads to greater consumption spending. Since consumption is a component of aggregate expenditures, aggregate demand increases as shown in Figure 13.4. Initially the tax reduction is likely to be interpreted as a transitory change, so the aggregate demand curve will shift further with time as the tax reduction is considered permanent.

## MONEY DEMAND EFFECTS

Do we conclude that tax reductions increase the level of real income temporarily with increased consumption, acting in much the same way as an increase in government spending? While the empirical evidence strongly suggests that government spending temporarily increases real income, there is little evidence to suggest that tax changes have much influence on real income, temporary or permanent. Therefore, something else must be occurring to counteract the rightward shift in aggregate demand shown in Figure 13.4.

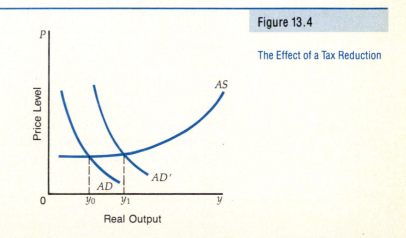

**Figure 13.4**

The Effect of a Tax Reduction

If money demand is responsive to private income increases, then an increase in private income could cause the money–income ratio to rise in a manner that offsets its fall due to the increase in consumer expenditures.[8]

Remember, nonmonetary demand shocks can increase income only if they cause a fall in the money–income ratio. Typically, this fall is induced by the rise in interest rates associated with a rightward shift in the *IS* curve. However, an increase in money demand shifts the *LM* curve to the left so that, other things equal, the interest rate rises, income falls, and the money–income ratio rises. Figure 13.5 illustrates the combined effects of the *IS* and *LM* shifts where they are just offsetting. Both shifts tend to raise interest rates, but there is no effect on total income because the induced rise in consumption is offset—at the higher interest rates—by lower investment spending. Therefore the aggregate demand curve of Figure 13.4, which shifted to the right initially with the fall in taxes, would be shifted left by the money demand effects. The lack of strong empirical evidence makes it difficult to say whether any net effect on real income remains.

## BALANCED-BUDGET FISCAL POLICIES

A balanced budget occurs when government spending equals taxes.

**balanced-budget fiscal policy**
A fiscal policy that leaves the deficit (or surplus) unchanged

The federal government budget is said to be balanced if government spending equals taxes. In this event, the federal deficit (borrowing plus money creation) is zero. Fiscal policy which leaves the deficit unchanged from its present position—that is, equal changes in government spending and taxes—is called **balanced-budget fiscal policy**.

In introductory courses, students are taught that since an increase in government spending raises aggregate expenditures directly by an equal amount, but an increase in taxes lowers aggregate expenditures only indirectly through lower consumption spending by an amount equal to the MPC times the tax change, there will be a net increase in aggregate demand and equilibrium income following a balanced-budget increase in spending. Such treatments ignore the potential offsets to the individual effects of government spending and taxes that we have discussed. Since there are theoretical uncertainties regarding the individual effects of taxes and government spending, and in addition, the empirical literature is weak with regard to the effect of taxes, we can make no strong statements regarding the net effects of balanced-budget fiscal policies. It is possible for

---

[8]James M. Holmes and David J. Smyth analyzed this money demand effect in ''The Specification of the Demand for Money and the Tax Multiplier,'' *Journal of Political Economy*, 80 (January/February 1972), 179–85.

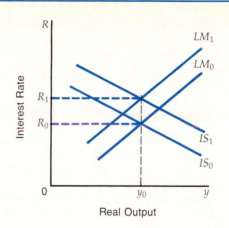

Figure 13.5

The Effect of a Tax Reduction When Money Demand Is Increased

any particular change to be mildly expansionary, mildly contractionary, or have no effect whatsoever.

The reader may be wondering why the empirical evidence on the effects of tax adjustments is weak. First, there are few historical episodes of tax reductions financed by borrowing. It is likely that when taxes have fallen, consumers have expected that tax increases will follow; so they have not responded to tax-induced rises in transitory income in the same way they would respond to other transitory income increases. Finally, pure fiscal policy changes holding the money growth rate constant are very rare. A stimulative fiscal policy is normally combined with a stimulative monetary policy which will finance part of the higher government spending or lower taxation. In order to avoid confusion of the effects of monetary and fiscal policy, researchers must account for both. The studies cited in the sections above, which yield evidence on the lack of a long-run real effect of higher government spending, used statistical techniques that could separate the individual contributions of monetary and fiscal policy. Unfortunately, such techniques have not provided convincing evidence regarding tax effects.

## 13.4 OTHER AGGREGATE DEMAND SHOCKS

So far we have discussed macroeconomic shocks connected with government decisions like changes in the growth rate of money or changes in government spending and taxation. Now we will consider aggregate demand shocks which could arise in the private sector. These shocks involve sudden changes in the basic behavioral relationships: the money multiplier, the demand for money function, the investment function, and the consumer-expenditure function. A shift in the money multiplier is considered a monetary shock; a shift in any of the next three relationships is a nonmonetary demand shock.

## SHIFTS IN THE MONEY MULTIPLIER

In Chapter 3, equation (3.3) expressed the nominal money supply $M$ as being equal to the product of the *money multiplier* $\mu$ and nominal base money $B$:

$$M \equiv \mu B \qquad\qquad (13.4)$$

Using the growth rate rule for products, the growth rate of nominal money is equal to the sum of the growth rates of the money multiplier and base money:

$$\hat{M} \equiv \hat{\mu} + \hat{B} \qquad\qquad (13.5)$$

We have been assuming that the money-multiplier growth rate was some given constant, so that changes in the growth rate of base money cause identical changes in the money supply. While this is usually a reasonable view of the economy, there are two important exceptions: periods of reserve requirement changes and banking panics.

reserve requirement
**Legally required fraction (set by the Fed) of deposits that banks must hold as base money**

   The Federal Reserve System sets the legally required fraction of deposits which banks must hold on reserve. If the **reserve requirement** is increased (decreased), the money multiplier falls (rises). While the Fed rarely changes reserve requirements, when it does, offsetting changes in nominal base money are made so that the nominal money supply is unaffected. The one time that changes in reserve requirements caused an important monetary policy shock occurred between August 1936 and May 1937. During this period, reserve requirements were doubled without an offsetting change in base money. The resulting sharp decline in the money supply growth rate was sufficient to stop the recovery from the Great Depression and begin the recession of 1937–38.

   Besides changes in the reserve–deposit ratio, the money multiplier can also change if the currency–deposit ratio is altered. Such changes arise most dramatically from *banking panics*, where the public is afraid that the banking system may fail. When a bank failed due to poor management, rumors would spread that other banks that held deposits in the closed bank might also go bankrupt. A *run* on these other banks would then occur. Depositors would descend on the suspect banks demanding their money. Since any bank only keeps a small fraction of their deposits as reserves, it becomes very difficult to meet such demands, and thus such banks often fail. Until the mid-1930s, banking panics were the most important source of macroeconomic shocks. The rise in the ratio of currency to deposits causes the money multiplier to plunge, which, if the central bank does not provide more base money, causes the money supply to fall as well. Over time, as public confidence in the banking system is restored, the money multiplier returns to its original growth path.

We have already studied the adjustment pattern of nominal and real income following a money shock, so we know that an unexpected fall in nominal money caused by a money multiplier drop will lead to a drop in both real income and the price level in the short run. To avoid such costly shocks resulting from banking panics, the Federal Deposit Insurance Corporation (FDIC) was established in 1934. The FDIC insures deposits up to $100,000, so the banking system is no longer as subject to panics caused by a lack of public confidence. As a result, changes in the money multiplier arising from the public are no longer an important source of macroeconomic shocks.

## SHIFTS IN THE DEMAND FOR MONEY

The steady-state growth path of the money–income ratio reflects the growth of real income, the payments technology, and money substitutes. A radical technological or institutional innovation can lead to a sudden change in the steady-state growth path of the money–income ratio. For instance, suppose that a new financial asset is developed which leads people to switch from money to the new money substitute. If the Fed maintains a constant growth rate of the nominal money supply, then the resulting excess money balances would be similar to the case of an unexpected increase in the money supply given constant money demand. Such shifts in money demand during the 1970s and 1980s have been attributed to several new financial assets, but economists are not yet in agreement as to what has happened during this recent period.

An example of this last statement is associated with a large increase in the money-income ratio $K$ during 1982. According to the Council of Economic Advisors, such a change is "historically atypical" considering the steady fall in $K$ over the past 35 years and is likely due to "regulatory changes that provide new financial opportunities—like the introduction of nationwide interest-bearing negotiable order of withdrawal (NOW) accounts—or because of changes in asset preferences—like the increased demand for money market mutual funds instead of long-term securities."[9] An alternative view is sug-

---

[9]*Economic Report of the President*, 1983, p. 22.

gested by John A. Tatom of the Federal Reserve Bank of St. Louis. Tatom considers the large increase in the money–income ratio to be quite consistent with the historical behavior of *K* around recessions and finds nothing "atypical" about the pronounced change in 1982.[10] Such disagreements need to be resolved because the Council of Economic Advisors looks to the rise in the money–income ratio as a factor explaining a slowdown in GNP. They suggest that, had the shift in *K* not occurred, "it is likely that real GNP would have increased enough to have ended the recession sometime before the final quarter of 1982."[11]

Although sudden changes in the steady-state level or growth rate of the money–income ratio may be an occasional source of macroeconomic disturbances, such disturbances are rare. If the money–income ratio was subjected to frequent shifts from the demand side of the market, then Federal Reserve monetary policy would be very difficult to formulate. If Fed economists could not predict the demand for money with any degree of accuracy, then the Federal Open Market Committee would be at a loss to choose a money growth rate consistent with noninflationary economic growth.

## SHIFTS IN INVESTMENT DEMAND

John Maynard Keynes was concerned about fluctuation in investment spending as a major source of macroeconomic shocks. Traditionally, Keynesian economists have argued that investment demand is very unstable because the expectations of business firms about future returns from investment are very fragile and unstable. When firms are optimistic about the future, investment demand will be high. Pessimism among entrepreneurs will lower investment demand. Shifts in investment demand, which are financed by borrowing, are equivalent to an equal shift in real government spending financed by borrowing, at least in the short run. A wave of optimism could cause an investment demand shock that raises nominal and real incomes relative to their steady-state growth paths.

The controversy surrounding the investment function is whether changes in expectations and the consequent shifts in investment

---

[10]See John A. Tatom, "Was the 1982 Velocity Decline Unusual?" *Federal Reserve Bank of St. Louis Review*, 65 (August/September 1983), 5–16.

[11]*Economic Report of the President*, 1983, p. 21.

spending are truly autonomous or are they dependent on other macroeconomic events. If changing expectations and investment are autonomous, then changes in real investment could *cause* business cycles. However, if expectations change due to other macroeconomic shocks, then changes in investment spending are caused by other variables and cyclical variation in real investment is simply part of the transmission, and therefore a symptom, of the basic causes of business cycles. Evidence in favor of the latter view arises when we consider that there appears to be no period in which investment demand shifts in the absence of other macroeconomic shocks.

## SHIFTS IN CONSUMER EXPENDITURES

A great deal of work has been devoted to understanding the consumption function. While this function was originally difficult for economists to describe well, work over the past 40 years has culminated in a view which leaves little room for significant autonomous shifts. It is safe to conclude that the consumer expenditure function is not an important source of macroeconomic shocks in the United States.

## 13.5 AGGREGATE SUPPLY SHOCKS

We can have shifts in behavioral functions affecting the supply side of the market just as the shifts in the previously discussed functions affected aggregate demand. On the supply side we are concerned with the aggregate production function and the labor supply function.

## SHIFTS IN THE AGGREGATE PRODUCTION FUNCTION

The aggregate production function could vary significantly from year to year in a small agricultural country as fluctuations in the weather affect the yields from crops. In a large country like the United States, such factors as the random effects of weather are unimportant. While particular industries may undergo rapid technological change that acts as a production function shock, such sectoral effects will not carry over to the economy as a whole in a large diversified economy. Similarly, worker slowdowns or strikes in a large diversified economy also are largely confined to individual sectors. Overall, then, shocks originating from the aggregate production function seem unimportant for the United States.

## SHIFTS IN THE LABOR SUPPLY FUNCTION

There is no evidence that the labor supply function jumps around in a manner causing macroeconomic disturbances. Changes in the trend growth rate of the labor supply occur much too gradually to be a source of shocks.

Most economists point to the 1973–74 disruption in the supply of foreign oil to the United States as the best recent example of a supply shock. This oil price shock certainly originated on the supply side of the market, as a reduction in the supply of oil from the OPEC nations forced the price of oil up dramatically. In terms of our behavioral functions, oil may be viewed as an input in the aggregate production function. An increase in the relative price of oil will cause the aggregate supply curve to decrease so that, theoretically, output falls and price increases. Yet as we learned in Sections 7.7 and 8.4, there is a disagreement among economists regarding the importance of the oil price shock in reducing output and raising prices. If the evidence is not clear-cut on the effects of this widely recognized supply-side event, it is probably safe to conclude that aggregate supply shocks have not been an important source of macroeconomic disturbances in the United States.

*Historically, aggregate supply shocks have not been an important source of disturbances in the U.S.*

## SUMMARY

**1** Demand shocks resulting from government policy decisions are called policy shocks, while shocks resulting from unexpected shifts in behavioral functions are called behavioral demand shocks.

**2** If higher government spending causes decreases in private spending which either partially or completely offset the government spending change, then crowding out occurs.

**3** An unexpected increase in debt-financed government spending will cause nominal and real income growth to rise, at first, above their steady-state growth rates. Over time, they undershoot their steady-state rates and then eventually grow at the steady-state rates once again.

**4** The effect of lowered taxes is to increase consumer spending with the magnitude of the increase, depending upon whether the change is perceived as permanent or transitory.

**5** Balanced-budget fiscal policy attempts to create equal changes in government spending and taxes so that the deficit remains unchanged.

**6**  Shocks to the money multiplier may be caused by shifts in the reserve requirement set by the Fed or shifts in the currency–deposit ratio that arise out of banking panics.

**7**  While Keynesian economists have emphasized shifts in investment demand as an important source of macroeconomic shocks, it is not clear whether such shifts are autonomous or a result of other macroeconomic shocks.

**8**  It seems unlikely that shifts in money demand or in the consumption function have accounted for a significant number of macroeconomic shocks.

## EXERCISES

1. Why does the government budget identity include the *levels* of government spending and taxes and the *rates of change* of base money and government debt?

2. Why would we expect the effect of a tax decrease financed by borrowing to have smaller effects on nominal income than an equal increase in government spending and borrowing?

3. Federal Reserve policy was once aimed at keeping interest rates within some desirable range. This was done by buying back government bonds with new high-powered money if the interest rate rose above target and selling government bonds, thereby withdrawing high-powered money, if the interest rate fell below target. How could fiscal policy affect money supply growth in this framework? Suppose government spending financed by borrowing is increased (think what will happen to the interest rate if the nominal growth of the money supply is constant).

4. Why are gradual shifts in behavioral functions incorporated in the analysis of steady-state equilibrium instead of being treated as macroeconomic shocks?

5. Banking panics often increased the desired reserve–deposit ratio of bankers, who felt the threat of panics more keenly for some years afterward. As the actual reserve–deposit ratio was adjusted to the new desired reserve–deposit ratio, what would happen to the money multiplier.

6. How does an increase in investment demand increase interest rates and nominal income?

7. Graph and explain the adjustment pattern of the growth rates of nominal income, real income, and the money–income ratio, following an unexpected decrease in government spending.

## REFERENCES FOR FURTHER READING

Andersen, Leonall C., and Jerry L. Jordan, ''Monetary and Fiscal Actions: A Test of Their Relative Importance in Economic Stabilization.'' *Federal Reserve Bank of St. Louis Review*, 50 (November 1968), 11–24.

Blinder, Alan S. ''Temporary Income Taxes and Consumer Spending.'' *Journal of Political Economy*, 89 (February 1981), 26–53.

Carlson, Keith M., and Roger W. Spencer, ''Crowding Out and Its Critics.'' *Federal Reserve Bank of St. Louis Review,* 57 (December 1975), 2–17.

Stein, Jerome L. *Monetarism*. Amsterdam: North–Holland, 1976.

# TAX RATES, AGGREGATE SUPPLY, AND TAX REVENUES

In Section 13.3 we learned that tax changes will exert their major influence on the economy through changes in consumer expenditures. Aside from such demand–side effects, there is a potential to influence aggregate supply as well. Since income taxes reduce the workers' return from working, higher taxes will encourage workers to work less and consume more leisure, and thus will tend to reduce efficiency in the economy. Lower taxes, on the other hand, will lead to a greater work effort as individuals are able to keep more of what they earn. This negative relationship between work and leisure would be reversed if the labor supply curve were backward bending, but at higher tax levels wasteful tax avoidance and evasion increases so that measured income subject to tax decreases.[1] We should therefore expect that higher tax rates will shift the aggregate supply curve to the left while lower tax rates shift the aggregate supply curve to the right.

Figure E13.1 illustrates these aggregate supply effects. Initially, we have equilibrium at price level $P$ and real income $y$. If tax rates increased, there would be a decrease in aggregate supply like the shift from $AS$ to $AS_1$. This would bring about a higher price level $P_1$ and a lower level of real output $y_1$. If tax rates fell, then the aggregate supply curve would shift to the right, out to $AS_2$. This shift would cause a lower price $P_2$ and a higher real income $y_2$.

---

[1]Recall that the "underground economy" grows relative to measured NNP as tax rates increase (see End of Chapter Essay 2).

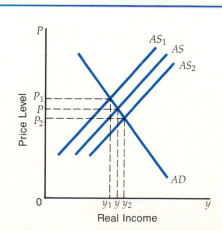

**Figure E13.1**

The Effect of Higher ($S_1$) and Lower ($S_2$) Taxes on Aggregate Supply

The Laffer Curve

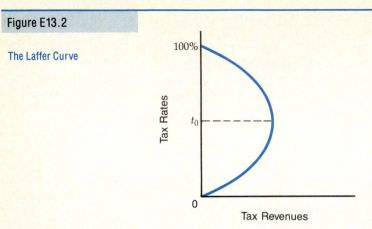

The change in output associated with a change in tax rates has implications for tax revenues. In the early 1980s it became popular to refer to the relationship between tax rates and tax revenues as the *Laffer curve*, named after the Pepperdine University economist Arthur Laffer. Figure E13.2 displays a typical Laffer curve. If the tax rate is zero, then there will be zero tax revenues. As tax rates increase, tax revenues increase up to a point. In Figure E13.2, we see that a tax rate of $t_0$ will maximize tax revenues. Once the rate of taxation exceeds $t_0$, the decrease in aggregate supply caused by the higher tax rate will lower tax revenues. As tax rates continue to rise, output continues to fall until, at a rate of 100 percent, no one will work, and thus there is no income to tax, so tax revenues equal zero again.

The argument underlying the Laffer curve was popularized in 1981 with the so-called *supply-side economics*. Several of President Reagan's economic advisers urged a reduction in tax rates as an incentive to produce more, thereby stimulating output and consequently increasing tax revenues. These "supply-siders" based their recommendations on a belief that the U.S. economy was in the downward-sloping, prohibitive tax region of the Laffer curve. While the supply-siders were certainly correct in arguing that tax rates affect work incentives, it appears that they were incorrect in their assessment of the position of the U.S. on a Laffer curve.

Don Fullerton of Princeton University constructed a Laffer curve for the U.S. economy.[2] The exact nature of the curve will differ based upon

[2]Don Fullerton, "On the Possibility of an Inverse Relationship Between Tax Rates and Government Revenues," *Journal of Public Economics*, 19 (October 1982), 3–22.

the elasticity of labor supply with respect to the after-tax wage, but using what Fullerton considers a most reasonable estimate, we find the data of Table E13.1, which are plotted in Figure E13.3. The first entries in the table—a tax rate of 31.8 percent and total tax revenue of $360 billion—are what we actually observe for 1973. As tax rates rise above 31.8 percent, tax revenues rise until a maximum is reached. The maximum tax revenue is $722 billion at a tax rate of 78.8 percent. Beyond this point, as tax rates rise, tax revenues fall.

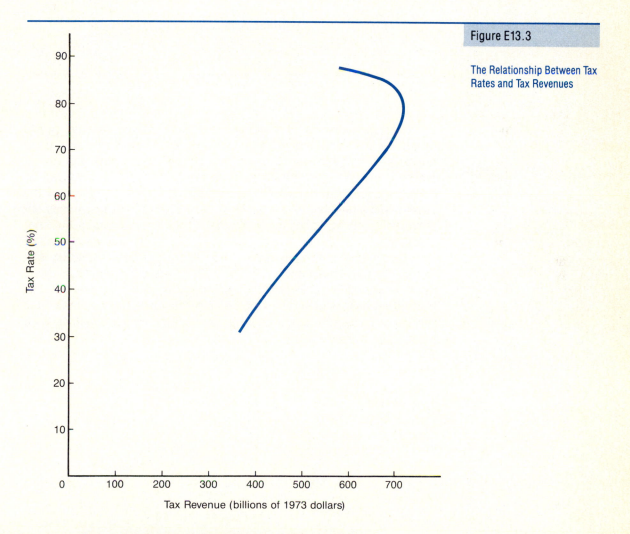

Figure E13.3

The Relationship Between Tax Rates and Tax Revenues

Source: Don Fullerton, "On the Possibility of an Inverse Relationship Between Tax Rates and Government Revenues," *Journal of Public Economics*, 19 (October 1982), 3–22.

| | | |
|---|---|---|
| *.318* | (observed figures) | *360* |
| .422 | | 439 |
| .499 | | 503 |
| .558 | | 556 |
| .605 | | 597 |
| .674 | | 658 |
| .722 | | 695 |
| .779 | | 721 |
| *.788* | (maximum revenue) | 722 |
| .797 | | 721 |
| .833 | | 698 |
| .875 | | 593 |

It appears that the U.S. could raise tax rates substantially before hitting the downward-sloping region of the Laffer curve. However, there are several things to keep in mind, like the political feasibility of tax increases versus the incentives to work. Also, the estimates derived by Fullerton should be considered as applicable for the short run. If the government alters the tax schedule in some significant way, we may observe shifts in the Laffer curve so that Fullerton's estimates no longer hold.

In conclusion, it appears that lower tax rates have little to do with increasing government revenue in the U.S., at least in the short run. While the incentive effects of lower tax rates on aggregate supply are certainly present, as suggested by the supply-siders, the notion that lower tax rates will produce a revenue bonanza to be used for funding government spending programs seems false.

# CHAPTER FOURTEEN

# MACROECONOMIC POLICY

## 14.1 MACROECONOMIC GOALS

The first step in the analysis of alternative macroeconomic policies is to identify the macroeconomic variables which measure the main public concerns. The most important macroeconomic issues were summarized in the Employment Act of 1946: "maximum employment, production, and purchasing power." Other specific macroeconomic issues that have been of concern from time to time include the balance of payments, interest rates, economic efficiency, economic growth, and environmental quality.

These various concerns may be translated into more specific goals. We can identify three separate groups of goals: those dealing with the stabilization of the economy in or near steady-state equilibrium, those dealing with the desired values of real steady-state variables, and those dealing with desired values of nominal steady-state variables.

A general definition of stabilization is keeping the economy in or near steady-state equilibrium. We want to avoid, or at least reduce, business cycles. Macroeconomic policy is aimed at reducing fluctuations in real income and the price level, and minimizing the associated fluctuations in the unemployment rate, industrial production, and the interest rate. A stable, predictable rate of economic growth allows individuals to make long-term plans and contracts without

Macro policy is aimed at reducing fluctuations in real income and the price level.

fear of unexpected fluctuations in unemployment and the price level. Section 14.2 will analyze stabilization policy.

Besides keeping the economy in steady-state equilibrium, we are concerned with *which* steady-state equilibrium. The key real macroeconomic variables are the natural unemployment rate and the growth path of real income. The main question is what, if anything, can macroeconomic policies do to raise the level or growth rate of real income or to lower the natural rate of unemployment? It is also important to consider the relation of the growth path of real income to other factors important to our well being, such as leisure and environmental quality.

The key steady-state nominal variable is the trend inflation rate. While the economy will eventually adjust so that real variables are independent of the inflation rate with superneutral money, we will prefer a low steady-state inflation rate if money is not superneutral. Besides aiming stabilization policy at minimizing fluctuations in the price level around the steady-state price level, macroeconomic policy may also be aimed at maintaining a low rate of inflation.

Macroeconomic policy attempts to move the economy closer to achieving these goals. Academic economists frequently think of policy as a set of rules—or a strategy or regime—which describes how the government will adjust its policy instruments (such as the money supply) in response to various conditions. In this view, policy analysis aims to find the set of rules or regime which best achieves the macroeconomic goals. Government economists and policymakers usually think of macroeconomic policy in terms of specific decisions to adjust specific policy instruments. Sections 14.2 and 14.3 pursue the strategic approach to policy analysis. Section 14.4 discusses the results of a number of particular policy decisions. The end-of-chapter essay examines a particular change in the set of rules which govern the Fed's monetary policy.

## 14.2 STABILIZATION POLICIES

### THE STABILIZATION PROBLEM

To stabilize the economy, government policy must work to offset the forces that move the economy from its steady-state level. However, if the policy produces too large an offsetting movement, the cure can be worse than the original problem and attempts at stabilizing the economy turn out to be destabilizing. The policymakers must be able to manipulate effective instruments of fiscal and monetary policy in both the appropriate direction and magnitude if they are to reduce fluctuations in the economy. Economists disagree as to whether or not stabilization policy can stabilize the economy and whether or not

| | Keynesians | Monetarists | Rational-Expectationists |
|---|---|---|---|
| Is stabilization possible? | Yes | Yes | No |
| Should stabilization be attempted? | Yes | No | No |

**Table 14.1**

Main Positions on Stabilization Policy

it should be attempted. The three main positions are summarized in Table 14.1. In general, Keynesians and monetarists agree that government policy possibly can stabilize the economy, while rational-expectationists believe that this simply cannot be done. Nonetheless, monetarists agree with rational-expectationists that the government should not intervene in an attempt to stabilize the economy. Clearly, there are basic differences over what can and should be done.

We can better understand the issues by using basic statistical theory to state the problem. In statistics classes students learn that one measure of the variability of a data series is the **variance**. The variance of real income, for instance, measures the degree to which real income varies about its average or *mean* value.[1] What could cause real income to vary in the first place? Suppose real income varies due to two sources of disturbances: autonomous and policy-induced. Autonomous changes arise in the private sector, like shifts in money demand or investment demand. Policy disturbances are caused by monetary or fiscal policy changes. Since real income changes arise from either autonomous private sources or official policy sources, we can write

**variance**
The extent to which a variable deviates from its average

$$\frac{y - y_e}{y_e} = y' = \alpha' + \pi'$$

(14.1)

where $y'$ represents *cyclical income*, measured as a fraction of equilibrium income; $\alpha'$ represents autonomous disturbances; and $\pi'$ repre-

---

[1]Specifically, the variance of a series is equal to the ratio of the sum of the squared deviations of each observation from the mean to the number of observations. For instance, if we observe the following real income figures: 60, 80, 100, 120, 140 for country A, while country B has data like 80, 90, 100, 110, 120, the mean or average value of income in each economy is 100. However computing the variance for A we have: $[(-40)^2 + (-20)^2 + (0)^2 + (20)^2 + (40)^2]/5 = 800$. For B the variance is $[(-20)^2 + (-10)^2 + (0)^2 + (10)^2 + (20)^2]/5 = 200$. Since A has income figures more widely dispersed about its mean than B, A will have a larger variance than B.

sents policy disturbances. Equation (14.1) indicates that if there were neither autonomous nor policy shocks, then real income would be not deviate from its normal or equilibrium value. However, cyclical income would also be zero if $\pi' = -\alpha'$. This would be the case if policy could perfectly offset autonomous disturbances.

In terms of the variability of income changes, there is a formula for the variance of a sum of two variables, like income in equation (14.1), which allows us to write

$$var(y') = var(\alpha') + var(\pi') + 2cov(\alpha', \pi') \qquad (14.2)$$

**covariance**
The degree to which two variables move together

where $var(\ )$ indicates the variance of the term in parentheses, and $cov\ (\alpha',\pi')$ represents the **covariance** between $\alpha'$ and $\pi'$. The covariance between two variables is a measure of the degree to which the variables move together. If when $\alpha'$ is above its mean, $\pi'$ is likely to be above its mean, the variables are said to have a *positive covariance*. If when $\alpha'$ is above its mean, $\pi'$ is likely to be below its mean, the variables are said to have a *negative covariance*. Looking at equation (14.2), we see that the variance of $y'$ is equal to the variance of $\alpha'$ plus the variance of $\pi'$ plus two times the covariance of $\alpha'$ with $\pi'$. If no stabilization is attempted, $var\ (\pi')$ and $cov\ (\alpha', \pi')$ are both zero so that $var(y') = var(\alpha')$. If a stabilization policy is implemented, then $var(\pi')$ is positive. So a stabilization policy must increase $var(y')$ over $var(\alpha')$ unless there is a negative covariance between $\alpha'$ and $\pi'$. This means that when $\alpha'$ is high, $\pi'$ must be low to offset the autonomous shock. If $\pi'$ could perfectly offset $\alpha'$, then the $2cov(\alpha',\pi')$ term in equation (14.2) would just offset $var(\alpha') + var(\pi')$ so that $var(y')$ equals zero.

There must be a negative covariance between autonomous shocks and policy responses for policy to be stabilizing.

Policy need not perfectly offset autonomous shocks to be stabilizing. As indicated by equation (14.2), a necessary condition for stabilization is that $cov(\alpha',\pi')$ be negative. This means that on average, the policymaker can see the proper direction for policy required to offset autonomous shocks. Realistically this is not easy to do, since there are long lags in putting policy into effect. Policy undertaken today is often based on a problem that was recognized in the past. Furthermore, the dynamic effects on the economy of a fiscal or monetary policy shock, as learned in Chapters 12 and 13, will be felt long after the policy is initially undertaken.

Even the creation of a negative covariance between autonomous shocks and policy shocks is no guarantee that policy will be stabilizing. While the negative covariance was said to be a necessary condition for stabilization, it is by no means sufficient. For the stabilization policy to work, it must not go too far—the policymaker could induce fiscal or monetary policy shocks that go far beyond offsetting the autonomous shocks and actually increase the variance of $y'$.

The policymaker really has two considerations: the direction and the magnitude of the policy shock. For a given ability to predict the correct direction for policy, larger policy moves increase $var(\pi')$ faster than $-cov(\alpha',\pi')$. The condition for stabilization policy to reduce $var(y')$ below $var(\alpha')$ is that

$$-2cov(\alpha',\pi') > var(\pi') \qquad (14.3)$$

If $cov(\alpha', \pi')$ is negative, this condition can always be met for small enough $var(\pi')$, but will be violated if $var(\pi')$ gets too large. Policymakers must not only be able to generally predict the right direction for policy, but must also be careful that their offsetting actions are not large enough to tip the boat over in the other direction.

It can be shown that the best possible ratio of income fluctuations with policy [$var(y')$] to income fluctuations with no policy [$var(\alpha')$] is:

$$\frac{var(y')}{var(\alpha')} \; 1 \; - \; [cor\,(\alpha',\pi')]^2 \qquad (14.4)$$

where $cor(\alpha', \pi')$ is the correlation coefficient between $\alpha'$ and $\pi'$, a measure of the accuracy with which the policymaker can judge the direction and relative magnitude of policy shocks required to offset autonomous shocks. A $cor(\alpha',\pi')$ of $-1$ is perfect while a $cor(\alpha',\pi')$ of $0$ indicates no ability to predict the right direction for policy.[2] Suppose that $cor(\alpha',\pi')$ equals $-.4$; then

$$\frac{var(y')}{var(\alpha')} = 1 - (-.4)^2 = 1 - .16 = .84,$$

so that optimal stabilization policy would reduce the variability of cyclical income by about 16 percent. However, if $var(\pi')$ were too large, $var(y')$ would be reduced by less than 16 percent or even increased.

---

[2]The covariance is related to the correlation coefficient by the formula

$$cov(\alpha',\pi') = (\sqrt{var(\alpha') \cdot var(\pi')} \cdot cor(\alpha',\pi')$$

So a $cor(\alpha',\pi')$ of $0$ means $cov(\alpha',\pi')$ is also $0$ and any stabilization policy—$var(\pi') > 0$—must *increase* the variance of $y'$ according to equation (14.2).

## THE ROLE FOR POLICY

We have just seen how government must offset the impact of autonomous shocks in order for its policy to be stabilizing. Economists are generally divided into three schools of thought on the ability of macroeconomic policy to stabilize the economy. We can identify a Keynesian view, a monetarist view, and a rational-expectationist view.

Keynesians advocate government intervention.

The traditional Keynesian view may be referred to as an *interventionist* or policy activist approach. This view holds that the private sector is characterized by recurring shocks which have large and long-lasting effects on key macroeconomic variables. Macroeconomic policy can then be aimed at offsetting these private sector disturbances. Most Keynesians will agree that, at times in the past, policy actions have been destabilizing. Still, they argue that policy can be stabilizing, and as we utilize better economic data and formulate better policies, we should become more adept at economic stabilization.

Monetarists argue against activist government policy.

Monetarists typically believe that the private economy is not a source of shocks with large or persistent effects. Furthermore, most monetarists are not convinced that the necessary negative correlation between autonomous changes and policy changes is large enough to warrant the risk of destabilizing policy and argue against activist government policy. Milton Friedman, in particular, has long argued for a **fixed-money growth rule** to be followed by the Fed, rather than discretionary changes in money growth. The idea is that the Fed could at best reduce the variance of income by only a few percentage points given a $cor(\alpha', \pi')$ that is only slightly negative because of the long time gap between the information that the Fed has about the economy and the ultimate effects of monetary policy on the economy. In fact, the Fed, as a political institution, has repeatedly bowed to pressure and taken bold actions against currently perceived problems, so that monetary policy has actually been destabilizing. By following a policy of maintaining a steady growth of the money supply, the Fed would only need to respond with changes in base money to changes in the money multiplier. Since only shocks to the money multiplier will induce policy actions, other macroeconomic shocks would be ignored. Many monetarists believe that such a Fed policy rule would do much more to stabilize the economy than would an activist monetary policy aimed at responding to every sort of autonomous shock. Even if the monetary authorities are capable of diagnosing the current economic malady, monetary policy works with a long and variable lag (see Section 11.3) and there is no assurance that today's policy action will prove to be stabilizing a year from now when the policy is still having an effect. The essay at the end of this chapter will consider how Federal Reserve policy has changed in recent years to be more consistent with the monetarist philosophy.

**fixed-money growth rule**
Requiring the Fed to maintain a fixed rate of growth of the money supply

## THE POLICY INEFFECTIVENESS CRITIQUE

So far we have identified Keynesians as those who favor active counter–cyclical policy measures in a belief that government has the ability to stabilize the economy. Monetarists seek a relatively limited use of policy, fearing that while it is possible for policy to be stabilizing, policymakers will do more to hurt the economy than benefit it. A third camp of macroeconomic thought, the *rational-expectationist* view, holds that the covariance between autonomous shocks and policy changes is zero so that it is impossible for policy to be stabilizing. This position sees no role for government policy.

With rational expectations, there may be no role for government to stabilize the economy.

This third view of macroeconomic policy is most closely associated with Thomas Sargent and Neil Wallace of the University of Minnesota and Robert E. Lucas, Jr., of the University of Chicago.[3] The essential idea of rational-expectationist theory is that only unexpected changes in policy will affect real income and the unemployment rate. What does this have to do with the required negative covariance between autonomous shocks and policy changes? If the policymakers respond to autonomous shocks in a regular systematic fashion, the public will come to expect the policy, thereby rendering it ineffective. Let's return to our aggregate demand–aggregate supply framework of Chapter 7 to see why this is true. There we learned that if expectations are realized, the equilibrium price will be the expected price $P^*$, and the equilibrium level of real output will be the normal level of real output $y_e$ (see the discussion surrounding Figure 7.11). Demand shocks change real output because they are, by definition, unexpected. If government policy measures are expected, then they will be incorporated into the expected price level and normal output. Furthermore, such expected changes in policy would not be termed "shocks"—a term reserved for unanticipated changes.

The only unexpected changes in policy must be due to the random element of erratic decisions of the policymakers and so must be uncorrelated with the state of the economy. In terms of equation (14.2), we can see that if policy has a zero covariance with autonomous shocks, any policy shocks must be destabilizing. With $cov(\alpha', \pi')$ equal to zero, equation (14.2) is:

$$var(y') = var(\alpha') + var(\pi') \qquad (14.5)$$

---

[3]Their very influential research in this area includes Thomas J. Sargent and Neil Wallace, "Rational Expectations, the Optimal Monetary Instrument, and the Optimal Money Supply Rule," *Journal of Political Economy*, 83 (April 1975), 241–54; and Robert E. Lucas, Jr., "An Equilibrium Model of the Business Cycle," *Journal of Political Economy*, 83 (December 1975), 113–45.

So the part of policy that is systematically and predictably related to the state of the economy has no effect on the economy. The unexpected part of the policy destabilizes the economy and should be avoided. So the rational expectations view also argues for the desirability of restricting the use of discretionary policymaking.

**Lucas supply curve**
An aggregate supply curve showing real income variations versus current price level relative to expected price level

The rational expectations view is conveniently summarized by the **Lucas supply curve**, so named because of the pioneering use of such approaches by Robert E. Lucas, Jr. The Lucas supply curve has real income varying from its normal level according to the current price level relative to the expected price level, or:

$$y = y_e + \delta((P/P^*) - 1) \qquad\qquad (14.6)$$

where $y$ is current real income, and $y_e$ is normal real income. $((P/P^*) - 1)$ indicates how the current price level $P$ varies from the expected price level $P^*$, and $\delta$ is an adjustment term indicating how real income adjusts to unexpected prices. According to equation (14.6), if price equals its expected value, then $P/P^*$ equals 1 so that $((P/P^*) - 1)$ is zero, and real income is equal to its normal level. If price is higher than expected, then output will be above its normal level, while lower than expected prices will result in income falling below its normal level. The key point is that only unexpected prices—caused by unexpected demand shifts—will have an effect on real income. If, after any private sector shock, the government tries to offset the shock in a predictable manner, the public will expect the policy so that it has no impact on real magnitudes and therefore cannot stabilize the economy.

The Lucas supply curve indicates that only unexpected prices change real income.

Figure 14.1 illustrates a hypothetical Lucas supply curve labeled $LS$. The vertical axis measures the ratio of the actual price $P$ to be expected price $P^*$. If actual price differs from what is expected due to unexpected shifts in aggregate demand, income will vary from its normal level $y_e$. If aggregate demand is equal to its expected value $AD(P^*)$, then the actual price will equal $P^*$ so that $P/P^*$ equals 1. The aggregate demand–aggregate supply equilibrium will occur at point 1 in Figure 14.1 and output will equal $y_e$. If aggregate demand is higher than expected, then the actual price level will exceed the expected price. This case is illustrated by the equilibrium occurring at point 2 in Figure 14.1. The new aggregate demand curve $AD(P')$ has a price level $P'$, greater than expected $P^*$, and since $P/P^*$ exceeds one, output is at the higher level $y'$. Finally, if aggregate demand is lower than expected, say $AD(P'')$, then the actual price level $P''$ is less than $P^*$, so $P''/P^*$ is less than one and output is at $y''$, which is less than the normal output $y_e$. This unexpectedly low price level is illustrated by the equilibrium point labeled point 3 in Figure 14.1.

Figure 14.1

The Lucas Supply Curve

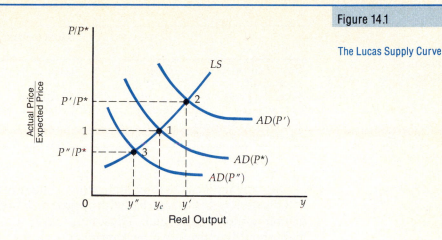

Contrary to strict rational-expectationist theory, the Lucas curve does provide an avenue through which government policy might have real effects and produce the negative relationship between autonomous shocks and policy changes required for stabilization. First, the macroeconomic variables to which policy responds may be observed after the relevant time for forming expectations. For instance, suppose that due to contracting practices, expectations formed today commit all parties to rigid wages and prices for the next year. In this case, an unforeseen event during the year can have real effects due to the inability of the contracting parties to respond to the change. So an autonomous shock occurring within the year may be met with a stabilizing policy response in the opposite direction. A second way for stabilizing policy to occur is if policymakers use information in setting policy that is not available to the private sector in forming expectations regarding government behavior. This could arise because government officials have access to official data, like the size of the money supply, before it is made public, or simply because the public believes that knowing what the government knows is not worth the cost.

Rational-expectationists generally argue that informational discrepancies between the public and policymakers are unimportant and that contracting problems can be eliminated by indexing. As a result, they believe that the covariance between policy and autonomous shocks is essentially zero. Monetarists and Keynesians believe that these elements make for a correlation coefficient $cor(\alpha', \pi')$ somewhat below zero.

Table 14.2 explains the positions of these groups by reference to their positions on potential gains and costs from stabilization. The

**Table 14.2**

Positions on Costs
and Benefits of
Stabilization Policy

|  | Keynesians | Monetarists | Rational-Expectationists |
|---|---|---|---|
| Size of correlation coefficient | $cor(\alpha',\pi')<<0$ | $cor(\alpha',\pi')<0$ | $cor(\alpha',\pi')=0$ |
| Potential gains | Large | Small | None |
| Potential costs | Small | Large | Small (?) |
| Should stabilization be attempted? | Yes | No | No |

Keynesians typically believe that $cor(\alpha',\pi')$ is substantially less than 0 (indicated by $<<0$) and that with appropriate institutions the costs of intervention will be small. Thus, they will propose that the government should continue to intervene in an attempt to stabilize the economy; nevertheless, some Keynesians propose specific institutional reforms to enhance the ability of stabilization policy to achieve its potential.

Monetarists might argue that $cor(\alpha',\pi')$ is at best, say, $-0.2$ and in practice has been close to zero, since policymakers have taken actions in response to political pressure—often in response to past shocks instead of those that will be having effects when their policy actions are instituted. Furthermore, the monetarists argue, the actions have been much too strong, so that even were the timing right they would still have been destabilizing. Since monetarists believe that these failures reflect not inept policymakers but irresistable political pressure, and that the best potential gain is trivial in magnitude, they want laws which constrain policymakers from taking actions beyond stabilizing money growth in the name of stabilization policy.

The rational-expectationists believe that stabilization policy is either systematic and ineffective or random and destabilizing. So they want to constrain policymakers to avoid random behavior and generally accept the monetarist proposal as doing this as well and as cheaply as any other. Thus, the rational-expectationists and monetarists agree on noninterventionist strategy but disagree on its rationale.

## MONETARY POLICY ISSUES

As our discussion of the Keynesian, monetarist, and rational-expectationist approaches indicates, economists differ with regard to the appropriate conduct of monetary policy. All can agree, however, that offsetting the effects of money multiplier changes with changes in money growth will stabilize the economy. In this particular instance, policymakers can very quickly recognize a private sector shock through changes in currency and demand deposits, and can quickly change high-powered money to offset the shock. (Some rational-expectationists argue that even offsetting money multiplier fluctuations has no effect; however, this systematic rule is as good as any other, so that they regard it as better than discretionary monetary policy).

Beyond this, economists tend to disagree on the appropriate monetary policy strategy. We consider only the most popular approaches here. These are to (1) stabilize the growth rate of the nominal money supply at some constant trend rate $\tilde{M}$, (2) stabilize the levels of nominal interest rates, and (3) vary the growth rate of the nominal money supply around a trend growth rate $\tilde{M}$ as warranted by conditions.

The first approach we already discussed with regard to the monetarist view of stabilization policy. This is the simplest approach. Choose a preferred nominal money supply growth rate on the basis of its steady-state effects and maintain the actual growth rate at that desired rate. Those who favor such a monetary policy tend to believe that the major fluctuations in business activity have been caused by fluctuations in the nominal money supply growth rate. Such fluctuations, it is argued, would be eliminated by a stable money supply growth rate. If the money supply grew at a constant rate, then nominal income growth would fluctuate only with shocks that vary the growth rate of the money–income ratio. Proponents of the constant money growth rule argue that, based on the historical record of fluctuations in the money–income ratio, a constant money growth economy would result in fluctuations in the annual growth rates of the money–income ratio and nominal income of no more than plus or minus 1.5 to 2 percentage points.

Historically, central bank policy has focused on the second strategy of stabilizing nominal interest rates rather than money supply growth. A constant interest rate policy works well as long as the only macroeconomic shocks that occur are associated with the money demand function and the money multiplier. In such a case, the pegged interest rate will result in the money supply varying to meet money demand.

An increase in money demand with a constant money supply would cause higher interest rates. To avoid this rise in interest rates, the central bank must increase the money supply to match the higher money demand. Figure 14.2 (a) illustrates the consequences of pegging nominal interest rates when money demand increases using the familiar *IS–LM* diagram of Chapter 5. Initially the economy is in equilibrium with interest rate $R_0$ and real income $y_0$. When money demand increases, the *LM* curve shifts left to $LM_1$, raising the interest

Monetarists prefer a steady growth of the money supply.

**Figure 14.2**

The Consequences of a Monetary Policy Aimed at Pegging Interest Rates
a) Increased Money Demand
b) Decreased Investment Spending

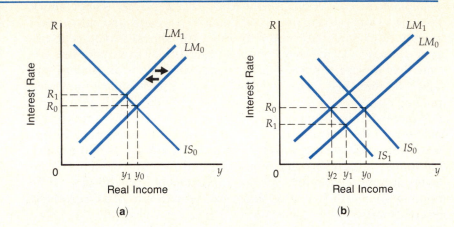

**Figure 14.2**

The Consequences of a Monetary Policy Aimed at Pegging Interest Rates
a) Increased Money Demand
b) Decreased Investment Spending

**pegged interest rate policy**
Setting fixed or target interest rates by varying the money supply as needed

rate to $R_1$ and lowering income to $y_1$. In order to hold the rate of interest at the desired level $R_0$, the money supply is increased so that the $LM$ curve shifts back to $LM_0$. In this case a policy of pegging interest rates stabilizes the economy by maintaining the real output level at $y_0$. A **pegged interest rate policy** would also require changes in base money so that money multiplier shocks would not shift the $LM$ curve. With only money demand and money multiplier shocks, the fixed interest rate strategy would stabilize the economy.

With other shocks, like investment, government spending, or consumption, the change in the money supply required to maintain the interest rate peg will reinforce the initial shock and thus prove destabilizing. For instance, suppose investment demand falls. With a constant money growth rate, the interest rate would tend to fall. To counteract this fall, the money supply growth rate must fall, which further reduces spending in the short run as we learned in Chapter 12. In this manner, the desire to hold interest rates fixed can reinforce nonmonetary shocks and be destabilizing. Figure 14.2(b) illustrates the $IS$–$LM$ representation of the decrease in investment spending. Initially there is equilibrium at $R_0$ and $y_0$. When investment spending decreases, the $IS$ curve shifts left to $IS_1$, lowering the interest rate to $R_1$ and income to $y_1$. To maintain the rate of interest at the desired level $R_0$, the money supply will decrease, shifting the $LM$ curve to $LM_1$. At the intersection of $IS_1$ and $LM_1$, we have the old equilibrium interest rate restored, but now the level of real income falls even further to $y_2$. So the policy of pegging interest rates with monetary policy is destabilizing.[4] In fact, the goal of maintaining fixed interest rates can result in an explosive reaction. The initial change in interest rates will be reversed in a relatively short time following the change in money growth (remember Section 12.4) so that the money growth rate must be lowered still further to maintain the desired interest rate. The process works in reverse if increased nominal money supply growth is used to lower interest rates. Most economists seem to agree that in the U.S., money demand shocks are relatively unimportant compared to nonmonetary shocks, so that a policy of maintaining fixed nominal interest rates is not advisable. The move away from such a policy is described in detail in the essay at the end of this chapter.

The final strategy to consider is the policy where money growth follows a trend with stabilizing deviations from trend allowed. The idea here is to stimulate the economy with higher money growth when it is sluggish and restrain spending with slower money growth when output is expanding rapidly. For this stabilization policy to work, the deviations of nominal income due to deviations from trend of nominal money growth must, on average, offset nominal income deviations due to autonomous shocks. Furthermore the deviations from trend nominal money growth must not be so large that they turn into a more important source of instability than the shocks they are meant to offset. As long as the policy is systematic and predictable, rational-expectationists maintain that it has no effects and is as good as constant money growth.

As already mentioned, many monetarists believe that a policy of changing money growth to combat autonomous disturbances may add to the variability of real income rather than reduce it. Since a monetary shock has significant effects on aggregate demand for a period of up to three or more years, it is easy to understand why these economists might worry about the ability of current policy decisions to produce a negative covariance between the policy effects and autonomous shocks that have yet to be realized. Furthermore, the policymaker is seldom responding to current conditions. Economic data are available with a lag of anywhere from one to four months, so the policymaker today is responding to conditions that existed from one to four months ago. Still, many economists favor the use of discretionary monetary policy changes to stabilize the economy. As usual, the debate is likely never to be settled, as each side can point to particular historical events that seemingly support its side. Those who support activist government intervention will acknowledge the excesses of past policy that have caused economic instability, but they then argue that we can learn from these past mistakes in order to formulate active stabilization policies today.

*Economists disagree over the appropriate use of discretionary monetary policy.*

---

[4]William Poole offered this critique of interest rate pegging in "Optimal Choice of Monetary Policy Instruments in a Simple Stochastic Macro Model," *Quarterly Journal of Economics*, 84 (May 1970), 197–216.

A related issue is the debate over "rules versus authorities." Some monetarists have argued that the Fed should have its discretionary powers limited by a legal statute requiring a fixed money supply growth rate. We saw that the argument for such a rule is based on a fear that with its current degree of independence, the Fed is subject to political pressures to aim monetary policy at achieving short-term results—like stimulating the economy before an election—at the long-run cost of a more unstable economy. The End of Chapter essay will consider the significance of a recent change in Fed operating procedures.

## FISCAL POLICY ISSUES

Just as there is debate over the ability of monetary policy to stabilize the economy, so is there debate regarding the stabilization potential of government spending and taxation. There are two issues in the fiscal policy debate: (1) Do the tools of fiscal policy have a significant effect on the growth rate of nominal income? (2) If they do, can they be altered rapidly enough to achieve stabilization? If fiscal policy has no effect, even temporarily, on nominal income, then it certainly cannot be used to promote, or harm, the stability of the economy. On the other hand, if fiscal policy does have some effects on nominal income, it is possibly, but not necessarily, true that fiscal policy can stabilize the economy.

Regarding the first issue, very few economists would doubt that an unexpectedly higher growth rate of government spending for goods and services will significantly increase aggregate demand. While there is disagreement regarding the absolute size of the effect and how long–lasting it is, there is general agreement that aggregate demand can be significantly changed by a change in government spending. The issue is not quite so clear for taxes. As we learned in Section 13.3, short-run variations in taxation may not have much of an effect on nominal income, due both to the change being perceived as transitory and offsetting changes in money demand.

The second issue—can fiscal policy be altered quickly enough to make stabilization possible—allows for doubts about the ability of fiscal policy to be used actively. Unlike monetary policy, which can be altered practically instantaneously, variations in government spending and taxes require much longer to accomplish. Once a problem is recognized, there is a decision lag during which Congress debates the merits of alternative policies. Following the passage of a particular policy, there is an action lag before the policy is carried out. This lag in carrying out fiscal policy makes stabilization difficult for the relatively short span of time over which the policy has effects. The necessary negative correlation between autonomous shocks and

Fiscal policy lags make stabilization difficult.

fiscal policy actions requires that there are reasonably accurate predictions of the autonomous shocks occurring when the policy takes effect. But since by definition, "shocks" are unpredictable surprises, this cannot occur. Current fiscal policy is a response to realized past and present shocks and therefore can only be stabilizing if enacted quickly enough to offset the current effects of such shocks. Rational-expectationists may argue that delays in enactment of fiscal policy may make it expected and so ineffective; only random variations in its implementation cause aggregate demand shocks and these are unsuited to stabilization.

Critics of an activist fiscal policy point out that relatively large variations in federal spending are required to obtain relatively small variations in nominal income. Such large variations in federal spending may imply much waste—greater perhaps than the value of any reduction in instability. While critics may point out such issues, the exact magnitudes involved are difficult to measure. Furthermore, fiscal policy involves more than just stabilization policy even though politicians often use stabilization as a justification for their proposals. Politicians will argue to cut programs that they oppose in any case "in order to fight inflation" and add programs that they support any way "in order to fight unemployment."

## 14.3 STEADY-STATE MACROECONOMIC POLICIES

### INVESTMENT ENHANCEMENT FOR ECONOMIC GROWTH

There are three basic variables which determine the growth path of real income: the investment–income ratio, the growth rate of labor, and the aggregate production function. Any policy influencing the steady-state growth path of real income must operate through one or more of these variables. Governments have often aimed to increase the investment–income ratio $i/y$ as a way to promote economic development. The most obvious way to increase the investment–income ratio is to increase the real government budget surplus. To see this, let's write real investment $i$ as being equal to real saving $s$, plus the real budget surplus $(t - g)$, less net exports, $x$, or:

$$i = s + (t - g) - x \tag{14.7}$$

Equation (14.7) is based on the idea that saving finances new securities issues by firms, government, and foreigners. The more saving, the higher investment spending. The larger the government surplus (a negative surplus is a deficit), the more saving is available for investment. The smaller net exports, the more saving is available for investment. This last effect is based on the notion that nations running a trade balance surplus (positive net exports) will be international creditors, as there must be a capital account deficit where the nation uses its earnings from goods exports to buy foreign securities.[5] Conversely, a nation with a trade deficit, or negative net exports will be a debtor nation that will sell securities to the rest of the world. Thus the smaller net exports, the greater the supply of domestic and possibly foreign savings made available to finance domestic investment.

Equation (14.7) indicates that given $s$ and $x$, fiscal policy can be used to generate a larger government budget surplus which will tend to stimulate investment. In Section 9.2 we saw that a higher investment–income ratio will result in a higher steady-state level—but not growth rate of real income at each point in time. Therefore fiscal policy can be used to permanently increase the level of real income and temporarily, during the adjustment period, increase the growth rate as well, unless there are fully offsetting movements in $s$, a possibility considered in the end-of-chapter essay for Chapter 15.

It should be realized that the use of government surpluses to raise real income is not without costs. The immediate effect will be less private (due to tax increases) and government spending for goods and services yielding current satisfaction. Of course the idea of saving and investment is to forego current consumption in order to enjoy greater future consumption, and as long as this policy is not carried too far, consumption will ultimately in fact be higher than it otherwise would have been.[6] It is a value judgment whether these future gains are sufficient to compensate for the short-run cost.

## ARE THERE LIMITS TO GROWTH?

At least since 1798, when Thomas R. Malthus published his pamphlet *An Essay on the Principle of Population*, there have been recurrent prophecies of the imminent cessation of economic growth. The basic idea is always the same. There is some kind of resource that is considered to be absolutely necessary for production, and this resource is

---

[5]Chapter 16 will cover international issues such as the balance of payments, so we will wait until then for a detailed discussion.

[6]This will be true as long as the real interest rate exceeds the real income growth rate.

available in fixed, or nearly fixed supply. Therefore, as soon as this resource is used up, output will begin to fall.

The reason that such prophets of doom are always wrong is that the "absolute necessity" never really is absolutely necessary. As resources become increasingly scarce, prices rise. The higher prices work to encourage conservation of the scarce resource and the discovery of substitutes. Doom is implied only if we are unable to adjust and adapt to changing conditions. While we cannot say with certainty that we will never run out of some critical resource, the force of history stands against the possibility.[7]

In a related area, many popular writers have seen a conflict between **environmental quality** and continuing economic growth. These writers also are mistaken. The problem is that we want firms and individuals to stop using or to use less of those productive processes which cause pollution and to substitute alternative, less offensive productive processes. For instance, to reduce acid rain, the coal-fired power plants of the Midwest need to drastically cut back production of pollutants. Such a change in production will shift down the aggregate production function, as shown in Figure 14.3. This means that less real output will be forthcoming from any given quantity of labor and capital. The steady-state growth rate of real income will be unchanged and equal to $\bar{\ell}$, but the level of income at each instant of time is lower because less is produced from any amount of labor and capital. In Figure 14.3, the less productive, non–polluting production change is illustrated by the shift from the production function $y/k = f_0(1\ell/k)$ to $y/k = f_1(1, \ell/k)$. For any given labor–capital ratio, like $(\ell/k)_0$, the output–capital ratio will fall, as in the fall from $(y/k)_0$ to $(y/k)_1$. Again, whether or not the reduction in goods and services available for consumption will be balanced by the value of improved environmental quality is a political decision.

**environmental quality**
Purity of surrounding air and water

## CHOOSING A STEADY-STATE INFLATION RATE

There are three issues associated with the choice of a steady-state inflation rate: the implications of alternative rates, the costs and benefits of moving from one rate to another, and the costs and benefits of variable steady-state inflation rates.

---

[7]An economic analysis of the market response to crisis is provided in Charles Maurice and Charles W. Smithson, *The Doomsday Myth: 10,000 Years of Economic Crises* (Stanford: Hoover Institution Press, 1984).

**Figure 14.3**

The Shift in the Aggregate Production Function Resulting From an Increase in Environmental Quality

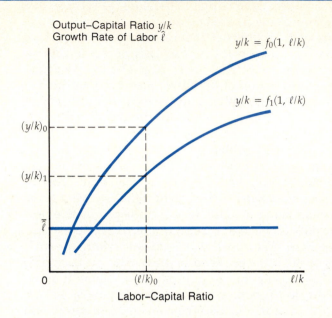

Output–Capital Ratio $y/k$
Growth Rate of Labor $\hat{\ell}$

$y/k = f_0(1, \ell/k)$

$y/k = f_1(1, \ell/k)$

$(y/k)_0$

$(y/k)_1$

$\bar{\hat{\ell}}$

$0$        $(\ell/k)_0$        $\ell/k$

Labor–Capital Ratio

## ALTERNATIVE INFLATION RATES

First we will consider the implications of alternative steady-state inflation rates. Modern folklore seems to include a belief that more inflation is bad. Yet this common belief among the populace is not so easy for the macroeconomist to see. Here we particularly focus on an anticipated inflation. If inflation is unanticipated due to, say, an unexpected increase in money growth, then the adjustment dynamics reviewed in Chapter 12 would occur. Furthermore, an unanticipated inflation would redistribute wealth from creditors to debtors as debtors repay, and creditors receive, dollars that are worth less than the dollars originally lent. But what if the inflation rate is held constant so that everyone correctly anticipates the rate? Is there any reason to prefer one rate of inflation over another?

At first it would seem that as long as all nominal values increase together, the rate of inflation would be of no consequence. There is no reason to be any more or less happy with an income of $10,000 per annum than with $100,000 if prices are ten times higher in the latter case. As long as we receive the same amount of goods and services, it shouldn't make any difference. In other words, unless different steady-state inflation rates imply some different real magnitudes, there is no reason to select one inflation rate over another.

There are three real implications that seem important: costs involved in economizing on money balances, costs involved in alternative means of financing government, and effects on the investment–income ratio. The government budget constraint indicates that government money creation is one way of financing government expenditures. The real amount of expenditures financed by money creation is found as the rate of change in nominal base money divided by the price level $\Delta B/P$. This can be written as:

$$\frac{\Delta B}{P} = \frac{\Delta B}{B} \frac{B}{P} = \hat{B}b$$

(14.8)

So $\Delta B/P$ is equal to the growth rate of nominal base money $\hat{B}$ times the real stock of base money $b$. The revenue from base money creation is sometimes referred to as the **inflationary tax on base money**, where the tax rate is $\hat{B}$ and the tax base is $b$.[8] As long as $b$ does not shrink too fast, increases in $\hat{B}$ can increase government revenue. What are the real costs of financing government with an inflation tax? Efforts involved in avoiding the tax are primarily related to economizing on money balances. This means holding less currency and using more demand deposits. While currency is part of base money, bank deposits are backed only by fractional reserves of base money. In addition to conserving on base money, the total demand for money may fall as receipts and expenditures are more closely matched.

These efforts at conserving money balances shift the production function downward, as resources that could be used to produce goods and services are devoted to managing money. Instead of hiring employees to manage cash flows, the firm might hire more production line workers. There could be a partial offset, though, if the revenue from the inflation tax is used to reduce other taxes. Since these other taxes involve costs of administration, avoidance, and incentives to work, a decrease in such taxes will tend to shift the production function upward. It is likely that regardless of whether the net shift

**inflationary tax on base money**
Revenue that accrues to government from issuing money

Money creation may act as an inflationary tax.

---

[8]Here we concentrate on real output effects of the inflationary tax. There is a literature on the government revenue creation aspects of the inflationary tax which considers the issue of the optimal inflation rate in terms of creating revenue. See Martin J. Bailey, "The Welfare Cost of Inflationary Finance," *Journal of Political Economy*, 64 (April 1956), 93–110; and Leonardo Auernheimer, "The Honest Government's Guide to the Revenue from the Creation of Money," *Journal of Political Economy*, 82 (May/June 1974), 598–606.

in the production function is up or down, the real effects of the inflation tax are quite small in magnitude.[9]

Several analysts have emphasized the effects of money growth on the investment–income ratio. Yet considering the magnitude of the potential effects of any drop in the steady-state value of the money–income ratio while the money stock is growing, changes in the investment–income ratio are likely to be slight.

Since higher inflation means higher nominal interest rates, should we prefer lower inflation in order to have lower interest rates? If the only reason for changes in interest rates is change in inflation rates, then there is no particular advantage to low or high nominal interest rates. Remember that what is relevant for economic decision-making is the real rate of interest, not the nominal rate. If nominal rates change strictly in proportion to changes in inflation, then real rates are constant.

To summarize, it is not all clear that any particular inflation rate is preferred over another. Calculations made for the United States suggest that for moderate inflation rates, say between 0 to 10 percent per annum, the annual gain or loss to the economy as a whole from the choice of any particular steady-state inflation rate is not likely to be as great as one tenth of a percent (0.001) of total income. Of course for very high rates of inflation, as experienced in Argentina and in Israel in the early 1980s, the costs of calculating monetary values like prices become very difficult as the inflation progresses. Cash registers and calculators often did not have enough capacity to deal with the immense size of the numbers required, so there were real costs of such a high inflation in terms of simply computing values used in day-to-day transactions. The Argentina solution was a currency re-

---

[9]Base money in the U.S. has averaged a bit under 6 percent of GNP recently. If the steady-state inflation associated with this base money–income ratio were 10 percent per year, the total revenue from this inflation would be about 0.6 percent of GNP. The difference between the waste associated with the inflationary tax and the waste associated with alternative revenue sources, such as the income tax, should be a reasonably small fraction of the revenue involved. Even if the difference were one sixth of revenue, the net difference in waste would be a bit less than 0.1 percent of GNP. Note, however, that the present value of the benefits of eliminating a steady-state inflation is this year's net waste divided by the difference between the real interest rate and the real-income growth rate. This present value can be a large multiple of the current year's loss; for details, see Martin S. Feldstein, "The Welfare Cost of Permanent Inflation and Optimal Short-Run Economic Policy," *Journal of Political Economy*, 87 (August 1979), 749–68.

form where 1000 old pesos were defined as being equal to one new peso, so goods previously selling for 100,000 pesos now sell for 100 pesos. However, in the realm of the moderate inflation rates of U.S. experience, such calculation costs are irrelevant and there seems to be no clear reason to choose any particular steady-state rate of inflation.

Such conclusions only apply in the case of inflation with no artificial constraints on price adjustments. The presence of price controls, usury laws, or other restrictions can lead to serious real inefficiencies in the economy. For instance, price controls enforced by the occupation troops in post–World War II Germany led to the effective abandonment of monetary exchange. Cognac and cigarettes were used to facilitate transactions. The restoration of money in exchange and the use of market-clearing money prices allowed resources to be allocated to their most valuable use and led to an increase of output of 50 percent in the last half of 1948 alone. With enforced price controls, real economic costs can only be avoided if prices remain below the controlled level. Therefore low (equilibrium) inflation rates would be very important to the successful functioning of the economy under price controls.

## CHANGING THE INFLATION RATE

If there is no clear reason to prefer one steady-state inflation rate over another, this does not imply that there is no cost associated with changing the rate of inflation. Consider what happens if the trend growth rate of nominal base money is increased by, say, 3 percentage points. First there is a boom as aggregate demand is increased. Whether it counts as a cost or benefit to trick people into taking jobs or selling products at wages and prices which would be otherwise unacceptable is a difficult question. But since people are indeed fooled into thinking they are better off than they really are, there is clearly a political benefit to those policymakers who directed the increased money growth. Likewise there would be a political cost to those who dared to engineer a decrease in nominal base money growth that caused a temporary fall in real income and unemployment. However, the cost of moving to a lower trend growth rate of the nominal money supply could be reduced by credible public announcements of the forthcoming slowing of money growth. If a program of reduced money growth was believable—incorporated in law, for instance—then expectations would be revised to be consistent with the announced program and expected growth in aggregate demand, prices, and wages would fall. If no one is fooled by the change in nominal money growth, then the temporary increase in unemployment following a decline in money growth should be eliminated.

Such credible government pronouncements are not observed in practice, so changes in money growth tend to have real effects. In addition to the dynamic adjustment in real variables following a change to a new inflation rate, we also have the transfer of wealth between creditors and debtors for loans already made. Of course any new loans will be at a nominal rate of interest consistent with the new rate of inflation.

## INFLATION VARIABILITY

The greatest problem with a monetary system such as exists in the U.S. is the potential variability in the inflation rate. A political decision can set the target rate of money growth and the temptations to increase the growth rate of nominal base money because of an impending election are great. The political costs of returning the nominal money supply to the previous growth path (and causing a recession) may well be sufficient to guarantee that it is never done. Making a long-term contract under such a monetary regime becomes risky. You don't know how or if the monetary growth target will change during the life of the contract, so it is difficult to count on any future real values resulting from future transactions. People react to this uncertainty by changing the contractual structure of the economy. By contracting for shorter periods or writing contracts in real terms, the inflation risk over the contract period is reduced. Labor contracts including "cost of living" raises are an example of attempts to keep real wages from falling due to inflation. One result of these arrangements is that the government will find it more difficult to cause either a boom or recession with monetary policy. Since there are fewer or shorter wage and price rigidities built into the system, the response to a new money growth rate would tend to be faster.

For a long time in the United States, it was relatively easy to predict the future price level because the money supply was tied to gold. In the early part of the twentieth century, the U.S. was on a gold standard so that the price level was simply the price of gold in terms of all other goods and services. This price level would change from time to time with new gold discoveries or mining techniques, but since the production of other goods and services generally kept pace, there was no persistent trend in the price level. The break from the gold standard occurred in several stages. In 1933 the official value of a dollar was changed from $1/20.67$ of a troy ounce of gold to $1/35$ of an ounce. This change in a dollar's value implied a 70 percent increase in the equilibrium price level of other goods and services. But the Fed did not allow the money supply to increase to a level consistent with this 70 percent increase during the Depression and war years. In fact, not until the middle of the Korean War was the U.S. price level 70 percent higher than it had been during the 1920s.

During the 1950s, as the nominal money supply grew, gold began to flow out of the United States. After 1933 we had maintained a high real value of gold by continuing large purchases of gold which we stored in Fort Knox. By the 1950s, rising prices had lowered the real value of gold at $35 per ounce to a level at which output was less than the amount that others than the U.S. government demanded. So to maintain the official price, the government had to supply the difference from its horde. At this time there was a requirement that the U.S. money supply be backed by gold to the extent of 25 percent of currency and deposits at the Fed. If too much gold was sold the Fed would have to cut back on the money supply. Instead, Congress repealed the gold reserve requirement for deposits in 1965 and for currency in 1968. This removed all guidance from the gold standard and opened the way for an entirely discretionary monetary policy. Since the Fed is now free to set the trend growth rate of the nominal money supply by any criterion it chooses, including political pressure from the President and Congress, predicting the price level 20 years from now is a political guessing game.

There does not appear to be any way to establish a stable, predictable growth rate of the nominal money supply under a system of completely discretionary policymaking by the Fed. Two suggested alternatives for controlling money growth are: a commodity standard and a legally fixed growth rate of the nominal money supply.

A commodity standard defines the price level in terms of some real good or bundle of goods. Besides gold, many other commodities have been recommended as a useful anchor for the money supply. With a commodity standard, as real production and money demand varies, the money supply varies in a way to maintain the set money price of the commodity. The fact that governments have chosen to abandon past commodity standards should cause serious doubts about the viability of such systems.

Rather than tie money growth to some real good, Congress could pass a law requiring a set growth rate for the money supply. A discussion of such a rate appears earlier in Section 14.2.

If a steady-state inflation rate is chosen, there must be some framework assuring that the choice be enforced. If no choice is made, then it is likely that there will be recurring periods marked by unanticipated money growth and money-induced business cycles. Of course the initial choice of a steady-state inflation rate is not obvious. Some argue for a gradual reduction in money supply growth to a rate consistent with zero inflation. Others argue that the advantages of zero inflation over moderate rates are small at best and that the short-run costs of reducing money growth to reach zero inflation outweigh any likely benefits. The research that will allow a definite answer to these issues has yet to be done. This is probably one more question in macroeconomics that will remain open to debate for a long time.

## 14.4 MACROECONOMIC POLICY TACTICS

Largely due to the influential work of Lucas, Sargent, and Wallace discussed in Section 14.2, academic macroeconomists have increasingly come to view macroeconomic policy in strategic terms. The "best" policy is one that reacts in a predictable way to a given set of circumstances, since any randomness in the behavior of policymakers unambiguously destabilizes the economy. Technical analysis along these lines focuses on what the optimal rules are and what institutional arrangements best enable and motivate those entrusted with following those rules to actually do so. The key empirical issue for this analysis is whether contracting lags and information differences are substantial so that the autonomous shock-policy correlation is large and negative as suggested by the Keynesians, small so that this correlation is trivial as argued by the monetarists, or zero as believed by the rational-expectations school.

Government officials, business economists and executives, and news analysts rarely if ever think of macroeconomic policy in these academic terms. Instead they tend to view macroeconomic policy as a set of decisions to deal with the current situations as now seems best to the decisionmakers—not as a preordained response to some explicit or implicit set of rules which describe the macroeconomic strategy of the government.

In part, these differences may simply reflect differences of perspective: just because a social scientist can predict the outcome of a social decision given the institutional rules does not mean that the individuals involved are not struggling with real issues so that the predicted outcome can occur. These differences also reflect the greater complexity of the world than of academic models: the full range of factors which determine macroeconomic policy is so large that any conceivable rule must be incomplete, requiring that at least apparant discretion enters into decision making.[10] Furthermore, policymakers are frequently making decisions to alter the basic strategic rules: how the economy *adjusts* from one set of policy rules to another is a difficult question with which practical people must contend.

Chapter 15 is concerned with the broader trends of U.S. macroeconomic development and the influence specific policy decisions have had upon the economy. So the practical approach to policy anal-

---

[10]Individual tastes and abilities may be important where a small number of individuals are making discretionary judgments. Philosophers can debate whether this is best described as discretion or an incomplete description of the rules which govern policy.

ysis is largely the subject of that chapter. Here we consider a few examples which illustrate the difficulties faced by policymakers in making their decisions. The End of Chapter Essay is concerned with a change in the rules which guide monetary policy and the surprising results of that change.

## THE KENNEDY TAX CUT

President John F. Kennedy's economic advisers were strongly Keynesian in orientation and persuaded by the simple Phillips curve analysis discussed in Section 8.1 above. They believed that the U.S. under President Eisenhower had chosen too high an unemployment rate and so they wanted to lower that rate even if the cost was a somewhat higher inflation rate.

One way these advisers proposed to increase output was by reducing taxes as illustrated in Figure 14.4. The expected increase in consumer spending would shift the *IS* curve to the right as illustrated in Figure 14.4(a) and shift the aggregate demand curve to the right as illustrated in Figure 14.4(b).

The Kennedy advisers believed that growth in average income had pushed people into higher and higher tax brackets so that taxes were higher than needed to finance current expenditures. They proposed to eliminate this "fiscal drag" by reducing all tax brackets: from 91 to 70 percent at the top down to a reduction from 20 to 14 percent for the bottom bracket. Following President Kennedy's assassination, Congress finally adopted his tax cut proposal effective from the spring of 1964.

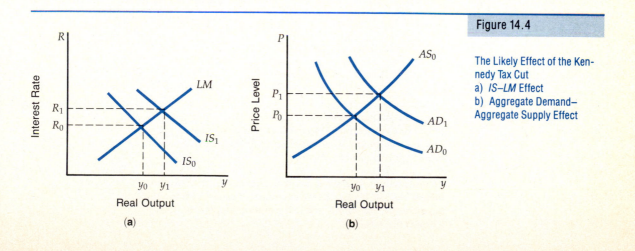

**Figure 14.4**

The Likely Effect of the Kennedy Tax Cut
a) *IS–LM* Effect
b) Aggregate Demand–Aggregate Supply Effect

Major tax cuts are rare events—the Mellon cuts of the 1920s and the Reagan cuts of the 1980s are the only comparable 20th century examples—so these tax cuts may qualify as a change in the rules of the game rather than policymaking as usual. Economists still are unsure what effect the cuts had on the economy. Output certainly increased over the next few years, but arguably by no more than would have been expected given the stimulative monetary policy and government spending increases which occurred at the same time.[11]

## FINANCIAL DEREGULATION AND MONETARY POLICY

With minor exceptions, between the Great Depression and 1980, banking laws and regulations effectively prohibited explicit payment of interest on checking accounts. Because banks invest most of the funds generated by these accounts in earning assets (bonds and loans), the high interest rates of the late 1970s and early 1980s created great competitive pressure to circumvent these regulations. As these evasions became widespread and open, it was clear that the old regulations could not continue. The Depository Institutions Deregulation and Monetary Control Act (DIDMCA) of March 1980 mandated phasing out the prohibition of interest-paying checking accounts. Limited interest payments were permitted beginning January 1, 1981, on so-called NOW accounts.[12] Super-NOW accounts with no interest limits on large balances were permitted from the end of 1982. DIDMCA and ensuing regulation made many other important changes in the structure of U.S. financial markets.

Such major structural shifts have been known to effect the demand for money both in the United States (during the 1930s) and abroad. Policymakers at the Fed and those whose livelihood depends on predicting future financial and macroeconomic events do not have the option of waiting until the late 1980s when sufficient data will have accumulated for academic economists to precisely define the nature of the money-demand shift or, indeed, to settle on the most reliable definition of money.

---

[11]The end-of-chapter essays for Chapters 13 and 15 discuss related issues concerning the effect of tax rate changes on revenues and aggregate supply and the effect of financing tax cuts by increased government borrowing.

[12]These accounts had previously been permitted on an experimental basis in the Northeast. A detailed discussion of interest payments on money is found in the end-of-chapter essay in Chapter 6.

James Lothian of Citicorp has presented evidence that base money is generally the best indicator of the future course of economies undergoing major changes in financial structure.[13] Since, even in normal times, base money is a rather imperfect guide to the future impact of monetary policy, most observers tried to do better. The Fed, for example, produced a money supply series adjusted for estimated shifts in money demand and formulated monetary policy for a while in terms of growth in this adjusted money series.

The idea behind the Fed's approach is illustrated in Figure 14.5. Since interest payments in services are likely less valuable to depositors than they would be in money, permitting (money) interest payments on checking deposits should increase the demand for those deposits in particular and money (including the deposits) in general. Recall from Section 5.3 that an increase in money demand shifts the *LM* curve to the left so that income would fall and interest rates rise at the expected price level as illustrated in Figure 14.5(a). Figure 14.5(b) illustrates the aggregate demand–aggregate supply effect. Before the regulatory change, price level $P^*$ (the expected price level) and output $y_e$ (the normal level of output) are established. The increase in money demand that comes with deregulation is associated

Financial deregulation should increase money demand.

[13]James R. Lothian, "The Demand for High-Powered Money," *American Economic Review*, 66 (March 1976), 56–88; confirmatory evidence from the U.K. (1979–1981) is found in Michael R. Darby and James R. Lothian, "British Economic Policy Under Margaret Thatcher: A Midterm Examination," *Carnegie-Rochester Conference Series on Public Policy*, 18 (Spring 1983), 157–207.

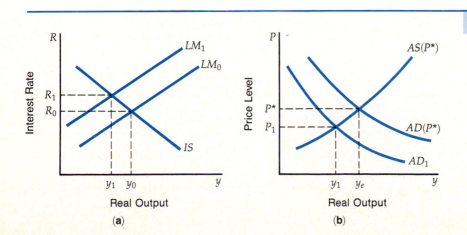

**Figure 14.5**

The Likely Effect of Financial Deregulation
a) *IS–LM* Effect
b) Aggregate Demand–Aggregate Supply Effect

with a decrease in spending so that aggregate demand shifts left and output falls to $y_1$.

The Fed would have liked to shift the *LM* curve back so as to offset the change in money demand. The problem is how to do that. Pegging interest rates is one obvious solution, but this was confounded by shifting inflationary expectations—would Reagan stick to his disinflationary program; would it work, how fast? Shifting inflationary expectations mean that the *IS* curve is moving at the same time as the *LM* curve, so that a fixed interest rate is not a safe way to achieve a particular desired level of aggregate demand.

When basic economic institutions are changed, policymakers and business economists usually end up relying on experience and intuition until sufficient data are accumulated to retool our statistical models. The simple analytical models that we have studied in this book do not give clear answers when many things are changing at once, but they still provide a useful framework for practical thinking about the possible implications of these changes.

## SUMMARY

1 Stabilization policy is policy aimed at keeping the economy in or near steady-state equilibrium.

2 A necessary condition for policy to be stabilizing is that policy changes and autonomous shocks have a negative correlation.

3 Keynesian economists tend to believe that although mistakes have been made in the past, policy can be used to stabilize the economy.

4 Monetarist economists tend to believe that discretionary policy has done more harm than good, and therefore they favor policy rules rather than discretion.

5 Rational expectations theory holds that any policy changes that affect real output will be destabilizing rather than stabilizing.

6 Monetary policy can be effective in offsetting the effects of money multiplier changes.

7 Interest rate pegging can be a stabilizing monetary policy when disturbances are largely due to shifts in money demand. If disturbances are predominantly nonmonetary, then pegging interest rates is destabilizing.

**8** Fiscal policy effects take too long to realize after a autonomous shock, so they are unlikely to be stabilizing.

**9** A larger government budget surplus will tend to stimulate private investment spending and lead to a rise in the investment–income ratio.

**10** A choice of greater environmental quality generally means a downward shift in the aggregate production function.

**11** The lack of any significant cost difference makes the choice between alternative moderate steady-state inflation rates relatively inconsequential, although the short-run costs of moving from one steady-state to another may be important.

## EXERCISES

1. What is the role of macroeconomic theory in the formulation of macroeconomic policy? Why can macroeconomics not tell whether a temporary increase in unemployment should be traded off for a permanent decrease in the inflation rate? Why is a knowledge of macroeconomics nevertheless valuable in formulating both the question and its answer?

2. If the rational expectations critique is correct, what are the implications of a plan to permanently reduce the unemployment rate by a series of unanticipated accelerations in the nominal money supply growth rate?

3. How can an activist monetary policy actually increase economic instability?

4. Why is it necessary that someone who advocates stabilization by active fiscal policy believe that fiscal policy can affect nominal income? Why do some people who believe that fiscal policy affects nominal income believe that fiscal policy cannot be used for stabilization? Is there any inconsistency in these views?

5. Why might an increased real government surplus imply an increased ratio of investment to income?

6. Explain and illustrate graphically how a monetary policy of pegging interest rates can in some cases be stabilizing, while in other cases is destabilizing.

7. What are the implications of the Lucas supply curve for stabilization policy?

## REFERENCES FOR FURTHER READING

Carlson, Keith M. "The Mix of Monetary and Fiscal Policies: Conventional Wisdom Vs. Empirical Reality." *Federal Reserve Bank of St. Louis Review*, 64 (October 1982), 7–21.

Friedman, Milton. "The Role of Monetary Policy." *American Economic Review*, 58 (March 1968), 1–17.

Gramlich, Edward M. "The Usefulness of Monetary and Fiscal Policy as Discretionary Stabilization Tools." *Journal of Money, Credit, and Banking*, 3 (May 1971), 506–32.

Hafer, R. W. "Monetary Policy and the Price Rule: The Newest Odd Couple." *Federal Reserve Bank of St. Louis Review*, 65 (February 1983), 5–13.

Lucas, Robert, and Thomas Sargent. "After Keynesian Macroeconomics." *After the Phillips Curve*, Boston: Federal Reserve Bank of Boston, 1978.

McCallum, Bennett T. "The Significance of Rational Expectations Theory." *Challenge*, January–February 1980.

# THE 1979–1982 CHANGE IN FED OPERATING PROCEDURES

As mentioned in Chapter 14, monetary policy has long been conducted by pegging interest rates. The Federal Open Market Committee (FOMC) would pick a narrow target band for the federal funds rate, and then the open market desk at the New York Fed would buy and sell bonds to maintain the interest rate within the target band. As was covered in the chapter, interest rate pegging can be destabilizing if the economy is subject to nonmonetary shocks.

From the mid-1960s, monetarists like Milton Friedman had argued that by setting money growth targets rather than interest rate targets, monetary policy would be more stabilizing. The Fed came to use money growth targets along with the Federal funds rate target: as long as the interest rate stayed within the target band, the open market desk was to pursue the target rate of money growth. By the late 1970s, pressures for interest rate shifts had resulted in unstable and rising money growth for several years, and the FOMC decided it was time for a change.

On October 6, 1979, the FOMC adopted a new set of operating procedures.[1] Rather than establish a money growth target via an interest rate peg, the open market desk was to control bank reserves with a view toward achieving the money growth target subject to an interest rate band five percentage points wide. The size of the interest band had gradually increased over the previous years, but this represented a doubling of permissible fluctuations in interest rates and the money supply now could be controlled without concern over interest rate movements.

Surprisingly, over the next three years the Fed in fact achieved more variability in money growth than over any similar period since World War II. The increased variability in money growth was reflected in increased variability in nominal income. This is illustrated in Tables E14.1 and E14.2. Until the Fed effectively abandoned these new procedures in the summer of 1982, monetary policy was more destabilizing and explained more of the quarter-to-quarter variation in nominal income than in any three-year period in the prior three decades.[2] This result would be predicted from

---

[1] An excellent analysis of the new procedures is provided by William Poole in "Federal Reserve Operating Procedures: A Survey and Evaluation of the Historical Record Since October 1979," *Journal of Money, Credit, and Banking*, 14 (November 1982), 575–96.

[2] See Milton Friedman, "Monetarism in Rhetoric and Practice," *Bank of Japan Monetary and Economic Studies*, 1 (October 1983), 1–14; and Milton Friedman, "Lessons from the 1979–82 Monetary Policy Experiment," *American Economic Review*, 74 (May 1984), 397–400. The latter article, from which Tables E14.1 and E14.2 were taken, notes that the real output effects were noticeable a quarter or two earlier than usual. This apparently reflects the unusually large swings in $\hat{M}$, which would result in larger swings in $y$.

| | M1 | Adjusted Monetary Base |
|---|---|---|
| 10 quarters prior to October 1979 | 1.59 | .94 |
| 10 quarters after October 1979 | 5.64 | 2.71 |

Note: The standard deviation is the positive square root of the variance of the variable for the indicated period. The larger the standard deviation, the greater the variability of money growth.

Source: Milton Friedman, "Lessons from the 1979–82 Monetary Policy Experiment," *American Economic Review*, 74 (May 1984), 397–400.

equation (14.2) in the text. The real question is why a policy aimed at controlling money growth would result instead in more volatile money growth.

The key factor seems to be that between 1968 and 1984, reserve requirements were computed on the basis of bank deposits as of two weeks before. The *lagged reserve accounting (LRA)* meant that the Fed could not control the quantity of bank reserves directly to adjust the quantity of money. Banks would hold whatever was required based on previous deposits, and the Fed determined what fraction of these reserves were borrowed. In order to reduce money if it was above target, the Fed would force banks to borrow more from the discount window. This would push up interest rates which would reduce the amount of deposits people want to hold. Unfortunately, the current response of demand deposits to week-to-week changes in interest rates is not very large. The Fed would push interest rates up greatly to reduce money with little effect; eventually people would begin to adjust deposits to persistently higher interest rates and soon money would drop below target and the Fed would repeat the process in the opposite direction.[3]

In conclusion, the adoption of monetarist goals without monetarist operating procedures—contemporaneous reserve requirements and base money control—resulted in the worst of both worlds. Interest rates *and* money growth fluctuated much more than when the Fed pegged interest rates. After reviewing the post-1979 policy, most monetarists

---

[3]On the operation of monetary policy under the 1979–82 procedures, see Warren L. Coats, Jr., "Recent Monetary Policy Strategies in the United States," *Kredit und Kapital*, Oct./Nov. 1981, 521–49; Jan G. Loeys, "Policy Invariance in the Financial Sector and the October 1979 Change in Monetary Policy," Ph.D. Dissertation, U.C.L.A. Department of Economics, 1981.

| Period for M1 | No. of Quarters | Annual Rate of Change | | |
| --- | --- | --- | --- | --- |
| | | Monetary Base | M1 | GNP One Quarter Later |
| 1978:4 to 1979:4 | 4 | 8.2 | 7.4 | 10.2 |
| 1979:4 to 1980:2 | 2 | 6.4 | 1.5 | 5.2 |
| 1980:2 to 1981:2 | 4 | 7.8 | 10.1 | 13.9 |
| 1981:2 to 1981:4 | 2 | 3.3 | 3.2 | 1.1 |
| 1981:4 to 1982:1 | 1 | 9.6 | 11.0 | 6.6 |
| 1982:1 to 1982:3 | 2 | 7.3 | 4.7 | 2.6 |
| 1982:3 to 1983:3 | 4 | 9.3 | 12.6 | 10.3 |

Source:   Milton Friedman, "Lessons from the 1979–82 Monetary Policy Experiment," *American Economic Review*, 74 (May 1984), 399.

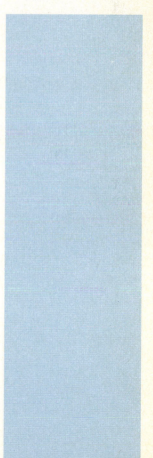

Swings in M1 and Nominal GNP One Quarter Later, Quarterly Data, 1979:1 to 1983:4

would argue that had the Fed consciously set out to discredit monetarism by claiming to be monetarist while acting in a decidedly nonmonetarist fashion, it could not have done a much better job at achieving that goal.

# CHAPTER FIFTEEN

# UNDERSTANDING U.S. MACROECONOMIC HISTORY

## 15.1 TWENTIETH-CENTURY GROWTH IN LABOR, OUTPUT, AND PRODUCTIVITY

The macroeconomic analysis presented in this text can be better appreciated by applying it to the study of the historical experience. In this manner, we gain an understanding of the effects of simultaneous and serial macroeconomic shocks and can observe the relative importance of different types of macroeconomic shocks. Throughout this chapter, dates are provided more for illustrating the timing relationships than for historical interest.

Any study of the macroeconomic experience is limited by data to relatively recent times. Many data series only exist since 1929 on a consistent basis—for instance, the national income accounts. Yet we can piece together some meaningful data from earlier times to allow a discussion of broad historical trends.

### GROWTH IN QUALITY-ADJUSTED HOURS WORKED

Column 2 of Table 15.1 reports data on total hours worked in the United States from 1900 to 1983. The values reported represent index numbers with a base year of 1958 equal to 100. We use such an index just as we did our price indexes discussed in Section 3.1. A value of 143 for 1983 means that actual hours worked in the U.S. economy in

1983 were 43 percent above the actual hours worked in 1958. A value of 57 in 1900 indicates that actual hours worked then were 43 percent below the total hours worked in 1958. Column 2 indicates that there has been an upward trend in hours worked through the years.

The problem with column 2 data is that it treats an hour of labor in 1900 as being identical to an hour of labor in 1983. We know, however, that the worker of today is more educated and highly skilled than the worker of yesteryear. Economists like to talk about investment in *human capital*, which refers to the education and training of the labor force that will allow greater future productivity. We can in fact adjust the data on hours worked to reflect some of the changes in the human capital that are put to use in each hour. By considering factors such as the education, age, sex, and immigrant status of the labor force, we can arrive at a revised measure of hours worked that we will refer to as *quality-adjusted hours worked*.[1] Column 3 of Table 15.1 lists this revised series. Notice that this quality-adjusted series starts lower and ends up higher than the unadjusted series. This reflects the investment in human capital increasing over time. While several factors entered into the determination of column 3, the change in the median number of school years completed by those 25 years and older is likely to be of particular interest to readers of this text. Column 4 of Table 15.1 lists these data. This very important element of human capital investment has increased dramatically since the turn of the century. From an average eighth grade education in 1900, schooling has become such an important part of job preparedness that by 1983, the average individual 25 and older had more than 12 years of education.

## GROWTH IN OUTPUT PER HOUR WORKED

Total output as measured by the gross private product of the U.S. is recorded in column 5 of Table 15.1. A common measure of the productivity of the economy is the output per hour of labor. If we divide column 5 by column 3, we have quality-adjusted output per hour as shown in column 6. Over the 1900–79 period, this measure of hourly productivity has had an average annual growth rate of 1.75 percent. While many recent economists have been concerned with a downward trend in U.S. productivity (see the essay at the end of Chapter 9), the growth rate of quality-adjusted output per hour reported in

Quality-adjusted output per hour has grown steadily over time.

[1]This section draws heavily from Michael R. Darby, "The U.S. Productivity Slowdown: A Case of Statistical Myopia," *American Economic Review*, 74 (June 1984), 301–22.

Table 15.1

United States Hours Worked, Output Per Hour, and Productivity

| 1. Year | 2. Hours Worked | 3. Quality-Adjusted Hours Worked | 4. Median School Years Completed | 5. Gross Private Product | 6. Output per Quality-Adjusted Hour |
|---------|-----------------|----------------------------------|----------------------------------|--------------------------|-------------------------------------|
| 1900 | 57.242 | 47.998 | 8.00 | 103.680 | 36.574 |
| 1901 | 59.715 | 50.085 | 8.01 | 115.835 | 39.159 |
| 1902 | 62.371 | 52.272 | 8.02 | 116.860 | 37.853 |
| 1903 | 64.111 | 53.635 | 8.03 | 122.717 | 38.740 |
| 1904 | 63.195 | 52.831 | 8.04 | 120.960 | 38.767 |
| 1905 | 66.309 | 55.332 | 8.05 | 130.039 | 39.793 |
| 1906 | 68.965 | 57.452 | 8.06 | 145.416 | 42.856 |
| 1907 | 70.522 | 58.603 | 8.07 | 147.612 | 42.649 |
| 1908 | 67.408 | 56.096 | 8.08 | 134.725 | 40.666 |
| 1909 | 71.163 | 59.304 | 8.09 | 151.566 | 43.274 |
| 1910 | 72.995 | 60.829 | 8.10 | 153.031 | 42.596 |
| 1911 | 74.369 | 61.997 | 8.11 | 158.010 | 43.154 |
| 1912 | 76.659 | 64.303 | 8.12 | 165.478 | 43.573 |
| 1913 | 77.300 | 64.432 | 8.13 | 172.068 | 45.217 |
| 1914 | 75.834 | 63.175 | 8.14 | 158.010 | 42.349 |
| 1915 | 75.193 | 62.868 | 8.15 | 162.256 | 43.699 |
| 1916 | 80.597 | 67.621 | 8.16 | 185.687 | 46.495 |
| 1917 | 82.337 | 69.434 | 8.17 | 178.365 | 43.496 |
| 1918 | 81.604 | 69.530 | 8.18 | 185.833 | 45.254 |
| 1919 | 79.040 | 67.311 | 8.19 | 193.448 | 48.662 |
| 1920 | 80.047 | 68.095 | 8.20 | 195.205 | 48.538 |
| 1921 | 72.079 | 61.371 | 8.22 | 190.666 | 52.604 |
| 1922 | 77.483 | 66.123 | 8.24 | 201.942 | 51.710 |
| 1923 | 83.619 | 71.484 | 8.26 | 229.765 | 54.423 |
| 1924 | 81.696 | 69.927 | 8.28 | 236.648 | 57.301 |
| 1925 | 84.627 | 72.632 | 8.30 | 242.066 | 56.430 |
| 1926 | 87.557 | 75.343 | 8.32 | 258.321 | 58.052 |
| 1927 | 87.099 | 75.131 | 8.34 | 260.518 | 58.712 |
| 1928 | 87.832 | 75.962 | 8.36 | 263.447 | 58.723 |
| 1929 | 89.572 | 77.667 | 8.38 | 279.702 | 60.977 |
| 1930 | 83.436 | 72.549 | 8.40 | 249.226 | 58.166 |
| 1931 | 76.475 | 66.580 | 8.42 | 228.274 | 58.052 |
| 1932 | 67.775 | 59.087 | 8.44 | 191.938 | 55.002 |
| 1933 | 67.042 | 58.520 | 8.46 | 186.810 | 54.050 |
| 1934 | 72.000 | 62.921 | 8.48 | 202.634 | 54.528 |
| 1935 | 75.900 | 66.401 | 8.50 | 223.293 | 56.938 |
| 1936 | 81.600 | 71.462 | 8.52 | 253.622 | 60.093 |
| 1937 | 86.700 | 75.999 | 8.54 | 270.032 | 60.161 |
| 1938 | 79.200 | 69.484 | 8.56 | 252.889 | 61.624 |
| 1939 | 83.300 | 73.135 | 8.58 | 276.478 | 64.010 |
| 1940 | 87.300 | 76.727 | 8.60 | 301.240 | 66.477 |
| 1941 | 94.700 | 83.480 | 8.67 | 346.660 | 70.312 |
| 1942 | 102.100 | 90.208 | 8.74 | 376.989 | 70.761 |
| 1943 | 105.800 | 93.226 | 8.80 | 399.700 | 72.594 |

Table 15.1

United States Hours Worked, Output Per Hour, and Productivity

| 1. Year | 2. Hours Worked | 3. Quality-Adjusted Hours Worked | 4. Median School Years Completed | 5. Gross Private Product | 6. Output per Quality-Adjusted Hour |
|---------|-----------------|----------------------------------|----------------------------------|--------------------------|-------------------------------------|
| 1944 | 104.400 | 92.731 | 8.87 | 420.358 | 76.754 |
| 1945 | 98.700 | 88.817 | 8.94 | 413.912 | 78.907 |
| 1946 | 99.700 | 90.704 | 9.01 | 403.069 | 75.242 |
| 1947 | 101.800 | 93.923 | 9.08 | 412.300 | 74.327 |
| 1948 | 102.600 | 94.926 | 9.16 | 431.500 | 76.967 |
| 1949 | 98.800 | 91.960 | 9.23 | 429.825 | 79.141 |
| 1950 | 100.500 | 93.849 | 9.30 | 470.050 | 84.805 |
| 1951 | 104.000 | 98.061 | 9.42 | 500.375 | 86.399 |
| 1952 | 104.700 | 100.012 | 9.55 | 515.275 | 87.236 |
| 1953 | 104.900 | 101.539 | 9.67 | 538.550 | 89.805 |
| 1954 | 100.600 | 98.431 | 9.80 | 531.825 | 91.484 |
| 1955 | 104.100 | 102.200 | 9.93 | 572.925 | 94.919 |
| 1956 | 105.600 | 104.057 | 10.06 | 584.85 | 95.166 |
| 1957 | 104.200 | 103.378 | 10.19 | 594.70 | 97.403 |
| 1958 | 100.000 | 100.000 | 10.33 | 590.60 | 100.000 |
| 1959 | 103.300 | 103.893 | 10.46 | 629.52 | 102.596 |
| 1960 | 104.500 | 105.538 | 10.60 | 641.95 | 102.990 |
| 1961 | 102.800 | 106.387 | 10.99 | 657.75 | 104.684 |
| 1962 | 104.800 | 111.287 | 11.40 | 697.77 | 106.167 |
| 1963 | 105.600 | 112.876 | 11.55 | 727.35 | 109.106 |
| 1964 | 107.700 | 115.742 | 11.70 | 767.55 | 112.286 |
| 1965 | 111.100 | 119.463 | 11.80 | 816.57 | 115.737 |
| 1966 | 113.906 | 123.261 | 12.00 | 863.97 | 118.681 |
| 1967 | 115.704 | 124.772 | 12.00 | 883.70 | 119.920 |
| 1968 | 117.416 | 127.142 | 12.10 | 925.65 | 123.272 |
| 1969 | 120.250 | 129.834 | 12.15 | 952.00 | 124.152 |
| 1970 | 117.680 | 127.015 | 12.20 | 949.50 | 126.575 |
| 1971 | 118.227 | 127.206 | 12.20 | 985.67 | 131.199 |
| 1972 | 121.801 | 130.250 | 12.20 | 1048.10 | 136.249 |
| 1973 | 126.573 | 135.403 | 12.30 | 1115.90 | 139.542 |
| 1974 | 127.448 | 136.016 | 12.30 | 1105.65 | 137.636 |
| 1975 | 122.619 | 130.721 | 12.30 | 1088.97 | 141.051 |
| 1976 | 126.236 | 134.864 | 12.40 | 1154.12 | 144.897 |
| 1977 | 132.075 | 140.578 | 12.40 | 1223.27 | 147.336 |
| 1978 | 140.018 | 148.357 | 12.40 | 1285.05 | 146.662 |
| 1979 | 145.081 | 154.452 | 12.50 | 1329.15 | 145.709 |
| 1980 | 143.743 | 153.116 | 12.50 | 1319.42 | 145.904 |
| 1981 | 143.448 | 152.797 | 12.50 | 1355.95 | 150.258 |
| 1982 | 140.711 | 150.914 | 12.60 | 1323.45 | 148.486 |
| 1983 | 143.285 | 153.636 | 12.60 | 1377.65 | 151.828 |

Sources: 1900–1979: Michael R. Darby, ''The U.S. Productivity Slowdown: A Case of Statistical Myopia,'' *American Economic Review*, 74, June 1984, 301–316.

1980–1983: Estimated by the authors using preliminary data and Darby's methods.

column 6 has been nearly constant, averaging 1.76 percent over the period 1900–29, 1.78 percent over the period 1929–65, and 1.65 percent over the period 1965–79.[2]

## SHORT-RUN PRODUCTIVITY MOVEMENTS

Looking beyond these long-run trends, we do find more substantial variations in hourly productivity growth. For instance, for the periods 1929–48, 1948–65, 1965–73, and 1973–78, we find quality-adjusted hourly productivity growth of 1.2, 2.4, 2.3, and 0.7 percent per annum, respectively. How do we explain this variation? It appears that certain institutional and business cycle factors account for these shorter period changes in productivity growth. Let's briefly consider each period in turn.

**1929–48** During the Great Depression and World War II, there was a very low ratio of investment to output. Laurits Christensen of the University of Wisconsin and Dale Jorgenson of Harvard University have estimated the growth rate of capital over this period at about 0.6 percent per annum.[3] This slow growth of capital produced an increase in the labor–capital ratio, and therefore reduced the productivity of labor.

**1948–65** Following the slow growth of the capital stock over 1929–48, there was a period of rapid catch-up between 1948 and 1965. Since the low rate of investment pushed the labor–capital ratio above its steady-state level in 1948, the period of rapid capital growth from 1948 to 1965 was required to return to the steady-state. Of course, as the labor–capital ratio fell over this period, labor productivity increased. Compared to the capital growth rate of 0.6 percent for the early period, Christensen and Jorgenson estimate that the capital stock grew at a rate of 4.0 percent annum over the period 1948–65.

---

[2]We look at these three subperiods because 1900–29 was a period of rapid employment growth where immigration was a dominant factor; 1929–65 was characterized by a tight limitation on immigration and a slow increase in employment growth; finally 1965–83 was a period of rapid employment growth due largely to the baby-boom children's coming of age.

[3]Laurits R. Christensen and Dale W. Jorgenson, "U.S. Input, Output, Saving and Wealth, 1929–1977," unpublished paper, Harvard Institute of Economic Research, December 1978.

**1965–83**   Earlier it was said that quality-adjusted hourly productivity growth grew at an annual rate of 2.3 percent over the period 1965–73 and 0.8 percent between 1973 and 1983. What accounts for this change? It appears that the reported data were biased by the presence of wage and price controls in the United States during the early 1970s. By holding prices artificially low, the controls overstated real output prior to their removal in 1973 and 1974. Estimating the understatement of prices during the period of controls, and computing the implied increase in real output, the adjusted annual growth of labor productivity is approximately 1.88 percent from 1965 to 1973 and 1.21 percent from 1973 to 1983—much different than the dramatic decline using the reported price data.[4]

Even after correction for price control biases, the 1973–83 adjusted productivity growth rate of 1.21 percent is below the 1900–65 trend of 1.75 percent. This probably reflects two other factors: First, the other years cited in this section were all selected as normal unemployment years so that no allowance for productivity effects of cyclical unemployment was needed. Typically, output varies more than hours worked over the business cycle; so productivity declines during recessions. In 1983, we estimated that cyclical unemployment would decrease measured productivity by about 2 percent.

Second, many economists also believe that there was a real drop in productivity around 1973 due to the effect of unexpectedly high oil prices. Robert Rasche of Michigan State University and John Tatom of the Federal Reserve Bank of St. Louis argue that higher oil prices will significantly lower the equilibrium level of output consistent with a given level of labor and capital, and will also induce a fall in the level of capital over time.[5] While the Nixon administration price controls contributed to an overstatement of the drop in productivity, we cannot rule out that the oil price shocks had real effects.

We have used three factors to explain recent slow adjusted labor productivity growth: price-control induced output measurement er-

---

[4]For an analysis of the effects of price controls see Michael R. Darby, "The U.S. Productivity Slowdown: A Case of Statistical Myopia," *American Economic Review*, 74 (June 1984), 301–22.

[5]See Robert H. Rasche and John A. Tatom, "Energy Resources and Potential GNP," *Federal Reserve Bank of St. Louis Review*, 59 (June 1977), 10–24, and "Energy Price Shocks, Aggregate Supply, and Monetary Policy: The Theory and International Evidence," *Carnegie–Rochester Conference Series on Public Policy*, 14 (Spring 1981), 9–93.

ror in 1973, cyclically low productivity in 1983, and the productivity effect of recent oil price increases. To illustrate how these add up, assume that the latter effect reduced the trend productivity *level* by 2 percent, although any particular number is controversial. Then we have:

| Factor | 1965–83 | 1973–83 |
|---|---|---|
| Adjusted labor productivity growth | 1.51% | 0.84% |
| 1973 price-control effect | 0.00% | 0.37% |
| 1983 cyclical effect | 0.11% | 0.20% |
| Oil-price effect | 0.11% | 0.20% |
| Totals | 1.73% | 1.61% |

The growth-rate impact is estimated by dividing the percentage effect on the level of productivity by the number of years in the period. As we see from the totals, these three effects can account for nearly all of the recent shortfall in adjusted labor productivity growth relative to the previous trend. As time passes, such special factors tend to average out or even reverse themselves, so that average productivity growth is more stable over longer periods of time.

## 15.2 THE GREAT DEPRESSION

Besides the broad sweep of history covered in the last section, no coverage of U.S. macroeconomic history would be complete without a discussion of the major economic event of the century—the Great Depression of 1929–33.

### SETTING THE STAGE

Our emphasis on the dynamic nature of macroeconomics requires that we first consider what was going on before 1929. The period from 1923 through 1928 was characterized by moderate fluctuations in the growth rate of the nominal money supply around an average rate of 4.4 percent per annum. In this section, we will use the M2 definition of the money supply, because the distinction between demand and time deposits was blurred until the Banking Acts of 1933 and 1935.

Between 1923 and 1928, there were two sequences consisting of a significant decrease in the money supply growth rate followed in a year by an increased growth rate. The decreases in growth rates started near the beginning of both 1923 and 1926 and caused the contractions of 1923–24 and 1926–27, respectively. These fluctuations

**375**

were small by previous standards, and the period as a whole was thought to reflect the improving skill and policy ability of the young Federal Reserve System.

The average growth rate of the money–income ratio over this period was nearly zero ($-0.1$ percent per annum), so the average growth rate of nominal income (4.5 percent per annum) differed only slightly from the averge growth rate of nominal money (4.4 percent per annum). The average growth rate of real income was a healthy 4.2 percent per annum, while the annual growth in the price level was 0.3 percent per annum. Actually, the period immediately preceding the Great Depression closely resembled the 1950s—nominal money growth fluctuations were large enough to cause recessions, but not so large as to cause any widespread, continuing macroeconomic problems.

Despite the frequent attempts of noneconomists to find reasons for the Great Depression, it should be stated that there was no more basic unsoundness in the economy in 1929 than there was in 1959. However, it can be said that the Fed misunderstood what was happening in the 1920s, and this faulty interpretation led to some disastrous policy decisions in the 1930s.

There was no basic problem existing in the 1920s to cause the Great Depression.

## THE FIRST TWO YEARS

The Great Depression started in a very undramatic fashion. The Fed had become concerned with what it supposed was undue speculation in the stock market. This stock market activity was attributed to unsound "speculative fever" and "easy credit," and the Fed hoped to eliminate these factors from the economy. In early 1928 the Fed embarked on a restrictive monetary policy by selling government securities and raising the discount rate. From April 1928 through November 1930, the money supply fell at an average growth rate of $-1.4$ percent per annum, a decrease of almost 6 percentage points compared to the previous average.

This sharp decrease in money growth would normally lead to a recession by early 1929. However, on most estimates of output, the recession did not begin until the summer of 1929. The official National Bureau of Economic Research date for the beginning of the contraction is August 1929. It may be that the booming stock market delayed the recession by inducing upward shifts in the aggregate expenditure function during early 1929, or stock market profits may have masked an earlier decline in output when statisticians later retrospectively constructed our output data. Despite the puzzling delay in its onset, by 1930 the economy was about what would be expected following a 6 percentage point drop in nominal money supply growth.[6] There was certainly no evidence that output was going to fall to the depths soon to follow.

To many people, the beginning of the Great Depression is marked by the stock market crash of October 1929. Is there anything special about this plunge in stock prices? Actually, there is little to distinguish the October 1929 crash from similar drops in stock prices occurring near the beginning of the 1937–38 and 1969–70 recessions. Stock prices in 1930 were actually 5.5 percent *higher* on average than they had been in 1928, and were only 19.2 percent lower than the 1929 average.

## THE COLLAPSE OF THE BANKING SYSTEM

Through November of 1930, the recession was severe, but certainly not so severe as to be classed as a depression. Then in November, a rash of rural bank failures in the Midwest shook confidence in the banking system and led to a banking panic.[7] As the ratio of currency to deposits rose, the money multiplier fell, leading to a fall in the money supply and a rise in interest rates. *Bank runs* became common, and as a bank exhausted its supply of readily marketable securities, it was left with its loans to customers as its only assets. One of the reasons the Fed was created was to prevent bank panics by serving as a *lender of last resort*. Yet rather than actively engage in this role to end the panic, the Fed had surprisingly little understanding of panic psychology and viewed the banks as failing due to bad management. As a result, 256 banks with deposits of $180,000,000 failed during November 1930. The panic became severe after the failure of the Bank of United States on December 11, 1930.

The Bank of United States was a commercial bank, but the name suggested some kind of official status to many people. It had deposits of over $200,000,000 and was a member of the Federal Reserve System. The failure of the Bank of United States seriously undermined the confidence in other commercial banks as well as the Federal Reserve System. In December of 1930, a total of 352 banks with deposits of $370,000,000 failed. As the money multiplier fell further, so did the nominal money supply. Over the November–January period, money supply growth averaged −12 percent per annum. In January,

*Bank runs caused the money supply to fall rapidly.*

---

[6]On these points, see James R. Lothian, "Comments on 'Monetarist Interpretations of the Great Depression,' " in Karl Brunner, ed., *The Great Depression Revisited* (Boston: Martinus Nijhoff Publishing, 1981); and Michael R. Darby, review of Brunner (op. cit.), *Journal of Money, Credit, and Banking*, 14 (May 1982), 293–95.

[7]See Section 13.4 for an analysis of banking panics.

the situation appeared to be stabilizing and the money multiplier and nominal money supply rose slightly in February. But in March 1931, the runs and bank failures resumed and continued intermittently until March 1933. The Fed took little corrective action so that the currency–deposit and reserve–deposit ratios rose with each crisis. Between March 1931 and March 1933, the currency–deposit ratio rose from 0.0964 to 0.2252 and the reserve–deposit ratio rose from 0.0807 to 0.1188. The result was a fall in the money multiplier from 6.278 to 3.720, a fall of some 41 percent. The Fed increased nominal base money by only 18.7 percent over this period and the net fall in the money supply was 29.7 percent.

Through March 1933, the pattern of monetary policy was one of falling nominal money supply growth rates. As would be expected, the cumulative effect on the economy of this series of restrictive shocks was devastating. Over the period from the money supply peak at April 1928 to the money supply trough of April 1933, the average growth rate of the nominal money supply was $-8.2$ percent per annum. Table 15.2 illustrates the deceleration of the money supply over this period. The growth rate of the nominal money supply drops from $-0.9$ percent per annum over the first two years to $-4.3$ percent, $-19.0$ percent, and $-15.9$ percent per annum over the next three years. Based on the available annual data, the average growth rate of nominal income from 1928 to 1933 was $-11.1$ percent per annum. This was divided between an average growth rate of real income of $-6.0$ percent and an average rate of inflation of $-5.1$ percent. Following the increase in money growth from April 1932 (although still negative), real income growth in the summer of 1932 rose to zero, and by March 1933 was positive.[8]

---

[8]Since data on real income in this period are only available on an annual basis, intrayear changes must be inferred from industrial production changes.

| Period | Growth Rate |
|---|---|
| April 1928 to April 1929 | $-1.0\%$ |
| April 1929 to April 1930 | $-0.9\%$ |
| April 1930 to April 1931 | $-4.3\%$ |
| April 1931 to April 1932 | $-19.0\%$ |
| April 1932 to April 1933 | $-15.9\%$ |

**Table 15.2**

Growth Rates of the Money Supply (M2) 1928–33

Source: Calculated from data in Milton Friedman and Anna Jacobson Schwartz, *Monetary Statistics of the United States* (New York: NBER, 1970), pp. 24–29.

The large drop in real income after 1929 meant that employment also fell dramatically. The unemployment rate went from about 3-¼ percent in 1929 to about 22-½ percent in 1932. The money–income ratio $K$ also behaved as we would expect. During the first year after the April 1928 decrease in money growth, $K$ fell. This initial fall was followed by a rise past its steady-state growth path. In 1929 $K$ was about 6 percent below the 1928 level. It then rose to a 1932 peak of about 30 percent above the 1928 level before beginning a gradual decline.[9]

We have yet to mention fiscal policy during the Great Depression. During 1930 and 1931, fiscal policy was actually very expansive due to a large increase in real government spending and borrowing relative to their low beginning levels. In 1932, taxes were increased and government expenditures reduced. Then in 1933, real federal expenditures were sharply increased, but real state and local expenditures were reduced by more. Given the limited data and the overwhelming monetary shock, it is difficult to detect any effects of nonmonetary shocks. Keynesian economists have emphasized falling investment demand as a macroeconomic shock, but given the relative constancy of consumer and government expenditures, monetary policy must operate primarily by reducing investment if real income is to fall.

An important question posed by Milton Friedman and Anna Schwartz is, "Why was monetary policy so inept?"[10] While there are many possible answers, Friedman and Schwartz suggested that the main cause was the vacuum left by, and the power struggle resulting from, the death of Governor Benjamin Strong, who was head of the Federal Reserve Bank of New York and a dominant figure on the Federal Open Market Committee. Following Strong's death in 1928, there was no clear leadership within the Federal Reserve System, so

---

[9]American postwar recessions have been generally too brief and shallow for this effect to be noted in Chapter 11, but recall that the money–income ratio $K$ actually adjusts to its desired value $K^d$ rather than its steady-state value $K_s$. In a deep recession $K^d$ significantly exceeds $K_s$ because (1) interest rates are very low and (2) decreases in *transitory* income decrease money demand much less than proportionately. This induced increase in the money–income ratio causes nominal income growth to slow by more than nominal money growth over the course of a severe recession or depression.

[10]Our understanding of the Great Depression was aided immensely by the publication of Friedman and Schwartz's *A Monetary History of the United States, 1867–1960* (Princeton University Press for the National Bureau of Economic Research, 1963).

the Fed was ill-prepared to take strong action when needed. There are several other stories attempting to explain the Fed's poor performance, but these are really not essential to understanding how macroeconomic shocks affect the economy.

## THE BANKING HOLIDAY OF 1933

In January 1933 another peak in the pattern of bank failures was reached. As panic spread, many states declared *bank holidays*—closing the banks to protect their deposits. On March 6, 1933, President Roosevelt closed all the nation's banks. The failure of the Federal Reserve to act in support of the banking system had caused the most severe and widespread banking suspension in American history.

Beginning March 13th, banks were permitted to reopen upon license from the Secretary of the Treasury.[11] Only banks that were clearly "sound" were licensed to reopen. This certification process restored some of the lost confidence in the banking system and ended the bank runs. By March 15, 1933, 68.6 percent of the banks, with 87.3 percent of the nation's total deposits, were licensed and open. About half of the unlicensed banks, with one quarter of the unlicensed bank deposits on March 15, 1933 were reopened by the end of 1933. With public confidence in the banking system restored, the currency–deposit ratio began falling instead of rising.

*Official bank closings followed by licensed reopenings ended the bank runs.*

## THE RECOVERY

Real income bottomed out starting in the summer of 1932. By early 1933, a definite recovery was under way. The speed of the recovery was hastened by an expansionary money shock following the banking holidays' restoration of confidence. Table 15.3 illustrates how much more rapidly money grew after April 1933 than during the pre-1933 period displayed in Table 15.2. This increase in the money growth rate is due to: (1) an increased, though still negative, growth rate of the money multiplier and (2) an increased growth rate of base money.

*The recovery began in 1933.*

The increased growth rate of the money multiplier was due to the change in the growth of the currency–deposit ratio from positive to negative. The new confidence in banks led to a return of the currency–deposit ratio toward its normal level. A major factor in maintaining public confidence was the establishment of the Federal Deposit Insurance Corporation (FDIC) in 1934. The value of the FDIC

*The FDIC promoted confidence in the banking system.*

---

[11]Banks that were not members of the Federal Reserve System were issued licenses by state banking officials.

Table 15.3

| Period | Growth Rate |
|---|---|
| April 1933 to April 1934 | 8.3% |
| April 1934 to April 1935 | 12.6% |
| April 1935 to April 1936 | 10.5% |
| April 1936 to April 1937 | 7.9% |

Source: Calculated from data in Milton Friedman and Anna Jacobson Schwartz, *Monetary Statistics of the United States*, (New York: NBER, 1970), pp. 28–31.

in preventing runs and banking panics is based more on its actual operation than on its legal contract with depositors. The federal government has no legal liability to bail out the FDIC if its reserves are exhausted by a bank panic, which was a real possibility in the early years. Furthermore, depositors are insured only up to a legal maximum amount—originally $2,500, but currently $100,000. Usually, a very large fraction of total deposits are uninsured, so it may appear that such uninsured deposit holders could still cause a serious run leading to bank failures. In practice, the FDIC has eliminated most of the incentive for bank runs so that general banking panics have become a thing of the past. This is true because the FDIC rarely allows a bank to go bankrupt. Instead, the FDIC arranges a merger of a mismanaged bank into a well–managed bank and compensates the well-managed bank for any losses incurred in the takeover.

Even though the currency–deposit ratio was falling, the money multiplier still fell (although at a lower rate than before) because of a more than offsetting rise in the reserve–deposit ratio. Bankers had been rapidly increasing their reserve–deposit ratio since it became apparent that the banker who relied on the Fed for borrowing during a panic was very likely to fail. From October 1930 to April 1933, the reserve-deposit ratio rose at an average growth rate of 16.3 percent; from April 1933 to June 1935, the growth rate was 19.7 percent; from June 1935 through July 1936, there was no particular trend up or down. The net effect of the rising reserve–deposit ratio and falling currency–deposit ratio was an average growth rate of the money multiplier of − 1.6 percent per annum between April 1933 and April 1936, this compared to an average growth of − 20.7 percent per annum between October 1930 and April 1933.

An additional factor that bolstered money growth was an increase in the official price of gold from $20.67 to $35.00 per ounce. This change occurred in several steps between April 1933 and January 1934. The significance of the rise in the price at which the United States would buy or sell gold is that much gold was sold to the U.S. at the higher price. To pay for the gold, new base money was created, and it turned out that the growth rate of base money between April

1933 and April 1936 was 12.2 percent per annum. The net effect on money supply growth is detailed in Table 15.3.

Following the rise in money growth, the resulting recovery in real income was dramatic. The average growth rate of real income between 1933 and 1937 was 9.0 percent per annum. Yet despite this very rapid recovery, real income in 1937 was only about the same as in 1929. If real income had grown at the long-run trend growth rate of about 3.1 percent per annum from 1929 on, real income in 1937 would have been about 28 percent higher than in 1929. In other words, 1937 real income was about 22 percent below the estimated steady-state level. Figure 15.1 compares the actual growth path of real income for 1929–46 with the estimated steady-state growth path.

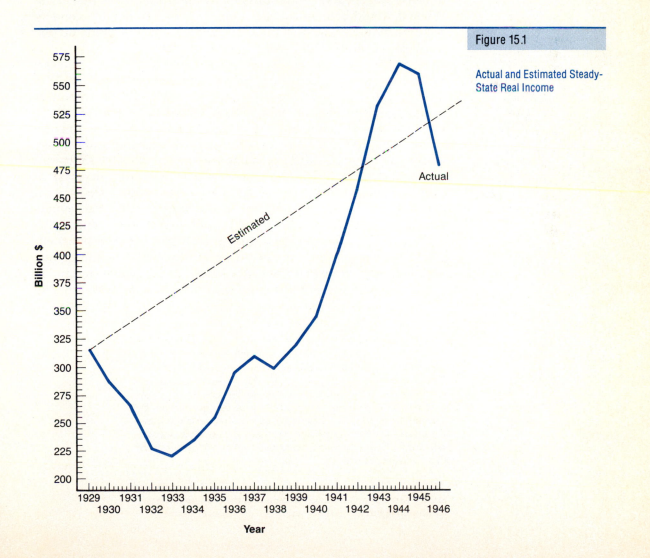

Figure 15.1

Actual and Estimated Steady-State Real Income

To most people, the very disturbing feature of the Great Depression was the high unemployment rates that were experienced. From a 1929 unemployment rate of 3.2 percent, the unemployment rate rose above 20 percent in 1932 and 1933, and was still at a very high rate of more than 9 percent in 1937. Table 15.4 reports the Depression-era unemployment rate data.[12] While 9.1 percent in 1937 is substantially less than the 22.5 percent of 1932, it was still quite high by historical standards. Some economists believe that the record shows normal progress on reemploying the millions of unemployed until the Fed stalled the recovery by doubling reserve requirements between August 1936 and May 1937. Others believe that the recovery was surprisingly slow and point to such factors as the large number of bankruptcies and certain possibly counterproductive new laws. While it would be interesting to know whether or not an economy recovers more slowly after a massive depression,[13] certainly no one wants to repeat the experiment to settle the debate!

Between 1929 and 1937, employment rose by almost 6 percent; 1937 real income, in contrast, was about 1½ percent below its 1929 level. The discrepancy is explained by the abnormally low amount of capital people had to work with in 1937. Between 1929 and 1933, there was considerable disinvestment in capital instead of the normal increase. This was due to the experienced fall in saving. If the short-run marginal propensity to consume is about 0.4, then the short-run marginal propensity to save is 0.6. So a $1 transitory decrease in private income will reduce saving by $.60. The fall in transitory income during the Great Depression was so great that the saving–income ratio fell from a normal 10 percent to 0.1, −10.7, and −10.4 percent in 1931, 1932, and 1933, respectively. Since government deficits were rising during this period, real investment by the private sector fell even more than the saving–income ratio would suggest, to −5.5, −15.6, and −14.6 percent of private income, respectively. Not

---

[12]The unemployment rate data for 1934–41 come from Michael R. Darby, "Three and a Half Million U.S. Employees Have Been Mislaid; Or, An Explanation of Unemployment, 1934–1941," *Journal of Political Economy*, 84 (February 1976), 1–16. The original data from the Bureau of Labor Statistics counted workers employed by government works programs like the WPA as being unemployed. By considering these workers as employed—as they certainly were— it appears that the original data overstated the unemployment rate during 1934–41 by 4 to 7 percentage points, and understated the speed of the recovery.

[13]Robert W. Clower and Axel Leijonhufvud of U.C.L.A. have long argued that a depression would so disrupt the economy that its equilibrating forces would be weakened and recovery slow.

Table 15.4

The United States
Unemployment Rate
1928–41

| Year | Unemployment Rate |
|------|-------------------|
| 1928 | 4.2% |
| 1929 | 3.2% |
| 1930 | 8.7% |
| 1931 | 15.3% |
| 1932 | 22.5% |
| 1933 | 20.6% |
| 1934 | 16.0% |
| 1935 | 14.2% |
| 1936 | 9.9% |
| 1937 | 9.1% |
| 1938 | 12.5% |
| 1939 | 11.3% |
| 1940 | 9.5% |
| 1941 | 6.0% |

Source: See footnote 12.

until 1936 was saving sufficient to finance—barely—positive net investment. A result of this very low rate of capital growth was a slow growth of real income in the early stages of the recovery.

Table 15.5 presents an overview of important variables during the Depression era. In this table we can see that the pace of recovery was anything but even. In fact, following the initial recovery in the mid-1930s, by summer of 1936 the Fed became concerned about inflation. Between 1933 and 1936, the rate of inflation averaged 2.8 percent per annum and the 1936 price level was approximately 15 percent below the 1929 level. Still the Fed felt compelled to double reserve requirements for commercial banks in several steps between August 1936 and May 1937. As a result, money growth between July 1936 and April 1938 was only 0.8 percent per annum. This drop in money growth led to a recession in 1937–38 that interrupted the recovery. In April 1938, reserve requirements were reduced and money supply growth increased to an average rate of 10.0 percent per annum through December 1941. Since real income growth had, for so long, been below the steady-state growth rate, it grew at a 6.5 percent per annum rate from 1937 through 1941—about twice the steady-state rate.

The Great Depression provides a startling example of the destabilizing potential of macroeconomic policy. Had the Fed not followed the overly restrictive monetary policy just described, the recession that began in 1929 would never have developed into the major prolonged contraction that was experienced. As was discussed in Chapter 14, those who favor activist government stabilization policies argue that we have learned from past mistakes so that present and

Table 15.5

Macroeconomic Data of the Great Depression Era

| Year | Money Supply M | Nominal Income Y | Real Income y | Price Level P | Unemployment Rate u | Interest Rate R |
|------|------|------|------|------|------|------|
| 1928 | 100.0 | 100.0 | 100.0 | 100.0 | 4.2% | 3.97% |
| 1929 | 100.4 | 106.3 | 106.7 | 100.4 | 3.2 | 4.42 |
| 1930 | 98.5 | 93.2 | 96.7 | 97.7 | 8.7 | 2.23 |
| 1931 | 92.0 | 78.2 | 89.2 | 88.3 | 15.3 | 1.40 |
| 1932 | 77.7 | 59.9 | 76.9 | 78.5 | 22.5 | 0.88 |
| 1933 | 69.4 | 57.4 | 75.3 | 76.8 | 20.6 | 0.52 |
| 1934 | 74.0 | 67.1 | 81.1 | 83.3 | 16.0 | 0.26 |
| 1935 | 84.2 | 74.5 | 88.4 | 84.9 | 14.2 | 0.14 |
| 1936 | 93.7 | 85.0 | 100.3 | 85.3 | 9.9 | 0.14 |
| 1937 | 98.4 | 93.2 | 105.0 | 89.5 | 9.1 | 0.45 |
| 1938 | 98.0 | 87.3 | 100.7 | 87.3 | 12.5 | 0.05 |
| 1939 | 106.1 | 93.3 | 108.3 | 86.8 | 11.3 | 0.02 |
| 1940 | 118.9 | 102.8 | 116.4 | 88.9 | 9.5 | 0.01 |
| 1941 | 134.6 | 128.3 | 134.4 | 96.2 | 6.0 | 0.10 |

Notes: $M, Y, y$, and $P$ are all indices (1928 = 100.0).
     1929 data for $Y, y, P$, and $u$ are questionable.

Sources:  $M, R$: *Long Term Economic Growth, 1860–1970*, series B111, B82
       $Y, y, P$: *National Income and Product Accounts of the U.S., 1929–74*, with 1928 data
          from $M$ and $R$ source.
       $u$: Darby, *Journal of Political Economy*, 1976.

future policy can be used to provide a more stable economy. Those who favor a minimum of government intervention in free markets would argue that the past teaches us the dangers of allowing well-intentioned policymakers to have free rein. While economists can agree on many factual statements regarding the Great Depression, the lesson it holds for today is a more open question.

## 15.3 THE POSTWAR ERA

We skip the war years of 1942–46 because the data are too unreliable to allow for a close inspection of any dynamic macroeconomic effects. For example, price controls and black markets make both price level and real income data very suspect. When price controls were removed in 1946, the large jump in the price index demonstrated the degree to which the price index was out of touch with reality.

The postwar era can be divided into two distinct parts. (1) The first contains the period up to 1962 during which the country returned to a pattern of economic equilibrium disturbed by occasional recessions. During this period, there was no persistent tendency for the growth rate of the nominal money supply to increase or decrease over time. (2) Since 1962, there has been a rising trend of money growth. Throughout much of this period, the economy was experiencing a new money shock before the adjustment to the previous one was completed. This period is of particular interest because of several dramatic points at which fiscal policy moves in one direction and monetary policy in the opposite direction. This permits comparison of the relative power of monetary and fiscal policy. When we refer to monetary policy in this section we will mean the narrow M1 definition.

## THE REBIRTH OF MONETARY POLICY

The Fed came out of World War II with a commitment to support government securities prices by buying and selling all the securities offered at certain pegged interest rates. A policy of maintaining pegged interest rates implies that nominal money supply growth will take on any value necessary, given other economic conditions, to maintain the peg. If the pegged interest rate is set below the rate which would be established by the free market, then interest rate pegging can lead to runaway inflation. With a peg set too high, interest rate pegging can lead to runaway deflation. Consider what would happen if the Fed tried to establish too low an interest rate. Private investors would not be willing to buy all of the government securities, so the Fed would have to buy some of them with newly issued base money. Over time, the new base money will cause the expected rate of inflation to rise and so interest rates will rise by the expectations effect. In trying to counteract this inflation-fueled rise in the rate of interest, the Fed buys even more government securities with new base money, which in turn breeds still more inflation. It is easy to imagine a hyperinflation arising from this scenario.

Figure 15.2 illustrates the effects of pegging interest rates at disequilibrium levels using the *IS–LM* framework. In panel (a), the free market rate of interest is $R_0$, where the initial curves, $IS_0$ and $LM_0$, intersect. Suppose the Fed chooses to peg the interest rate at $R_1$. With $IS_0$ and $LM_0$, interest rate $R_1$ will clearly not be sustained. The Fed is able to lower the interest rate from $R_0$ to $R_1$ by increasing the money supply so that the LM curve shifts right to $LM_1$. This increase in the money supply will tend to increase actual and expected inflation, which will cause interest rates to rise. How does the Fed maintain $R_1$ in the face of market pressure for higher interest rates? The money supply must increase farther, leading to a new rightward shift in $LM$. However, this new increase in the money supply will cause still more

Following World War II, the Fed pegged interest rates.

Figure 15.2

Pegged Interest Rates and
Money Supply Changes
a)  Peg Below the Free Market
Rate
b)  Peg Above the Free Market Rate

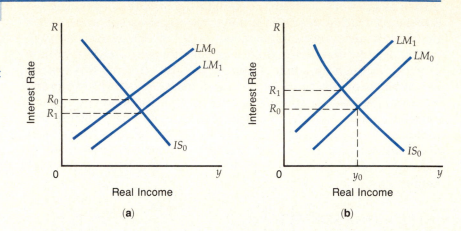

(a)                                                     (b)

inflation, so that new pressure for higher interest rates must be met
with still another monetary expansion. If this vicious circle continues
unchecked, the ultimate result is hyperinflation.

If the Fed attempts to peg interest rates above the free market
rate, we have the case illustrated by Figure 15.2(b). With a free market
interest rate $R_0$ determined by the initial curves $IS_0$ and $LM_0$, the Fed
must decrease the money supply so that the LM curve shifts left, like
the shift to $LM_1$, for a higher interest rate $R_1$ to exist. Such a fall in the
money supply will tend to lower prices. A lower expected rate of inflation would cause the interest rate to fall so that the Fed must lower
the money supply again to maintain $R_1$. Thus, the Fed now faces a
vicious circle of falling prices, falling interest rates, and a falling
money supply. It should be obvious that an attempt at pegging interest rates away from the free market rates can lead to a situation where
monetary policy feeds unacceptably high inflation or deflation.

It turns out that interest rates were pegged near equilibrium
until about the start of the Korean War. The peg established for long-
term government bonds was 2.5 percent per annum. Such a low
nominal interest rate (low by historical standards) was acceptable
because of widespread expectations of renewed worsened depression. With a negative expected inflation rate, 2.5 percent was an
attractive yield. When the Korean War began in June 1950, such low
inflation expectations were quickly eliminated. The pressure for rising interest rates led to the Fed purchasing securities and increasing
nominal base money at a higher rate. After a dramatic confrontation
with the Treasury and the President, the Fed's freedom to determine
monetary policy without regard to any bond price supports was announced in the Treasury–Federal Reserve Accord of March 1951.

Despite the accord, Fed policy up through the late 1960s continued to be formulated in terms of pegging the level of interest rates at

an unannounced and often changing level. The Fed judged its policy as stimulative or restrictive depending on whether the interest rate peg chosen was low or high by historical standards. Since policy is actually stimulative or restrictive depending on whether money growth is high or low, the interest rate pegging would give stimulative or restrictive money growth only if the nominal interest rate which would otherwise exist is unchanged when the Fed alters its desired pegged rate. For instance, if the initial rate of interest is 6 percent per annum, and then the Fed decides to peg interest rates at 4 percent, the lower peg will be attainable by increasing money growth. But if interest rates in the free market had fallen from 6 to 4 percent with a constant Fed policy, the new lower interest rate would be consistent with the old growth rate of money. In the former case, the lower interest rate is associated with a stimulative monetary policy, while in the latter case, the lower interest rate involves no change in monetary policy.

## MACROECONOMIC TRENDS AND CYCLES, 1947–62

During the stable money period of 1947–62, there was a constant trend growth rate of the nominal money supply of 1.9 percent per annum. While actual money growth fluctuated around this trend, it did not vary much. The average growth rate of nominal income was 6.0 percent per annum, so the average growth rate of the money–income ratio was −4.1 percent per annum.

The growth in nominal income was divided between an average inflation rate of 2.4 percent per annum and an average real income growth of 3.6 percent per annum. We may question the accuracy of these figures because of the Korean War price controls that likely overstated real income and understated price level growth in the early 1950s. Still we would expect real income to grow above the steady-state rate during the period following World War II. During the Great Depression, real income fell far below its steady-state growth path and was about 10 percent below it in 1941. Even though much of the capital stock purchased by the government during war time was converted to the production of private goods, real income in 1947 was still 13 percent below its steady-state level (assuming that the steady-state growth rate since 1929 equalled 3.1 percent per annum). This low level of output was due to low investment rates during the 1930s and World War II. Following the war, then, we would expect both physical and human capital resources to grow more rapidly than normal to catch up with their steady-state growth paths, so that real income must also grow more rapidly to catch up to the steady-state. By 1962, half of the percentage difference between real income and its steady-state growth path was eliminated.

The negative growth rate of the money–income ratio $K$ in the postwar period has concerned many macroeconomists. One cause of this fall in $K$ has no doubt been the introduction and steady growth of money substitutes such as savings and loan accounts, and more recently, money-market mutual funds. This effect is supported by the fact that $K$ has fallen more slowly for broader definitions of money, which include more of the potential "near-monies," than for narrowly defined M1. The upward trend in interest rates may also account for some of the decline in $K$. Figure 15.3 illustrates how $K$ has fallen over time as interest rates have risen. In the early 1980s, as interest rates fell, $K$ increased slightly.

---

**Figure 15.3**

The Money–Income Ratio and Interest Rates

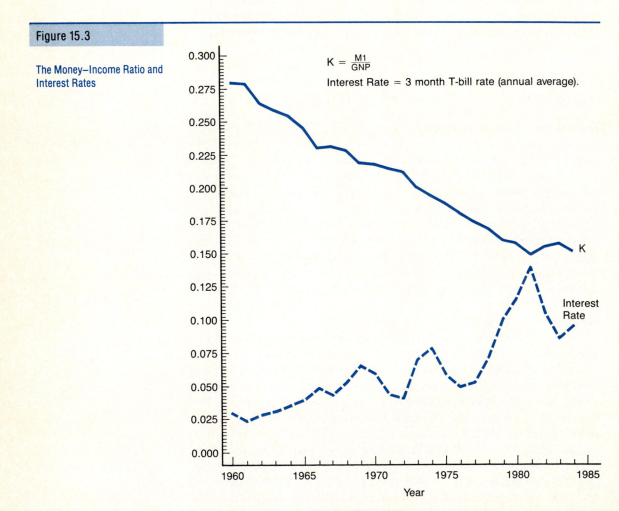

$$K = \frac{M1}{GNP}$$

Interest Rate = 3 month T-bill rate (annual average).

**Source:** *Economic Report of the President,* 1985.

Table 15.6

Business Cycles as Identified
by the NBER
1947–62

| Peak | November 1948 | 11-month contraction |
| Trough | October 1949 | 45-month expansion |
| Peak | July 1953 | 13-month contraction |
| Trough | August 1954 | 35-month expansion |
| Peak | July 1957 | 9-month contraction |
| Trough | April 1958 | 25-month expansion |
| Peak | May 1960 | 9-month contraction |
| Trough | February 1961 | |

The National Bureau of Economic Research (NBER) has identified four contractions between 1947 and 1962, as noted in Table 15.6. These are periods where real income growth turned negative. The immediate cause of the 1948–49 recession was a sharp decrease in the growth rate of the money supply. The Fed had been pegging interest rates on short-term government securities at very low levels since 1941. Maintaining these interest rates meant buying short-term Treasury bills with newly created base money. As the interest rate peg was raised to a more realistic level in 1947 and 1948, the Fed was able to stop buying Treasury bills. As a result, the growth rate of the money supply averaged −1.1 percent per annum compared to a 3.5 percent growth rate the previous year. At this same time, fiscal policy was stimulative through the third quarter of 1949, with rising federal expenditures and falling budget surpluses.

Unlike the Fed response to the recession of 1929–33, the growth of the nominal money supply did not continue to fall. Instead, the Fed lowered interest rates below the official pegged levels so that nominal money supply growth rose slightly to 0.0 percent in 1949. The normal return to the natural employment level of real income following the recession was sufficiently strong to overcome a restrictive fiscal policy that started in the third quarter of 1949 and continued until the start of the Korean War.

During the Korean War, interest rates rose due to increased government spending and a higher expected inflation rate. The average growth rate of the money supply was 4.5 percent per annum during 1950, 1951, and 1952. By the beginning of 1953, rising concern about inflation convinced the Fed to adopt a restrictive monetary policy. Raising the peg on long-term bonds allowed the Fed to follow a policy of reducing money supply growth to about 1.1 percent per annum during 1953. This was combined with a restrictive fiscal shock due to the large drop in defense spending at the end of the Korean War in the third quarter of 1953, and the recession of 1953–54 followed.

In early 1954, the growth rate of the nominal money supply increased to an average rate of 2.7 percent per annum for the year.

The combination of monetary stimulus and normal recovery from the recession made 1955 a boom year of rapid recovery. In fact, by mid-1955, the economy had apparently surpassed the natural employment level. Real income growth then slowed while the price level adjusted upward during 1956. This is the characteristic pattern presented in Chapter 12, where increased money growth is followed with a lag by increased real income growth, which is in turn followed by a more rapid rate of inflation.

The growth rate of the nominal money supply gradually decreased to 2.2 percent for 1955, 1.2 percent for 1956, and − 0.7 percent per annum for 1957. Real income growth started to slow in 1956, and the recession of 1957–58 began in July 1957.

In November 1957, the Fed reversed its policy of rising interest rates and lowered the interest pegs through April 1958. The resulting growth rate of the money supply from January 1958 to August 1959 was 4.1 percent per annum. As the economy began to recover from recession, the Fed moved the interest rate upward. Then a steel strike occurred in the summer of 1959. By itself, such a strike would have had only short-run effects in terms of reducing the demand for credit as inventories were drawn down. However, when combined with the suddenly higher interest rate peg, the strike-induced decline in borrowing led to a decline in money growth to a rate of − 1.7 percent per annum between July 1959 and June 1960. The recession beginning in May 1960 can be related to the unintended impact on the money supply of the previous year's steel strike.

Real income growth was quite rapid over the 1947–62 period.

Overall, throughout the period 1947–62, real income growth was very rapid by historical standards. The fluctuations in growth that occurred were due to a "stop–go" monetary policy caused by the Fed's reacting with a lag to the ill effects of its previous policy. The major fiscal policy shock of this period was the drop in real government spending associated with the end of the Korean War which contributed to the recession of 1953–54.

## THE RISE OF INFLATION, 1963–80

The 1963–80 period was one of increasing money growth and inflation.

As a whole, the period 1963–80 can be characterized as a period of increasing growth rates of the nominal money supply. While the average annual rate of money growth was 5.8 percent over the entire period, the rate increased from an annual average of 4.8 percent between 1963 and 1969, to 5.8 percent from 1969 to 1975, and finally 7.1 percent between 1975 and 1980.

The average growth rate of nominal income over the whole period was 8.7 percent per annum. This was divided between a 3.3 percent growth rate of real income and a 5.4 percent rate of inflation. Looking at the trends over time, Table 15.7 shows how the rate of

Table 15.7

Growth Rates of Nominal Income, Price Level, and Real Income 1967–80

|  | Nominal Income Growth $\hat{Y}$ | Price Level Growth $\hat{P}$ | Real Income Growth $\hat{y}$ |
|---|---|---|---|
| 1963–80 | 8.7% | 5.3% | 3.4% |
| 1963–69 | 7.6% | 3.2% | 4.5% |
| 1969–75 | 8.3% | 6.2% | 2.1% |
| 1975–80 | 10.6% | 7.0% | 3.6% |

inflation increased over the whole period, while real income growth fluctuated around the trend over the period of 3.4 percent per annum. By the end of 1965, real income had finally achieved the steady-state path of real income found by assuming a steady-state growth rate of 3.1 percent since 1929. It must be emphasized that a 3.1 percent per annum growth rate of real income is no more than a historical average used to estimate the underlying concept.

Before examining the period 1963–80 in more detail, we should be aware that the wage and price controls in existence from August 1971 through April 1974 distorted the reported data on output and prices. Cheating on the price controls probably resulted in a reported price index lower than the true price index. It has been estimated that the price index was reduced between 3 and 4.5 percent at the peak impact of the controls in late 1972.[14]

The recession of 1960–61 had contributed to the election of President John Kennedy. Kennedy's economic advisers were convinced that a tax reduction was needed to stimulate the economy. Since the Federal government ran a budget surplus in 1960, it was argued that fiscal policy was exerting a restrictive influence on the economy. President Kennedy's chief economic adviser, Walter Heller, argued that there was a **fiscal drag** operating which could be alleviated by a tax cut. The tax cut, which was proposed in 1962, was finally enacted in March 1964. The period of the mid-1960s is generally considered to be the highpoint of Keynesian economics in the United States. Keynesians had argued that a cut in taxes would stimulate aggregate demand and lower unemployment—this is in fact exactly what happened. As we shall soon see, the aggregate demand prescriptions of the Keynesians did not enjoy a long-lived popularity. The behavior of

**fiscal drag**
As income rises, tax rates rise so that income growth is lower than if tax rates had been constant

[14]See Michael R. Darby, "Price and Wage Controls: Further Evidence," in K. Brunner and A. Meltzer (eds.), *Carnegie–Rochester Conference Series*, vol. 2, (Amsterdam: North–Holland, 1976).

the economy often appears to conform to simple Keynesian models for brief episodes. Over time, experience reveals that the world we live in calls for a broader view of macroeconomics.

Real income grew very rapidly in the period 1963–69: 4.5 percent. The growth rate of the nominal money supply increased by 2 percentage points in 1963 and by another percentage point in 1964 and then grew at a constant rate in 1965. Throughout this 1963–66 period, nominal and real income grew very rapidly. Nominal money supply growth then stopped during the last half of 1966. The accelerating growth rate of nominal money had come about because the Fed pegged interest rates at a low level to stimulate the economy. As interest rates tended to rise, the Fed "leaned against the wind" by increasing the rate of nominal money creation. The accelerating inflation that resulted finally convinced the Fed that it must tighten. As a result, the nominal money supply was constant from June 1966 to January 1967. The first half of 1967 may be characterized as a "minirecession"—there was a downturn in real income, but it was not of long enough duration to qualify as an official contraction as classified by the NBER. The impact of the minirecession on the economy was trivial, but it did have a significant impact on economic thought.

Following the publication of Milton Friedman and Anna Schwartz's *Monetary History of the United States, 1867–1960*, there was considerable debate regarding the impact of monetary versus fiscal policy. Friedman and Schwartz presented a "monetarist" analysis that differed from the predictions of "fiscalists" like the Keynesians. The minirecession was not surprising to the monetarists due to the earlier drop in the growth rate of the money supply. Fiscalists predicted further rapid growth of real income because of the ongoing rapid increases in real government spending largely financed by borrowing. The 1964 tax cut was followed by a rapid growth in defense spending due to the Vietnam War. The large deficit led most fiscalists to expect rapid economic growth rather than recession. The evidence from the 1967 minirecession did much to popularize the views of the monetarists.

At the first evidence of falling industrial production, the Fed responded by increasing money growth. During 1967, the growth rate of the money supply rose to 7.7 percent per annum. The acceleration of money supply growth during 1967 and the first half of 1968 had caused monetarists to predict continued rapid growth of nominal income in the last half of 1968. The fiscalists predicted a slowdown or recession because of a very large tax increase passed in June 1968. President Johnson had been advised by his chief economic adviser, Gardner Ackley, to raise tax rates in 1966 to help fund the Vietnam War. Johnson delayed any tax increase, feeling that such a move would be damaging politically, until 1968. As a result of the tax increase, the President's Council of Economic Advisers forecast a

recession in mid-1968 for the next year. The tax increase, together
with the cessation of growth of real government spending, did in fact
stop the normal fall in the money–income ratio during the second
half of 1968, but this was not enough to outweigh the money supply
acceleration, so real income continued growing. Monetarist views
became more influential. Keynesians who had once argued that
money was unimportant for macroeconomic policymaking now began to develop a broader view of macroeconomics. It was also about
this time that the Fed, which had engineered the money supply acceleration because of fears of fiscal "overkill," began a slow process
of de–emphasizing interest rate pegs and introducing money supply
growth as the guide to open market operations.

Accelerating inflation was widely believed to have been an important issue in the Democratic loss of the Presidency in 1968. Beginning in January 1969, the Fed reduced the growth rate of the money
supply to 3.2 percent per annum. The fact that by 1969, a 3.2 percent
rate of money growth was considered restrictive, is indicative of the
acceleration of money growth that had continued since 1962. Fiscal
policy also was restrictive during 1969, and in November 1969, a
recession began. The recession of 1969–70 (the trough occurred in
November 1970) was widely viewed as further evidence of the importance of monetary policy. However, it seems that an important channel of influence was a sharp fall in the expected rate of inflation
caused by the Fed's willingness to reduce money supply growth and
cause a recession. Many borrowers and lenders believed—erro-
neously, it turns out—the claims by federal officials that monetary
restraint would be maintained until inflation was eliminated. This
change in inflation expectations lowered the rate of interest even
further than the normal cyclical fall. Short-term interest rates fell by
3 percentage points (from 7.82 to 4.87 percent per annum) during
1970. A decrease in expected inflation will shift investment demand
down as a function of the *nominal* interest rate.[15]

The major event of the early 1970s was the so-called Economic
Stabilization Program (ESP) announced by President Nixon on August 15, 1971. Although properly termed wage and price controls, the
ESP controls generally permitted prices to rise in proportion to costs
and only applied to some wages (by July 1972, the wages of 56 percent
of the labor force had been exempted from the controls). The wage
controls were effective only for union wages, so that the ESP turned
out to be little more than an antitrust program for unions. As the
normal loss of real income due to the monopoly power of unions is

---

[15]Section 7.6 explains the effects of such a downward shift in investment demand in an aggregate demand–aggregate supply
framework, where such a shift leads to decreases in spending.

generally estimated to be somewhat less than 1 percent of GNP, an increase of ½ percent of GNP is likely a high estimate of real income gains from ESP after allowance is made for the waste of misallocation in a few industries under special rules and for administrative costs. Nevertheless, reported real income in the first quarter of 1973 was about 4 percent higher than could be accounted for by applying Okun's law to the 0.9 percentage point decline in the unemployment rate from the second (pre-ESP) quarter of 1971. The likely explanation for this is that firms underreported their actual prices to give the appearance of complying with the price controls. About 1½ percentage points of this apparent understatement of the price level (and overstatement of real income) was worked off by the third quarter of 1973 under Phase III of the ESP. At this point, controls were reformulated to place a real constraint on prices as well as wages. The increasing economic dislocations quickly led business executives to join unionists in opposing the ESP. The controls were gradually removed beginning in January 1974, with final abolition in April 1974.

Because of the distorting effects of the price controls, the reported data in the early 1970s are suspect. We can estimate substitute real income figures by using Okun's law to relate real income to changes in unemployment. These estimates are used in Table 15.8 to present a division of the growth rate of nominal income into its real income and price level growth components. Table 15.8 presents the estimated alternative data next to the official data. The corrected real income data suggest a more even growth of real income than the reported data, while the corrected inflation data indicate a slower rise in the inflation rate.

**Table 15.8**

Growth Rates of Nominal Income Components, Both Reported and Corrected For Price Control Bias, 1971–74

| Year | Nominal Income Growth $\hat{Y}$ | Reported Real Income Growth $\hat{y}$ | Corrected Real Income Growth $\hat{y}$ | Reported Price Level Growth $\hat{P}$ | Corrected Price Level Growth $\hat{P}$ |
|---|---|---|---|---|---|
| 1971 | 9.1% | 4.5% | 4.4% | 4.6% | 4.7% |
| 1972 | 11.1% | 7.0% | 4.7% | 4.1% | 6.4% |
| 1973 | 10.6% | 3.3% | 4.6% | 7.2% | 6.0% |
| 1974 | 6.9% | −3.5% | −2.7% | 10.4% | 9.6% |

Source: Reported data from Department of Commerce. Corrected data from Michael R. Darby, "Wage and Price Controls: Further Evidence," in K. Brunner and A. Meltzer (eds.), *Carnegie–Rochester Conference Series*, vol. 2 (Amsterdam: North–Holland, 1976).

From December 1971 through June 1973, the Fed—apparently less concerned about inflation because of the ESP—accelerated money supply growth to an average rate of 8.0 percent per annum. At the same time, fiscal policy was expansionary as a result of both the expiration of the temporary tax surcharge imposed in 1968 and a further tax reduction bill signed in December 1971 that generated a larger federal government budget deficit. While inflation was being artificially controlled by the ESP, the rapid growth of money was creating strong inflationary pressures. This situation has been compared to holding an ice cube to a thermometer when the temperature is 100 degrees: while the thermometer records a cool temperature, everyone knows that in reality the heat is still present. The inflationary pressures from rapid growth of the money supply led to the breakdown of the ESP, and the Fed responded by cutting money supply growth to 4.6 percent per annum from June 1973 to December 1973, 6.0 percent per annum for the next six months, and 1.3 percent per annum from June 1974 to January 1975.[16] Thus, a recession would have been anticipated beginning about the second quarter of 1974 and then worsening through the year due to the near cessation of monetary growth in the last half of 1974.

Matters grew more complex because of the establishment of an oil cartel and a temporary embargo on Arab oil sales to the United States in late 1973. It appears that the oil embargo had about the same impact on the economy as a major strike. This impact is illustrated by the corrected real income data underlying Table 15.8. Compared to the fourth quarter of 1973, real income was about 0.7 percent lower in the first quarter of 1974, but 0.1 percent higher in the second quarter. Since this second-quarter growth rate is below the steady-state rate, it appears that some residual effects of the oil cartel were still being felt at the same time that the recession induced by lower money growth was beginning. The official data show a 1.5 percent fall in real income from the fourth quarter of 1973 to the second quarter of 1974. This partly reflects the ending of the ESP and overstatement of real income. Even so, real income growth was practically

---

[16]The erratic money growth rate in 1974 occurred because the Fed's operating instructions were aimed at a peg for the federal funds market interest rate (a market for short-term interbank lending). The peg was originally set to achieve a particular growth rate of the money supply. However, after several large bank failures, the risk associated with federal funds lending caused an increase in the federal funds interest rate from December 1973 to July 1974. As the interest rate increased, nominal money supply growth increased in order to maintain the interest rate peg. From July 1974 to January 1975, the interest rate fell and led to a decrease in money supply growth.

nil, mainly because of the oil embargo and cartel. The remainder of 1974 corresponds to the classical pattern of a monetary contraction.

It should be realized that there was a lack of agreement regarding the causes of the recession in 1974. While events are consistent with the monetarists view that the recession was caused by a drop in money growth, Keynesians saw the recession as a result of the increase in oil prices. Since the recession was associated with high inflation, many economists saw the 1974 recession as an indicator of the failure of Keynesian theory and its emphasis on the demand side of the market. Figure 15.4 shows that there is no way to shift the aggregate demand curve with a constant aggregate supply to generate both falling income and rising prices. If aggregate demand increases from $AD_0$ to $AD_1$, price increases from $P_0$ to $P_1$ and real income increases from $y_0$ to $y_1$. There is no way to shift aggregate demand without the price and income effects moving in the same direction. Those who did not subscribe to the monetarist view of the causes of the recession pointed to the oil price increases as a supply shock. A decrease in aggregate supply will lower output and raise the price level as illustrated in Figure 15.5. Since oil is an important input in the production of many goods and services, a rise in its price will shift the aggregate supply curve to the left, as in the move from $AS_0$ to $AS_1$ in Figure 15.5. At the new equilibrium, there is a higher price level $P_1$ and lower real income $y_1$. Such an aggregate supply shift could explain an "inflationary recession" as was experienced in 1974.

Following the 1974 recession, real income grew rapidly until the end of the decade. The period from 1975 to 1979 can be characterized as one of convergence to the steady-state equilibrium path of real income. However, this period can also be characterized as a time of rising inflation. The decrease in money growth responsible for the 1974 recession was also responsible for moderating inflation rates.

**Figure 15.4**

Aggregate Demand, Prices, and Income

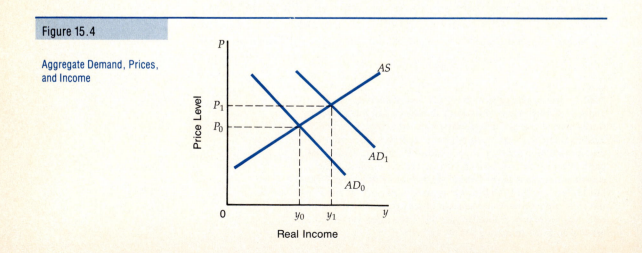

Figure 15.5

The Effects of Higher World Oil Prices on Aggregate Supply

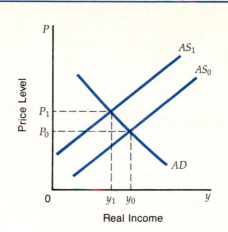

The rate of inflation fell to 4.6 percent in 1976, before rising steadily after that due to an increasing rate of money growth from 1975 on. By 1980 the inflation rate had reached 10.2 percent—a rate that was considered politically unacceptable.

## CONTROLLING INFLATION, 1980–84

With inflation the clearly identified enemy of the early 1980s, it should not be surprising that real output growth was very weak during this period. In fact, there were two successive recessions, in 1980 and 1981–82. Several factors have been identified as potential causes of the brief recession in the spring of 1980. First there was a decrease in money growth. But to complicate matters, in March 1980 the Fed imposed credit controls that restricted the availability of certain forms of credit.[17] In addition, world oil prices doubled in 1979–80, depressing real income.

The early 1980s were characterized by a falling inflation rate.

---

[17]President Carter's anti–inflation program, announced on March 14, 1980, included the application by the Fed of special restraints on credit growth. These restraints involved reserve requirements and special deposit requirements on some types of consumer credit, an interest surcharge on banks that borrowed frequently from the Fed, a special deposit requirement on money market funds, and a voluntary restraint program for the growth of commercial bank loans. The effects of such credit controls are considered in Brian A. Maris, "Indirect Evidence on the Efficacy of Selective Credit Controls: The Case of Consumer Credit," *Journal of Money, Credit, and Banking,* August 1981, 388–390, and in Lazaros E. Molho, "On Testing the Efficacy of Selective Credit Controls," *Journal of Money, Credit, and Banking,* February 1983, 120–22.

While there is some problem in identifying the individual contributions of the factors leading to the short recession of 1980, it is likely that restrictive monetary policy halted the recovery that began in mid-1980. While the money stock grew at a 7.4 percent rate in 1979 and a 7.2 percent rate in 1980, the rate of growth fell to 5.1 percent in 1981. One result of this downward shift in money growth following the 10.2 percent inflation rate of 1980 was the establishment of record-high nominal interest rates. Table 15.9 lists the interest rate on United States Treasury bills over the period 1976–84. To illustrate the pattern of change during the 1980–82 period, the average rate for the first month of each quarter is given. Table 15.9 also includes the rate of inflation over each year. As the inflation rate rose over the late 1970s, interest rates rose to accommodate higher expected rates of inflation. The decreases in money growth that brought on the recessions of 1980 and 1981–82 would be expected to have temporary effects of raising interest rates before rates seek a new level consistent with new inflation expectations. Here, in fact, is one of the striking features of the period: even though inflation rates fell dramatically through 1982, the nominal rate of interest remained very high so that real interest rates seemed to be at rates never before experienced.

**Table 15.9**

Interest Rates and Inflation Rates, 1976–84

| Period | Nominal Interest Rate* | Inflation Rate† |
|---|---|---|
| 1976 | 5.0% | 5.2% |
| 1977 | 5.3% | 5.8% |
| 1978 | 7.2% | 7.4% |
| 1979 | 10.0% | 8.6% |
| Jan. 1980 | 12.0% | |
| Apr. 1980 | 14.0% | 10.2% |
| Jul. 1980 | 8.1% | |
| Oct. 1980 | 11.6% | |
| Jan. 1981 | 14.7% | |
| Apr. 1981 | 13.6% | 8.9% |
| Jul. 1981 | 14.7% | |
| Oct. 1981 | 13.9% | |
| Jan. 1982 | 12.4% | |
| Apr. 1982 | 12.8% | 4.3% |
| Jul. 1982 | 11.9% | |
| Oct. 1982 | 7.8% | |
| 1983 | 8.6% | 3.8% |
| 1984 | 9.6% | 3.6% |

*Rate on 3-month Treasury bills.
†Annual percentage change in the implicit GNP deflator.

Can we be sure that the recession of 1981–82 was caused by falling money growth? Since the federal budget deficit was very large ($57.9 billion) in 1981 and much larger still in 1982 ($110.6 billion), fiscal policy could hardly be termed restrictive. Furthermore, one of the hypothesized culprits behind the 1980 recession—oil prices— could not explain the contraction of 1981–82, because real oil prices were falling throughout the period.

We learned in Chapter 12 that there would be a cyclical adjustment to a restrictive monetary shock. The **disinflation** policy of the early 1980s was essentially a policy of slowing the growth of the nominal money supply. We would expect that when money growth is slower than expected, real output will fall and unemployment will rise as part of the early adjustment to the negative money shock. After the adjustment is complete, the unemployment rate will return to the natural rate consistent with the return to the steady-state rate of real income growth. If, in the long run, the growth of real income is independent of both the inflation rate and growth rate of the money supply (i.e., money is superneutral), are there any costs of disinflation—the process of lowering the inflation rate? The costs are sustained in the early part of the adjustment process when real income and unemployment rise.

What were the costs associated with the disinflation of the early 1980s? First we must realize that there was a very rapid process of disinflation. Table 15.10 presents data on inflation as measured by the consumer price index (CPI) along with data on the cost of such disinflation, like the higher unemployment rate and lower real income growth. Notice that in terms of the CPI, the inflation rate was cut in half from 1981 to 1982. After 5 years of rising inflation rates through 1979, there was a moderate reduction in 1980, a sizeable reduction in 1981, and a very dramatic reduction in 1982. By 1983, the

disinflation
Extended falling inflation rates

Disinflation was accompanied by rising unemployment.

| Table 15.10 |
| --- |

Inflation, Unemployment Rates, and Real Income Growth 1979–84

| Year | Inflation Rate* | Unemployment Rate† | Real Income Growth‡ |
| --- | --- | --- | --- |
| 1979 | 12.8% | 6.0% | 1.4% |
| 1980 | 12.5% | 7.3% | −0.8% |
| 1981 | 9.6% | 8.8% | 1.6% |
| 1982 | 4.4% | 10.8% | −1.5% |
| 1983 | 3.3% | 8.2% | 6.3% |
| 1984 | 4.1% | 7.2% | 5.7% |

*4th-quarter to 4th-quarter change in the CPI.
†December figure.
‡4th-quarter to 4th-quarter change in real GNP.

rate of inflation was at its lowest level in a decade. The change from 12.5 percent in 1980 to 4.4 percent in 1982 was not achieved without incurring short–run costs. As the rate of inflation slowed, the unemployment rate started to climb, reaching a peak of 10.8 percent of the civilian labor force in December 1982. Looking beyond 1982, we can see that the beneficial part of the adjustment process begins to be realized—a period of falling inflation alongside falling unemployment rates. In fact, the recovery from the 1981–82 recession was quite rapid. There has not been a drop in the unemployment rate comparable to the drop from the December 1982 high since the early 1960s.

The pronounced drop in the unemployment rate during 1983 is likely to be due to more than just the strength of the recovery. From December 1982 to November 1983, the civilian labor force grew at a slower rate than during any of the previous seven recovery periods. It appears that the drop in unemployment was not only a result of the recovery increasing employment, but was also hastened by a slowdown in the number of individuals seeking employment. These latter changes may be attributed to the end of the entry into the labor force of the baby-boom generation.

The fact that disinflation policies are not costless is consistent with the dynamic view of the economy presented in earlier chapters. Reducing inflation involves a short-run adjustment period of rising unemployment and falling output, during which the rate of inflation is only moderated slightly. Eventually, as the inflation rate falls to and temporarily below the new steady state consistent with the new money growth rate, the unemployment rate falls and real output rises back to the natural or steady-state paths. This later stage of the adjustment process was consistent with events in the United States in 1983–84.

In 1985, the Fed started a very active policy of increasing the money supply to fight off economic sluggishness. This policy also was targeted to drive down interest rates to lower the desirability to foreigners of investing in this country; this policy lowered the value of the dollar in order to stimulate exports and production. Many predicted 1986 would see higher inflation.

## 15.4 HISTORICAL OVERVIEW

### MONETARY POLICY

The history of monetary policy since the Federal Reserve System was created is one of stop-and-go money growth policies as the monetary authorities attempt to conduct policy aimed at stabilizing the business cycle. It is important to realize that many mistakes have been made—our review of the Great Depression in Section 15.2 reviews the most disastrous episode in Federal Reserve history. Yet economists generally believe that the Fed Governors have operated in the manner that they thought best for the nation. In other words, while mistakes have been made, the policies were formulated with the best of intentions.

It is easy today to study the monetary policy followed in the 1930s or even the 1970s and point out ways that the Fed has been destabilizing rather than stabilizing. It is, of course, quite another matter to formulate policy today to achieve the optimal macroeconomic performance in the future. As a result of the long and variable lag in the effect of monetary policy on the economy, some economists like Milton Friedman have argued that an activist monetary policy, even though well intentioned, will not reduce the variability of the macroeconomy. So the prescription is one of stable money growth at some fixed growth rate.

Once past the Great Depression and World War II, U.S. monetary policy was largely aimed at pegging interest rates at levels that changed according to the Fed's view of business conditions. Overall, from the end of World War II until the mid-1960s, the rate of money growth was fairly stable and low. From the mid-1960s until 1980, there was an upward trend in the money growth rate along with rising inflation.

From 1979 to 1982 the Fed changed its operating procedure so that interest rate pegging was de-emphasized and targets would instead be set for the rate of money growth. The period from 1981–84 was one of disinflation, as the rate of money growth was low relative to the previous decade.

## FISCAL POLICY

Not surprisingly, the most notable fiscal policy episode of the past 50 years has been related to war. The end of the Great Depression coincides with the massive increase in government spending and deficits needed to finance World War II. The real federal deficit during World War II hit a peak at more than five times the largest deficit of the Depression era.

Moving beyond the expansionary fiscal policy of World War II, the next important fiscal policy effects were also related to war. The Korean War generated a rapid increase in spending in the 1950–53 period. At the conclusion of the war in 1953, government spending dropped dramatically so that large federal budget surpluses were realized in the mid-1950s.

From the point of view of the policymaker, the federal tax cut of 1964 appeared to be a landmark since it stimulated economic growth and provided a false sense that the influential Keynesian economic advisers knew how to "fine-tune" the economy. Such confidence was steadily eroded as fiscal policy came in conflict with monetary policy in a couple of well-publicized episodes that proved the Keynesian forecasters wrong. For instance, a tax increase in 1968 led economists trained in the Keynesian tradition to expect a recession. But at the same time there was an expansionary monetary policy that appeared to dominate the fiscal policy. This is an important episode in that it caused many fiscalists to question their view of macroeconomics and broadened the appeal of monetarism.

The last two decades have provided several interesting special cases for economists to examine, only one of which is a result of U.S. government action: the wage and price controls imposed by President Nixon in 1971. It appears now that the major effect of the controls was to underreport the true rate of inflation and overstate the growth of real income in the early 1970s. The second special case is the large jump in oil prices occurring in 1973–74. The effect of rising international oil prices is to lower real output, although economists disagree on the magnitude of the real output effect.

As we move into the 1980s, the major fiscal policy issue of the early to mid-1980s is the size of the federal deficit. The end-of-chapter essay will address the question: do government deficits matter? For now, let's consider how the role of the United States government has changed through the years.

Many of the government expenditures with which we are most familiar are relatively new when viewed in the sweep of more than 200 years of United States government operation. Social Security did not exist prior to 1935. Food stamps were first made available in 1964. Many people today do not realize that private charity once cared for most of the low-income people now covered by government welfare spending. Over time, the federal government has broadened its role in the economic lives of Americans. As has become most apparent by the huge budget deficits of the 1980s, this growing role for government does not come cheaply. Not only are new programs enacted through time, but existing programs are "indexed" to the rate of inflation in order to protect beneficiaries from a loss of purchasing power. Table 15.11 lists the federal government programs that are indexed. Why do most of the programs first include cost-of-living adjustments in the 1970s? Prior to the 1970s, the United States enjoyed relatively stable prices. For instance, while in existence since 1935, Social Security benefits were not indexed until 1975.

Indexing is important because it builds a minimum increase in government spending into every year's budget. While most citizens believe that there should be some minimum level of support for those who can not take care of themselves, there is some threshold beyond

Table 15.11

Major Federal Programs Indexed for Inflation

| Program | Year Enacted | First Indexed in | Share of 1983 Budget |
|---|---|---|---|
| Social Security | 1935 | 1975 | 21.4% |
| Federal Employee Compensation | 1916 | 1977 | 13.5% |
| Civil Service Retirement and Disability | 1920 | 1965 | 2.6% |
| Military Retirement | * | 1964 | 2.0% |
| Food Stamps | 1964 | 1971 | 1.5% |
| Supplemental Security Income | 1972 | 1975 | 1.1% |
| Railroad Retirement | 1936 | 1975 | 0.5% |
| Veterans' Pensions | * | 1979 | 0.5% |
| Child Food Care | 1968 | 1975 | 0.4% |
| School Lunch | 1946 | 1973 | 0.3% |
| Coal Miners' Benefits | 1969 | 1969 | 0.2% |

which taxpayers become extremely averse to further government spending increases. The debate surrounding the large government budget deficits of the 1980s suggests that many taxpayers feel a restraint on government spending is in order. We will consider the importance of government budget deficits in the end-of-chapter essay. The point here is simply that fiscal policy has built-in rigidities in the form of popular programs with guaranteed cost-of-living raises that severely limit the discretionary powers of the policymaker.

## SUMMARY

**1** The trend growth rate of quality-adjusted output per hour has been quite constant over the 1900–83 period.

**2** The period prior to the Great Depression was similar to the 1950s—nominal money growth fluctuations were large enough to cause recessions, but not so large as to cause any continuing problems.

**3** The Great Depression began with a restrictive monetary policy in 1928 aimed at reducing the ''speculative fever'' perceived by the Fed.

**4** After November of 1930, what was a recession turned into a depression after the drop in the money multiplier, caused by banking panics, lowered money supply growth substantially.

**5** To restore confidence in the banking system, a banking holiday was declared in March 1933, followed by a government certification that banks allowed to reopen were sound.

**6** During much of the postwar era, monetary policy was established by the Federal Reserve pegging interest rates.

**7** The period 1947–62 was characterized by relatively stable money growth and moderate inflation rates. The fluctuations in growth that occurred were due to a "stop–go" monetary policy caused by the Fed's reacting with a lag to the ill effects of previous policy.

**8** The period 1963–80 can be characterized as a period of increasing money supply growth and increasing inflation.

**9** The disinflation policies of the early 1980s led to recessions in 1980 and 1981–82.

## EXERCISES

1. During the Great Depression, Fed officials claimed that the depression could not be blamed on them because the fall in the money supply was simply a response to falling money demand due to falling income. Indeed, they claimed that monetary policy was easy because interest rates on Treasury securities were low and money was a larger fraction of income. What is wrong with this argument?

2. How can a bank go bankrupt during a banking panic and then still have enough assets to pay off all depositors with something left over for the stockholders?

3. If the Fed tried to maintain a low interest rate peg with rapid base money creation, what would rising inflation expectations mean for future base money creation?

4. When analyzing changes in productivity as measured by output per hour of labor, why is it important to adjust hours worked for changes in the quality of labor?

5. How do banking panics lead to a decrease in the money supply?

6. After considering the historical evidence on the effects of monetary policy on the economy, what sort of monetary policy would you advise if you were in charge of the Federal Reserve Board (Chapter 14 reviewed the popular alternatives)?

## REFERENCES FOR FURTHER READING

Brunner, Karl, ed. *The Great Depression Revisited.* Boston: Martinus Nijhoff, 1981.

Coats, Warren L., Jr. "Recent Monetary Policy Strategies in the United States." *Kredit and Kapital*, October 1981.

Friedman, Milton, and Anna Jacobson Schwartz. *A Monetary History of the United States, 1867–1960.* Princeton: Princeton University Press for the NBER, 1963.

Raiff, Donald L. "Slowdowns and Recessions: What's Been Government's Role?" *Federal Reserve Bank of Philadelphia Business Review*, October 1975.

# DO GOVERNMENT BUDGET DEFICITS MATTER?

If government spending exceeds tax revenues, should we be concerned? In the early 1980s, economists spent a great deal of time trying to analyze the effects of government budget deficits. This is not because deficits are something new. To the contrary, deficit spending has been a regular feature of the U.S. experience for over two decades. The last measured budget surplus occurred in 1969. The macroeconomic importance of deficits has long been a topic of interest and study, but such interest took on new dimensions in the early 1980s due to a fundamental change—beginning in 1982, the United States began a series of deficits of unprecedented proportions. Table E15.1 underscores the magnitude of these new deficits relative to past experience.

In traditional Keynesian analysis, budget deficits, whether caused by higher $g$ or lower $t$, stimulate the economy; the very large deficits of 1982–83 may have contributed to a strong recovery from the 1981–82 recession. So where is the cost or harmful impact of a large deficit? First we must realize that we are in uncharted territory, as there has been no past peacetime experience with deficits of the magnitude at hand, so no one can claim to know for sure what the effect of these deficits will be. However, one popular belief is that large budget deficits will slow the growth of the nation's capital stock. This hypothesis is seen quite clearly by

Table E15.1

Federal Budget Surpluses or Deficits ( − ) 1947–84

| Fiscal Year | Budget Deficit | Fiscal Year | Budget Deficit |
|---|---|---|---|
| 1947 | $3.9 billion | 1966 | −3.8 |
| 1948 | 12.0 | 1967 | −8.7 |
| 1949 | .6 | 1968 | −25.2 |
| 1950 | −3.1 | 1969 | 3.2 |
| 1951 | 6.1 | 1970 | −2.8 |
| 1952 | −1.5 | 1971 | −23.0 |
| 1953 | −6.5 | 1972 | −23.4 |
| 1954 | −1.2 | 1973 | −14.8 |
| 1955 | −3.0 | 1974 | −4.7 |
| 1956 | 4.1 | 1975 | −45.2 |
| 1957 | 3.2 | 1976 | −66.4 |
| 1958 | −2.9 | 1977 | −44.9 |
| 1959 | −12.9 | 1978 | −48.8 |
| 1960 | .3 | 1979 | −27.7 |
| 1961 | −3.4 | 1980 | −59.6 |
| 1962 | −7.1 | 1981 | −57.9 |
| 1963 | −4.8 | 1982 | −110.6 |
| 1964 | −5.9 | 1983 | −195.4 |
| 1965 | −1.6 | 1984 | −175.4 |

referring to the national-income-accounts (NIA) identity relating investment to saving:

$$I = S - (G - T) - X$$

This says that investment is equal to private saving less the deficit and net exports. A higher government deficit competes with private sector borrowing, so that interest rates rise to ration out the funds not borrowed by the government. This is the way in which private investment is crowded out by the deficit as originally covered in Section 13.2. According to the Council of Economic Advisors, "The magnitude of the potential crowding out of private investment is immense. During the past two decades, the net saving of households and businesses totaled only about 7 percent of GNP. Prospective deficits of more than 6 percent of GNP would represent virtually all of current net saving. Even though existing saving would be augmented by borrowing from abroad and by some increase in the private saving rate, the reduced rate of capital formation would be very substantial."[1]

If, in fact, the large deficits do retard capital growth, then future output and real wages would be lower than otherwise as a result. This effect could be avoided in two ways: (1) Net exports X measures net American investment abroad or, if it is negative, net foreign investment in the United States. If X decreased by the amount of the increase in the government deficit, then investment and future output would not be affected. However, American earnings from abroad would decline and we might even have to pay a substantial portion of output to foreign investors. (2) Private saving could increase by enough to finance the increased deficits without any reduction in investment.

A number of economists believe that the second possibility, increased private saving, is likely to occur in sufficient magnitude to offset any substantial effect on investment. One reason why this might occur is that the NIA government deficit and private saving measures are not properly adjusted for inflation. Specifically, the entire nominal payment on the national debt is included in the deficit and private saving. But part of this payment merely compensates for the decline in the real value of the government bonds. If we are concerned with command over real goods and services, this amount is not a real cost to the government nor real income and saving for the public.[2] This line of reasoning shows that to obtain the real deficit we cannot simply deflate the NIA deficit by the GNP deflator. A measure of the real deficit would be the increase over the year in the real (deflated) value of government debt outstanding. Table E15.2 presents this measure with signs reversed to conform to the convention

---

[1]*Economic Report of the President*, 1983, p. 27.

| | Real Debt at End of Year | | Decrease from Prior Year | |
|---|---|---|---|---|
| Year | 1972 $ Billions | % of GNP | 1972 $ Billions | % of GNP |
| 1945 | 661.3 | 117.8 | − 93.0 | − 16.6 |
| 1946 | 521.1 | 108.7 | 140.2 | 29.3 |
| 1947 | 445.9 | 94.6 | 75.2 | 16.0 |
| 1948 | 405.3 | 82.6 | 40.6 | 8.3 |
| 1949 | 410.0 | 83.8 | − 7.8 | − 1.6 |
| 1950 | 404.5 | 75.4 | 8.6 | 1.6 |
| 1951 | 383.7 | 66.1 | 20.8 | 3.5 |
| 1952 | 386.6 | 64.2 | − 2.6 | − 0.4 |
| 1953 | 388.9 | 62.2 | − 2.6 | − 0.4 |
| 1954 | 386.6 | 62.6 | 2.2 | 0.4 |
| 1955 | 379.1 | 57.5 | 7.5 | 1.1 |
| 1956 | 358.6 | 53.3 | 20.6 | 3.1 |
| 1957 | 346.0 | 50.5 | 12.6 | 1.8 |
| 1958 | 353.4 | 51.8 | − 7.4 | − 1.1 |
| 1959 | 358.5 | 49.6 | − 5.2 | − 0.7 |
| 1960 | 350.5 | 47.4 | 8.1 | 1.1 |
| 1961 | 357.1 | 47.1 | − 6.6 | − 0.9 |
| 1962 | 360.1 | 44.9 | − 3.0 | − 0.4 |
| 1963 | 360.6 | 43.2 | − 0.4 | 0.0 |
| 1964 | 364.0 | 41.5 | − 3.5 | − 0.4 |
| 1965 | 359.1 | 38.6 | 4.9 | 0.5 |
| 1966 | 356.6 | 36.1 | 2.5 | 0.3 |
| 1967 | 365.3 | 36.0 | − 8.6 | − 0.9 |
| 1968 | 356.6 | 33.6 | 8.7 | 0.9 |
| 1969 | 335.9 | 30.8 | 20.6 | 1.9 |
| 1970 | 328.8 | 30.2 | 7.1 | 0.7 |
| 1971 | 339.1 | 30.1 | − 10.3 | − 0.9 |
| 1972 | 340.7 | 28.7 | − 1.6 | − 0.1 |
| 1973 | 329.5 | 26.2 | 11.1 | 0.9 |
| 1974 | 313.2 | 25.1 | 16.4 | 1.3 |
| 1975 | 354.7 | 28.7 | − 41.5 | − 3.4 |
| 1976 | 390.3 | 30.0 | − 35.6 | − 2.7 |
| 1977 | 406.9 | 29.7 | − 16.7 | − 1.2 |
| 1978 | 412.6 | 28.6 | − 5.6 | − 0.4 |
| 1979 | 406.2 | 27.4 | 6.4 | 0.4 |
| 1980 | 415.0 | 28.2 | − 9.8 | − 0.7 |
| 1981 | 424.7 | 28.1 | − 9.7 | − 0.6 |
| 1982 | 478.9 | 32.2 | − 54.2 | − 3.6 |
| 1983 | 541.6 | 35.3 | − 62.7 | − 4.1 |

Data courtesy of Brian Horrigan, Federal Reserve Bank of Philadelphia. Real debt is interest-bearing federal debt issued by the Treasury or a wholly owned federal agency, exclusive of that part held by the Treasury or an agency; the Federal Reserve System is treated as part of the public for this measure.

that surpluses are positive and deficits negative. We see in the table that the real debt has been generally declining since the end of World War II and that recent deficits are not so exceptional.[3]

A second reason for optimism about the effects of deficits is the view that rational consumers can and will undo the effects of government borrowing. This "Ricardian equivalence" view argues that for society as a whole, it makes no difference whether the government issues tax receipts or bonds to finance given government expenditures. Only if people consume more when they receive bonds instead of tax receipts will investment be affected. (If consumer spending is unchanged, $S$ rises by the same amount as $G - T$ when a tax cut is financed by borrowing.) Rational consumers will not increase their spending, it is argued, because that would result in lower future private income.[4]

In opposition to these optimistic views, a number of economists have attributed high real interest rates during 1982 and 1983 to the large deficits. Why do deficits lead to high interest rates? First, there is the Keynes-

---

[2]The details and issues of correcting the NIA for the increase in nominal debt required to keep the real debt constant are discussed in Jeremy J. Siegel, "Inflation-Induced Distortions in Government and Private Saving Statistics," *Review of Economics and Statistics*, 61 (February 1979), 83–90; Gregory V. Jump, "Interest Rates, Inflation Expectations, and Spurious Elements in Measured Real Income and Saving," *American Economic Review*, 70 (December 1980), 990–1004; Phillip Cagan, "The Real Federal Deficit and Financial Markets," *The AEI Economist*, November 1981, pp. 1–16; and Michael R. Darby and James R. Lothian, "British Economic Policy Under Margaret Thatcher: A Midterm Examination," *Carnegie-Rochester Conference Series on Public Policy*, 18 (Spring 1983), 157–207.

[3]Robert J. Barro argues that recent deficits are in fact about what would be expected from the American experience since the 1920s and recent levels of inflation and the unemployment rate (as an indicator of the cyclical portion of the deficit). See his "U.S. Deficits since World War I, *Scandanavian Journal of Economics*, in press 1985; and also his "A Deficit Nearly on Target," *Wall Street Journal*, January 19, 1985. There are other problems with the NIA measure of the deficit. For example, it does not include such items as increases in the unfunded liabilities of the social security system, which may dwarf even the recent nominal deficit figures.

[4]See the evidence for this view cited in footnote 2 to Chapter 13.

ian impact of government borrowing competing with private borrowing and thereby putting upward pressure on interest rates. Yet there is perhaps an inflation expectations effect as well. If the financial market participants believe that the Fed will create base money to help finance the deficit, or attempt to peg interest rates at lower levels, then current interest rates may be high even though the current inflation rate is low. The current nominal interest rates simply include a high inflation expectations effect. Steven Holland has shown that *after-tax* real interest rates were about the same before 1971 as since 1980;[5] so it may be that economists should concentrate on explaining why these rates were so low during the 1971–80 period of inflation.

Considering the evidence of recent years, it does not appear that the recent U.S. deficits have had any significant effect in terms of crowding out private investment. As Figure E15.1 illustrates, investment has increased substantially in the early 1980s. In fact, nonresidential fixed investment set a postwar record by growing at a 16.8 percent annual rate during the first 6 quarters of real economic growth following the 1981–82 recession.

---

[5]See A. Steven Holland, "Real Interest Rates: What Accounts for Their Recent Rise?," *Federal Reserve Bank of St. Louis Review*, December 1984, 18–29.

**Figure E15.1**

**U.S. Investment Spending**

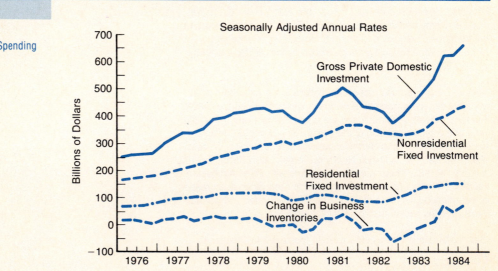

Seasonally Adjusted Annual Rates

**Source:** Department of Commerce, Council of Economic Advisers

The major effect of the deficit appears to have fallen on the international sector, specifically the U.S. balance of trade. We will delay our discussion of these effects until the next chapter, when the importance of the rest of the world is covered in detail.

In summary, it does appear that government budget deficits can have real effects, if not on the steady-state growth rate of real output, then at least on its level. The recent U.S. budget deficits do not appear to have crowded out private investment. If such crowding out did occur, however, the bulk of the adjustment cost to the deficit could fall on industries that are closely related to capital investment expenditures, like the steel and machinery industries, and other industries that produce durable goods.

# CHAPTER SIXTEEN

# MACROECONOMICS AND THE OPEN ECONOMY

## 16.1 MONEY IN INTERNATIONAL TRADE

So far, this text has considered only one international factor—net exports as an element of aggregate demand. While we have not assumed that the domestic economy was a *closed economy*—one that does not transact with the rest of the world—we have overlooked some interesting and important linkages that exist between *open economies* (those that have international transactions). The act of international trade in goods and services gives rise to international financial flows of securities and money.

### FOREIGN EXCHANGE AND EXCHANGE RATES

**foreign exchange**
Foreign-currency denominated bank deposits and actual foreign currency

A foreign exchange rate is the price of one money in terms of another.

Since Mexicans use pesos, Japanese use yen, and U.S. residents use dollars, international trade requires that domestic money be exchanged for foreign money. **Foreign exchange** is foreign-currency denominated bank deposits and actual foreign currency. The foreign exchange market refers to the trading of foreign-currency denominated deposits by large commercial banks. The price of one currency in terms of another is the foreign *exchange rate* between the two currencies. For instance, if the U.S. dollar price of British pounds is $1.10, then we say that the dollar–pound exchange rate is 1.10.

Just as with other prices, exchange rates are set by supply and demand. However, we will see in Section 16.3 that this is not just the free market supply and demand, as central banks and governments also buy and sell currencies, sometimes with a view toward establishing an exchange rate peg.

If a U.S. firm makes a purchase of a machine from a British manufacturer for £100,000, how many dollars will this cost? It depends upon the current exchange rate. This rate, known as the **spot exchange rate**, will indicate how much 1 pound will cost, so by multiplying times 100,000 we find the dollar value of £100,000. Suppose the spot rate equals 1.10; then £100,000 = $110,000, so the machine will sell for $110,000. Note that as exchange rates change, the domestic currency price of foreign goods change. If the dollar *appreciated* on the foreign exchange market, then the dollar would be worth more in terms of other currencies. If the dollar-pound rate went to 1.05, then £100,000 = $105,000, and the price of the British machine to the U.S. importer falls by $5,000. So an appreciation of the domestic currency will make foreign goods cheaper to domestic residents. But from the foreign point of view, domestic goods are now more expensive to foreign buyers as the dollar appreciation makes dollars more expensive to foreigners.

If the dollar *depreciates* relative to the pound, say the dollar-pound rate rises to 1.20, then the dollar is worth less in terms of pounds or (the same thing) the pound is worth more in terms of dollars. Now the British machine selling for £100,000 will require a dollar equivalent of $120,000. Therefore, as the domestic currency depreciates, foreign goods become more expensive to domestic residents while domestic goods become cheaper to foreigners. In Section 16.3 we will consider how exchange rate fluctuations affect the pattern of international trade. Figure 16.1 illustrates how the value of the dollar has changed over time relative to several major currencies.

What if the U.S. firm doesn't have to pay for the machine now, but instead has 90 days until payment is due? The firm could wait 90 days and then purchase the £100,000 at the then prevailing spot rate. The problem with this strategy is that the exchange rate could change in an unexpected manner. If there is an unexpected appreciation of the dollar, then pounds will be cheaper in 90 days and the firm will pay fewer dollars to buy the machine than originally expected. But an unexpected dollar depreciation would lead to a rise in the number of dollars required to buy the machine. To avoid this uncertainty with regard to the future spot exchange rate, the firm could arrange now to buy pounds for delivery in 90 days in the *forward exchange market*. The price established now for delivery of a currency at some time in the future is the **forward exchange rate**. For instance, the firm might

**spot exchange rate**
The foreign exchange rate of a currency for immediate delivery

**forward exchange rate**
The price established now for delivery of a currency at some time in the future

Figure 16.1

The Foreign Exchange Value of the Dollar Against Selected Foreign Currencies

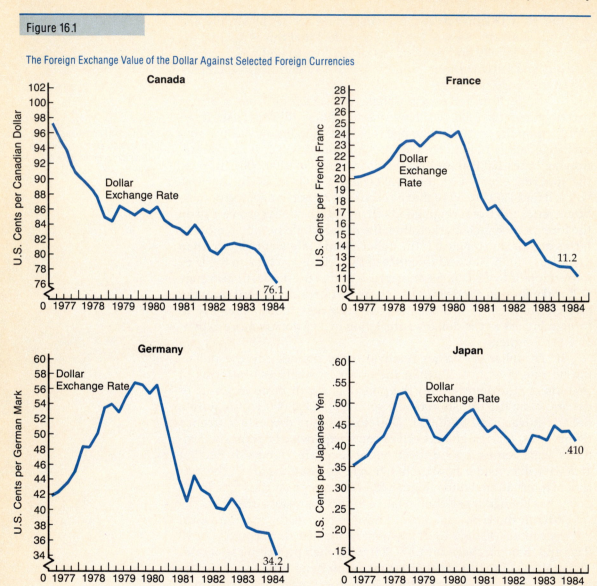

**Source:** *International Economic Conditions*, Federal Reserve Bank of St. Louis.

find that it could buy pounds forward for 1.12. In this case, £100,000 to be received in 90 days will cost $112,000 with certainty. By using the forward exchange market, the firm has eliminated any uncertainty regarding the dollar price of the machine it wants to purchase.

## THE BALANCE OF PAYMENTS

The **balance of payments** is a financial statement where all of a nation's international transactions are recorded. The balance of payments as actually recorded by the United States Department of Commerce is more detailed than we need to be concerned with, but a simplified quarterly summary of the balance of payments is presented in Table 16.1. Balance of payments transactions are conveniently divided into current account and capital account transactions. The first four columns of Table 16.1 represent current account trade in merchandise and services. Note that definitions of the various accounts are provided in the legend to the table. Column 5 gives the balance on the current account. A positive balance indicates that exports exceeded imports and thus there was a *surplus*, while a negative balance indicates imports greater than exports or a *deficit*.

The rest of the table deals with capital flows. Here we mean financial assets and not the usual macroeconomic meaning of the word capital, i.e., manmade instruments of production used to make other things. If the U.S. sold more financial securities to the rest of the world than it purchased, there would be a capital account surplus. While capital account transactions are classified into many different categories, of particular interest is the last column—the monetary base effect. We have analyzed changes in base money as the primary determinant of money supply changes; therefore, insofar as the balance of payments changes base money, it also changes the money supply. This is an important channel through which international transactions may have an effect on the domestic economy.

Since merchandise exports earn foreign exchange while merchandise imports mean outflows of foreign exchange, it is often argued that macroeconomic policy should be aimed at maximizing the merchandise trade surplus. Is this a good policy? Recalling the Chapter 2 discussion of national income accounting, a higher trade balance surplus is associated with higher GNP. The fact that aggregate demand can be increased by increasing the balance of trade is the point often focused on by policymakers. But it is impossible for every nation to run a larger trade surplus. Since one country's export is another country's import, on a global basis the sum of all balance of trade surpluses must be matched by an equal amount of trade balance deficits, globally, trade must be balanced. Even though it is impossible for all countries to run trade surpluses, many observers argue that nevertheless, it is better to run trade surpluses than deficits. But is this necessarily true? If the United States' current account deficit is financed by a capital account surplus, then, in effect, the U.S. is buying real goods and services from the rest of the world in exchange

**balance of payments**
A financial accounting statement that shows all of a nation's international transactions

The balance of payments is a balance sheet where transactions with the rest of the world are recorded.

Table 16.1

Quarterly Series U.S. International Transactions$^a$ Seasonally Adjusted (Millions of Dollars)

|  |  | Trade Flows | | | | | |
|---|---|---|---|---|---|---|---|
| Quarters | | Merchandise Exports | Merchandise Imports | Service Exports | Service Imports | Current Account Balance | Direct Investment Abroad |
| 1981 | I | 60,793 | 65,275 | 32,993 | 23,672 | 3,344 | 2,045 |
|  | II | 60,031 | 67,373 | 34,503 | 24,852 | 742 | 5,657 |
|  | III | 57,812 | 66,214 | 35,270 | 25,067 | −83 | 1,181 |
|  | IV | 58,383 | 66,224 | 34,838 | 24,426 | 585 | 797 |
| 1982 | I | 55,636 | 61,739 | 34,125 | 25,397 | 564 | 346 |
|  | II | 54,996 | 60,850 | 35,794 | 26,704 | 1,434 | −1,163 |
|  | III | 52,241 | 65,319 | 34,691 | 26,467 | −6,596 | −161 |
|  | IV | 48,344 | 59,698 | 32,496 | 25,332 | −6,621 | −2,031 |
| 1983 | I | 49,350r | 58,206r | 31,581r | 24,829r | −3,665r | 324r |
|  | II | 48,757r | 63,462r | 32,867r | 15,301r | −9,747r | −934r |
|  | III | 50,429r | 68,607r | 34,968r | 26,749r | −12,074r | −4,549r |
|  | IV | 51,667p | 70,478p | 34,614p | 27,995p | −15,291p | −2,448p |

$^a$The signs in this table do *not* indicate whether a particular transaction is an inflow or an outflow. In this table a negative sign indicates a reduction in the stock of a particular class of assets during a particular time period.

$^b$Not seasonally adjusted, quarterly averages of end-of-month data. Beginning first quarter 1979, official U.S. holdings of assets denominated in foreign currencies are revalued monthly at market exchange rates. As of July 1980 the monetary base effect includes the addition of official U.S. holdings of Swiss franc denominated assets. Consequently, this series after July 1980 is not directly comparable to that reported for previous periods.

p–preliminary, r–revised.

Merchandise Exports and Imports: the current dollar value of physical goods which are exported from and imported into the United States.

Service Exports and Imports: receipts and reinvestment of earnings on United States investments abroad and payments and reinvestment of earnings on foreign investments in the United States (interest, dividends and branch earnings), sales and purchases of military equipment, expenditures for U.S. military stations abroad, and payments and receipts associated with foreign travel and transportation.

Current Account: the sum of merchandise and service exports less merchandise and service imports and unilateral transfers, which are private transfers representing gifts and similar payments by Americans to foreign residents and government transfers representing payments associated with foreign assistance programs.

Direct Investment: private sector capital transactions which result in the ownership of 10 percent or more of the voting securities or other ownership interests in foreign enterprises by U.S. residents either by themselves or in affiliation with others, including reinvested earnings of incorporated foreign affiliates of

## Capital Flows

| Direct Investment in U.S. | Security Purchases Abroad | Security Purchases in U.S. | Bank Claims on Foreigners | Bank Liabilities to Foreigners | U.S. Government Assets Abroad | Foreign Official Assets in U.S. | Monetary Base Effect[b] |
|---|---|---|---|---|---|---|---|
| 2,775 | 488 | 3,809 | 11,664 | −3,793 | 5,890 | 5,517 | 2,344 |
| 4,528 | 1,547 | 4,336 | 14,981 | 8,071 | 2,374 | −2,999 | 210 |
| 4,702 | 705 | 323 | 15,293 | 16,494 | 1,278 | −5,880 | −547 |
| 9,993 | 2,896 | 1,685 | 41,913 | 21,382 | 711 | 8,792 | −100 |
| 2,081 | 581 | 2,601 | 32,551 | 25,685 | 1,896 | −3,061 | −242 |
| 2,892 | 546 | 4,529 | 38,653 | 24,778 | 2,621 | 1,930 | 119 |
| 2,636 | 3,331 | 1,784 | 20,631 | 10,977 | 3,296 | 2,642 | 389 |
| 2,781 | 3,527 | 4,232 | 17,511 | 2,823 | 2,884 | 1,661 | 980 |
| 2,054 | 1,808 | 5,898 | 15,935 | 10,588 | 1,840 | 49 | −342 |
| 2,230 | 3,222 | 5,700 | −5,166r | 919 | 1,146 | 1,973r | −487 |
| 3,165r | 1,543r | 2,853r | 2,025r | 15,068r | 659 | −2,581r | −1,232 |
| 2,065p | 912p | 2,736p | 12,172p | 24,720p | 2,429p | 6,642p | 505 |

U.S. firms; private sector transactions which result in the ownership of 10 percent or more (before 1974, 25 percent or more) of the voting securities or other ownership interests in U.S. enterprises by foreigners, including reinvested earnings of incorporated U.S. affiliates of foreign firms.

Security Purchases: U.S. private sector net purchases of foreign equity and debt securities with no contractual maturity or a maturity of more than one year; foreign private sector and international financial institutions net purchases of U.S. equity and debt securities with no contractual maturities or maturities of more than one year and U.S. Treasury securities.

Bank Claims and Liabilities: changes in claims on private sector foreigners (loans, collections outstanding, acceptances, deposits abroad, claims on affiliated foreign banks, foreign government obligations, and foreign commercial and finance paper) and liabilities to private sector foreigners and international financial institutions (demand, time, and savings deposits, certificates of deposit, liabilities to affiliated foreign banks, and other liabilities) reported by U.S. banks for their own accounts and for the custody accounts of their customers.

U.S. Government Assets Abroad: changes in U.S. official reserve assets (gold, special drawing rights, foreign currency holdings, and reserve position in the International Monetary Fund) and changes in other U.S. government assets abroad.

Foreign Official Assets in U.S.: foreign official agencies' net purchases of U.S. government securities, obligations issued by U.S. government corporations and agencies, securities issued by state and local governments, and changes in liabilities to foreign official agencies reported by U.S. banks.

Source: Federal Reserve Bank of St. Louis

for dollar denominated financial assets. This makes more goods and services available to U.S. consumers now, which is, in itself, desirable.

Whether it is better to have trade deficits or surpluses at any particular time is best answered by . . . it depends on the current overall macroeconomic situation. Suppose, for example, that the United States had a relatively low rate of domestic saving compared to the rest of the world. Unless foreigners financed some American investment, interest rates in the U.S. would rise relative to rates available abroad. This inflow of foreign investment will mean a capital account surplus which is balanced by a trade account deficit. This is desirable in that the foreign money is needed to augment domestic savings and the amount of loanable funds. We see that the balance of trade cannot be evaluated by itself as being good or bad.

## 16.2 INTERNATIONAL PARITY CONDITIONS

Parity conditions are equations which state the circumstances under which particular prices will be equal or "on par" in different countries when allowance is made for differences in currency units. Parity conditions would hold exactly if both countries were part of the same market and if the prices were accurately measured for identical goods or identical baskets of goods. The parity conditions will not hold exactly if transportation costs or trade barriers such as tariffs make the countries separate but related markets or if the goods are not truly identical. These factors imply that the parity conditions can be applied in practice only with a generous margin for error, but the conditions are still a useful summary of basic international relationships.

### PURCHASING POWER PARITY

Since an exchange rate is the price of one money in terms of another, as the values of the money change in terms of domestic purchasing power, so too should the foreign exchange value. The value of domestic money is equal to the reciprocal of the domestic price level $1/P$. This represents the value of goods and services that must be given up to obtain one unit of domestic currency. Likewise the reciprocal of the foreign price level $1/P^F$ represents the value of foreign currency in terms of foreign goods. If the price of foreign currency in terms of domestic currency, the exchange rate $E$, is determined by these relative values, it may be written as:

$$E = \frac{1/P^F}{1/P} = \frac{P}{P^F}$$

(16.1)

So the domestic currency price of foreign currency is equal to the ratio of the domestic price level to the foreign price level. Equation (16.1) is referred to as *absolute purchasing power parity*. Sometimes equation (16.1) is expressed in a form known as the *law of one price*:

$$P = EP^F \tag{16.2}$$

In this form we see that the price of goods, adjusted by the exchange rate should be the same worldwide. While Frenchmen use francs and Italians lire, when goods are expressed in a common currency they should sell for the same price. The exchange rate is the factor used to convert different currencies into a common basis.

*If goods sell for the same price internationally, the law of one price holds.*

**Purchasing power parity** (PPP) has been studied by countless researchers. The consensus is that absolute PPP does not hold very well in the real world. There are many reasons why this is true; for example, goods are not homogenous all over the world, shipping costs would have goods sell for different prices in different countries, and tariffs create artificial price differentials.[1]

**purchasing power parity** The same good in different countries will sell for the same price when prices are stated in terms of a common currency

Another statement of purchasing power parity relates percentage changes in the exchange rate to inflation differentials. If we compute the growth rates of each side of equation (16.1) we have (remembering our rules for the growth rate of a ratio):

$$\hat{E} = \hat{P} - \hat{P}^F \tag{16.3}$$

So the percentage appreciation or depreciation of a currency is given by the difference between the domestic and foreign inflation rates. This is known as *relative purchasing power parity*. Relative PPP tends to hold better in the real world than absolute PPP. Relative PPP is considered by many to be an indicator of the long-run trend growth in the exchange rate. If we can forecast inflation differentials, then there is an implied exchange rate change. It would be a mistake, however,

---

[1]There are many studies explaining why deviations from PPP should be observed and these studies suggest several reasons in addition to those mentioned above. For example, see Jacob Frenkel, "The Purchasing Power Parity: Doctrinal Perspective and Evidence From the 1920s," *Journal of International Economics*, May 8, 1978, 169–91; Lawrence H. Officer, *Purchasing Power Parity and Exchange Rates: Theory, Evidence, and Relevance* (Greenwich, Conn.: JAI Press, 1982); Michael Melvin and David Bernstein, "Trade Concentration, Openness, and Deviations From Purchasing Power Parity," *Journal of International Money and Finance*, December 1984, 369–76; and Stephen P. Magee, "Contracting and Spurious Deviations from Purchasing Power Parity," in J. A. Frenkel and H. G. Johnson, eds., *The Economics of Exchange Rates* (Reading, Mass.: Addison-Wesley, 1978).

to refer to PPP as a theory of the exchange rate. Prices and exchange rates are determined simultaneously by other factors like monetary policy. If domestic money growth is higher than foreign, then the money growth differential is the ultimate cause of the higher domestic inflation rate and the depreciating exchange rate.

## INTEREST RATE PARITY

A "parity" relation is a relation that must hold for some prices to be equal or "on par." In the case of purchasing power parity, if domestic prices rise faster than foreign, domestic goods will become expensive relative to foreign and demand for foreign goods will increase while the demand for domestic goods falls. This will mean an increase in demand for foreign currency relative to domestic in the foreign exchange market and a consequent depreciation of the domestic currency until domestic and foreign price differentials are just offset. This activity of buying in the cheapest market as conditions change is known as goods **arbitrage**. While demanders always prefer a lower to a higher price, PPP does not hold well because price differentials are not eliminated quickly in goods markets. Goods are not homogeneous, it takes time to order and purchase goods, and many goods are sold on a contractual basis so that the parties are not free to alter agreed upon prices and quantities for the duration of the contract.

These conditions that lead to deviations from PPP are much less important in markets for financial assets. As a result, we find that domestic and foreign financial assets yield very nearly the same return, or that **interest rate parity** (IRP) holds quite well. To see the logic for IRP, let's consider an investor with a choice of investing in a domestic or a foreign security.

By investing in a domestic asset, a domestic resident will earn the domestic interest rate $R_d$. Foreign assets pay the foreign rate of interest $R_f$, but this is not the total return to a domestic investor. First the domestic resident will have to exchange domestic currency for foreign currency before buying the foreign security. Then the return from the foreign asset must eventually be converted back to domestic currency. For instance, suppose a U.S. investor will receive £1000 in 3 months. The investor could wait and exchange the pounds for dollars at the spot exchange rate prevailing in 3 months, or the investor could sell the pounds in the forward market so that the dollar value of the £1000 pounds to be received in 3 months is known with certainty now. Therefore, the total return from the foreign investment is the foreign interest rate $i_f$ plus the *forward premium* or *discount* on the pound $(F - E)/E$, where $F$ is the forward exchange rate. A currency is said to be selling at a forward premium if the forward price of the currency exceeds the spot price. The currency is selling at a forward discount if the forward price of the currency is less than the spot

**arbitrage**
The activity that equalizes the cost of a good in different markets by buying the good in the cheap market and reselling it in the expensive market

**interest rate parity**
Similar financial assets in different countries yield the same return in terms of a given currency

price. For instance, if the forward dollar price of pounds is $F = 1.80$, while the spot price is $E = 1.75$, then the pound is said to be selling at a premium against the dollar. This means that the dollar must be selling at a discount against the pound.

Interest rate parity is said to hold when the domestic asset yields a return equal to the foreign asset, or:

$$R_d = R_f + (F - E)/E \qquad (16.4)$$

This relation will hold only for comparable assets available internationally. We would not expect the return on a very risky corporate bond to be comparable to the return on a riskless government bond. But for comparable assets, equation (16.4) will hold. If not, investors would buy the higher return security and sell the lower return security, thus raising the return on the low return security and lowering the return on the high return security until the parity condition is established. This buying and selling behavior, known as *arbitrage*, continuously occurs so that only brief and fleeting deviations from interest rate parity would ever be observed for identical bonds. Debate continues over whether or not government bonds of different countries can be identical given the risks of currency controls and whether or not the forward rate is equal to the expected value of the future exchange rate. But international economists agree that interest rate parity holds much more exactly than purchasing power parity.

Another way of expressing the interest parity relation is:

$$R_d - R_f = (F - E)/E \qquad (16.5)$$

This says that the interest differential between domestic and foreign securities is equal to the forward premium ($F > E$) or discount ($F < E$) on the foreign currency. Interest rate parity is the way that interest rates are linked internationally via the foreign exchange market.

## 16.3 MACROECONOMIC IMPACTS OF INTERNATIONAL TRADE AND FINANCE

### EXCHANGE RATE SYSTEMS AND HISTORY

The implications of international events for the domestic economy will depend upon the institutional framework regarding the foreign exchange rate system. First we will consider the basic types of exchange rate systems and then we will evaluate the macroeconomic implications.

**gold standard**
An international financial system in which currency values are stated in a fixed ratio to gold and thus exchange rates are fixed

**Bretton Woods system**
An international financial system (1944–71) in which fixed exchange rates prevailed

**International Monetary Fund**
A lending agency that provides short-term loans to countries having balance-of-payments problems

International monetary history discussions frequently begin with the **gold standard** that existed between 1880 and 1914. Under a gold standard, exchange rates are fixed between currencies. Each currency has an established value in terms of gold—one troy ounce of gold was worth $20.67—and therefore each currency will have an implicitly fixed rate of exchange with other currencies. Under such a system, gold will serve as an international money. Any balance of payments disequilibrium will be remedied by international gold flows. A country running a deficit will find itself losing gold to surplus countries. These gold outflows will tend to lower the money supply and the price level of the deficit country, while the gold inflows will raise the money supply and price level of the surplus countries. This change in national price levels will bring about changes in the pattern of trade that will restore international equilibrium. Falling prices in the deficit country and rising prices in the surplus country will lead to an increase in deficit-country net exports and a decline in surplus-country net exports until the initial trade imbalance is eliminated.

With a strict gold standard, money growth is constrained by the increase in the gold stock. As a result, prices tended to be stable for long periods of time. Many who favor some sort of commodity money standard, as discussed in Chapter 14, often refer to the policy discipline enforced by such a standard and point to the long-run price stability of the gold standard as an example.

The gold standard effectively ended with World War I. Not until 1944 was there another well-defined, long-lasting international monetary system. Near the end of World War II, an international conference at Bretton Woods, New Hampshire, marked the beginning of the **Bretton Woods system** of fixed exchange rates. Under the Bretton Woods system, each country was pledged to maintain the value of its currency by buying and selling foreign exchange. A country lacking sufficient foreign exchange reserves to support its exchange rate could turn to a new institution created at the Bretton Woods Conference: the **International Monetary Fund** or IMF. The IMF was to provide short-term financing assistance to countries experiencing temporary balance of payments difficulties.

IMF loans are made subject to conditions regarding changes in domestic economic policy. IMF staff members prescribe the changes in policy required that will return the troubled country to sound health. If a country experienced a "fundamental" balance of payments disequilibrium, then a currency *devaluation*, or permanent depreciation of the troubled currency, was allowed.[2] Therefore, the fixed exchange rate system was really an *adjustable peg* system. Countries were to maintain fixed exchange rates unless there was a permanent shift in their international competitive position. In the face of such permanent changes, exchange rate adjustments were allowed.

The failure of deficit countries to devalue on a timely basis contributed to the downfall of the Bretton Woods system. There were recurring foreign exchange crises in the late 1960s and early 1970s, when it became obvious that a currency value was out of line. The longer the problem government delayed an obviously needed devaluation, the greater the problem became, as speculators would take positions in the foreign exchange market—selling the weakening currency for stronger currencies. This speculation caused even greater pressure for the devaluation. Table 16.2 lists the exchange rate arrangements and adjustments for the major developed nations during the Bretton Woods era.

[2]This is for the typical case of chronic balance-of-payments deficits; permanent appreciations were used occasionally for chronic balance-of-payments surpluses.

**Table 16.2**

Exchange Rates Over the Bretton Woods Era

| Country | Exchange Rates* |
|---|---|
| Canada | Floated until May 2, 1962, then pegged at C$1.081 = $1. Floated again on June 1, 1970. |
| France | No official IMF parity value after 1948 (although the actual rate hovered around FF350 = $1) until December 29, 1958 when rate fixed at FF493.7 = $1 (old francs). One year later, rate was FF4.937 = $1 when new franc (one new franc was equal to 100 old francs) was created. Devaluation to FF5.554 = $1 on August 10, 1969. |
| Germany | Revalued on March 6, 1961 from DM4.20 = $1 to DM4.0 = $1. Revalued to DM3.66 = $1 on October 26, 1969. |
| Italy | Pegged at Lir625 = $1 from March 30, 1960 until August 1971. |
| Japan | Pegged at ¥360 = $1 until 1971. |
| Netherlands | Pegged at F13.80 = $1 until March 7, 1961 when revalued at F13.62 = $1. |
| United Kingdom | Devalued from $2.80 to £ to $2.40 = £ on November 11, 1967. |

*Relative to the U.S. dollar.

The major traded curren-
cies now follow managed
floating.

**managed float**
An international financial system in which exchange rates
freely float by supply and demand within target ranges controlled by central banks

The 1971–73 period was one of transition. The Bretton Woods system of fixed exchange rates was ended, but the onset of generalized floating exchange rates could not be said to exist until March 1973. In March 1973, the major traded currencies began what is called a **managed float**. Exchange rates are set partly by the free market supply and demand for each money, with rates floating to whatever value will clear the market. We say that rates are set "partly" by the free market because central banks also intervene in the market to establish desired rates. The managed float is a system where central bank management of exchange rates modifies the free market outcome.

## ADJUSTMENT WITH PEGGED EXCHANGE RATES

A system of fixed exchange rates requires that all nations follow a similar monetary policy. As indicated by the purchasing power parity analysis, when inflation rates diverge, there is pressure for the exchange rate to change. How can monetary policy be coordinated internationally with a fixed exchange rate system? Under the Bretton Woods system, the U.S. dollar was the world's dominant currency, so maintaining fixed exchange rates meant following a monetary policy similar to that of the U.S.

Countries experiencing slower rates of inflation would tend to run balance of trade surpluses against the United States as their goods became less expensive relative to U.S. goods. Remember the law of one price: $P = EP^F$. If the domestic price level $P$ is increasing faster than the foreign price level $P^F$, and the exchange rate $E$ is held constant, then foreign goods become cheap relative to domestic goods and the domestic economy runs a trade deficit while the foreign economy runs a trade surplus.

With fixed exchange rates, international money flows eliminate disequilibrium.

What happens to prevent this domestic deficit from continuing? In other words, what is the process of adjustment to balance of payments disequilibrium? To maintain the pegged exchange rate, it is necessary for the two nations to have similar inflation rates. As the foreign country experiences a balance of payments surplus, it experiences inflows of foreign exchange and this inflow of money tends to increase the foreign money supply. In this manner, the foreign country can passively find that its money supply grows at a similar rate to the dominant-currency country—the currency it pegs to.

If the foreign central bank resists the increase in money growth by reducing the rate of growth of base money through restrictive open market operations, then the inflation differential and consequent money flows will increase even further. Under a fixed or pegged exchange rate regime, international money flows serve as the vehicle that maintains the exchange rate peg. If countries act to *sterilize* the impact of the money flows in order to follow a monetary policy independent of the dominant currency country, then the exchange rate ultimately will have to change. Sterilization occurs when the central bank conducts open market operations that offset international reserve flows, so that base money is determined by the central bank independent of foreign monetary policies.

## ADJUSTMENT WITH FLEXIBLE EXCHANGE RATES

The propensity for nations to choose independent monetary policies makes an exchange rate peg unworkable. With flexible or floating exchange rates, each central bank can choose a money growth rate consistent with domestic policy goals. Countries choosing relatively fast money growth rates will have depreciating currencies while countries choosing relatively slow money growth rates will have appreciating currencies.

Under a pure free-market float, there would be no balance of payments disequilibrium or international money flows because the exchange rate would adjust to where private exports of goods and services just equal their imports. With a managed float, the exchange rate may be kept from the free-market level by central bank intervention. The central banks' activity will result in a managed float having the characteristics of both a pegged rate system and a float: there are international flows of money along with exchange rate fluctuations. In general, it will still be true that countries choosing lower rates of inflation will have currencies that appreciate in value while currencies that have higher rates of inflation will depreciate. Such ongoing exchange rate adjustments are the natural results of inflation differentials.

The world does not always work along the lines of the purchasing power parity, at least in the short run. This was particularly evident in the early 1980s, when the United States had higher inflation rates than West Germany, Japan, and Switzerland and still the dollar appreciated against the mark, yen, and Swiss franc. What accounted for this surprisingly strong dollar? Most observers attribute the dollar's strength to U.S. real interest rates, which were very high by historical standards. United States monetary policy in the early 1980s was aimed at controlling inflation. In Chapter 15 we learned that the rate of inflation dropped dramatically between 1980 and 1983. Yet even though inflation fell, nominal interest rates remained quite high, which meant that real interest rates would rise. The higher real interest rates in the United States made security purchases more attractive there than in foreign countries; as a result, investment funds poured into the U.S. from abroad. A byproduct of this popularity of dollar denominated securities was an increased demand for dollars on the foreign exchange market, as foreigners had to exchange foreign currency for dollars before buying U.S. securities. So as the demand for U.S. securities increased, the dollar appreciated on the foreign exchange market.

## U.S. BUDGET DEFICITS AND THE BALANCE OF PAYMENTS AND EXCHANGE RATES

This dollar appreciation in excess of the inflation differential made U.S. goods more expensive relative to foreign goods and caused a large U.S. balance of trade deficit. Many economists have generally blamed the very large federal government budget deficits and consequently large borrowing requirements for the high real interest rates. In this case, the infusion of foreign investment funds was desirable, as it helped to supplement U.S. private saving in providing the government borrowing needs and minimized the private investment crowding out caused by the budget deficit. We see then that the large capital account surplus required to help finance the federal budget deficit simultaneously caused an appreciation of the dollar and a large trade deficit.[3]

The end-of-chapter essay for Chapter 15 postponed discussion of the possibly major impact of the large Reagan-era deficits until we discussed in this chapter the relationship between the domestic economy and the rest of the world. The next-to-last paragraph tied the large U.S. budget deficit to the foreign exchange appreciation of the dollar. The tremendous demand for credit arising from U.S. Treasury borrowing is cited frequently as a cause of high real interest rates in the United States. However, rather than inflows of foreign savings financing the deficit, as is commonly believed to be true, it seems that the major change in lending was a shift in the lending of U.S. financial institutions. Figure 16.2 illustrates the dramatic change in lending. The high real return in the U.S. (whatever its origin) decreased foreign lending by U.S. institutions as lending was directed inward. Figure 16.2 shows the change in U.S.-owned for-

---

[3]See Charles Piggott and Michael Hutchison, "Misaligned Dollar," *Federal Reserve Bank of San Francisco Weekly Letter*, January 20, 1984, for an analysis of the dollar appreciation in the early 1980s.

Figure 16.2

U.S. Financial Transactions
with the Rest of the World

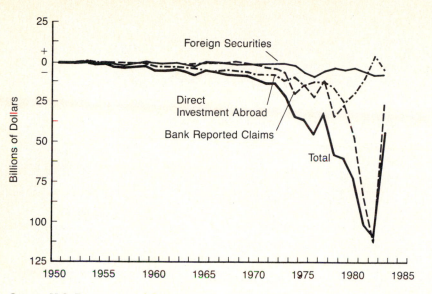

Source: U.S. Department of Commerce.

eign assets. The heavy line representing total assets owned is dominated by the dramatic shift in commercial bank activity (illustrated
by the dashed line). In 1982, U.S. commercial bank lending abroad
equaled approximately $112 billion. In 1983, U.S. commercial banks
loaned approximately $25 billion abroad.

Since foreign lending to the U.S. did not change very much but
U.S. lending abroad fell, there was a large surplus on the capital
account of the U.S. balance of payments. As the demand for foreign
currencies fell relative to the demand for dollars due to the change in
international lending, the dollar appreciated in value relative to other
currencies. This capital account surplus and dollar appreciation contributed to what some economists believe is the major effect of the
large U.S. budget deficits—a very large balance of trade deficit.

Figure 16.3 illustrates how the merchandise trade balance
dropped dramatically in the early 1980s. Why did the difference between the value of goods exported and the value of goods imported
increase considerably? As the dollar appreciated due to the change
in capital flows, U.S. goods became more expensive to foreign buyers
while foreign goods became cheaper to U.S. buyers. This change in
the price of goods traded internationally caused U.S. exports to fall
relative to U.S. imports. The resulting balance of trade deficit was
unparalleled in U.S. history.

Figure 16.3

U.S. Merchandise Transactions with the Rest of the World

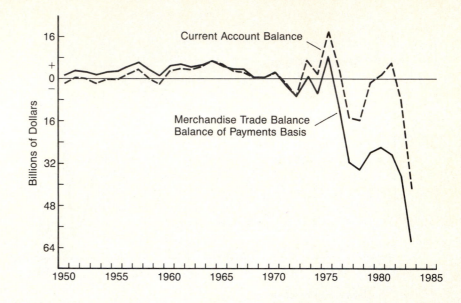

## 16.4 THE MONETARY APPROACH TO THE BALANCE OF PAYMENTS AND EXCHANGE RATES

Now that we have discussed in general terms the response of the balance of payments and exchange rates to international disequilibrium, it is time to look at a specific view of the adjustment mechanism. The *monetary approach to the balance of payments and exchange rates* became quite popular in the 1970s. Since this approach emphasizes money demand and supply, it is a useful approach for us to consider in a macroeconomics text. The basic insight of the monetary approach is that international pressures will be reflected in the money market and the process of adjustment can be described in terms of changes in base money or changes in exchange rates.

It is useful to divide base money *B* into a *domestic credit* component and an **international reserves** component. In this framework, the central bank controls domestic credit through domestic open market operations, while international transactions give rise to flows of foreign exchange that become the international reserves held by the central bank. For instance, suppose a British exporter receives payment in dollars. This payment is presented to a commercial bank and exchanged for British pounds. If the commercial bank has no current use for the dollars, they are presented to the English central bank (the Bank of England) and exchanged for pounds. The Bank of

**international reserves**
Financial assets, including foreign exchange and gold, which may be used to settle international debts

England buys the foreign currency from the commercial bank by increasing the commercial bank's reserve deposit with the Bank. So as the Bank accumulates international reserves (the dollars), base money expands. The total of British base money is found by summing international reserves (denoted here by $R$) plus domestic credit ($D$):

$$B = R + D \qquad (16.6)$$

These new meanings for the symbols $R$ and $D$ are standard in this literature and are maintained for the remainder of this chapter.

The monetary approach analysis differs according to the exchange rate regime—with fixed exchange rates, the adjustment process occurs through international reserve flows, and we have the monetary approach to the balance of payments (MABP).[4] This approach is summarized by the following equation:

$$\Delta R = \Delta(M^d/\mu) - \Delta D \qquad (16.7)$$

This MABP equation says that the change in international reserves is determined by the difference between the change in domestic base money demand ($M^d/\mu$) and the change in domestic credit $D$.[5] If the central bank is increasing domestic credit faster than domestic residents demand, then there will be an excess supply of money. Equation (16.7) indicates that if $\Delta D$ is greater than $\Delta(M^d/\mu)$, then $\Delta R$ will be negative, or the country will experience a loss of international reserves via balance of payments deficits. On the other hand if $\Delta(M^d/\mu)$ exceeds $\Delta D$, then there is an excess demand for money and $\Delta R$ is positive, so that the nation experiences reserve inflows through a balance of payments surplus.

---

[4]The monetary approach to the balance of payments is properly applied only to the countries which actively maintain the fixed exchange rate. The United States, even under the Bretton Woods System, determined its domestic money growth with little or no regard to the balance of payments. Generally, if $n$ countries are linked by fixed exchange rates, one central bank will determine the price level for all $n$ countries while the remaining central banks will maintain the $n-1$ independent exchange rates. See Michael R. Darby, "The United States as an Exogenous Source of World Inflation under the Bretton Woods System." in Michael R. Darby, James R. Lothian et al., *The International Transmission of Inflation*, A N.B.E.R. Monograph (Chicago: University of Chicago Press, 1983).

[5]If we divide the demand for money by the money multiplier $\mu$, we get the amount of base money required to fulfill the demand, which we can (loosely) call base money demand.

The MABP assumes that $\Delta D$ is exogenously determined by central bank policy while $\Delta(M^d/\mu)$ is determined by prices, real income and the interest rate. At least in the long run, real income will be at its normal level while prices and interest rates will be determined by their values in the rest of the world through the parity conditions. With fixed exchange rates, countries would not run chronic balance of payments deficits if they did not follow policies of inflationary money growth in excess of money demand growth. The balance of payments is the vehicle through which money demand is adjusted to money supply. If the domestic money market is not in equilibrium, then international reserve flows will adjust to provide the equilibrium.

With flexible exchange rates, we have the monetary approach to the exchange rate (MAER):

$$\hat{E} = \hat{M} - (\hat{K} + \hat{y} + \hat{P}^F) \tag{16.8}$$

Equation (16.8) has the appreciation or depreciation of the domestic currency price of foreign currency (the exchange rate) determined by the difference between the growth rate of the domestic nominal money supply and the growth rate of the domestic nominal money demand *if* the domestic inflation rate equaled the foreign inflation rate. It is obtained by substituting the basic inflation equation (10.3) into the relative purchasing power parity equation (16.3). With flexible exchange rates, the central bank does not buy or sell foreign exchange; so the exchange rate adjusts to where the balance of payments is zero and there are no international reserve flows. In this case the money market disequilibrium is resolved through exchange rate appreciation or depreciation. If the central bank follows a policy of money supply growth in excess of money demand growth at the foreign inflation rate, then the exchange rate will depreciate causing the domestic currency price of foreign currency to rise. If the central bank is following a tight money policy of slow $\hat{M}$ relative to $\hat{K} + \hat{y} + \hat{P}^F$, then $\hat{E}$ will fall, or the domestic currency will appreciate. This is the common-sense supply and demand result in any market— if supply increases relative to demand, the currency value falls; if supply decreases relative to demand, the currency value rises.

What about a managed float where there are both exchange rate fluctuations and reserve flows? The analysis becomes a bit more complicated because we can no longer think of the central bank as rigidly pursuing either a money growth or exchange rate goal alone, with the other variable adjusting passively. Suppose that change in reserves, that is, the amount by which the bank intervenes in the for-

Domestic money market equilibrium may be achieved through international reserve flows or exchange rate changes.

eign exchange market, is proportional to the difference between the bank's target $\hat{E}^*$ and the actual growth in the exchange rate $\hat{E}$:

$$\Delta R = a(\hat{E}^* - \hat{E}) \qquad (16.9)$$

The central bank will likely raise or lower actual money growth $\hat{M}$ relative to its target $\hat{M}^*$, depending on whether its foreign exchange intervention is causing an inflow or outflow of reserves:

$$\hat{M} = \hat{M}^* + b(\Delta R) \qquad (16.10)$$

Combining these two equations with equation (16.8), we find that the growth rate of the exchange rate is

$$\hat{E} = \frac{ab}{1 + ab} \hat{E}^* + \frac{1}{1 + ab} [\hat{M}^* - (\hat{K} + \hat{y} + \hat{P}^F)] \qquad (16.11)$$

This equation tells us that the exchange rate's growth rate is a weighted average of the central bank's exchange rate goal and the exchange rate growth implied by its money goal. More weight is put on the exchange rate goal as the responsiveness $a$ of intervention to exchange rate movements and the responsiveness $b$ of money growth to the balance of payments increase.[6]

We have purposely kept the analysis of the monetary approach at a simple level in order to emphasize the forest and not the trees.[7] In our discussions of monetary policy in previous chapters, we emphasized the impact on domestic interest rates, income, and prices. Now we see how domestic monetary policy decisions can also affect the balance of payments and exchange rates. In an increasingly integrated world, the international consequences of domestic policies become ever more important.

---

[6]Money growth $\hat{M}$ can be shown to be a similar weighted average of the money growth implied by the bank's exchange rate target and its money growth target. See Michael R. Darby, "Monetary Policy in the Large Open Economy," in Albert Ando, Hidekazu Eguchi, Roger Farmer, and Yoshio Suzuki, eds., *Monetary Policy in Our Times* (Cambridge: M.I.T. Press, 1985)

[7]There is a voluminous literature on the monetary approach. A good introductory exposition of the basic model is provided by Michael Connolly in "The Monetary Approach to An Open Economy: The Fundamental Theory," in Putnam and Wilford (eds.), *The Monetary Approach to International Adjustment* (New York: Praeger, 1978).

## 16.5 THE ABSORPTION APPROACH TO THE BALANCE OF TRADE

A nation's balance of trade may be viewed as the difference between what the economy produces and what it takes for domestic use or absorbs. To see this, consider the national income accounting identity originally appearing in Chapter 2:

$$Y \equiv C + I + G + X, \tag{16.12}$$

or national income or output is equal to total expenditures—the sum of consumption $C$, investment $I$, government spending $G$, and net exports $X$. Net exports, remember, is equal to exports minus imports. If we define total domestic spending or **absorption** $A$ as being equal to the sum of consumption plus investment plus government spending, or:

**absorption**
Domestic aggregate demand or $C + I + G$

$$A = C + I + G, \tag{16.13}$$

then national income may be written as $Y = A + X$. Net exports, then, can be seen as being equal to output minus absorption:

$$X = Y - A \tag{16.14}$$

Equation (16.14) indicates that if $Y$ exceeds $A$, then total domestic production exceeds the amount of output consumed at home and the nation will export the rest of its output and run a balance of trade surplus (positive net exports). On the other hand, if absorption exceeds domestic production, then $A$ exceeds $Y$ causing net exports to be negative and a balance of trade deficit. In this latter case, the excess of domestic demand over domestic production will be met through imports.

Net exports will increase with an increase in output and/or a decrease in absorption.

Economists have generally used the absorption approach to analyze the effects of devaluation, or an official depreciation of a currency's value, on the balance of trade in the short run. The traditional analysis assumes that a devaluation can improve a country's trade balance if there are unemployed resources. The devaluation will make the domestic goods cheaper to the rest of the world. If there are unemployed resources, then $Y$ will increase as resources are put to work to meet the foreign demand. If the devaluation occurs when an economy has few unemployed resources, then the increased demand of foreigners for domestic goods will only create a rise in the price level. In this case, the lack of unemployed resources constrains $Y$ from increasing sufficiently in the short run to meet the foreign demand. Therefore, domestic prices are bid up for the goods and services currently being produced.

The absorption approach is an analysis of the balance of trade. In the previous section we learned that the monetary approach considered the broader range of both trade and capital flows. The absorption approach would only be a theory of the overall balance of payments in a world without capital flows. Perhaps in a time of primitive capital markets, understanding the determinants of the balance of trade was sufficient to understand the domestic consequences of international economic relationships. In the modern day this is not true. We must be careful to remember that the absorption approach is strictly a theory of the trade balance.

## SUMMARY

**1** Foreign exchange is foreign-currency denominated bank deposits and actual foreign currency.

**2** The price of one currency in terms of another is the foreign exchange rate.

**3** An appreciation of the domestic currency makes domestic goods more expensive to foreign residents while a depreciation makes domestic goods cheaper.

**4** A nation's international transactions are recorded in the balance of payments.

**5** If goods sell for a common price worldwide when stated in terms of a common currency, the law of one price holds.

**6** Relative purchasing power parity suggests that the percentage change in the exchange rate is equal to the difference between the domestic and foreign inflation rates.

**7** Interest rate parity holds when the domestic interest rate is equal to the foreign interest rate plus the forward premium or discount.

**8** Under a gold standard, balance of payments disequilibria will be remedied through changes in the national money supplies caused by international gold flows and the consequent price level changes.

**9** Following World War II, the Bretton Woods conference established a new international monetary system of fixed exchange rates.

**10** By the early 1970s, the Bretton Woods system collapsed due to the differential monetary policies followed by individual nations.

**11**  In the early 1980s, the dollar appreciated against several currencies with lower inflation rates because of high real interest rates in the U.S.

**12**  With fixed exchange rates, an excess supply (demand) of money will be reflected in international reserve outflows (inflows).

**13**  With flexible exchange rates, an excess supply (demand) of money will lead to an exchange rate depreciation (appreciation).

**14**  If output exceeds (is less than) absorption, net exports are positive (negative).


## EXERCISES

1. What is interest rate parity and why does it hold?

2. Carefully explain why, other things equal, a reduction in U.S. money supply growth implies a stronger dollar on the foreign exchange market.

3. Using the interest parity relation of Chapter 16 and the Fisher equation relating interest rates and inflation, show how exchange rate changes may be related to inflation differentials. Under what conditions will the forward premium equal the inflation differential between two countries?

4. Suppose the dollar interest rate is 20 percent, the pound interest rate is 15 percent, and the spot dollar price of pounds is $2.00.

   **a.** What do you expect the 12 month forward rate to be?

   **b**. If the 12 month forward rate is actually $2.15, what would profit-maximizing investors do?

5. According to the monetary approach to the balance of payments, what would happen to the domestic balance of payments if, other things equal, domestic income increased? (Hint: income is a determinant of money demand).

6. Suppose that during a period of pegged exchange rates, Germany is running a balance of payments surplus that is causing pressure for an appreciation of the mark. What can the German central bank do to maintain the pegged exchange rate?

7. Suppose that in London, the pound price of dollars is 0.4, and in Paris, the franc price of dollars is 4. What is the implied pound price of francs in these two markets.

8. Suppose the current spot exchange rate is 250 yen per dollar, and the current forward exchange rate is 230 yen per dollar.

   a. Is the dollar selling at a premium or discount relative to the yen?

   b. Is the yen selling at a premium or discount relative to the dollar?

   c. What can you say about the dollar interest rate relative to the yen interest rate?

9. How do the implications of the absorption approach differ according to whether or not there is full employment?

## REFERENCES FOR FURTHER READING

Kubarych, Roger M. *Foreign Exchange Markets in the United States*. New York: Federal Reserve Bank of New York, 1978.

McKinnon, Ronald I. *Money in International Exchange*. New York: Oxford, 1979.

Melvin, Michael. *International Money and Finance*. New York: Harper and Row, 1985.

## AN EARLY STATEMENT OF THE MONETARY APPROACH TO THE BALANCE OF PAYMENTS

Now that we have reached the end of the text, it is interesting to note that we can, in a sense, come full circle and return to the year 1752 to see a statement of the monetary approach to the balance of payments put forth by David Hume. In his "Of the Balance of Trade," Hume describes the nature of the monetary adjustment mechanism to a domestic excess demand for money. In his analysis, the excess demand is eliminated by balance of payments surpluses leading to international reserve inflows until monetary equilibrium is restored. Let us briefly consider Hume's problem and its resolution:

> Suppose four-fifths of all the money in Great Britain to be annihilated in one night, and the nation reduced to the same condition with regard to specie, as in the reigns of the Harrys and Edwards, what would be the consequence? Must not the price of all labour and commodities sink in proportion, and everything be sold as cheap as they were in those ages? What nation could then dispute with us in any foreign market, or pretend to sell manufactures at the same price, which to us would afford sufficient profit? In how little time, therefore, must this bring back the money which we had lost, and raise us to the level of all neighboring nations? Where, after we have arrived, we immediately lose the advantage of the cheapness of labour and commodities; and the farther flowing in of money is stopped by our fullness and repletion.[1]

In Hume's analysis, when the nominal supply falls, the price level must also fall to equate the real amount of money supplied to the real amount demanded. In a closed economy, the story might end here, although we would expect the dynamic adjustment to the negative money shock to involve changes in real income and unemployment in the short run. In the open economy, like 18th-century England or the United States under the gold standard, the story does not end with the lower domestic price level. With domestic goods selling for lower prices than other nations' comparable products, domestic exports should rise so as to encourage international reserve (gold in Hume's time) inflows. As the domestic

---

[1]David Hume, "Of the Balance of Trade," as reprinted in R. N. Cooper, ed., *International Finance* (Baltimore: Penguin, 1969).

money supply rises following the reserve inflows, the domestic price level rises until equilibrium is restored. With fixed exchange rates, as exist under a gold standard, purchasing power parity requires similar price levels in competing nations. Once the price levels are similar, there will be no further reserve flows and balance of payments equilibrium will be restored.

After all of the modern macroeconomic literature reviewed in our textbook, and all of the modern macroeconomic pioneers cited in these pages, it is noteworthy to consider the contributions and level of understanding of the classical economists like Hume. While the modern macroeconomist has added much to our understanding of how economies work, the basic forces were well understood by the 18th century classicists.

# INDEX

## Relation of national income and personal income, 1929–84
[Billions of dollars; quarterly data at seasonally adjusted annual rates]

| Year or quarter | National income | Corporate profits with inventory valuation and capital consumption adjustments |
|---|---|---|
| 1929 | 84.8 | 9.0 |
| 1933 | 39.9 | −1.7 |
| 1939 | 71.4 | 5.3 |
| 1940 | 79.7 | 8.6 |
| 1941 | 102.7 | 14.1 |
| 1942 | 135.9 | 19.3 |
| 1943 | 169.3 | 23.5 |
| 1944 | 182.1 | 23.6 |
| 1945 | 180.7 | 19.0 |
| 1946 | 178.6 | 16.6 |
| 1947 | 194.9 | 22.3 |
| 1948 | 219.9 | 29.4 |
| 1949 | 213.6 | 27.1 |
| 1950 | 237.6 | 33.9 |
| 1951 | 274.1 | 38.7 |
| 1952 | 287.9 | 36.1 |
| 1953 | 302.1 | 36.3 |
| 1954 | 301.1 | 35.2 |
| 1955 | 330.5 | 45.5 |
| 1956 | 349.4 | 43.7 |
| 1957 | 365.2 | 43.3 |
| 1958 | 366.9 | 38.5 |
| 1959 | 400.8 | 49.6 |
| 1960 | 415.7 | 47.6 |
| 1961 | 428.8 | 48.6 |
| 1962 | 462.0 | 56.6 |
| 1963 | 488.5 | 62.1 |
| 1964 | 524.9 | 69.2 |
| 1965 | 572.4 | 80.0 |
| 1966 | 628.1 | 85.1 |
| 1967 | 662.2 | 82.4 |
| 1968 | 722.5 | 89.1 |
| 1969 | 779.3 | 85.1 |
| 1970 | 810.7 | 71.4 |
| 1971 | 871.5 | 83.2 |
| 1972 | 963.6 | 96.6 |
| 1973 | 1,086.2 | 108.3 |
| 1974 | 1,160.7 | 94.9 |
| 1975 | 1,239.4 | 110.5 |
| 1976 | 1,379.2 | 138.1 |
| 1977 | 1,550.5 | 167.3 |
| 1978 | 1,760.3 | 192.4 |
| 1979 | 1,966.7 | 194.8 |
| 1980 | 2,116.6 | 175.4 |
| 1981 | 2,363.8 | 189.9 |
| 1982 | 2,446.8 | 159.1 |
| 1983 | 2,646.7 | 225.2 |
| 1984 | 2,959.4 | 284.5 |

Source: Department of Commerce, Bureau of Economic Analysis.